United States
Catholic Catechism
for Adults

United States Catholic Catechism for Adults

UNITED STATES CONFERENCE OF CATHOLIC BISHOPS

United States Conference of Catholic Bishops
Washington, D.C.

The *United States Catholic Catechism for Adults* was developed by the Ad Hoc Committee to Oversee the Use of the *Catechism of the Catholic Church* of the United States Conference of Catholic Bishops (USCCB). It was approved by the full body of bishops at its November 2004 General Meeting, received the subsequent *recognitio* of the Holy See, and has been authorized for publication by the undersigned.

Msgr. David J. Malloy, STD
General Secretary, USCCB

ISBN-10: 1-57455-450-6
ISBN-13: 978-1-57455-450-2

First printing, July 2006
Second printing, September 2006

CONTENTS

Part III. Christian Morality: The Faith Lived

Part IV. Prayer: The Faith Prayed

Conclusion and Appendices

Acknowledgments

Scriptural Index

Index

PREFACE:
OUR FIRST U.S. BISHOP

On the Feast of the Assumption in 1790, the first bishop of the United States was ordained. The event occurred in St. Mary's Chapel at the Weld family's ancestral home, Ludworth Castle, in England. The Weld family had been Catholic for centuries, remaining so during and after the Reformation. Bishop Charles Walmsley was the ordaining prelate. Fr. John Carroll of Maryland chose this historic setting for his ordination.

John Carroll was born in 1735 to a wealthy, landowning family in Rock Creek, Maryland. He attended a Jesuit school in St. Omer in France. After his graduation, he entered the Jesuit Order, became a priest, and taught in France at the Order's schools. For most of his young adult life as a Jesuit priest, John Carroll was a teacher of religion and other subjects. After the suppression of the Jesuits in 1773, he became a parish priest and continued his calling to communicate the Gospel through preaching and teaching. His love of teaching endured throughout his life.

At forty years of age, Fr. Carroll returned to his mother's home in Rock Creek, and served as a parish priest there as the mounting conflict between England and the colonies came to a head. Following the Revolutionary War, Fr. Carroll was chosen as the first bishop of Baltimore, Maryland; he was ordained on August 15, 1790. For the next twenty-five years, he set the direction for the Catholic Church in the United States. Bishop Carroll forged a creative role for the Church in a new type of country.

One year after he became a bishop, he convened a synod—a formal meeting of his priests—to address pastoral needs of the diocesan Church and to make sure that the universal practice of the Church was being carried out in the United States. On November 7, 1791, twenty priests assembled at the bishop's house in Baltimore. The first session of the synod dealt with rules for administering Baptism and Confirmation. Another session developed guidelines for the admission of children to their first Holy Communion. Before receiving the Sacrament, children were expected to have reached the age of reason, to have received full instruction in Christian doctrine, and to have gone to Confession.

The fourth session dealt with the need for priests to receive approval from the bishop to hear confessions. During the fifth session, an extensive discussion was held about pastoral concerns regarding the Sacrament of Matrimony. The synod proved to be a success and received widespread praise at home and abroad. The synod's manner of governance helped shape the provincial and plenary councils of Baltimore well into the nineteenth century and beyond. The issues reflected Bishop Carroll's commitment to being an attentive teacher, bishop, and shepherd.

Throughout the years that followed, Bishop Carroll proceeded to influence the establishment of Catholic schools, the institution of religious congregations, and the creation of new dioceses and parishes. He was also effective at organizing his wide-ranging diocese, which included the nation's original thirteen states, the Northwest Territory, and later the vast territory of the Louisiana Purchase. He set the stage for the Church's strong community in the United States; he built a firm foundation upon which it could and did grow.

In 1808, on the same day that the Holy Father established the dioceses of Boston and Bardstown, the See of Baltimore was made an archdiocese. As a result, Carroll became the first archbishop in the United States.

During his time as bishop and then archbishop of Baltimore, the uniquely American policy of religious freedom began to take shape. The Declaration of Independence began with a presupposition of faith in God. The first article of the Bill of Rights prohibited Congress from making laws respecting an establishment of religion or prohibiting the free exercise of religion.

Archbishop Carroll died in 1815. Catholicism had made great progress under his twenty-five years of episcopal leadership. The number of Catholics increased four times over. The number of clergy to serve them doubled. Archbishop Carroll established three seminaries for the training of priests, three colleges for men, and several academies for women. With his encouragement, St. Elizabeth Seton's Sisters of Charity spread throughout the East Coast and onto the frontier. Other religious

SPANISH, FRENCH, AND NATIVE AMERICAN CATHOLICS

Within a few years of the first voyage of Christopher Columbus, the presence and influence of the Catholic Church were already evident in areas of the "New World" that would eventually become parts of the United States. The vast lands of what would become the continental United States were home to Native Americans as well as Spanish-speaking Catholics in California, Colorado, Arizona, New Mexico, Texas, and Florida, and in parts of Arkansas, Oklahoma, and the Olympic Peninsula in the state of Washington. Similarly, French-speaking Catholics found their home in the huge territory encompassed by the Louisiana Purchase and also in the American heartland and the Pacific Northwest, where Native Americans were evangelized by French Jesuit missionaries. From the early years of the sixteenth century, Mass was celebrated in the lands that are now Florida, Texas, and states of the U.S. Southwest. The first Catholic martyr in this land was a Franciscan missionary priest, Fr. Juan de Padilla, OFM, who was killed in 1542 because of his evangelization efforts among the natives of Quivira in what is present-day Kansas.

Not long afterwards, dioceses began to be established in the lands of the present-day United States. Catholic life, the preaching of the Gospel, the reception of the Sacraments, the celebration of the Eucharist, and the teaching and witness of Catholicism also began to grow in those parts of the continent that would become the Thirteen Colonies.

By the time Bishop John Carroll was appointed as shepherd to the nascent Catholic community in the United States (Catholics numbered about 35,000 in a national population of four million), Catholicism was flourishing in many parts of the continent. Throughout this text we will cite examples of the continuing religious impact of the nation's first Catholic generations.

congregations of men and women came from Europe and flourished. Archbishop Carroll guided the infant Church in the United States with faith, intelligence, and kindness.

Throughout the text of this *United States Catholic Catechism for Adults*, stories are presented to invite reflection on Catholic teaching. So it seems appropriate to use the story of Archbishop Carroll as the preface. He always acted to fulfill his role as a faithful teacher and shepherd, a concern shared by the U.S. bishops of today.

ABBREVIATIONS

Church Documents

AG   Second Vatican Council, *Decree on the Church's Missionary Activity (Ad Gentes Divinitus)*

CCC   *Catechism of the Catholic Church*

CCEO   *Code of Canons of the Eastern Churches (Codex Canonum Ecclesiarum Orientalium)*

CIC   *Code of Canon Law (Codex Iuris Canonici)*

DD   Pope John Paul II, *Day of the Lord (Dies Domini)*

DS   H. Denzinger and A. Schonmetzer, *(Enchiridion Symbolorum)*

DV   Second Vatican Council, *Dogmatic Constitution on Divine Revelation (Dei Verbum)*

EE   Pope John Paul II, *On the Eucharist (Ecclesia de Eucharistia)*

EN   Pope John Paul VI, *On Evangelization in the Modern World (Evangelii Nuntiandi)*

EV   Pope John Paul II, *The Gospel of Life (Evangelium Vitae)*

FC   Pope John Paul II, *On the Role of the Christian Family in the Modern World (Familiaris Consortio)*

GS   Second Vatican Council, *Pastoral Constitution on the Church in the Modern World (Gaudium et Spes)*

HV   Pope Paul VI, *On the Regulation of Birth (Humanae Vitae)*

LG   Second Vatican Council, *Dogmatic Constitution on the Church (Lumen Gentium)*

NA   Second Vatican Council, *Declaration on the Relation of the Church to Non-Christian Religions (Nostra Aetate)*

NMI   Pope John Paul II, *At the Close of the Great Jubilee of the Year 2000 (Novo Millennio Ineunte)*

PO   Second Vatican Council, *Decree on Priestly Life and Ministry (Presbyterorum Ordinis)*

RCIA   Rite of Christian Initiation of Adults

RVM   Pope John Paul II, *On the Most Holy Rosary (Rosarium Virginis Mariae)*

SC   Second Vatican Council, *Constitution on the Sacred Liturgy (Sacrosanctum Concilium)*

UR   Second Vatican Council, *Decree on Ecumenism (Unitatis Redintegratio)*

UUS   Pope John Paul II, *On Commitment to Ecumenism (Ut Unum Sint)*

Books of the Bible

Old Testament			Jon	Jonah
Gn	Genesis		Mi	Micah
Ex	Exodus		Na	Nahum
Lv	Leviticus		Hb	Habakkuk
Nm	Numbers		Zep	Zephaniah
Dt	Deuteronomy		Hg	Haggai
Jos	Joshua		Zec	Zechariah
Jgs	Judges		Mal	Malachi
Ru	Ruth			
1 Sm	1 Samuel			
2 Sm	2 Samuel		New Testament	
1 Kgs	1 Kings		Mt	Matthew
2 Kgs	2 Kings		Mk	Mark
1 Chr	1 Chronicles		Lk	Luke
2 Chr	2 Chronicles		Jn	John
Ezr	Ezra		Acts	Acts of the Apostles
Neh	Nehemiah		Rom	Romans
Tb	Tobit		1 Cor	1 Corinthians
Jdt	Judith		2 Cor	2 Corinthians
Est	Esther		Gal	Galatians
1 Mc	1 Maccabees		Eph	Ephesians
2 Mc	2 Maccabees		Phil	Philippians
Jb	Job		Col	Colossians
Ps	Psalms		1 Thes	1 Thessalonians
Prv	Proverbs		2 Thes	2 Thessalonians
Eccl	Ecclesiastes		1 Tm	1 Timothy
Sg (Song)	Song of Songs		2 Tm	2 Timothy
Wis	Wisdom		Ti	Titus
Sir	Sirach		Phlm	Philemon
Is	Isaiah		Heb	Hebrews
Jer	Jeremiah		Jas	James
Lam	Lamentations		1 Pt	1 Peter
Bar	Baruch		2 Pt	2 Peter
Ez	Ezekiel		1 Jn	1 John
Dn	Daniel		2 Jn	2 John
Hos	Hosea		3 Jn	3 John
Jl	Joel		Jude	Jude
Am	Amos		Rev	Revelation
Ob	Obadiah			

INTRODUCTION

[The Catechism of the Catholic Church] is meant to encourage and assist in the writing of new local catechisms, which must take into account various situations and cultures, while carefully preserving the unity of faith and fidelity to Catholic doctrine.

—Pope John Paul II, *The Deposit of Faith* (*Fidei Depositum*), IV, no. 4

On October 11, 1992, Pope John Paul II published his apostolic constitution *The Deposit of Faith*, promulgating the *Catechism of the Catholic Church* (CCC). He chose the publication date to mark the thirtieth anniversary of the opening of the Second Vatican Council.

Pope John Paul II envisioned the *Catechism* as a sure and authentic reference text for teaching Catholic doctrine and particularly for preparing local catechisms. The bishops of the United States subsequently discussed in depth what they might do to follow the pope's call to prepare a local catechism. It would need to take into account the local situation and culture, while at the same time preserving the unity of faith and fidelity to Catholic teaching found in the *Catechism of the Catholic Church*. In June 2000, the bishops determined that a national adult catechism would be an effective way to achieve this goal.

Before describing the content and approach of this adult catechism, several preliminary matters need to be presented. First, it should be noted that historically the term *catechism* has acquired a variety of meanings. It comes from a Greek word that means "to echo." Before the invention of the printing press in 1450, in the Church and elsewhere learning was mainly an oral experience. A Church teaching would be recited, and the listener would be instructed to "echo" it, or repeat it, until it was learned. This way of learning has been around since before the Church. Jewish teachers from both before and after the time of Jesus taught the Scriptures by again and again asking the learner to repeat verses.

The invention of the printing press made it possible to adapt the "speak and echo" method of catechesis into a question-and-answer approach that could be fixed in print. The Church adopted this approach. It is especially evident in the influential catechisms of St. Peter Canisius (1521-1597) and St. Robert Bellarmine (1542-1621).

THE *ROMAN CATECHISM,* 1566

A third development in catechisms occurred when the bishops at the Council of Trent in 1563 undertook the production of a printed catechism that would be a comprehensive, systematic presentation of Catholic teachings. St. Pius V completed this work and published it as the *Roman Catechism* in 1566. It sought to present Catholic truths from the viewpoint of their inherent coherence and value for instructing the faithful. It became the enduring sourcebook for local catechisms up to its last edition in 1978.

Until the second half of the twentieth century, for millions of Catholics in the United States the word *catechism* meant the *Baltimore Catechism*, which originated at the Third Plenary Council of Baltimore in 1884 when the bishops of the United States decided to publish a national catechism. It contained 421 questions and answers in thirty-seven chapters. The *Baltimore Catechism* gave unity to the teaching and understanding of the faith for millions of immigrant Catholics who populated American cities, towns, and farms. Its impact was felt right up to the dawn of the Second Vatican Council in 1962.

At that time, Blessed John XXIII articulated a vision for the Fathers of the Second Vatican Council that charged them to guard and present more effectively the deposit of Christian doctrine in order to make it more accessible to the Christian faithful and all people of goodwill in the contemporary world.

THE *CATECHISM OF*
THE CATHOLIC CHURCH, 1992

Eventually, it became clear that the development of a new universal cate-chism would be beneficial, especially since there has been significant growth in issues and insights in the Church and in society since 1566. In 1985, a synod of bishops was convened in Rome to celebrate the twenti-eth anniversary of the conclusion of the Second Vatican Council. Many of the synod fathers expressed the desire for a universal catechism that would be a reference book for the catechisms that would be prepared in various regions. The proposal was accepted, and the outcome was the *Catechism of the Catholic Church*, published in 1992. A new edition, which contained some modifications, was released in 1997.

This *Catechism of the Catholic Church* is arranged in four parts: "The Profession of Faith"; "The Celebration of the Christian Mystery"; "Life in Christ"; and "Christian Prayer." Its content is faithful to Apostolic Tradition, Scripture, and the Magisterium. It incorporates the heritage of the Doctors, Fathers, and saints of the Church. At the same time, it illuminates, with the light of faith, contemporary situa-tions, problems, and questions.

The *Catechism* begins with God's Revelation, to which we are called to respond in faith, worship, moral witness, and a life of prayer. The entire text is guided by the fact that Christian life is rooted in the cre-ative and providential outpouring of the Holy Trinity. The *Catechism* centers itself on the saving life, teachings, death, and Resurrection of Jesus Christ, the Son of God and Son of Mary. This text is a work by and of the Church.

The goal of the *Catechism of the Catholic Church* is to help facili-tate the lifelong conversion of the whole person to the Father's call to holiness and eternal life. At its heart is the celebration of the Christian mysteries, especially the Eucharist and the life of prayer. Users of the *Catechism* are called to witness Christ, the Church, and God's Kingdom of salvation, love, justice, mercy, and peace in the world.

While the *Catechism* is addressed to a number of audiences—bish-ops, priests, teachers, writers—it is meant for all the faithful who wish to deepen their knowledge of the Catholic faith. Further, it is offered to every person who wants to know what the Catholic Church teaches.

UNITED STATES CATHOLIC CATECHISM FOR ADULTS

The *United States Catholic Catechism for Adults* is an adaptation of the *Catechism of the Catholic Church*, and it is presented to Catholics of the United States who are members of both Latin and Eastern Churches, with the understanding that the Eastern Churches may develop their own catechisms for adults emphasizing their own traditions.

This text follows the *Catechism*'s arrangement of content: "The Creed"; "The Sacraments"; "Moral Life"; and "Prayer." It emphasizes the Trinity, Jesus Christ, the Sacraments, moral principles, and the heritage of the Doctors and saints of the Church. It is an organic and systematic expression of the Apostolic Tradition, expressed in an inspired way in Sacred Scripture and authoritatively interpreted by the Magisterium of the Church. This text also reflects the sacramental language, practice, and discipline of the Eastern Churches to the degree necessary to provide basic information to Latin Catholics about the Eastern Churches.

The Structure of Each Chapter of This Book

1. Story or Lesson of Faith
2. Teaching: Its Foundation and Application
3. Sidebars
4. Relationship of Catholic Teaching to the Culture
5. Questions for Discussion
6. Doctrinal Statements
7. Meditation and Prayer

CANONIZATION

A canonization today is the Church's official declaration, through the decision of the pope, that a person is a saint, truly in heaven and worthy of public veneration and imitation. The process begins by naming the person "Venerable," a "Servant of God" who has demonstrated a life of heroic virtue. The next stage is beatification, by which a person is named "Blessed." This step requires one miracle attributed to the intercession of the Servant of God. For canonization, a second miracle is needed, attributed to the intercession of the Blessed and having occurred after the individual's beatification. Miracles are not required for martyrs. The pope may dispense with some of the formalities or steps in the process.

1. Stories or Lessons of Faith

The Saints and the Beatified of America accompany the men and women of today with fraternal concern in all their joys and sufferings, until the final encounter with the Lord. With a view to encouraging the faithful to imitate them ever more closely and to seek their intercession more frequently . . . the Synod Fathers proposed . . . that there be prepared "a collection of short biographies of the Saints and the Beatified of America, which can shed light on and stimulate the response to the universal call to holiness in America."

—Pope John Paul II, *The Church in America*
(*Ecclesia in America*), no. 15

The preface and most of the chapters start with stories of Catholics, many from the United States. As far as possible, this *United States Catholic Catechism for Adults* relates the Church's teachings to the culture of the United States, both to affirm positive elements in our culture and to challenge the negative. One way of doing this is found in the stories that begin each chapter. Most of these narratives are biographical sketches of American saints or other outstanding Catholics who represent the variety of racial and ethnic witnesses to the Catholic way of life. These stories give us glimpses of how Catholics participated in the unfolding of American culture from colonial days to the present. Those chosen for these examples are Catholics whose lives or actions illustrate a particular Church teaching. From the earliest days of the Church when St. Athanasius wrote the life of St. Anthony of the Desert, it was clear that telling stories about saints and holy people encourages others to want to be like them and is an effective way of teaching Catholic doctrine.

2. Teaching: Its Foundation and Application

In each chapter, the introductory story is followed by a presentation of a particular teaching. This foundational teaching provides expositions on aspects of the Creed, the Sacraments, the Commandments, and prayer. A few comments about each of these sections are in order.

A. Creed: The Faith Professed

When we pray or recite the Creed, we can be reminded that Catholicism is a revealed religion. God is the author of our faith. All that we are expected to believe is summed up in the revelation of Jesus Christ. God has spoken all that is necessary for our Salvation in Jesus, the Word made flesh. God also gives us the gift of faith that enables us to respond, accept, and live out the implications of Divine Revelation. In this first section of the book, the roles of Apostolic Tradition, Scripture, and Magisterium are clearly outlined.

B. Sacraments: The Faith Celebrated

The second section of this text deals with the celebration of the Christian mystery in the liturgy and the Sacraments. Through the Sacraments the Holy Spirit makes available to us the mysteries of God's revelation in Christ. The saving gifts of Christ's ministry are encountered in the liturgy and are available to us. This is evident in the Sacraments

FATHERS AND DOCTORS OF THE CHURCH

The title "Father of the Church" has been given to those whose sanctity and teaching served to help others understand, defend, and pass on the Faith. Those who have achieved this distinction lived from the earliest days of the Church up to the last Father in the West (present-day Western Europe), St. Isidore of Seville (sixth century), and the last Father in the East (present-day southeastern Europe and Asia Minor), St. John Damascene (seventh century).

The golden age of the Fathers in the fourth and fifth centuries included such figures as St. Basil, St. John Chrysostom, St. Athanasius, and St. Gregory Nazianzen in the Eastern Church, and St. Jerome, St. Ambrose, and St. Augustine in the Western Church.

The title "Doctor of the Church" has been applied to persons from any era in the Church's history whose sanctity and writings have had a profound influence on theological and spiritual thought. Doctors of the Church include such figures as St. Thomas Aquinas, St. Catherine of Siena, St. Anthony of Padua, St. Teresa of Ávila, St. John of the Cross, St. Robert Bellarmine, and St. Thérèse of Lisieux.

of Initiation (Baptism, Confirmation, the Eucharist), the Sacraments of Healing (Penance and the Anointing of the Sick), and the Sacraments at the Service of Communion (Marriage and Holy Orders). Through the Sacraments, God shares his holiness with us so that we, in turn, can make the world holier.

C. Christian Morality: The Faith Lived

The third section of this text offers an extensive exposition of the foundations of the Christian moral life. Themes of covenant, grace, happiness, sin, forgiveness, virtues, the action of the Holy Spirit, the call to love God and neighbor, the dignity of the person, and the Church's social teachings are part of the foundational elements for morality. Subsequently, when the Ten Commandments are presented, it is easier to see how the Covenant with God comes first and how the Commandments are ways in which we live out this Covenant. In the Sermon on the Mount, Jesus presents to us a summary of the New Covenant in the Beatitudes. Hence, the Commandments are more than moral laws; our commitment to living them flows from our response to the Covenant we have with God, as members of the Church strengthened by the Holy Spirit.

D. Prayer: The Faith Prayed

The last section of this text bears an essential relationship to the second section on the liturgy, which is the prayer life of the Church herself. This section deals with vocal prayer, meditation and contemplation, and the types of prayer—adoration, petition, intercession, thanksgiving, and praise. A special chapter is devoted to a commentary on the Our Father, which is the Lord's Prayer. It seemed suitable here to acknowledge the special link between doctrine and prayer so that a Church teaching is not seen as an abstract idea, and so that prayer not be without a solid doctrinal foundation.

3. Sidebars

The doctrinal section in each chapter is followed by a sidebar composed of three questions with answers taken from the *Catechism of the Catholic Church*. This is one of several ways in which the reader is drawn to explore the extensive resources of the universal *Catechism*. Throughout the text, other sidebars on various topics appear where appropriate.

4. Relationship of Catholic Teaching to the Culture

The next section in each chapter returns to the theme of relating Church teaching for a diverse U.S. society. There are many issues to address such as human dignity, fairness, respect, solidarity, and justice. Each chapter contains a reflection on how its teaching can apply to our culture. Sometimes there are positive elements; at other times, challenges are to be met. Issues such as disbelief, relativism, subjectivism, and differences about morality highlight conflicts between Church teachings and the culture. The purpose of this section in each chapter is to point to the way in which the Church proclaims salvation to the culture, based on confidence in the validity and relevance of Catholic teaching.

It might also be helpful to note that in keeping with cultural practice in the United States, the text uses horizontally inclusive language, that is, describing human persons according to both male and female genders. The only exceptions to this practice are when the *Catechism* or some other source is quoted directly. References to God in this text maintain traditional usage.

5. Questions for Discussion

Following the section of each chapter that addresses aspects of faith as applied to U.S. culture are questions that allow the readers to explore personal and communal ways of internalizing the teaching of the Church.

6. Doctrinal Statements

Following both a story of faith and a concise review of the Church's teaching and its relation to the culture, each chapter contains a review of points of doctrine covered in the chapter.

7. Meditation and Prayer

As far as possible, this book is meant to draw the reader into a prayerful attitude before God. Every chapter concludes with a meditation drawn from a saint or spiritual writer. A catechism needs to be more than a summary of teachings. God has called all of us to prayer and holiness. Doctrines are distillations of prayer and thought made possible by the Holy Spirit's guidance of the Church. Prayer is the gate that leads us to a deeper understanding of the Word of God and to the hidden treasures of doctrinal teachings. A formal prayer is presented at this point in each chapter. It is usually drawn from the Church's liturgy or from traditional prayers of the Church so that the reader may become more familiar with the prayer life of the universal Church. There is also a collection of some traditional Catholic prayers in the appendix.

Glossary

Finally, an alphabetized glossary of many terms appears at the end of this book. The definitions are brief. It is recommended that readers also consult the *Catechism of the Catholic Church*, which has an extensive glossary. While studying the *United States Catholic Catechism for Adults*, readers can consult these glossaries for definitions of words that are not familiar to them.

CONCLUSION

It is our hope that this *United States Catholic Catechism for Adults* will be an aid and a guide for deepening faith. It may serve as a resource for the Rite of Christian Initiation of Adults and for the ongoing catechesis of adults. It will also be of interest for those who wish to become acquainted with Catholicism. Finally, it can serve as an invitation for all the faithful to continue growing in the understanding of Jesus Christ and his saving love for all people.

PART I

THE CREED:
THE FAITH PROFESSED

1 MY SOUL LONGS FOR YOU, O GOD (Ps 42:2)

THE HUMAN QUEST FOR GOD
—CCC, NOS. 27-43

ONE WOMAN'S QUEST

Elizabeth Bayley came from a wealthy, Episcopalian, New York family. Born in 1774, two years before the signing of the Declaration of Independence, she came into a world of conflicting loyalties—royalists and revolutionaries. Her father threw in his lot with the American Revolution.

At sixteen, Elizabeth fell in love with William Magee Seton, a wealthy businessman. Three years later, in early 1794, she married William and in time gave birth to three girls and two boys. The couple was married for only a few years before a series of problems began to affect the family. By 1801, William's business had failed and so had his health.

William and Elizabeth accepted an offer from the Fillichi family of Livorno, Italy, to come there to help William recover. However, shortly after arriving in Italy in late 1803 with his wife and eldest daughter, William died. The Fillichis comforted the widow and child and impressed them both with their strong Catholic faith. While in Italy, Elizabeth spent much time visiting various Catholic churches and spending time in them praying in front of the Blessed Sacrament.

After about six months, Elizabeth returned to New York, where she was reunited with her other children, and she decided to become a Catholic. A year later, she was received into full communion with the Catholic Church on March 4, 1805, by Fr. Matthew O'Brien, pastor of St. Peter's Church in lower Manhattan. Her family and friends abandoned her, but Antonio Fillichi—who was in New York at this time—supported her.

Now she needed to make a living and support her family. She wanted to open a school. She received an invitation from Bishop John Carroll to start a school for girls near St. Mary's Seminary on Paca Street in Baltimore. This became the groundwork of a career that would lead her to become the foundress of the American Sisters of Charity and that would lay the basis for the United States Catholic school system. She provided free education for the poor while also accepting tuition from those who could afford it.

Cecilia O'Conway of Philadelphia joined her effort. They discussed starting a religious congregation to ensure the future of their ministry. Bishop Carroll supported the idea. In a short time, their dream became a reality. Property was purchased at Emmitsburg, Maryland. Other women joined Elizabeth and Cecilia, and together they formed the nucleus of the new community. Mother Seton—as she was now known—founded orphanages in Philadelphia and New York. Her successors went on to establish a stunning array of charitable services.

Mother Seton did not neglect her own children. Her daughters were educated in her school. Her sons received their schooling at Georgetown College. She encouraged her son William to become a banker. Instead, he chose to be a merchant seaman. Eventually he settled down, married, and had two sons, one of whom became an archbishop.

Elizabeth Ann Seton died in 1821 at the age of forty-six, and she was canonized in 1975 as the first native-born North American saint. Her feast day is celebrated on January 4.

St. Elizabeth Seton and her journey of faith point to the reality that in all of us there is a longing to know God and to draw closer to him. The story of how she responded to that longing is a suitable introduction to our opening lesson on the human longing and capacity for God.

THE UNIVERSAL DESIRE FOR GOD

The desire for God is written in the human heart, because man is created by God and for God.

—CCC, no. 27

People have always asked fundamental questions: Who am I? Where did I come from? Where am I going? Why do I need to struggle to achieve my goals? Why is it so hard to love and be loved? What is the meaning of sickness, death, and evil? What will happen after death?

These questions relate to human existence. They also move one to ask questions about the divine because they pertain to God's existence. When asked with ever deeper reflection, they uncover an inner sense of longing for God. They challenge our minds, but the mind's answers are not always sufficient. We must also become aware of the mysterious yearning of the human heart.

God has planted in every human heart the hunger and longing for the infinite, for nothing less than God. St. Augustine, a theologian from the fifth century, said it best: "Our heart is restless until it rests in you" (St. Augustine, *The Confessions*, bk. 1, chap. 1, 1; cf. CCC, no. 30).

How is our quest for God awakened? God first pursues us; this spurs us to search for him for whom we were made. The *Catechism* presents three paths through which every person can come to God: creation, the human person, and Revelation. In the next chapter, Revelation will be presented as the greatest and most essential path to God. He is discovered also through creation and through the mystery of our inner life.

THROUGH CREATION

The heavens declare the glory of God.

—Ps 19:2

Ever since the creation of the world, his invisible attributes of eternal power and divinity have been able to be understood and perceived in what he has made.

—Rom 1:20

St. Augustine asks us to look at the beauty of the world and let it open us to God. "Question the beauty of the earth, question the beauty of the sea . . . question the beauty of the sky. . . . All respond, 'See, we are beautiful.' Their beauty is a profession. These beauties are subject to change. Who made them if not the Beautiful One who is not subject to change?" (St. Augustine, Sermon 241, no. 2; cf. CCC, no. 32).

Throughout the history of the Church, Christians have seen the universe as evidence of God's existence. The order, harmony, and beauty of the world point to an intelligent Creator. The purposefulness of creation from the inanimate to human life similarly points to a wise Creator. The fact that all visible things come to be and eventually pass out of earthly existence points to an eternal Creator who has no beginning and no end and who sustains all that he has created (cf. CCC, no. 32).

THROUGH THE HUMAN PERSON

I praise you, so wonderfully you made me.

—Ps 139:14

Every human person seeks to know the truth and to experience goodness. Moral goodness appeals to us. We treasure our freedom and strive to maintain it. We hear the voice of our conscience and want to live by it. We long for absolute happiness.

These experiences make us aware of our souls and our spiritual nature. The more we become aware of these truths, the more we are drawn to the reality of God who is the Supreme Good. These are the seeds of eternity within us that have their origins only in God. St. Augustine confirmed this insight when he prayed, "That I may know myself, that I may know you."

Since this is true, why have so many not found God?

Many reasons account for the lack of familiarity with God. The presence of so much suffering and pain in the world disheartens some and moves them to rebel against the idea of a God who would let this happen. Some do not know who God is because no one has shared the good news of his self-revelation with them. Ignorance of religion or indifference to it is another cause.

The scandalous behavior of some believers frequently drives honest seekers away from religion. Sinful conduct weakens the ability of

FROM THE CATECHISM

1. How have people expressed their quest for God throughout history?

In many ways, throughout history down to the present day, men have given their expression to their quest for God in their religious beliefs and behavior: in their prayers, sacrifices, rituals, meditations, and so forth. These forms of religious expression, despite the ambiguities they often bring with them, are so universal that one may well call man a *"religious being"* (cf. Acts 17:26-28). (CCC, no. 28)

2. What do we mean by "proofs" for God's existence?

Created in God's image and called to know and love him, the person who seeks God discovers certain ways of coming to know him. These are also called proofs for the existence of God, not in the sense of proofs in the natural sciences, but rather in the sense of "converging and convincing arguments," which allow us to attain certainty about the truth. These "ways" of approaching God from creation have a twofold point of departure: the physical world and the human person. (CCC, no. 31)

3. Can we know God?

The Church teaches that the one true God, our Creator and Lord, can be known with certainty from his works, by the natural light of human reason (cf. First Vatican Council, can. 2 §1: H. Denzinger and A. Schonmetzer, *Enchiridion Symbolorum* [DS] 3026). (CCC, no. 47)

many to assume responsibility for their actions and causes them to hide from God (cf. Gn 3:8; Jn 3:19ff.). Others may resist acknowledging God because they do not wish to follow and obey God. Still others may allow their lives to become so cluttered, hectic, or busy that there is little room for God.

Throughout history, people have yearned for God. Despite obstacles and occasions of violent opposition to belief in God, millions of people have continued to search for God. The spiritual dynamism of the human heart, having its origin in God, endures in countless and inspiring ways. Often just when the shadows of doubt and skepticism appear to have laid the great search to rest, our yearning for God surges again to witness to the light of God's inherent attractiveness in human life.

A GENERATION OF SEEKERS

Religious seekers in the United States live within a culture that in some important ways provides support for belief in God while at the same time also discourages and corrodes the faith in practice. It is encouraging that many are finding the move to secularism to be an unsatisfactory approach and continue to search for a deeper meaning in life.

Particularly encouraging is that a number of young people, who had once drifted away from faith, today are seeking a connection with a church community. Among the many causes of this hunger for God, two stand out: the experience of having children who need a proper education and upbringing, and the experience of one's own longing for direction, meaning, and hope.

Catholicism in the United States continues to attract thousands of new members each year as the Holy Spirit works through the Church to awaken a thirst for the Lord. The Rite of Christian Initiation of Adults, the pastoral process for initiating new members into the Church, is ministering to great numbers of seekers. The Church is leading them to knowledge of the truths of faith, to the celebration of the Seven Sacraments, to commitment to the moral life—including the forming of a social conscience—and to the practice of prayer, and at the same time, the Church responds to their desire for community.

The Church does more than welcome new members; she forms disciples. Seekers can begin to find in the Church fulfillment of their heart's desires. They are invited to undertake a spiritual journey that is focused on Jesus Christ and his Kingdom of salvation, love, justice, and mercy. Jesus reminds us that this Kingdom is already in our midst, and as his disciples we are called to assist him in bringing it to its fullness.

This is the Church's invitation to seekers who want to discover a satisfying answer to their spiritual hungers. Her invitation is rich: to seekers, old and new, and to those who might label themselves as alienated or indifferent, the Church offers Jesus Christ and his love, the fulfillment of hope. The Church offers a way of belonging that teaches truths that free one from sin and its power. The Church initiates members into an intimate relationship with God—indeed, into a participation in the divine life—where one will find genuine joy and fulfillment. This is all possible because of Jesus Christ and his love.

FOR DISCUSSION

1. What are you looking for in life? What are your goals and ideals? How do God and the Church play a part in what you are seeking? How is your life a journey toward God?
2. As a seeker, how do you look for truth? When you hear of truth or behold beauty or experience goodness, what do you think? If you seek for God, what has made this possible? What have you found in your search thus far?
3. As a Catholic, how are you searching for God? Why does seeking God keep your relationship with him dynamic? How does the Church help you in your search for God? How does your family affect your faith?

DOCTRINAL STATEMENTS

- God has planted in every human heart the hunger and longing for the infinite—for nothing less than himself.
- Only in God will we find the truth, peace, and happiness for which we never stop searching. Created in God's image, we are called to know and love the Lord.
- God can be known with certainty from his works in creation and from the spiritual nature of the human person by the light of natural

reason, although there are many difficulties in coming to this knowledge because of humanity's historical and sinful condition.

- By our openness to goodness and truth, our experience, our sense of moral goodness, our listening to the voice of conscience, and our desire for happiness, we can discern our spiritual soul and can come to see that this could only have its origin in God.

- We can speak of God even if our limited language cannot exhaust the mystery of who he is.

- While we can come to know something about God by our natural power of reason, there is a deeper knowledge of God that comes to us through Divine Revelation.

MEDITATION

Where did I find you, that I came to know you? You were not within my memory before I learned of you. Where, then, did I find you before I came to know you, if not within yourself, far above me? . . .

Late have I loved you, O Beauty ever ancient, ever new, late have I loved you! . . . Created things kept me from you; yet if they had not been in you they would not have been at all. [O eternal truth, true love and beloved eternity. You are my God. To you I sigh day and night.] . . . You were with me but I was not with you. Created things kept me from you; yet if they had not been in you they would not have been at all. You called, you shouted, and you broke through my deafness. You flashed, you shone, and you dispelled my blindness. You breathed your fragrance on me; I drew in breath and now I pant for you. I have tasted you; now I hunger and thirst for more. You touched me, and I burn for your peace.

—St. Augustine, *The Confessions*, bk. 10, chap. 26, 27.37

PRAYER

As the deer longs for streams of water,
    so my soul longs for you, O God.
My being thirsts for God, the living God.
    When can I go and see the face of God?
My tears have been my food day and night,
    as they ask daily, "Where is your God?"
Those times I recall
    as I pour out my soul,
When I went in procession with the crowd,
    I went with them to the house of God,
Amid loud cries of thanksgiving,
    with the multitude keeping festival.
Why are you downcast, my soul;
    why do you groan within me?
Wait for God, whom I shall praise again,
    my savior and my God.

—Ps 42:2-6

God loves each one of us as if there were only one of us to love.

—St. Augustine

2 GOD COMES TO MEET US

GOD REVEALS A PLAN OF LOVING GOODNESS
—CCC, NOS. 50-67

GOD REVEALS HIS HOLY NAME

 Moses was tending the flock of his father-in-law Jethro, the priest of Midian. Leading the flock across the desert, he came to Horeb, the mountain of God. There an angel of the Lord appeared to him in fire flaming out of a bush. As Moses looked on, he was surprised to see that the bush, though on fire, was not consumed. So he decided, "I must go over to look at this remarkable sight to see why the bush is not burned."

When the Lord saw him coming over to look at the sight more closely, God called out to him from the bush, "Moses! Moses!"

Moses answered, "Here I am."

God said, "Come no nearer! Remove the sandals from your feet, for the place where you stand is holy ground. I am the God of your father, the God of Abraham, the God of Isaac, the God of Jacob. The cry of the Israelites has reached me and I have truly noted that the Egyptians are oppressing them. Come now! I will send you to Pharaoh to lead my people, the Israelites out of Egypt."

But Moses said, "Who am I that I should go to Pharaoh and lead the Israelites out of Egypt?"

God answered, "I will be with you; and this shall be your proof that it is I who have sent you: when you bring my people out of Egypt, you will worship God on this very mountain."

"But," Moses said to God, "when I go to the Israelites and say to them, 'The God of your fathers has sent me to you,' if they ask me 'What is his name?' what am I to tell them?"

God replied, "I AM WHO AM." Then he added, "This is what you shall tell the Israelites: I AM sent me to you. . . . This is my name forever; this is my title for all generations."

But Moses said to the LORD, "If you please, LORD, I have never been eloquent, neither in the past, nor recently, nor now that you have spoken to your servant; but I am slow of speech and tongue."

The LORD said to him, "Who gives one man the gift of speech and no such gift to another? Is it not I, the LORD? Go then! It is I who will assist you in speaking and will teach you what you are to say."

Yet Moses persisted, "If you please, LORD, send someone else."

Then the LORD relented, "Have you not your brother, Aaron the Levite? I know that he is an eloquent speaker. He shall speak to the people for you. He shall be your spokesman. I will assist both you and him and teach the two of you both what you are to do." (adapted from Exodus 3:1-15; 4:10-16)

The Old Testament is filled with numerous occasions where God reveals himself, such as he does to Moses in this passage from Exodus. The event of God's self-disclosure to Moses at the burning bush is an excellent introduction to the mystery of God's revelatory acts, a truth of our faith that is the focus of this chapter.

GOD REVEALS HIS LOVING PLAN TO SAVE US

By natural reason man can know God with certainty, on the basis of his works. But there is another order of knowledge, which man cannot possibly arrive at by his own powers: the order of divine revelation.

—First Vatican Council, *Dogmatic Constitution on the Catholic Faith* (*Dei Filius*), no. 1870

Through the use of reason, we can learn much about God from both creation and conscience, but Revelation enables us to learn about God's inner life and his loving plan to save us from sin and share in his divine life. No amount of unaided thinking could penetrate such a mystery. God freely chose to share this hidden mystery with us. God's sharing was an act of friendship for us, revealing himself as one reveals his or her heart to a friend. Love does such things.

God's Revelation unfolded gradually throughout history. "Wishing to open up the way to heavenly salvation, he manifested himself to our first parents from the very beginning. After the fall, he buoyed them up with the hope of salvation, by promising redemption" (Second Vatican Council, *Dogmatic Constitution on Divine Revelation* [*Dei Verbum*; DV], no. 3; cf. Gn 3:15).

God continued over the succeeding centuries to provide providential care for those he created in his image and likeness. He called Abraham to make of him a great nation, a chosen people through whom salvation would come to the world. In the encounter of God with Moses, God reveals himself as "I AM WHO AM." These words reveal something about God, who, nevertheless, still remains mysterious. God is revealed as the source of all that is, but who he is will be revealed still further as he continues his loving work for his people. The prophets, in reflecting on God's actions, will make clearer the nature of God. But the clearest Revelation will come in Jesus Christ.

"In times past, God spoke in partial and various ways to our ancestors; in these last days he spoke to us through a son" (Heb 1:1-2). This Son was Jesus Christ, the fullness of Revelation. Wonderful indeed is this mystery of our faith in Jesus Christ, as we say in professing it, "[He] was manifested in the flesh, / vindicated in the Spirit; / seen by angels; / proclaimed to the Gentiles, / believed throughout the world, / taken up in glory" (1 Tm 3:16).

Revelation is the self-disclosure of the living God. God shows himself by both great deeds, as narrated for us in Scripture, and by the words that illumine the meaning of these deeds (see DV, no. 2). In Revelation, the tremendous gulf between God and the human race is bridged. More profoundly God desires to have an intimate relationship with all people. The process of Revelation, which took centuries to unfold, reached its magnificent fulfillment in the life, death, and Resurrection of Jesus Christ.

Revelation is the act by which God speaks to and forms a covenant people.[1] The covenant between God and humanity was first established with Noah after the great Flood, when God in his mercy promised that never again would there be a catastrophe that threatens the existence of all of humanity. God entered into a covenant later with Abraham and then with the people of Israel at the time of their exodus from slavery in Egypt under the leadership of Moses. He affirmed that they will always be his people.

This is the grand drama of the dialogue between God and his people that takes place in the lived history of the people encompassed by his love. It includes the people's inspired interpretation of historical events that reflects an ever greater understanding of God's will and presence as they advanced on their pilgrimage through the centuries.

It requires faith to respond to God's revealing word and to perceive the divine action in history. There are those who do not have faith or who consciously reject living in faith. They cannot or will not perceive God's presence or action in the world and sometimes scoff at or ridicule those who do. But for many people, God makes faith possible and with the guidance of the Holy Spirit faith helps those people to grow in an appreciation of how God has worked in history to love and save us.

God's Revelation disturbed and changed the patriarchs, prophets, Apostles, and others. When Moses encountered God in the burning bush, Moses trembled and took off his shoes, for he stood on holy ground (cf. Ex 3:1-6). Isaiah beheld the glory of God, and when the vision disappeared he saw himself in a brand-new light, "Woe is me, I am doomed! For I am a man of unclean lips" (Is 6:5). Faced with the revelation of divine power in Jesus, Peter begged, "Depart from me, Lord, for I am a sinful man" (Lk 5:8). Revelation calls for a response of faith and conversion, not just in times past, but today as well.

Because the Christian covenant is definitive, there will be no new public Revelation until the final glorious manifestation of Jesus Christ at the end days (DV, no. 4). All that is needed for salvation has already

---

1   A covenant was originally a treaty in which an overlord and a vassal accepted certain responsibilities toward each other. In the Old Testament, this idea of covenant became the primary analogy for the relationship between God and his people.

FROM THE CATECHISM

1. How does God freely reveal himself?
This he does by revealing the mystery, his plan of loving goodness, formed from all eternity in Christ, for the benefit of all men. God has fully revealed this plan by sending us his beloved Son, our Lord Jesus Christ, and the Holy Spirit. (CCC, no. 50)

2. What response to Revelation did God plan for men and women?
By revealing himself, God wishes to make them capable of responding to him, and of knowing him, and of loving him far beyond their own natural capacity. (CCC, no. 52)

3. If Revelation is complete, what is the next step?
Even if Revelation is already complete, it has not been made completely explicit; it remains for Christian faith gradually to grasp its full significance over the course of the centuries. (CCC, no. 66)

been revealed. What are called *private revelations*, that is, messages such as those given by the Blessed Virgin Mary at Lourdes and Fatima, add nothing to what was publicly revealed up and through Christ but can help inspire a more profound commitment to what has been revealed through public Revelation.

THE GOSPEL AND CULTURE

The split between the Gospel and culture is without a doubt the drama of our time.

—Pope Paul VI, *On Evangelization in the Modern World*
(*Evangelii Nuntiandi*), no. 20

Religion does not exist in a vacuum. It operates in a given culture at a particular moment in time. The understanding of a living God who has revealed a loving plan to save us takes place in real time. There is much in our culture that is good and favorable to faith and morality. The freedom to practice our faith is a treasured principle in our society.

But there are troubling developments. Most history today is taught from a secular viewpoint. Such a prevailing attitude often makes it hard for believers to realize there is a starting point in God's Revelation for understanding human history. The culture in which we live is, in many ways, individualistic, secular, and materialistic. This poses a challenge to Christians and other believers who are asked to respond in faith to God who has revealed himself. It often requires great patience and much virtue to live a faith-filled life, to hand on Gospel values to children and others, and to interact with people—often the young—whose lives are affected by counter-Christian cultural currents.

In many ways, attitudes and actions in the United States have fostered a "culture of disbelief." The First Amendment, which prohibits the establishment of a state religion, has been interpreted in such a way that it excessively marginalizes religion. Society has reached the stage in which people of faith are pressured to act publicly as though religion does not matter. This has caused many believers to think their faith is strictly a private matter and that it should have no influence on society and politics.

The Church's response is to bring the Gospel into our culture in order to build on what is positive in it and to change what is not. This is one aspect of evangelization, the proclamation of the Gospel to all peoples. It assumes that we first must be evangelized ourselves, calling each other to an intimate relationship with Jesus Christ. It means embracing truth, beauty, and goodness wherever it can be found in our society, while at the same time removing falsehood and injustice from our land.

We must remember that all is not darkness. There are rays of light in our culture shed by Jesus, the Light of the World. There are seeds of the Word in our society sown by Jesus, the tireless Sower of love and truth. We do not work alone. The Holy Spirit is our teacher and guide.

Cultural change is slow, but it can take place through perseverance and God's grace. Evangelizers need a broad vision as well as wisdom, courage, fortitude, and perseverance. Evangelizing a culture relies on deep insight into the mysteries of our faith and a keen vision for understanding the basis of our culture.

Culture is not just an abstraction; it is the sum of the beliefs, attitudes, and practices of individuals and communities. Evangelizing a culture means dealing with people. It involves more than persuading people of the truth of Christ and the Church. Sharing the Gospel with others means offering them its transforming power, not just for their minds, but also for their hearts. In our daily prayer, we need to lift up our fellow citizens and their needs to God's loving concern for them.

The Catholic Church provides us with numerous ways to witness and teach the truth and love of Jesus Christ. Church history shows that the renewal of faith is frequently accompanied by a return to the truths of the faith and witnessing to those truths. Such a renewal of faith will gradually influence our culture.

FOR DISCUSSION

1. When friends and family members converse with one another, what do they reveal about themselves? What does God reveal of himself to us in treating us as friends and family members? How does God's Revelation give meaning to our lives?
2. What is meant when we say that we have a "revealed" religion? What are positive features in our culture? How can culture be converted and transformed by the Gospel?
3. What would help you to spend more time reading and praying over God's revealed word in Scripture? Why can we say that growth in our faith will strengthen us to affect public policy with our beliefs?

DOCTRINAL STATEMENTS

• Revelation is the self-disclosure of the living God and his plan to save us. Revelation shows us that God desires to have an intimate and loving relationship with everyone.
• The process of Revelation took centuries to unfold. God gradually communicated the divine mystery by words and deeds.

- From the beginning, God established a personal relationship with our first parents. After the Fall, he encouraged them with the hope of Salvation by promising them Redemption.
- God's Revelation resulted in a relationship with people that is called a *covenant* in Scripture. Scripture tells us that God entered into a covenant with Noah and all living beings (cf. Gn 9:16).
- Revelation is an act by which God speaks to and forms a covenant people beginning with Abraham. He then chose Moses through whom the divine law was given to the covenant people.
- Through the prophets God prepared the covenant people to look forward to the coming of the Messiah who would bring the salvation destined for all people.
- Revelation reached its fullness in God's Son, Jesus Christ. The Son is the Father's definitive Word. No new public revelation will occur before the final, glorious manifestation of Jesus Christ.
- God's Revelation is transmitted to us by Apostolic Tradition and Scripture. This is the topic of our next chapter.

■ MEDITATION ■

Jesus Christ is the definitive revelation of God:

> Christ, the Son of God made man, is the Father's one, perfect, and unsurpassable Word. In him he has said everything; there will be no other word than this one. St. John of the Cross, among others, commented strikingly on Hebrews 1:1-2: "In giving us his Son, his only Word (for he possesses no other), he spoke everything to us at once in this sole Word—and he has no more to say . . . because what he spoke before to the prophets in parts, he has now spoken all at once by giving us the All Who is His Son. Any person questioning God or desiring some vision or revelation would be guilty not only of foolish behavior but also of offending him, by not fixing his eyes entirely upon Christ and by living with the desire for some other novelty."

—CCC, no. 65, citing St. John of the Cross,
The Ascent of Mount Carmel, 2, 22, 3-5

PRAYER

Your word, LORD, stands forever;
    it is firm as the heavens.
Through all generations your truth endures;
    fixed to stand firm like the earth.
Your word is a lamp for my feet,
    a light for my path.

—Ps 119:89-90; 105

Make every effort to supplement your faith with virtue.

—2 Pt 1:5

3 PROCLAIM THE GOSPEL TO EVERY CREATURE (Mk 16:15)

THE TRANSMISSION OF DIVINE REVELATION
—CCC, NOS. 74-133

HANDING ON THE FAITH

Blessed John XXIII (pope from 1958 to 1963) believed that the Church needed a pastoral renewal that would enable the Church to minister more effectively to contemporary society. In his time he sensed that new ways were needed to communicate Christian doctrine to reveal the inherent attractiveness of the Gospel, while protecting its integrity. He said in his address to the bishops at the opening of the Second Vatican Council in 1962, "Christian doctrine should be guarded and taught more efficaciously." When he spoke about the Church's being the source of unity for all peoples, he based his teaching on Jesus Christ, the one and only Savior who prayed at the Last Supper, "that they may all be one, as you, Father, are in me, and I in you" (Jn 17:21). In his opening address to the bishops on October 11, 1962, Blessed John XXIII explained his vision for the Second Vatican Council, the twenty-first Ecumenical Council.[2] He proposed five points for achieving this goal:

1. *Be filled with hope and faith. Do not be prophets of gloom.*
"Divine Providence is leading us to a new order of human relations,

---

2   An Ecumenical Council is a gathering of bishops from around the world called together by the pope or approved by him. The Second Vatican Council was held from 1962 to 1965.

which by men's own efforts and even beyond their very expectations, are directed toward God's superior and inscrutable design."

2. *Discover ways of teaching the faith more effectively.* "The greatest concern of the ecumenical council is this: that the sacred deposit of Christian doctrine should be guarded and taught more efficaciously."

3. *Deepen the understanding of doctrine.* Authentic doctrine "should be studied and expounded through the methods of research and the literary forms of modern thought. The substance of the ancient doctrine and deposit of the faith is one thing, and the way in which it is presented is another."

4. *Use the medicine of mercy.* "Errors vanish as quickly as they arise, like fog before the sun. The Church has always opposed these errors. Frequently she has condemned them with the greatest severity. Nowadays, the Spouse of Christ prefers to make use of the medicine of mercy rather than that of severity. She considers that she meets the needs of the present day by demonstrating the validity of her teaching rather than by condemnation."

5. *Seek unity within the Church, with Christians separated from Catholicism, with those of non-Christian religions, and with all men and women of goodwill.* "Such is the aim of the Second Vatican Ecumenical Council which . . . prepares, as it were, and consolidates the path toward that unity of mankind where truth reigns, charity is the law and whose extent is eternity." ((Blessed) Pope John XXIII, *Rejoice, O Mother Church* (*Gaudet Mater Ecclesia*), opening address at the Second Vatican Council (October 11, 1962))

Pope John Paul II noted that the Second Vatican Council owes much to the immediate past. He wrote the following:

The Second Vatican Council was a providential event. It is often considered as a new era in the life of the Church. This is true, but at the same time it is difficult to overlook the fact that the Council drew much from the experience of the immediate past, especially from the intellectual legacy left by Pius XII. In the history of the Church the "old" and the "new" are always closely interwoven. Thus it was for the Second Vatican Council and for the activity of the popes connected with the Council, starting with John XXIII, continuing with Paul VI and John Paul I, up to the present Pope. (Pope John Paul II, *On the Coming of the Third Millennium (Tertio Millennio Adveniente)*, no. 18)

❧ ⟡ ❧

TRANSMITTING GOD'S REVELATION

Sacred Tradition and Sacred Scripture, then, are bound closely together and communicate one with the other. For both of them, flowing out from the same divine well-spring, come together in some fashion to form one thing and move towards the same goal.

—CCC, no. 80, citing DV, no. 9

Blessed John XXIII and the Second Vatican Council itself illustrate how the Church constantly draws upon Tradition and Sacred Scripture. This chapter examines these foundations of Church teaching because it is through Tradition and Scripture that the Church knows God's Revelation and transmits it from one generation to another.

SACRED TRADITION

Jesus Christ, the divine Son of God become man, is the fullness of Revelation by his teaching, witness, death, and Resurrection. On the road to Emmaus, the risen Jesus showed the two disciples how the teachings of the prophets were fulfilled in him and proclaimed by his own lips. Just before his Ascension, Christ commissioned the Apostles to preach the Gospel to all whose hearts would be open to receive them. The revealed Word of God in the Gospel would be for everyone a source of saving truth and moral discipline.

He commanded the Apostles to proclaim and witness his Kingdom of love, justice, mercy, and healing, foretold by the prophets and fulfilled in his Paschal Mystery. Jesus sent them the Holy Spirit to enable them to fulfill this great commission, to give them needed courage, and to help them in their evangelizing work.

THE BIBLE

The Church accepts and venerates the Bible as inspired. The Bible is composed of the forty-six books of the Old Testament and the twenty-seven books of the New Testament. Together these books make up the Scriptures. The unity of the Old and New Testaments flows from the revealed unity of God's loving plan to save us. The books of the Old Testament include the Pentateuch, historical books, the books of the Prophets, and the Wisdom books. The New Testament contains the four Gospels, the Acts of the Apostles, and letters from St. Paul and other Apostles and concludes with the Book of Revelation.

The *canon* of the Bible, which is a term that refers to the books the Bible contains, was fixed within the first centuries of the Church. These books that make up both the Old and New Testaments were identified by the Church as having been divinely inspired. At times, people challenged the divinely inspired character of some of the books in the Bible. In 1546, the Council of Trent declared that all the books in both the Old and New Testament were inspired in their entirety. This declaration was subsequently confirmed by both the First Vatican Council (1869-1870) and the Second Vatican Council (1962-1965). Those books whose divinely inspired character was challenged appear in non-Catholic Bibles identified as either the "Deuterocanonical Books" or the "Apocrypha."

Graced by the Holy Spirit, the Apostles did what Jesus commanded them. They did this orally, in writing, by the heroic sanctity of their lives, and by ensuring that there would be successors for this mission. The first communication of the Gospel was by preaching and witness. The Apostles proclaimed Jesus, his Kingdom, and the graces of salvation. They called for the obedience of faith (hearing and obeying God's Word), the reception of Baptism, the formation of a community of believers, gathering for the Eucharist, and generosity to the poor.

The Apostles chose men to be bishops to succeed them and handed on to them "what they received from Jesus' teaching and example and what they learned from the Holy Spirit" (CCC, no. 83). The pope and bishops in union with him are successors of the Apostles and inherit the responsibility of authoritative teaching from them. We call this teaching office the *Magisterium*. "The task of giving an authentic interpretation of the Word of God, whether in its written form or in the form of Tradition, has been entrusted to the living, teaching office of the Church alone" (CCC, no. 85, citing DV, no. 10).

All the faithful share in understanding and handing on revealed truth. "The whole body of the faithful cannot err . . . in matters of belief. This characteristic is shown in the supernatural appreciation of faith (*sensus fidei*) on the part of the whole people, when, 'from the bishops to the last of the faithful,' they manifest a universal consent in matters of faith and morals" (CCC, no. 92, citing Second Vatican Council, *Dogmatic Constitution on the Church* [*Lumen Gentium*; LG], no. 12). Another way of understanding this truth is the principle that the Holy Spirit, dwelling in the Church, draws the whole body of the faithful to believe what truly belongs to the faith. "By this appreciation of the faith, aroused and sustained by the Spirit of truth, the People of God, guided by the sacred teaching authority (*magisterium*), and obeying it, receives not the mere word of men, but truly the word of God (cf. 1 Thes 2:13), the faith once for all delivered to the saints (cf. Jude 3)" (LG, no. 12).

Tradition is the living transmission of the message of the Gospel in the Church. The oral preaching of the Apostles and the written message of salvation under the inspiration of the Holy Spirit (Bible) are conserved and handed on as the Deposit of Faith through the Apostolic Succession in the Church. Both the living Tradition and the written Scriptures have their common source in the revelation of God in Jesus Christ. This is particularly important to understand and believe when one is faced with the postmodern attitude that Tradition cannot be trusted, and that what the Church teaches as Tradition is really just a reflection of particular judgments and biases. Knowing that what Tradition teaches has its ultimate

THE GOSPELS

The four Gospels and the rest of the New Testament were written down over time by those Apostles and others associated with them who worked under the inspiration of the Holy Spirit (see CCC, no. 76, citing DV, no. 7). Among all the books of Scripture, the Gospels hold a special place of honor because they tell us about Jesus Christ, his person and message. The Gospels were formed in three stages:

1. *The life and teachings of Jesus*: The Church affirms that the Gospels faithfully hand on what Jesus did and taught for our salvation (cf. CCC, no. 126, citing DV, no. 19).
2. *The oral tradition*: What Jesus said and did, the Apostles preached to others. They brought to their preaching a deeper understanding of what they had experienced, having been instructed by the events of Christ's life and enlightened by the Holy Spirit (cf. CCC, no. 126, citing DV, no. 19).
3. *The written Gospels*: "The sacred authors, in writing the four Gospels, selected certain of the many elements which had been handed on, either orally or already in written form; others they synthesized or explained with an eye to the situation of the churches, while sustaining the form of preaching, but always in such a fashion that they have told us the truth about Jesus" (CCC, no. 126, citing DV, no. 19).

foundation in Jesus Christ helps a person of faith to respond to Tradition with trust. The theological, liturgical, disciplinary, and devotional traditions of the local churches both contain and can be distinguished from this Apostolic Tradition (cf. CCC, Glossary, "Tradition").

SACRED SCRIPTURE

Sacred Scripture is inspired by God and is the Word of God. Therefore, God is the author of Sacred Scripture, which means he inspired the human authors, acting in and through them. Thus, God ensured that the authors taught, without error, those truths necessary for our salvation. *Inspiration* is the word used for the divine assistance given to the human authors of the books of Sacred Scripture. This means that guided by the Holy Spirit, the human authors made full use of their talents and abilities while, at the same time, writing what God intended. There are many in modern society who find incredible the belief that Scripture contains the inspired word of God and so reject the Bible as a collection of stories and myths. There are others who profess belief in the Triune God and are even identified as "Scripture scholars" who work to "demythologize" the Scriptures, that is, they remove or explain away the miraculous as well as references to God's revealing words and actions. It is important to understand in the face of such challenges to Scripture that it is not simply the work of human authors as some critics allege, but truly the Word and work of God.

INTERPRETATION OF SCRIPTURE

When interpreting Scripture, we should be attentive to what God wanted to reveal through the authors for our salvation. We need to see Scripture as a unified whole with Jesus Christ at the center. We must also read Scripture within the living Tradition of the whole Church, so that we may come to grasp a true interpretation of the Scriptures. The task of giving an authoritative interpretation of the Word of God has been entrusted to the Magisterium. Last, we need to remember and recognize that there is a coherence of the truths of faith within Scripture (cf. CCC, nos. 112-114).

The Church recognizes two senses of Scripture, the literal and the spiritual. In probing the literal meaning of the texts, it is necessary to determine their literary form, such as history, hymns, wisdom sayings, poetry, parable, or other forms of figurative language. "The *literal sense* is the meaning conveyed by the words of Scripture and discovered by exegesis [the process scholars use to determine the meaning of the text], following the rules of sound interpretation: 'All other senses of Sacred Scripture are based on the literal'" (CCC, no. 116, citing St. Thomas Aquinas, *Summa Theologiae* I, 1, 10).

The spiritual senses of Sacred Scripture derive from the unity of God's plan of salvation. The text of Scripture discloses God's plan. The realities and events of which it speaks can also be signs of the divine plan. There are three spiritual senses of Scripture:

1. The *allegorical sense.* We can acquire a more profound understanding of events by recognizing their significance in Christ; thus the crossing of the Red Sea is a sign or type of Christ's victory over sin and also of Christian Baptism.
2. The *moral sense.* The events reported in Scripture ought to lead us to act justly. As St. Paul says, they were written "for our instruction" (1 Cor 10:11).
3. The *anagogical sense.* . . . We can view realities and events in terms of their eternal significance, leading us toward our true homeland: thus the Church on earth is a sign of the heavenly Jerusalem. (CCC, no. 117)

The Church's Scripture scholars are expected to work according to these principles to develop a better understanding of Scripture for God's people. Interpretation of Scripture is ultimately subject to the judgment of the Magisterium, which exercises the divine commission to hold fast to and to interpret authoritatively God's Word.

OTHER BIBLICAL INTERPRETATIONS

Our response to God's call to holiness involves regular, prayerful study of Scripture. "Such is the force and power of the Word of God that it can serve . . . the children of the Church as strength for their faith, food for the soul, and a pure and lasting font of spiritual life" (CCC, no. 131, citing DV, no. 21).

Catholic biblical scholars have made distinguished contributions to scriptural studies. Their outstanding service to the Church has assisted believers to grow in their faith by an authentic understanding of Scripture. Two of the various challenges they face come from interpretations posed, on the one hand, by those who interpret the Bible only in a literal fashion, and, on the other hand, by those who deny the supernatural aspects of the Gospels.

FROM THE CATECHISM

1. Why must Revelation be transmitted?
God "[wills everyone] to be saved and to come to the knowledge of the truth": that is, of Christ Jesus. Christ must be proclaimed to all nations and individuals, so that this revelation may reach to the ends of the earth. (CCC, no. 74, citing 1 Tm 2:4; cf. Jn 14:6)

2. How is Apostolic Tradition linked to Apostolic Succession?
Christ the Lord . . . commanded the apostles to preach the Gospel. (CCC, no. 75, citing DV, no. 7; cf. Mt 28:19-20; Mk 16:15)

In order that the full and living Gospel might always be preserved in the Church the apostles left bishops as their successors. They gave them "their own positions of teaching authority." (CCC, no. 77, citing DV, no. 7; St. Irenaeus, *Adv. Haeres*)

3. Why does the Church venerate Scripture?
The Church has always venerated the Scriptures as she venerates the Lord's Body. She never ceases to present to the faithful the bread of life, taken from the one table of God's Word and Christ's Body. In Sacred Scripture, the Church constantly finds her nourishment and her strength. (CCC, nos. 103-104; cf. DV, no. 21)

Biblical Literalism

In the United States a certain number of Christians of many denominations—often called *Fundamentalists*—have adopted the supremacy of Scripture as their sole foundation. They also approach Scripture from a viewpoint of private interpretation. This they do in the strictest literal sense without appreciation of the various literary forms that the biblical authors used within the specific cultural circumstances in which they were writing.

The Church's response to Fundamentalism is that Revelation is transmitted by Apostolic Tradition and Scripture together. The Church and Apostolic Tradition existed before the written New Testament. Her Apostles preached the Gospel orally before writing it down. The Apostles appointed bishops to succeed them with the authority to continue their teaching. Scripture alone is insufficient. Authoritative teaching is also needed. That is given to us by the Church's teaching office. Catholics, then, accept Scripture and Tradition as one "sacred deposit of the Word of God" (CCC, no. 97, citing DV, no. 10). Although this sets us apart from those who believe only in the Bible as their source of revelation, Catholics accept and honor both Scripture and Tradition "with equal sentiments of devotion and reverence" (CCC, no. 82, citing DV, no. 9).

In response to biblical literalism, the Church holds that "the books of Scripture firmly, faithfully and without error, teach that truth which God, for the sake of our salvation, wished to see confided to the sacred Scriptures" (DV, no. 11). At the same time, the Church recognizes that the interpreter of Scripture needs to attend to the literary forms—such as poetry, symbol, parable, history, song, or prayer—in which the Bible is written. The interpreter "must look for that meaning which the sacred writer . . . given the circumstance of his time and culture, intended to express and did in fact express, through the medium of a contemporary literary form" (DV, no. 12).

Historical Reductionism

Another challenge comes from scholars and others who deny the supernatural aspects of the Gospels, such as the Incarnation, Virgin Birth, miracles, and the Resurrection. We call this *reductionism* because it reduces all Scripture to the natural order and eliminates the reality of divine intervention.

The Church's Pontifical Biblical Commission has dealt with approaches of this kind in its publications *Instruction on the Historical Truth of the Gospels* and *The Interpretation of the Bible in the Church*.

The Pontifical Biblical Commission lists five unacceptable assumptions found in forms of scriptural interpretation:

1. the denial of a supernatural order;
2. the denial of God's intervention in the world through revelation;
3. the denial of the possibility and existence of miracles;
4. the incompatibility of faith with historical truth;
5. an almost *a priori* denial of the historical value of the nature of the documents of revelation. (Pontifical Biblical Commission, *Historical Truth of the Gospels* [1964], no. 5)

The Church approaches Scripture as God's revealed Word. Its authors wrote under the guidance and inspiration of the Holy Spirit. The Bible is more than a human work; it is God's words put into human words. It will always be a fountain of faith for those who read it in a spirit of prayer.

FOR DISCUSSION

1. Read again Blessed John XXIII's thoughts about sharing and spreading the faith in a more effective way. How would they help you share your faith with others? What is both consoling and challenging about the way God has chosen to transmit his Revelation?
2. Why might you say it makes perfect sense for Jesus to commission followers to carry on his saving vision? How do leaders of the Catholic Church continue the vision of Jesus in our times?
3. How does the Church help you to understand the Bible? How do the bishops in communion with the pope ensure that the full and living Gospel will always be preserved in the Church?

DOCTRINAL STATEMENTS

*   Jesus Christ, the fullness of Revelation, entrusted his mission to the Apostles. They transmitted Christ's Gospel through their witness, preaching, and writing—under the guidance of the Holy Spirit—meant for all peoples until Christ comes in glory.

- Divine Revelation is transmitted through Apostolic Tradition and Sacred Scripture, which flow from the same divine wellspring and work together in unity toward the same goal.
- "The Church, in her doctrine, life and worship, perpetuates and transmits to every generation all that she herself is, all that she believes" (DV, no. 8, §1). This is what is meant by the term *Tradition*.
- Because of the divine gift of faith, God's People as a whole never ceases to receive and reflect on the gift of Divine Revelation.
- The teaching office of the Church, the Magisterium—that is, the pope and the bishops in communion with him—has the task of authoritatively interpreting the Word of God, contained in Sacred Scripture and transmitted by Sacred Tradition.
- Sacred Scripture is inspired by God and truly contains the Word of God. This action of God is referred to as *Inspiration*.
- God is the author of Sacred Scripture, inspiring the human authors, acting in and through them. Thus God ensured that the authors taught divine and saving truth without error.
- The Catholic Church accepts and venerates as inspired the forty-six books of the Old Testament and the twenty-seven books of the New Testament. The unity of the Old and New Testaments flows from the revealed unity of God's loving plan to save us.
- Our response to God's Revelation is faith, by which we surrender our whole selves to him.

MEDITATION

Go Gladly to the Sacred Text Itself: From the Second Vatican Council on the Bible

[We] forcefully and specifically exhort all the Christian faithful . . . to learn the "surpassing knowledge of Jesus Christ" (Phil 3:8) by frequent reading of the divine scriptures. "Ignorance of the Scriptures is ignorance of Christ" (St. Jerome). Therefore, let them go gladly to the sacred text itself, whether in the sacred liturgy, which is full of the divine words, or in devout reading, or in such suitable exercises and various other helps which, with the approval and guidance of the pastors of the Church, are happily spreading everywhere in our day. Let them remember, however, that prayer should accompany the reading of sacred Scripture, so that a dialogue takes place between God and man. . . .

Just as from constant attendance at the Eucharistic mystery the life of the Church draws increase, so a new impulse of spiritual life may be expected from increased veneration of the Word of God.

—DV, no. 25-26

PRAYER

Let your scriptures be my chaste delight . . .
O Lord, perfect me and reveal those pages to me!
See, your voice is my joy. Give me what I love . . .
May the inner secrets of your words be
laid open to me when I knock.

This I beg by our Lord Jesus Christ in whom are hidden all the treasures of wisdom and knowledge (Col 2:3). These are the treasures I seek in your books.

—St. Augustine, *The Confessions*, bk. 11, chap. 2, nos. 2-4

Hold fast to the traditions you were taught,
either by an oral statement or by a letter of ours.

—2 Thes 2:15

4 BRING ABOUT THE OBEDIENCE OF FAITH

FAITH AS THE HUMAN RESPONSE TO GOD'S REVELATION
—CCC, NOS. 142-197

MISSIONARY TO THE AMERICAN PEOPLE

Isaac Thomas Hecker was born in New York City in 1819 to John and Caroline Freund Hecker, who were both immigrants from areas in present-day Germany. Isaac was one of three sons born into the family. Though his mother was known to have had ties to the Methodist Church, none of the boys seem to have been given any religious instruction. Nor did Isaac receive a formal education. Instead, he educated himself. This thirst for knowledge began his journey of faith.

As a young adult, Isaac found himself drawn to the plight of the working class. At first, he tried his hand at politics, but was soon disheartened with the political climate of his age, which was largely driven by a thirst for power rather than a concern for one's fellow man. Eventually, at the inspiration of his friend Orestes Brownson, Isaac was baptized by Bishop John McCloskey in New York in January of 1844.

Isaac's zeal for the faith grew. Only a year after his Baptism, he joined the Redemptorists in Belgium and was ordained a priest in 1849. Returning to the United States in 1851, Isaac was determined to bring the Catholic faith to others. He became one of the foremost lecturers in the United States on the Catholic faith, filling auditoriums beyond capacity in New York, Boston, Detroit, Chicago, St. Louis, and other cities. He saw his mission as evangelical: to bring the fullness of faith to the non-Catholic—and many times, hostile anti-Catholic—population of America.

In 1857, Isaac Hecker made a trip to Rome in order to seek a resolution to a difficulty that had arisen between the American Redemptorists and their superiors. The meeting did not go well and resulted in the expulsion of Isaac and four others from the order. Blessed Pius IX, having been informed of the plight of Hecker and his companions, dispensed them from their vows to the Redemptorists and encouraged them to found a new congregation with a missionary emphasis. Soon thereafter, Isaac Hecker became the first superior of "The Missionary Society of Saint Paul the Apostle," later known as the Paulists.

Throughout his life Isaac diligently worked to promote evangelization in American culture, particularly through the print media. He organized the Catholic Publication Society and became the founder of *The Catholic World* magazine, the director of Catholic Youth, and the author of three books. He did all this while continuing to be the first superior of the Paulists and preaching tirelessly to thousands across the country.

The motivation behind these efforts was always the drive to teach everyone the beauty and truth of the Catholic faith. It was the love of this faith that led Isaac Hecker to dedicate his life to serving Christ and Catholic Americans. Today the Paulists, following in the footsteps of their founder (who died in 1888 after a long illness), are present in parishes, campus ministry, major city information centers, publishing, and electronic, print, and broadcast media.

Knowing our faith and then sharing it with others is the responsibility of every Catholic. Fr. Isaac Hecker is a good example of one who lived out that responsibility.

IN THE ACT OF FAITH WE RESPOND TO GOD'S LOVING REVELATION

By his Revelation, "the invisible God, from the fullness of his love, addresses men as his friends, and moves among them, in order to invite and receive them into his own company." The adequate response to this invitation is faith.

—CCC, no. 142, citing DV, no. 2

God makes himself known to us through Revelation in order both to give us something and to draw a response from us. Both this gift of God and our response to his Revelation are called *faith*. By faith, we are able to give our minds and hearts to God, to trust in his will, and to follow the direction he gives us. St. Paul describes this response as the "obedience of faith" (Rom 16:26). We have many examples of faith. For instance, in Scripture we read of Abraham, who trusted in God's promise to make of him a great nation, and of Moses who, in faith, responded to God's call to lead his people out of slavery in Egypt to the Promised Land. The Virgin Mary is the perfect model of faith. From her "yes" to God at the Annunciation to her silent assent at the Cross, Mary's faith remained firm. No wonder we hear Mary's faith acclaimed in the Gospels, "Blessed are you who believed that what was spoken to you by the Lord would be fulfilled" (Lk 1:45).

Our response to God in faith is an act so rich in meaning that the *Catechism* explores its complexity in a number of ways.

BELIEVE IN THE LORD JESUS (ACTS 16:31)

Our faith life is a grace or a gift that brings us into a personal, loving union with the Father, Son, and Holy Spirit. This grace enables us both to hear the Word of God and to keep it. The qualities of faith listed here remind us of the basic ways in which we express our belief in God and that challenge us to apply our faith in our daily lives:

1. *Faith is a personal and communal relationship.* "Faith is first of all a personal adherence . . . to God. At the same time, it is a free assent to the whole truth that God has revealed" (CCC, no. 150). A personal faith says, "*I* believe in God." This is an act of belief in the one, true, and living God. It is as though we gather all that we are, and gratefully give our hearts and minds to God. We have a personal relationship with the Triune God, Father, Son, and Holy Spirit. But faith is also communal. It is not just a private act. In the assembly of believers at Mass, we profess our faith together and join our hearts as we experience ourselves as the Body of Christ. Our personal faith

brings us into a relationship with God's people, and the faith of the entire people strengthens us in our relationship with God.

2. *Faith seeks understanding and is a friend of reason.* Faith as a grace or gift from God makes it possible to gain some understanding of all that he has revealed to us, including the totality of his plan as well as the many mysteries of faith. Growth in understanding God's Revelation is a lifelong process. Theology and catechesis help us. We never completely understand these divine mysteries, but we often gain insight into them. In this context, faith and reason work together to discover truth. To ever suppose that human thought or scientific research can or should be in conflict with faith is a mistaken approach because this position denies the basic truth that everything has been created by God. Scholarly and scientific research that is carried out in a manner faithful to reason and to moral law will not conflict with truth as revealed by God (see CCC, no. 159).

3. *Faith is necessary for salvation.* "Believing in Jesus Christ and in the One who sent him for our salvation is necessary for obtaining that salvation" (CCC, no. 161). "Faith is necessary for salvation. The Lord himself [teaches]: 'He who believes and is baptized will be saved, but he who does not believe will be condemned'" (CCC, no. 183, citing Mk 16:16).[3]

4. *Faith is a gift of grace.* God not only speaks to us, he also gives us the grace to respond. To believe in Revelation we need the gift of faith. Peter was able to see that Jesus was the Messiah, not from "flesh and blood," that is, not by means of reason or common sense, but by the grace of the Father (cf. Mt 16:16-18). When by faith and Baptism we enter the Church, we already share in eternal life. Faith perceives this in ever deepening ways, as through a glass darkly (cf. 1 Cor 13:12).

5. *Faith is a free, human act.* Faith is a gift of God which enables us to know and love him. Faith is a way of knowing, just as reason is. But living in faith is not possible unless there is action on our part. Through the help of the Holy Spirit, we are able to make a deci-

---

3 For the Church's teaching about the salvation of those who have not known Christ or the Gospel, see CCC, no. 1260, and Chapter 11 of this book.

sion to respond to divine Revelation, and to follow through in living out our response. God never forces his truth and love upon us. He reveals himself to us as free human beings, and our faith response to him is made within the context of our freedom. At Capernaum, Jesus asked the Apostles, "Do you also want to leave?" Peter answers for them, "Master, to whom shall we go?" (Jn 6:67-68). Peter's response is freely sought and freely given. The same is true with each of us.

6. *Faith believes with conviction in a message.* We have seen that faith is a relationship with God. Now we note that it is also belief in a message. This message is found in Scripture and Tradition and is transmitted to us through many means such as liturgical prayers and the Creeds. Faith fills us with conviction because God guarantees the truthfulness of what he revealed. "Our Gospel did not come to you in word alone, but also in power and in the Holy Spirit and [with] much conviction" (1 Thes 1:5). The Spirit assists us to be believers. "Faith is the realization of what is hoped for and evidence of things not seen" (Heb 11:1).

THE FAITH PILGRIMAGE

Faith is therefore both a relationship with God as well as an engagement with the truths that he reveals. In other words, faith refers to both the act by which we accept God's word and the content of what he has revealed to us.

Abraham, whom the Church calls our "father in faith," and Mary, the first among all disciples, show by their acts of trust in God that faith is a process of growth, day by day. Like any other relationship, our faith communion with God develops in stages. It is a journey, a pilgrimage. On this journey, there will be periods of temptation, worry, shadows, and darkness. Many saints experienced such tests. But Jesus has sent us the Holy Spirit to enlighten and guide us on the way.

Our faith encounter with God's revealed message takes time and maturity to probe its meaning and gain some hint of the awe and majesty to which divine truths point. There is brilliant light as well as shadows. We are pilgrims of love and truth ever seeking and longing for closer union with God.

FAITH REQUIRES SUBMISSION

John Henry Cardinal Newman (1801-1890) often wrote about faith and its implications. He was born and raised in England. As a child, he was exposed to Protestant Christianity in a very general sense. Around the age of fifteen, he had a conversion experience that led him ultimately to seek ordination as an Anglican priest. Even before his ordination, which took place when he was twenty-three, Newman served as a fellow at Oxford, where his teaching, preaching, and writing caused him to reassess his strong anti-Catholic position. He entered the Catholic Church in 1845, was ordained a priest in 1847, and eventually was named a cardinal in 1879. He spent much of the rest of his life teaching and writing about the Catholic faith and the Catholic Church. His influence at the university level drew many others to follow him into the Catholic Church. Because of Cardinal Newman's university work and the success of his efforts to teach the faith, centers of Catholic faith and worship at secular colleges and universities are often called Newman Centers.

In 1849, the then-Fr. Newman published an essay in which he wrote of the necessity of trusting in God's Word and submitting in faith to the teaching authority of the Church. Newman's words can be read and reflected upon in light of contemporary trends towards deciding for oneself what to believe:

> [In the time of the Apostles] . . . A Christian was bound to take without doubting all that the Apostles declared to be revealed; if the Apostles spoke, he had to yield an internal assent of his mind. . . . Immediate, implicit submission of the mind was, in the lifetime of the Apostles, the only, the necessary token of faith. . . No one could say: "I will choose my religion for myself, I will believe this, I will not believe that; I will pledge myself to nothing; I will believe

just as long as I please, and no longer; what I believe today I will reject tomorrow, if I choose. I will believe what the Apostles have as yet said, but I will not believe what they shall say in time to come." No; either the Apostles were from God, or they were not; if they were, everything that they preached was to be believed by their hearers; if they were not, there was nothing for their hearers to believe. To believe a little, to believe more or less, was impossible; it contradicted the very notion of believing. (John Henry Newman, "Faith and Private Judgment," in *Discourses to Mixed Congregations* [1849])

The ultimate goal of a life of faith is eternal union with God in heaven. Through the gift and experience of faith, we are able not only to look ahead to what awaits us, but also to experience here some of God's divine life, "a taste in advance" of our sharing life with him forever (see CCC, no. 163). While living a life of growing in faith might seem like a waste of time and energy to skeptics and non-believers, both because the objects of faith cannot always be proven and because faith often "produces" little of measurable value, believers know the strength, the wisdom, the confidence and hope that a life of faith gives.

CHALLENGES TO FAITH

The culture of the United States has been strongly influenced by the eighteenth-century Enlightenment, or Age of Reason. That philosophy coincided with the scientific revolution and was based on the premise that reason and common sense should be our only guides. Its religious counterpart was Deism, which claimed that while God exists, he simply created the world and then left us to our own devices.

The founding fathers of our country were influenced by the Enlightenment and the promises of science. Though some were attracted to Deism, they supported freedom of religion and noted the value of

FROM THE CATECHISM

1. Why do we say faith is both personal and communal?
Faith is a personal act—the free response of the human person to the initiative of God who reveals himself. But faith is not an isolated act. No one can believe alone just as no one can live alone. You have not given yourself the faith as you have not given yourself life. The believer has received faith from others and should hand it on to others. (CCC, no. 166)

2. What should we recall about the *formulas* of faith such as those found in the creeds?
We do not believe in formulas, but in those realities they express, which faith allows us to touch. . . . All the same we do approach these realities with the help of formulations of the faith which permit us to express the faith and hand it on, to celebrate it in community, to assimilate and live on it more and more. (CCC, no. 170)

3. What role does the Church play in handing on the faith?
The Church, "the pillar and [foundation] of truth," faithfully guards "the faith which was once for all delivered to the saints." She guards the memory of Christ's words; it is she who from generation to generation hands on the apostles' confession of faith. (CCC, no. 171, citing 1 Tm 3:15; Jude 3)

religion for the stability of society and the moral order. In fact, they expected that faith would affect the social order.

Despite some major problems that the Church faced in this country, the Catholic faith grew and prospered here. But the early influence of the Enlightenment in this country's origins continues in unexpected ways and presents troubling issues for faith. The country's foundational principle of religious freedom, originally meant simply to preserve the independence and dignity of both church and state, has evolved into a "wall" of separation that seems to say that faith should have no impact on the state or society.

The Church, however, continues to apply principles flowing from her faith to public policy, most notably in her teaching on the dignity of the human person and the culture of life. The Church's advocacy for the poor, the elderly, children, and immigrants are further examples of the Church's commitment to advance social justice in America. The Church's unflagging pro-life stand is an outstanding example of calling our society and government to protect life from conception to natural death.

Deism, or at least a form of it, has been replaced by an ideological secularism, a belief that we are self-sufficient and self-explanatory and do not need religious faith. The Church's response to this ideological secularism is helped by joining with thoughtful people who are raising basic questions: Who are we? What is the meaning of suffering, evil, and death? Why has modern progress not eliminated them? What is the value of our country's achievements in light of their cost to human dignity and life?

These questions point us to the transcendent origins of humanity. The resulting discussion can awaken the seeds of eternity planted by God in each soul.

Finally, we need to affirm again our faith that Jesus Christ can show all of us the way—believers to stronger faith, and others to be brought to faith. When we are newly aware of the Holy Spirit's power to transform us and others, we will have both the energy and imagination to find paths to faith for those in need. We always need to rediscover the truth that the key to our history is to be found in Jesus, the Lord of history. Beneath all the rapid changes in our culture, there are still many people who possess and live enduring values rooted in Christ, who "is the same yesterday, today, and forever" (Heb 13:8). We need to rely on our faith in Christ when we reflect on the mystery and dignity of man and woman, and as we address challenges to faith and its relationship to culture.

FOR DISCUSSION

1. In what ways do you find it difficult to be open about your faith in public situations? How have you been able to apply your faith to family issues, community development, and political decisions?
2. What steps might you take to make your faith more effective in our culture? What help in this regard do you expect from the Church?
3. Who are outstanding models of faith that inspire you to deeper faith and practice? How is your faith bringing you closer to God and to a deeper understanding of his message?

DOCTRINAL STATEMENTS

- Faith is a gift from God. He not only enters a relationship with us but also gives us the grace or help to respond in faith.
- In faith we surrender our whole being to God who has revealed himself to us. This involves the assent of the intellect and will to the Revelation that God has made in words and deeds.
- By faith, we enter a relationship of trust in God as well as belief in the message of truth that he has revealed.
- Faith is a free, conscious, human act. Faith is a way of knowing just as reason is, though it is different from reason. Faith involves the whole of the human being. Aided by the Holy Spirit we exercise faith in a manner that corresponds to our human dignity.
- Faith is a supremely personal act: "I believe." It is also communal, occurring within the life and worship of the Church. In the assembly of believers at Mass, as we join together in the Profession of Faith (or Creed), we experience ourselves as the Body of Christ.
- By faith we believe with conviction in all that is contained in the Word of God, written or handed down, which the Church proposes for belief as divinely revealed.
- Faith is necessary for salvation. "Believing in Jesus Christ and the One who sent him for our salvation is necessary for obtaining that salvation" (CCC, no. 161).

- We have two forms of the Creed that we use for prayer and worship: the Apostles' Creed, the ancient baptismal Creed of the Church of Rome; the Nicene Creed, from the first two Ecumenical Councils—Nicea in 325 and Constantinople in 381.
- A Creed is a brief, normative summary statement or profession of Christian faith. Creeds are also called Symbols of Faith.

MEDITATION

"The obedience of faith" (Rom 13:26; cf. 1:5; 2 Cor 10:5-6) "is to be given to God who reveals, an obedience by which man commits his whole self freely to God, offering the full submission of intellect and will to God who reveals," and freely assenting to the truth revealed by Him. To make this act of faith, the grace of God and the interior help of the Holy Spirit must precede and assist, moving the heart and turning it to God, opening the eyes of the mind and giving "joy and ease to everyone in assenting to the truth and believing it." To bring about an ever deeper understanding of revelation the same Holy Spirit constantly brings faith to completion by His gifts.

—DV, no. 5

PRAYER

"I believe" (Apostles' Creed) is the faith of the Church professed personally by each believer, principally during Baptism. "We believe" (Niceno-Constantinopolitan Creed) is the faith of the Church confessed by the bishops assembled in council or more generally by the liturgical assembly of believers. "I believe" is also the Church, our mother, responding to God by faith as she teaches us to say both "I believe" and "We believe."

—CCC, no. 167

The Apostles' Creed is so called because it is rightly considered to be a faithful summary of the apostles' faith. It is the ancient baptismal symbol of the Church of Rome. Its great authority arises from this fact: it is "the Creed of the Roman Church, the See of Peter, the first of the apostles, to which he brought the common faith."

—CCC, no. 194

The Niceno-Constantinopolitan or Nicene Creed draws its great authority from the fact that it stems from the first two ecumenical Councils (in 325 and 381). It remains common to all the great Churches of both East and West to this day.

—CCC, no. 195

The Apostles' Creed

I believe in God, the Father Almighty, creator of heaven and earth.

I believe in Jesus Christ, his only Son, our Lord. He was conceived by the power of the Holy Spirit and born of the Virgin Mary. He suffered under Pontius Pilate, was crucified, died, and was buried. He descended into hell. On the third day he rose again. He ascended into heaven, and is seated at the right hand of the Father. He will come again to judge the living and the dead.

I believe in the Holy Spirit, the holy catholic Church, the communion of saints, the forgiveness of sins, the resurrection of the body, and the life everlasting. Amen.

Nicene Creed

We believe in one God, the Father, the Almighty, maker of heaven and earth, of all that is, seen and unseen.

We believe in one Lord, Jesus Christ, the only Son of God, eternally begotten of the Father, God from God, Light from Light, true God from true God, begotten, not made, one in Being with the Father. Through him all things were made. For us men and for our salvation he came down from heaven: by the power of the Holy Spirit he was born of the Virgin Mary, and became man.

For our sake he was crucified under Pontius Pilate; he suffered, died, and was buried. On the third day he rose again in fulfillment of the Scriptures; he ascended into heaven and is seated at the right hand of the Father. He will come again in glory to judge the living and the dead, and his Kingdom will have no end.

We believe in the Holy Spirit, the Lord, the giver of life, who proceeds from the Father and the Son. With the Father and the Son, he is worshiped and glorified. He has spoken through the Prophets.

We believe in one, holy, catholic and apostolic Church. We acknowledge one baptism for the forgiveness of sins. We look for the resurrection of the dead, and the life of the world to come. Amen.

Faith is the assurance of things hoped for,
the conviction of things not seen.

—CCC, no. 146, citing Heb 11:1

5 I BELIEVE IN GOD

AN INTELLECTUAL CATHOLIC

When the brilliant Orestes Brownson embraced the Catholic faith in the middle of the nineteenth century, he wrote that an intelligent Catholic mind is served by the teaching authority of the Church in the same way that a seafarer is guided by maps and charts. Brownson was among a group of restless religious seekers whose last stops before Catholicism were Unitarianism and Transcendentalism.[4]

Brownson was born in Stockbridge, Vermont, in 1803. He and his twin sister were the youngest of six children. His father died when Orestes was a child. Poverty forced his mother to put him in a foster home for several years. He had memorized large portions of Scripture by the time he was fourteen. In 1827 he married Sally Healy. He became a preacher in the Universalist church, and seven years later changed to a Unitarian minister.

Later, he was attracted to a group of thinkers called Transcendentalists. They included Henry David Thoreau, Ralph Waldo Emerson, Margaret Fuller, and Elizabeth Peabody. They held that God was somehow immanent in human nature and in the human soul. They were reacting against

---

4   Unitarianism is a monotheistic system of belief not compatible with the Catholic faith that holds for universal salvation and that sees reason and conscience as the basis for any practice of faith. Transcendentalism is a philosophical approach that asserts that there are spiritual realities beyond what we see and that we know these realities through intuition.

what they perceived as a Calvinist view of an angry God and depraved human nature. The movement lasted about a dozen years, but its vision had a much longer influence. It is best remembered in Emerson's aphorisms on self-improvement, Thoreau's essays, and the short-lived Brook Farm communal experience.

In seeking to justify the divine quality of people, Brownson was frustrated by the fact of human sinfulness. The premise of natural goodness was not enough. He found a satisfying answer in the Catholic doctrines of the Incarnation and Redemption. He and his family were baptized Catholic by Bishop John Fitzpatrick in Boston on October 20, 1844.

For most of the next twenty-six years, he published his magazine quarterly *The Review*, writing most of the articles himself. As a journalist and critic, he examined the important religious, moral, and political issues of his time. When he founded *The Review*, he said, "I hoped to startle. I made it a point to be as paradoxical and extravagant as I could without doing violence to my own reason and conscience." Since he switched positions often, he was at times denounced by liberals for his conservatism and by conservatives for his liberalism.

Throughout his career, Brownson stressed the Church's mission of renewal and the responsibilities of Catholics toward culture and civilization. He died on April 17, 1876. He is buried in the crypt of Sacred Heart Basilica on the campus of the University of Notre Dame.

Brownson's story is of interest to us because his journey of faith led him to acknowledge the self-revelation of God as Father, Son, and Holy Spirit. While he struggled with the mystery of God, he also pondered the mystery of evil. He found the satisfying response in the gift of faith that brought him to Catholicism.

GOD IS HOLY MYSTERY

It is right and just to sing of You, to bless You, to praise You, to thank You, to worship You—for You are God ineffable, inconceivable, invisible, incomprehensible, always existing and ever the same, You and Your only begotten Son and Your Holy Spirit.

—Anaphora of the Liturgy of St. John Chrysostom

God "dwells in unapproachable light, whom no human being has seen or can see" (1 Tm 6:16). Revelation tells us that he is living and personal, profoundly close to us in creating and sustaining us. Though he is totally other, hidden, glorious, and wondrous, he communicates himself to us through creation and reveals himself through the prophets and above all in Jesus Christ, whom we meet in the Church, especially in Scripture and the Sacraments. In these many ways, God speaks to our hearts where we may welcome his loving presence.

We do not confuse the word *mystery* with the term as it applies to a detective story or a scientific puzzle. The mystery of God is not a puzzle to be solved. It is a truth to be reverenced. It is a reality too rich to be fully grasped by our minds, so that while it continues to unfold, it always remains mostly beyond our comprehension. The mystery of God is present in our lives and yet remains hidden, beyond the full grasp of our minds.

God, who always remains beyond our comprehension, has shown himself to us throughout the history of salvation. His relationship with Israel is marked by all kinds of loving deeds. He, ever faithful and forgiving, is ultimately experienced by human beings through his Son, Jesus Christ, and the Holy Spirit. His love is stronger than a mother's love for her child or a bridegroom's for his beloved. St. John proclaims, "God is love" (1 Jn 4:8). Jesus has revealed that God's very being is love.

GOD IS THE TRINITY

The mystery of the Holy Trinity is the central mystery of the Christian faith and of Christian life.

—CCC, no. 261

The Old Testament shows God as one, unique, without equal. "Hear, O Israel! The LORD is our God, the LORD alone" (Dt 6:4; Mk 12:29). He created the world, made a covenant with his people, and is the Father of the poor, the orphan, and the widow.

In the Creeds, we profess our faith in God as "Father almighty." His fatherhood and power illumine each other by his care for us, by adopting us as sons and daughters in Baptism and by being rich in mercy to forgive our sins. Scripture constantly praises the universal power of God as the "mighty one of Jacob" and the "LORD of hosts" (Gn 49:24; Is 1:24ff.). God's power is loving, for he is our Father.

> God's parental tenderness can also be expressed by the image of motherhood, which emphasizes God's immanence, the intimacy between Creator and creature. The language of faith thus draws on the human experience of parents, who are in a way the first representatives of God for man. But this experience also tells us that human parents are fallible and can disfigure the face of fatherhood and motherhood. We ought therefore to recall that God transcends the human distinction between the sexes. He is neither man nor woman: he is God. He also transcends human fatherhood and motherhood, although he is their origin and standard: no one is father as God is Father. (CCC, no. 239)

Jesus revealed God as *Father* in a new sense. God is Father in his relation to Jesus, his only begotten Son. At the Last Supper, Jesus calls God "Father" forty-five times (cf. Jn 13-17). The Son is divine, as is the Father (cf. Mt 11:27). In a later chapter, Jesus as the Second Person of the Trinity will be discussed further.

Before the Passion, Jesus promised to send the Holy Spirit as teacher, guide, and consoler. The Spirit's appearance at Pentecost and at other events in the New Testament gives ample evidence of the Holy Spirit as the third Person of the Trinity. This, too, will be discussed in a later chapter.

The mystery of the Holy Trinity is the central mystery of the Christian faith and life. God reveals himself as Father, Son, and Holy Spirit. The doctrine of the Trinity includes three truths of faith.

First, the Trinity is One. We do not speak of three gods but of one God. Each of the Persons is fully God. They are a unity of Persons in one divine nature.

Second, the Divine Persons are distinct from each other. Father, Son, and Spirit are not three appearances or modes of God, but three identifiable persons, each fully God in a way distinct from the others.

Third, the Divine Persons are in relation to each other. The distinction of each is understood only in reference to the others. The Father cannot be the Father without the Son, nor can the Son be the Son without the Father. The Holy Spirit is related to the Father and the Son who both send him forth.

All Christians are baptized in the name of the Father and of the Son and of the Holy Spirit. The Trinity illumines all the other mysteries of faith.

GOD IS CREATOR OF HEAVEN AND EARTH

The first line of the Bible says, "In the beginning when God created the heavens and the earth" (Gn 1:1). The first three chapters of the Book of Genesis have shaped the religious thought of Jews and Christians; indeed they have shaped the literature of the Western world—about God as "Creator of heaven and earth" (Apostles' Creed), "of all that is seen and unseen" (Nicene Creed), and about the creation of the human race, of the Fall, and of the promise of salvation through the story of Adam and Eve. These three chapters must be read by anyone who wants to understand the meaning of the world and humanity.

Catechesis on creation is of major importance. Where do we come from? Where are we going? These two questions about our origin and our end are the underlying issues of the human search for meaning. These are the questions that the Bible helps us to answer.

Beginning with Genesis, all Scripture states the following truths in relation to God's work of creation:

- *God created the world out of his wisdom and love.* Creation is not the result of blind fate or complete chance.
- *God made the universe "out of nothing."* This means that the world is not a "part" of God or made from some pre-existing substance. The world depends on God for its existence; God is independent of his creation and distinct from it, even though creation is sustained in existence by his Providence: "In him we live and move and have our being," as St. Paul preached to the people of Athens (Acts 17:28).

- *Creation reflects God's goodness and wisdom.* The creation story in Genesis affirms the goodness of creation: "God looked at everything he had made, and found it very good" (Gn 1:31). Because the universe is destined for the human family, whom he calls to a personal relationship with himself, it is ordered in a way that allows the human intellect to perceive God's hand working in and through it. As the *Dogmatic Constitution on Divine Revelation* (*Dei Verbum*) of the Second Vatican Council teaches, "God who creates and conserves all things by his Word (see Jn 1:3), provides men with constant evidence of himself in created realities" (DV, no. 3; see Rom 1:19-20).

The answers to questions about the origins of the world and humanity provided by God's own Revelation are intimately linked with the meaning and purpose of the world and humanity. This provides a distinctive worldview that differs dramatically from those shaped by other philosophies and points of view. In Pantheism, the development of the world is identified with the development of God. In Dualism, our origins are explained by the perpetual conflict of good and evil. According to Deism, God abandons the world, once made, to itself. There is also materialism, in which the world is understood to have come from pre-existing matter that developed naturally and not as a result of any type of divine action or plan.

THE ANGELS

It is a truth of faith that God, the "maker . . . of all that is seen and unseen," created a realm of spiritual beings who do not share the limitations of a physical body and yet exist as the result of his all-powerful, loving act of creation. We call these spiritual beings *angels*. "As purely spiritual creatures angels have intelligence and will: they are personal and immortal creatures, surpassing in perfection all visible creatures, as the splendor of their glory bears witness" (CCC, no. 330). Angels glorify God and work for our salvation. The Church celebrates the memory of certain angels (St. Michael, St. Gabriel, and St. Raphael) who were God's messengers.

Some of the angels turned against God and were driven out of heaven and into hell. Their leader is called Satan, and they are referred to as devils or demons in Scripture. They tempt us to evil (cf. CCC, nos. 391, 1707). But their power is limited and is never greater than God's.

THE VISIBLE WORLD

In the first of two creation stories (cf. Gn 1–2:4), Scripture describes the creation of the visible world as a succession of six days of divine "work," after which God "rested" on the seventh day, the Sabbath. From the earliest times, Christian writers and biblical scholars have been aware that the language in the story is symbolic, for the six "days" of creation could hardly be solar days, since Genesis says that the sun was not made until the fourth day. The sequence of creation reported in Chapter 1 of the Book of Genesis is not literal or scientific, but poetic and theological. It describes a hierarchy of creatures in which human beings are the summit of visible creation. By ending the sequence of creation with the Sabbath, the story points to the adoration of God the Creator as the focal point of all the works of creation. "The heavens declare the glory of God; / the sky proclaims its builder's craft" (Ps 19:1).

The *Dogmatic Constitution on Divine Revelation* of the Second Vatican Council reminds us that "in Sacred Scripture, God speaks through human beings in human fashion," and that if we are "to ascertain what God has wished to communicate to us, [we] should carefully search out the meaning which the sacred writers really had in mind" (DV, no. 12). It goes on to say, "In determining the intention of the sacred writers, attention must be paid, *inter alia* [among other things], to literary forms." Chapters 1 and 2 of Genesis use symbolic language to convey fundamental truths about God and ourselves.

It may be helpful to recall how important symbols are in everyday human life. Being a unity of body and spirit, we express and perceive spiritual realities through material symbols. God also speaks to us through visible creation: light and darkness, wind and fire, water and earth, trees and their fruit. Scripture uses all these to speak of God and to symbolize his greatness and his nearness.

In language, symbols are often used to communicate a truth. Symbolic language in Scripture, as in literature in general, may use poetry, parable, story comparisons or metaphors, or other literary forms. In today's world, we often use novels, films, plays, songs, and other creative works to communicate reality in a manner that simple factual presentations cannot do as effectively.

Through the stories of creation in Chapters 1 and 2 of Genesis, God reveals himself as the Creator of all that exists, showing particularly a tender love for the high point of his creation, man and woman. The majesty and wisdom of God's creation are celebrated in the eloquence of the prophets, the lyricism of the Psalms, and the Wisdom writings of the Old Testament. Through his Incarnation, death, and Resurrection, Jesus Christ renews all creation, making it his own and filling it with the Holy Spirit.

DIVINE PROVIDENCE

God guides his creation toward its completion or perfection through what we call his *Divine Providence*. This means that God has absolute sovereignty over all that he has made and guides his creation according to the divine plan of his will. At the same time, both the evidence of the world that we discover by our human endeavors and the testimony of Sacred Scripture show that for the unfolding of his plan, God uses secondary causes, including the laws of physics, chemistry, and biology, as well as the cooperation of our own human intellect and will. The Father of all continues to work with his Son, who is eternal Wisdom, and with the Holy Spirit, who is the inexhaustible source of life, to guide creation and humanity to the fullness of God's truth, goodness, and beauty.

THE REALITY OF EVIL

If God has created all things to be good and cares providentially for his creation, why does evil exist? There is no quick answer to this challenging question. Christian faith, after centuries of reflecting on the answers revealed in the Bible, provides the only comprehensive answer. This answer includes the drama of sin, the love of God who sent his only Son to be our Redeemer and Savior, and the call of God to sinful humanity to repent and to love him in return.

We may ask why God did not create a world so perfect that no evil could exist in it. God freely willed to create a world that is not immediately at its state of ultimate perfection, but one that must journey toward that perfection through time. "In God's plan this process of becoming involves the appearance of certain beings and the disappearance of others, the existence of the more perfect alongside the less perfect, both constructive and destructive forces of nature" (CCC, no. 310). Physical evil can thus exist alongside physical good because creation has not reached its ultimate perfection. On this journey, created realities remain limited and thus subject to decay and death.

As intelligent and free creatures, both angels and human beings must make their way to their ultimate destinies by using their intellect and will to make free choices. They can and must choose between loving God—who has shown his love for them in creation and Revelation—and loving something else. Thus moral evil—the evil of sin—can also exist in this state of journeying (cf. CCC, nos. 309-313). God permits such moral evil in part out of respect for the gift of freedom with which he endowed created beings. But his response to moral evil is an even greater act of love through the sending of his Son who offers his life to bring us back to God. "Christ has ransomed us with his blood, and paid for us the price of Adam's sin to our eternal Father. . . . O happy fault, O necessary sin of Adam, which gained for us so great a Redeemer!" (Easter Proclamation [*Exsultet*] at the Easter Vigil).

St. Catherine of Siena said, to "those who are scandalized and rebel against what happens to them": "Everything comes from love, all is ordained for the salvation of man, God does nothing without this goal in mind" (*Dialogue on Providence*, chap. IV, 138).

ISSUES OF FAITH AND SCIENCE

Catholic philosophy and theology have traditionally held that the human intellect comes to know the truth through scientific discovery and philosophical reasoning and can even come to a knowledge of God and many of his purposes through an understanding of created realities.

The *Pastoral Constitution on the Church in the Modern World* (*Gaudium et Spes*; GS) of the Second Vatican Council teaches that "methodical research in all branches of knowledge, provided it is carried out in a truly scientific manner and does not override moral laws, can never conflict with the faith, because the things of the world and the things of faith derive from the same God. The humble and persevering investigator of the secrets of nature is being led, as it were, by the hand of God in spite of himself, for it is God, the conserver of all things, who made them what they are" (CCC, no. 159, citing GS, no. 36).

This does not mean that there have not been conflicts between science and religion. For example, in the seventeenth century, Galileo, building on previous discoveries, held firmly to the conviction that the earth moves around the sun. This was not acceptable to many of his contemporaries including Church authorities. As a result, he was subjected to a Church investigation and placed under house arrest for the rest of his life. Pope John Paul II ordered a study of Galileo's case, which resulted in his exoneration in 1992.

In modern times, the scientific teaching on evolution has also led to conflict with some Christians. Since 1925, the celebrated "Scopes monkey trial" in Dayton, Tennessee, has had a lasting effect on the popular understanding about evolution. The famous orator and frequent presidential candidate William Jennings Bryan argued from the principles of a literalist interpretation of the Bible. Clarence Darrow, his agnostic counterpart, ridiculed his approach as contrary to scientific progress. Through subsequent dramatic presentations like *Inherit the Wind*, on stage and in film, this debate fixed in the American mind the mistaken notion that in the debate over evolution, the only choice is between biblical literalism and Darwinism, when, in fact, there are some who recognize physical and biological evolution as the work of the divine Creator.

The Catholic Church, however, has continued to uphold the principle that there is no intrinsic conflict between science and religion. In his 1950 encyclical *Concerning Some False Opinions Threatening to*

FROM THE CATECHISM

1. What does faith in God mean?

It means coming to know God's greatness and majesty. It means living in thanksgiving. It means knowing the unity and true dignity of all men. It means making good use of created things. It means trusting in God, even in adversity. (CCC, nos. 222-227)

2. Why does the Creed begin with God?

Our profession of faith begins with *God*, for God is the First and the Last, the beginning and the end of everything. The [Creed] begins with God the *Father*, for the Father is the first divine person of the Most Holy Trinity; our Creed begins with the creation of heaven and earth, for creation is the beginning and foundation of all God's works. (CCC, no. 198)

3. What is the importance of God's Revelation about creation?

Creation is the foundation of "all God's saving plans," the "beginning of the history of salvation" that culminates in Christ. Conversely, the mystery of Christ casts conclusive light on the mystery of creation and reveals the end for which "in the beginning God created the heavens and the earth": from the beginning, God envisioned the glory of the new creation in Christ. (CCC, no. 280, citing the *General Catechetical Directory*, no. 51, and Gn 1:1)

Undermine the Foundations of Catholic Doctrine (*Humani Generis*), Pope Pius XII applied this principle to the controversial theories of evolution, which have often been used in a materialistic or agnostic sense to argue against any divine intervention in the work of creation: "The [Magisterium] of the Church does not forbid that, in conformity with the present state of human sciences and sacred theology, research and discussions, on the part of [people] experienced in both fields, take place

FROM POPE JOHN PAUL II

The Bible itself speaks to us of the origin of the universe and its makeup, not in order to provide us with a scientific treatise but in order to state the correct relationship of humanity with God and the universe. Sacred Scripture wishes simply to declare that the world was created by God. (Pope John Paul II, Address to the Pontifical Academy of Sciences [October 3, 1981])

with regard to the doctrine of evolution, in as far as it inquires into the origin of the human body as coming from pre-existent and living matter" (no. 36). At the same time, Pope Pius XII reiterated the doctrine that each human soul is immortal and individually created by God.

Pope John Paul II made a further commentary on this question in his 1996 Message to the Pontifical Academy of Sciences. While acknowledging the scientific evidence in favor of evolution, he cautioned that the theories of evolution that consider the human soul the seat of the intellect and will by which the human person comes to know and love God "as emerging from forces of living matter" would not be compatible with the truth about the dignity of the human person as taught in Revelation. This position does not conflict with the nature of scientific methodology in the various fields, since their method is one of observation and correlation. The spiritual dimension of the human person is of a different order that is related to yet transcends the material world and that is not reducible simply to the physical aspects of our being, which can be more readily studied by the scientific method.

Among scientists, a lively debate about aspects of Darwin's theory of natural selection as the key to evolutionary hypothesis continues. Christian faith does not require the acceptance of any particular theory of evolution, nor does it forbid it, provided that the particular theory is not strictly materialistic and does not deny what is essential to the spiritual essence of the human person, namely that God creates each human soul directly to share immortal life with him. At a popular level in our country, heated controversy still engages people on both sides of the issue, especially in regard to what is appropriate in the education of their children. This debate is often fueled, on the one hand, by "creationist" or fundamentalist biblical opinions that do not take into account the literary forms of the Bible and the primary theological purpose of its teaching, and on the other hand by the use of theories of evolution to support a materialist and anti-religious interpretation of the world and humanity. The Bible is not a scientific textbook and should never be read as such; rather it reveals what God wants us to know for the sake of our salvation.

FOR DISCUSSION

1. Knowing that God is rich in mercy and that he is love, how does this affect your attitude toward him? Toward your neighbor?
2. How did God progressively reveal his mystery as a unity of three Persons? How would you teach the doctrine about God to others?
3. What are some practical ways you would reply to creationists and atheistic evolutionists? Why is the dialogue between religion and science necessary and valuable?

DOCTRINAL STATEMENTS

- God is a holy mystery. As the Byzantine Church sings, "You are God, ineffable, inconceivable, incomprehensible, always existing and ever the same, You and Your only begotten Son and Your Holy Spirit" (Anaphora of the Liturgy of St. John Chrysostom).
- The Old Testament reveals God as One, unique, and without equal. "Hear, O Israel! The LORD is our God, the LORD alone!" (Dt 6:4; Mk 12:29).
- Our faith in God, the only One, leads us to adore him as our origin and destiny and to love him with all our hearts.
- God is truth. "And now, O Lord GOD, you are God and your words are truth" (2 Sm 7:28). His words cannot deceive. This is why we can trust his truth and fidelity. St. John goes further when he writes, "God is love" (1 Jn 4:8).

- The mystery of the Holy Trinity is the central mystery of the Christian faith and life. God alone reveals himself as Father, Son, and Holy Spirit.
- Jesus revealed God as *Father* in a new sense. God is Father in relation to his only Son. The Son is divine, as is the Father. The Father testified to the unique relationship of Jesus to him as his Son at the baptism in the Jordan and at the Transfiguration: "This is my beloved Son" (Mt 3:17, 17:5).
- Before the Passion, Jesus promised to send the Holy Spirit as teacher, guide, and consoler. The revelation of the Holy Spirit at Pentecost and in the rest of the New Testament testify to his divinity.
- We do not speak of three gods in the Trinity, but of one God. Father, Son, and Spirit are not three modes of God, but three distinct Persons who are the same divine being. They are also in relation to each other, for all three Persons work together in the works of creation, Redemption, and sanctification.
- God is almighty. The Church often addresses God as almighty, believing that nothing is impossible with him. He shows almighty power by converting us from our sins and by restoring us to grace.
- For some, the presence of evil in the world raises questions. However, God sheds some light of understanding on the mystery of evil through the death and Resurrection of his Son. Faith in the Resurrection gives us hope. Full understanding will come only in eternal life.
- God alone created the universe freely and without any help. No creature can create or call into being something or someone "out of nothing," as he did.
- God created the world to show forth and share divine glory. We are called to share in his truth, goodness, and beauty.
- God keeps the world in existence by the power of the Son and by the Holy Spirit as giver of life. Through Divine Providence God guides all creatures with wisdom and love to their final goal.
- Angels are spiritual creatures who glorify God and work for our salvation. The Church venerates angels who help her on the pilgrimage to God and protect every human being.
- Some angels turned against God and were driven from his presence. Led by Satan and followers, called devils, they tempt us to evil.

MEDITATION

God's Providential Care

God has a special love for every human person and a special plan for each of us. Often enough, God's plan is not what we would expect. Look at the lives of great people like Pope John Paul II or Blessed Teresa of Calcutta. During World War II, Karol Wojtyla (Pope John Paul II) was a laborer and an actor, but led by God, he entered an underground seminary. Born in Albania, Blessed Teresa found herself seeking out the dying in the gutters of Calcutta. Have the lives of these two unfolded according to their original plans? Surely not. If and when we accept God's love in our lives, he can ask surprising and sometimes challenging things of us.

Why do so many of us tend to brush aside God's plan for us in our lives? It seems to be because we find it hard to imagine how he can be so loving to us, especially in awkward surroundings. Yet if the divine Word of God could become one of us by taking on our human nature with the cooperation of a young woman in Nazareth, God can surely touch our lives.

PRAYER

Act of Faith

O my God, I firmly believe that you are one God
in three divine Persons, Father, Son and Holy Spirit;
I believe that your divine Son became man and died for our sins,
and that he will come to judge the living and the dead.
I believe these and all the truths which the Holy Catholic
    Church teaches,
because you have revealed them,
who can neither deceive nor be deceived.

My Lord and my God, give me everything
that brings me closer to you.

—St. Nicholas of Flüe

6 MAN AND WOMAN IN THE BEGINNING

THE CREATION OF MAN AND WOMAN, THE FALL AND THE PROMISE
—CCC, NOS. 355-421

THE HOUSE OF MERCY

On the night before she died in 1926, Rose Hawthorne Lathrop (now known as Mother Alphonsa) wrote a letter to the editor of the New York Times about her work with penniless patients with terminal cancer:

Many people know nothing of our work with the cancerous poor, and if accosted by a person asking for a donation would give a sum out of politeness, mentally asking, "What unheard of thing is this?" We are practical enough to want everyone to know what it is and to give a bit because their hearts are touched, to help us build this house of mercy.[5]

This angel of mercy, foundress of the Servants of Relief for Incurable Cancer, was born in 1851, the youngest of three children of the famous novelist Nathaniel Hawthorne and his wife Sophia (Peabody). Soon after Rose's birth, the family moved to Liverpool, in England, where Nathaniel served as the American consul. At the end of his service, the family spent two years In Italy before returning to New England.

Nathaniel died four years later. Sophia took the family back to Europe. At age twenty, Rose married the nineteen-year-old George Lathrop in London in 1871. The young couple moved to Cambridge, Massachusetts,

---

5   In Diana Culbertson, OP, ed., *Rose Hawthorne Lathrop: Selected Writings* (Mahwah, NJ: Paulist Press, 1993), 83, 183.

where George worked as assistant editor of *The Atlantic Monthly*. During these years, Rose wrote poetry and short stories for magazines such as *Harper's Bazaar* and *Scribner's*. Their only child, Francis, died at age four. The Paulist Fr. Alfred Young received the Lathrops into the Catholic Church in 1891. George Lathrop died in 1898.

The story of a poor seamstress who died of cancer on Blackwell's Island occasioned the spiritual turning point for Rose. "A fire was then lighted in my heart, where it still burns. . . . I set my whole being to bring consolation to the cancerous poor." In Rose's time, cancer patients were marginalized by society much as patients with AIDS (Acquired Immune Deficiency Syndrome) have been in modern times. Yet Rose recognized that they were more than helpless poor people. They were made in the image of God.

Rose devoted the next thirty-three years of her life to caring for victims of incurable cancer. She proved to be an able administrator and fund-raiser, establishing a number of hospices for cancer victims in the New York area. Rose and her friend Alice Huber were living a semi-monastic existence in the city, when Dominican Fr. Clement Theunte received them as Third Order members.

Then, as Sr. M. Alphonsa and Sr. M. Rose, they established the Dominican Congregation of St. Rose of Lima, incorporated as the Servants of Relief for Incurable Cancer. They established a cancer hospice in Hawthorne, New York. Funds were sought by the then-Mother Alphonsa through her appeals in her magazine *Christ's Poor*. Other similar facilities were established around the country.

Mother Alphonsa composed essays that appeared in every issue of *Christ's Poor*. She believed it was possible for every parish to have two houses for the relief of the sick poor. She answered God's call with faith, energy, and imagination. Her spirit burns brightly to this day through her community and through the poor who still need such help.

This chapter focuses on two fundamental aspects of human nature as seen from the viewpoint of faith: we are made in the image of God and yet bear the impact of Original Sin. These truths account for the inner conflicts we experience. Made in the image of God, we find ourselves drawn toward him. As burdened by the effects of Original Sin, we experience the tendency that takes us away from God.

We chose the story of Rose Hawthorne Lathrop in this context, primarily because she saw the image of God in the cancerous poor of her day. She also shows us how we, urged on by God, can overcome the self-centeredness caused by Original Sin.

CREATED IN GOD'S IMAGE

God willed the diversity of his creatures and their own particular goodness, their interdependence, and their order. He destined all material creatures for the good of the human race. Man, and through him all creation, is destined for the glory of God.

—CCC, no. 353

"God created man in his image . . . male and female he created them" (Gn 1:27). In figurative and symbolic language, Scripture describes God's creating the first man and woman, Adam and Eve, and placing them in Paradise. They were created in friendship with God and in harmony with creation. The Church teaches that theirs was a state of original holiness and justice, with no suffering or death (cf. CCC, no. 376; GS, no. 18).

The first man and woman were qualitatively different from and superior to all other living creatures on earth. They were uniquely made in the image of God, as are all human beings, their descendants. What does this mean? God's image is not a static picture stamped on our souls. God's image is a dynamic source of inner spiritual energy drawing our minds and hearts toward truth and love, and to God himself, the source of all truth and love.

To be made in the image of God includes specific qualities. Each of us is capable of self-knowledge and of entering into communion with other persons through self-giving. These qualities—and the shared heritage of our first parents—also form a basis for a bond of unity among all human beings. To be made in God's image also unites human beings as God's stewards in the care of the earth and of all God's other creatures.

Another important aspect of our creation is that God has made us a unity of body and soul. The human soul is not only the source of physical life for our bodies but is also the core of our spiritual powers of knowing and loving. While our bodies come into being through physical processes, our souls are all created directly by God.

God created man and woman, equal to each other as persons and in dignity. Each is completely human and is meant to complement the other in a communion of persons, seen most evidently in marriage.

Finally, we need to recognize that God created the first humans in a state of original holiness and justice, so that we are able to live in harmony with his plan. By his gracious will, he enabled us to know and love him, thus calling us to share his life. Our first parents also had free will and thus could be tempted by created things to turn away from the Creator.

THE FALL

The doctrine of original sin is, so to speak, the "reverse side" of the Good News that Jesus is the Savior of all men, that all need salvation, and that salvation is offered to all through Christ.

—CCC, no. 389

Why is it that, with the best of intentions, we find it so difficult to do what is right? We can look for an explanation in the opening chapters of the Book of Genesis. Here the seemingly endless struggle between good and evil is described in the imagery of the serpent tempting Adam and Eve with the forbidden fruit.

God said to them, "You are free to eat from any of the trees of the garden except the tree of knowledge of good and bad. From that tree you shall not eat; the moment you eat from it, you are surely doomed to die" (Gn 2:16-17). The tempter, however, said, "You certainly will not die! No, God knows well that the moment you eat of it your eyes will be opened and you will be like gods who know what is good and what is bad" (Gn 3:4-5). Adam and Eve chose their own desires, based on a lie, over God's will and plan. Sin entered the world through this decision to choose themselves over God and his plan.

Through the Fall of Adam and Eve, the harmony of creation was also destroyed. If we continue to read the Book of Genesis, we see how Adam and Eve became aware of their sinful condition, were driven out of the garden, and were forced to live by the sweat of their brow. The beauty and harmony of God's creative plan was disrupted. This was not the way it was meant to be. Once sin entered into life and into our world, all harmony with God, with self, with each other, and with the world around us was shattered. We call the Fall and its results "Original Sin."

Each one of us is heir to Adam and Eve. Their sin shattered God's created harmony, not only for them but also for us. We experience the effects of Original Sin in our daily life. This explains why it is so difficult to do good or to do what we should.

UNDERSTANDING THE IMPACT OF ORIGINAL SIN

Scripture uses figurative language in describing the account of the Fall in Genesis 3 but affirms an event that took place at the beginning of human history. The language is figurative, but the reality is not a fantasy. The gift of freedom, given to the first man and woman, was meant to draw them closer to God, to each other, and to their destiny. God asked them—as he asks us—to recognize their human limits and to trust in him. In the temptation, they were lured into trying to surpass their being human. "You will be like gods" (Gn 3:5). They abused their freedom, failed to trust God, and disobeyed his command. They lost paradise and its gifts. And death became part of the human experience. For the people of ancient Israel, sin was a spiritual death that leads to separation from God, the source of life, and consequently, to the death of the body.

The sin of Adam and Eve has been called Original Sin since the time of St. Augustine (AD 354-430). But the Church's belief in an ancient alienation from God was part of Revelation from the start.

What is Original Sin? It is a deprivation, a loss of the original holiness and righteousness with which our first parents were created. When

God made them, he filled Adam and Eve with all the grace and virtue they would ever need, and they experienced a close relationship with God beyond our ability to know. Because of the unity of the human race, everyone is affected by the sin of our first parents, just as, in turn, humanity is restored to a right relationship with God by Jesus Christ. "Just as through one person sin entered the world, and by sin, death and . . . just as through the disobedience of one person the many were made sinners, so through the obedience of one the many will be made righteous. . . . Where sin increased, grace overflowed all the more" (Rom 5:12, 19, 20b). Though Original Sin has had far-reaching consequences, of greater consequence has been God's mercy to us through the death and Resurrection of Jesus Christ.

Do we commit Original Sin? "Original sin is a sin contracted and not committed—a state and not an act" (CCC, no. 398). Each of us inherits Original Sin, but it is not a personal fault of ours. It is a deprivation for each of us of original holiness and justice. This inheritance leaves us in a world that is subject to suffering and death, as well as in an environment in which the accumulated sins and failings of others disturb peace and order.

What is the effect of Original Sin upon us? Original Sin underlies all other sins and causes our natural powers of knowing and loving to be wounded. We are subject to ignorance, which makes it difficult for us to know the truth, and for some, even to believe that truth exists. We also endure suffering and death and have a disorder in our appetites and an inclination to sin. This inclination is called *concupiscence*. Because sin alienates us from each other, it weakens our ability to live fully Christ's commandment of love for one another.

It is Jesus Christ who frees us from Original Sin and our own actual sins. By Baptism, we share in the redemptive act of Jesus' death and Resurrection, are freed from Original Sin, and are strengthened against the power of sin and death. We are reconciled to God and made members of his holy people, the Church.

FROM THE CATECHISM

1. What are some implications of being made in the image of God?

Of all visible creatures only man is "able to know and love his creator" (GS, no. 12). He is "the only creature on earth that God has willed for its own sake" (GS, no. 24), and he alone is called to share, by knowledge and love, in God's own life. (CCC, no. 356)

2. What is the main result of Original Sin?

By his sin, Adam, as the first man, lost the original holiness and justice he had received from God, not only for himself but for all human beings. (CCC, no. 416)

3. Why didn't God prevent the first man from sinning?

God gave us free will and would not interfere with the use of our free will:

Christ's inexpressible grace gave us blessings better than those the demon's envy had taken away. (CCC, no. 412, citing St. Leo the Great, *Sermo* 73, no. 4)

UNDERSTANDING SIN

In recent times the comment frequently arises, What's happened to sin? Where has sin gone? There is a perceptible discomfort in our culture with the notion of sin as an evil for which we must give an account to God, our Creator, Redeemer, and Judge. This tendency applies not just to everyday evil acts, but even more so to Original Sin, something that seems to have little to do with us. The origin of this attitude may be found in an underdeveloped sense of Revelation: "Without the knowledge Revelation gives of God we cannot recognize sin clearly and are tempted to explain it as merely a developmental flaw, a psychological weakness, a mistake. . . . Only in the knowledge of God's plan . . . can we grasp that sin is an abuse of the freedom that God gives to created persons" (CCC, no. 387).

Connected with this is the popular notion or attitude of self-help. According to this attitude, all we need to do is fill the mind with lots of inspirational knowledge and reach out for insights. In this viewpoint, we are able to resolve all our shortfalls by ourselves. But sin is not a weakness we can overcome by our own effort. It is a condition from which we need to be saved. Jesus is our Savior.

Central to our journey of faith is the awareness of forces within us that oppose each other and cause us conflict. One drive flows from our being created in the image of God, with all the gifts and abilities that brings. The other force results from the effects of Original Sin, which can cause us to act with selfishness and malice. In his Letter to the Romans, St. Paul describes his own experience of this conflict: "What I do, I do not understand. For I do not do what I want, but I do what I hate. . . . For I do not do the good I want, but I do the evil I do not want" (Rom 7:15, 19). He had actually met the Risen Lord Jesus in an extraordinary vision on the Damascus Road and later saw eternal glory itself (cf. 2 Cor 12:2). But he still experienced the inner war within his soul caused by the aftereffects of Original Sin. In maddening frustration, he cried out, "Miserable one that I am! Who will deliver me from this mortal body?" (Rom 7:24). It was his faith that "where sin increased, grace overflowed all the more" (Rom 5:20).

No matter how sinful we human beings become, the desire for God never dies while we are on earth. No matter how holy we grow, the sting of evil always gnaws at us from the effects of Original Sin. St. Paul shared with us his spiritual struggle on the journey to holiness. He gives us courage. In Jesus Christ, we can overcome the power of sin, for it is the Lord's desire that all come to salvation.

FOR DISCUSSION

1. When you hear yourself described as being created in the image of God, what comes to your mind? What would help you perceive that being made in God's image encourages you to do good things? How should a person created in God's image live?

2. Why do you think some people are not comfortable with the teachings about Original Sin and their personal sins? St. Paul writes, "I do not do the good I want, but I do the evil I do not want" (Rom 7:19). He discovered an inner war between evil and good. In what ways could you identify with his analysis?

3. Why do some people think they can win salvation on their own? Why is that approach mistaken? Why is Jesus the answer to the need for salvation?

■ DOCTRINAL STATEMENTS ■

- God created man and woman in his image as his creatures called to love and to serve him and to care for creation.

- Each person is a unity of body and soul. God directly creates the immortal soul of each human being.

- God created human beings as male and female, equal to each other as persons and in dignity. Man and woman complement each other in a communion of persons.

- "Because of its common origin *the human race forms a unity* for 'from one ancestor [God] made all nations to inhabit the whole earth.' . . . 'This law of human solidarity and charity,' without excluding the rich variety of persons, cultures, and peoples, assures us that all men are truly brethren" (CCC, nos. 360-361, citing Acts 17:26 and Pope Pius XII, *Summi Pontificatus*, no. 3).

- Revelation teaches about the state of original holiness and justice of man and woman before sin. Their happiness flowed from their friendship with God.

- The account of the Fall in Genesis 3 uses figurative language, but it affirms a primeval event, a sin that took place at the beginning of history (cf. CCC, no. 390).

- Tempted by the Evil One, man and woman abused their freedom. They opposed God and separated themselves from him.

- "By his sin Adam, as the first man, lost the original holiness and justice he had received from God, not only for himself, but for all human beings" (CCC, no. 416).

- Adam and Eve transmitted to all future generations a human nature wounded by their sin and deprived of original holiness and justice. This deprivation is called Original Sin.
- Because of Original Sin, human nature is subject to ignorance, suffering, death, disorder in our appetites, and an inclination to sin—an inclination called concupiscence.
- But the victory over sin that Jesus accomplished has provided greater blessings than those taken away. "Where sin increased grace abounded all the more" (Rom 5:20). Baptism delivers us from Original Sin.
- Because every human being is made in the image of God, each one has a desire for union with God. Humanity has been reconciled to God by the redemptive death and Resurrection of Jesus Christ.

MEDITATION

Although set by God in a state of rectitude, man, enticed by the evil one, abused his freedom at the very start of history. He lifted himself up against God, and sought to attain his goal apart from him. Although they had known God, they did not glorify him as God, but their senseless minds were darkened and they served the creature rather than the creator (cf. Rom 1:21-25). What Revelation makes known to us is confirmed by our own experience. For when man looks into his own heart he finds that he is drawn towards what is wrong and sunk in many evils which cannot come from his good creator. Often refusing to acknowledge God as his beginning, man has also upset the relationship which should link him to his last end; and at the same time he has broken the right order that should reign within himself as well as between himself and other men and all creatures.

Man therefore is divided in himself. As a result, the whole life of men, both individual and social, shows itself to be a struggle, and a dramatic one, between good and evil, between light and darkness. Man finds that he is unable of himself to overcome the assaults of evil successfully, so that everyone feels as though he is bound by chains. But the Lord himself came to free and strengthen man, renewing him inwardly and casting out that "prince of this world" (John 12:31), who held him in the bondage of sin (cf. Jn 8:34). For sin brought man to a lower state, forcing him away from the completeness that is his to attain.

Both the high calling and the deep misery which men experience find their final explanation in the light of this Revelation.

—GS, no. 13

PRAYER

We adore you, O Christ, and we praise you.
Because by your holy Cross you have redeemed the world.

For every good work, every kindly thought, or tiny act of humble helpfulness, God gives a reward.

— *Rose Hawthorne Lathrop, 225*

7 THE GOOD NEWS: GOD HAS SENT HIS SON

SON OF GOD, SON OF MARY,
MYSTERIES OF CHRIST'S LIFE
—CCC, NOS. 422-570

A GOOD MAN IN OLD NEW YORK

"Pierre Toussaint, you are the richest man I know. Why not stop working?"

"Then, Madam, I should not have enough for others."

Pierre Toussaint was born in Haiti in 1766 and raised as a slave at a time when it was a French colony. A small group of slave owners made fabulous fortunes from trading sugar, coffee, indigo, tobacco, and fruit. Seven hundred thousand black slaves, brutally beaten and terrorized, made this possible.

Baptized and raised a Catholic, Toussaint was one of the lucky ones, a house slave instead of a farm hand. Treated humanely by the Berard family, he was brought with them to New York when they fled the upcoming slave rebellion. They arrived around the time that George Washington was inaugurated as the first president of the United States.

Berard assigned Pierre as an apprentice to a Mr. Merchant, one of the city's leading hairdressers. Pierre found he had a talent for this work and soon became a success at it. Wealthy women spent vast sums to acquire the elaborate hairstyles of the day. The Berards allowed Pierre to keep a portion of his earnings.

Back in Haiti the slaves rebelled and drove out the French government. An attempt to retake the country by Napoleon's invasion force failed. The Berards lost their property and source of income. Berard died and left his wife without much to live on. Toussaint quietly took over the support of Mrs. Berard and the household. In gratitude, she freed him from his slave status, after which he married Juliette Noel. He used his considerable income to support charitable causes. He conducted a fundraising effort among his rich clients of differing religious persuasions to build a Catholic orphanage. Mother Elizabeth Seton sent three sisters to start the orphanage. He ministered personally to victims of a plague.

He labored to dispel religious and racial prejudice in the city. One of his customers, Emma Cary, wrote about his dignity and Catholic witness:

> His life was so perfect, and he explained the teaching of the Church with a simplicity so intelligent and courageous that everyone honored him as a Catholic. He would explain the devotion to the Mother of God with the utmost clearness, or show the union of the natural and supernatural gifts in the priest.[6]

Pierre worked up to the last two years of his life before dying at age eighty-seven in 1853. Along with many others, the New York newspapers mourned his passing. The *New York Post* reported, "Toussaint is spoken of by all as a man of the warmest and most active benevolence." He was buried with his wife Juliette and niece Euphemia in Old St. Patrick's cemetery on Mott Street in New York.

Pope John Paul II declared him Venerable—an important step in Toussaint's cause for canonization—in December 1996. Since then his body has been reburied in the crypt of the archbishops in St. Patrick's Cathedral in New York City. If canonized he would become the first black U.S. canonized saint.

As a married man, he was able to show us how a spouse may admirably fulfill God's call to holiness. He was a true and heroic disciple of Jesus Christ.

Scripture tells us that no sooner had our first parents sinned than God hastened to promise them the hope of redemption. God loved us so much that he sent his only Son, Jesus Christ, to save us. In this chapter we review the mysteries of Jesus found in the Gospels and doctrinal teachings about him that were taught by early Councils of the Church. Venerable Pierre

---

6   Quoted in Boniface Hanley, OFM, *Ten Christians* (Notre Dame, IN: Ave Maria Press: 1979), 34.

Toussaint was motivated by profound love of Jesus Christ, and his inspiring story aptly leads us to a prayerful study of our blessed Lord.

GOSPEL PORTRAITS OF JESUS

If we want to know Jesus, we should know the Scripture. This is certainly true about the Gospels of Matthew, Mark, Luke, and John, which were written "that you may [come to] believe that Jesus is the Messiah, the Son of God, and that through this belief you may have life in his name" (Jn 20:31).

We ponder Christ's person and his earthly words and deeds in terms of *mystery*. His earthly life reveals his hidden divine Sonship and plan for our salvation. His parables, miracles, sermons, and wisdom sayings help us "to see our God made visible, and so we are caught up in love of the God we cannot see" (First Preface for Christmas).

The Gospels tell us a lot of what we know about Jesus. In two of the Gospels, we hear of his birth in the town of Bethlehem, to a young virgin named Mary. None of the Gospels tell much of the first thirty years of his life. We know he lived in the town of Nazareth with his mother and foster father, St. Joseph, and that he learned to be a carpenter like his foster father. The Gospels concentrate mostly on the events of his public life or ministry, which began when he was around the age of thirty. Jesus spent the last three years of his life traveling around the lands of ancient Israel, teaching the people of the Kingdom of God and confirming his identity as the Son of God through the miracles and wonders he performed. He gathered around him many disciples from whom he selected twelve who became the Apostles.

In the Gospels, we see and hear Jesus summon others to accept, live, and share the Kingdom of God. The proclamation of the Kingdom of God was fundamental to Jesus' preaching. The Kingdom of God is his presence among human beings calling them to a new way of life as individuals and as a community. This is a Kingdom of salvation from sin and a sharing in divine life. It is the Good News that results in love, justice, and mercy for the whole world. The Kingdom is realized partially on earth and permanently in heaven. We enter this Kingdom through faith in Christ, baptismal initiation into the Church, and life in communion with all her members.

The words of Jesus, expressed in his parables, the Sermon on the Mount, his dialogues, and the Last Supper discourse are calls to holiness through accepting his Kingdom and salvation. Jesus did not abolish the Law of Sinai, but rather fulfilled it (cf. Mt 5:17-19) with such perfection (cf. Jn 8:46) that he revealed its ultimate meaning (cf. Mt 5:23) and redeemed the transgressions against it (cf. Heb 9:15). The miracles and other deeds of Jesus are acts of compassion and signs of the Kingdom and salvation.

In the mystery of the Transfiguration, we gain a foretaste of the Kingdom. A hymn of the Byzantine liturgy spells it out for us:

> You were transfigured on a mountain. Your disciples contemplated your glory, Christ God, so that when they saw you crucified, they would understand that your passion was freely willed. They would announce to the world that you are truly the splendor of the Father. (*Kontakion* for the Feast of the Transfiguration, Byzantine tradition)

Above all it is in the Paschal Mystery, which is the saving Passion, death, and Resurrection of Jesus, that we participate most profoundly in the mystery of Christ. Here is the heart of the Kingdom and salvation to which we are called. In Christ, we die to self and sin. We rise to participate in his divine life through the Resurrection. This is made possible for us through the Sacraments.

Our access to the Gospels is made possible by doing faith-filled reading of the sacred texts, by listening to them in the Church's liturgy, and by witnessing their meaning in our lives and in the lives of others. We can benefit greatly from the number of available Scripture commentaries and Bible study groups that are sponsored by local parishes.

TRUE GOD AND TRUE MAN

Who is Jesus Christ? He is the Second Person of the Blessed Trinity, conceived by the Holy Spirit and born of the Virgin Mary. He is true God and true man.

> The unique and altogether singular event of the Incarnation of the Son of God does not mean that Jesus Christ is part God and part man, nor does it imply that he is the result of a confused mixture of the divine and the human. He became truly man while remaining truly God. . . . During the first centuries the Church had to defend and clarify this truth of faith against the heresies that falsified it. (CCC, no. 464)

Because of various heresies that departed from the Apostolic Tradition, the Church needed to defend and clarify the true being of Christ. The first major heretical movement, Gnosticism, denied the humanity of Christ. Its advocates taught that the body was an unworthy dwelling place for God. They thought that the Incarnation could not have happened. The Church asserted Christ's true coming in the flesh, born of the Virgin Mary. Moreover, in a real body, he truly suffered and died on the Cross.

> The son of God . . . worked with human hands; he thought with a human mind. He acted with a human will, and with a human heart he loved. Born of the Virgin Mary, he has truly been made one of us, like us in all things except sin. (GS, no. 22)

It is important to understand that Jesus had a human soul. He was also endowed with true human knowledge, which always worked in harmony with the divine wisdom to which Jesus' knowledge was united. Jesus also possessed a true human will, which always cooperated with his divine will.

A second major heresy, called Arianism because it was taught by a man named Arius, claimed that Jesus was not God. This Alexandrian priest argued that the "Word" which became flesh in Jesus was not God, but a created being, marvelous but created nonetheless. Arius and his disciples believed it was unfitting to even think that a human being could

CHRISTOLOGICAL TEACHINGS OF EARLY COUNCILS
(CF. CCC, NOS. 465-468)

Nicea (AD 325): Jesus Christ is the Son of God by nature and not by adoption. He is "begotten," not made, of the same substance as the Father.

Ephesus (AD 431): Since the one who was born of Mary is divine, Mary is rightly called "Mother of God."

Chalcedon (AD 451): Jesus Christ, Son of God, is true God and true man. His divine and human natures remain together without confusion, change, division, or separation.

Second Constantinople (AD 553): There is only one person—a divine person—in Jesus Christ. The human acts of Jesus are also attributed to his divine person.

be God. To counter Arius, the Council of Nicea (AD 325) reaffirmed the faith of the Church that Jesus was really God, "begotten, not made, of one substance with the Father."

A third heresy, Nestorianism, denied the unity of Jesus Christ as God and man. The Nestorians argued that the divine Son of God dwelled inside the human Jesus of Nazareth, but that they were not really one as one person. They insisted that Mary could be called "Mother of Jesus" but not "Mother of God," as if the man Jesus and the divine Son were two separate persons. The Council of Ephesus (AD 431) rejected this heresy and professed that Mary is the Mother of God, the *Theotokos* (Birth-giver of God; sometimes translated as "God-bearer"). Jesus Christ is the divine Son of God who became man in the womb of Mary. The one who was born of Mary is the same one—the same person—who has existed with the Father and the Holy Spirit from all eternity.

FROM THE CATECHISM

1. What does the name *Jesus* mean?
Jesus means in Hebrew: "God saves." . . . Since God alone
can forgive sins, it is God who, in Jesus his eternal Son
made man, "will save his people from their sins." (CCC, no.
430, citing Mt 1:21)

2. Why is Jesus called *Christ*?
The word "Christ" [*Christos*] comes from the Greek translation of the Hebrew *Messiah*, which means "anointed." It
became the name proper to Jesus . . . because he accomplished perfectly the divine mission that "Christ" signifies.
(CCC, no. 436)

3. How does Jesus model discipleship for us?
In all of his life, Jesus presents himself as *our model.* He is
"the perfect man," who invites us to become his disciples
and follow him. In humbling himself, he has given us an
example to imitate, through his prayer he draws us to
pray, and by his poverty he calls us to accept freely the
privation and persecution that may come our way. (CCC,
no. 520, citing GS, no. 38)

Understanding that Jesus is both fully human and fully divine is very
important. The Church has consistently defended this teaching against
attempts to present one or the other as somehow less. If the Crucifixion
and Resurrection were events that involved God only, then we are not
saved. If Jesus was not divine, he would have been just another good
man whose death and Resurrection would not have saved us. It is necessary to believe that the mystery of the Incarnation means that Jesus was
both fully God and fully man.

JESUS IS THE SAVIOR OF ALL

There is no salvation through anyone else, nor is there
any other name under heaven given to the human race
by which we are to be saved.

—Acts 4:12

At the beginning of the third millennium, the world celebrated global awareness and the diversity of cultures. The revolution in communications, transportation, and computer technologies is making us all aware of peoples and diversity in ways seldom experienced so directly in times past. The United States itself is a primary case study in continuing cultural diversity, especially witnessing the arrival of large numbers of Hispanics and Asians.

Amid the excitement generated by global awareness, it is helpful to point out that God's plan to save the world has been global from the very start. Christ's final words to his Apostles precisely present a global scale to their mission: "Go, therefore, and make disciples of all nations" (Mt 28:19).

The energetic missionaries of the Church have brought the Good News of Jesus Christ to every part of the world. Time after time the Church has incarnated the Gospel in yet another new and fascinating culture. If anyone is an expert in cultural pluralism, it is the Church, whose Gospel outreach has evangelized ancient Judea, Greece and Rome, Egypt and North Africa, the tribal communities that flowed into northern Europe, the Medieval and Renaissance worlds, the far-flung lands of Asia, and the new fields opened up by the discovery of America. In recent times, the Church's revitalized mission to Africa and Asia is yet another chapter in her proclamation of Christ to the world.

While we correctly celebrate the rich variety of cultures, we also are reminded that unity and harmony in Christ constitute the greatest value and hope for the human community. There should be no clash of cultures or civilizations, but rather the growth of universal respect for everyone's human dignity. We search for unity as we honor ethnic and cultural diversity. This is a unity that reflects the unity of the Holy

Trinity itself. The mission of the Catholic Church is the Lord's plan to unite all people in the love of Jesus Christ, the Savior of all. This unity can never detract from the uniqueness of cultures that pluralism recognizes and respects.

FOR DISCUSSION

1. Why is it important for you to appreciate the truth that the person, words, and deeds of Jesus as seen in the Gospel accounts are mysteries revealing to us the hidden plan of God for our salvation? Conversely, what happens when this is forgotten?
2. The New Testament and the early Church Councils affirm in faith that Jesus is true God and true man. What is the value for our faith life in appreciating this truth of Revelation? What happens if we forget any aspect of Christ's identity?
3. What is your experience of cultural diversity? How has such diversity influenced your sensitivity to others? Why is God's plan for the unity of all peoples through the love of Christ an even greater value?

DOCTRINAL STATEMENTS

- "The whole of Christ's life was a continual teaching: his silences, his miracles, his gestures, his prayer, his love for people, his special affection for the lowly and the poor, his acceptance of the total sacrifice of the Cross for the redemption of the world, and his Resurrection are the actualization of his word and the fulfillment of Revelation" (CCC, no. 561).
- The name *Jesus* means "God saves." "There is no other name under heaven given to the human race by which we are to be saved" (Acts 4:12). The title *Christ* means "anointed one" (*Messiah*).
- The title *Son of God* refers to the truth that Jesus Christ is the unique and eternal Son of the Father. At Christ's baptism and Transfiguration, the Father says of Jesus, "This is my beloved Son" (Mt 3:17; 17:5). To profess Jesus as *Lord* is to believe in his divinity.

- The only Son of the Father, the eternal Word, became man at the appointed time, without ceasing to be God. He was conceived by the Holy Spirit and born of the Virgin Mary.
- Jesus Christ is true God and true man united in one divine Person.
- "The son of God . . . worked with human hands; he thought with a human mind. He acted with a human will, and with a human heart he loved. Born of the Virgin Mary . . . he is like us in all things except sin" (GS, no. 22).
- In the Incarnation, we behold the mystery of the union of the divine and human natures in the one person of God's Son. Somehow, in a way we cannot completely grasp, Jesus had both human knowledge and a human will and divine knowledge and a divine will.
- As disciples of Christ, we are called to conform ourselves to him until he is formed in us.
- The mysteries of Christ's infancy and hidden life invite us to identify with Christ's obedience to Mary and Joseph as well as the example of his holiness in the daily work of family and work in the long years at Nazareth.
- The mysteries of Christ's public life draw us to learn discipleship from the teachings of his baptism, his temptation in the desert, his preaching and witness of the Kingdom of Heaven, his Transfiguration, his voluntary journey to Jerusalem to face his Passion, and his entry into Jerusalem, where he completed the work of our salvation through his death and Resurrection.

MEDITATION

Why Did the Word Become Flesh?

The Word became flesh to save us from sin and reconcile us to God. "For God so loved the world that he gave his only Son, so that everyone who believes in him might not perish but might have eternal life" (Jn 3:16).

By the Incarnation we are made aware of the depth of God's love for us. "In this way the love of God was revealed to us: God sent his only Son into the world so that we might have life through him" (1 Jn 4:9).

When the Son of God became man he became a model of holiness for us. "This is my commandment: love one another as I love you" (Jn 15:12).

God became man that we may partake in the divine nature. "He has bestowed on us the precious and very great promises, so that through them you may come to share in the divine nature" (2 Pt 1:4)

PRAYER

Lord Jesus Christ, Son of the living God,
have mercy on me, a sinner.

I can never cease to speak of Christ for he is our truth and
our light.

—Pope Paul VI

8 THE SAVING DEATH AND RESURRECTION OF CHRIST

THE PASCHAL MYSTERY, UNITY OF THE SAVING DEEDS
—CCC, NOS. 571-664

SINGING THE LORD'S PRAISES— WITH A CHALLENGE

At the funeral of Sr. Thea Bowman, on April 3, 1990, Fr. John Ford asked, "Who was Sister Thea?" Many answers were given. One said, "She challenged us to our own individuality, yet pleaded for us to be one in Christ. This was her eloquent song." Another called her "the springtime in everyone's life." She was praised as "the God-gilded voice sent dancing, swaying, sashaying into our lives."

Who was Sr. Thea?

Born as Bertha Bowman in 1937 in Yazoo City, Mississippi, the daughter of a physician, Theon E. Bowman, and a schoolteacher, Mary E. Coleman Bowman, Bertha thrived in a richly textured extended African American family. When local schools did not offer a good education, her mother enrolled her in a school run by the Franciscan Sisters of Perpetual Adoration of La Crosse, Wisconsin. Bertha converted to Catholicism at age ten, and six years later she entered the congregation that had taught her. In becoming a sister, she took the name *Thea.*

She became a teacher from 1959 to her death in 1990, first with elementary school students and then with a wider audience. She earned a graduate degree in English literature at The Catholic University in Washington, D.C. But no matter where she was, she carried in her heart and voice the songs, stories, and values of the rich cultural heritage of the

African American community of the rural South. Like a modern version of the singing poets of Scripture, the bards of ancient Greece, and the storytellers of Africa, she shared the Gospel and the gifts of black Americans with all who would listen. She demonstrated a social conscience on many occasions.

She spoke to the U.S. bishops on June 17, 1989, at their meeting at Seton Hall University in South Orange, New Jersey. Suffering from bone cancer, she spoke from a wheelchair. Among the many challenges she presented was one about Catholic schools.

> I've got to say one more thing. You-all ain't going to like this but that's all right. The Church has repeatedly asked black folk, what do you want, what can the Church do for you? And black folk all over the country are saying, help us to education. We need education. The way out of poverty is education. We can't be Church without education, because ignorance kills and cripples us. Black people are still asking the Church for education. ("To Be Black and Catholic," *Origins* (July 6, 1989): 117)

At the conclusion of her speech—received by the bishops as a warm and moving message—she asked the bishops to join her in singing "We shall overcome," with their arms joined to bring them closer together. She often said, "We do not want to change the theology of the Church. We just want to express theology within the roots of our black spiritual culture" (quoted in Mary Queen Donnelly, "Sr. Thea Bowman (1937-1990)," *America* (April 25, 1990)).

As we proceed to reflect on the death and Resurrection of Jesus, we find that the compelling story of Sr. Thea Bowman shows that she was a witness to this mystery of Christ. She bore her cross courageously and still could sing alleluias from her wheelchair—living the Paschal Mystery every day. Nearing the end of her life she said, "Let us stretch ourselves, going beyond our comfort zones to unite ourselves with Christ's redemptive work. Let us break bread together. Let us relive the holy and redemptive mystery" (quoted in Catholic News Service, "Sr. Thea Bowman's Posthumous Plea: Really Live Holy Week" (March 30, 1990)).

LIFT HIGH THE CROSS

In suffering and death his humanity became the free and perfect instrument of his divine love which desires the salvation of men.

—CCC, no. 609

In a number of ways, Jesus warned his followers that pain and death would be an essential part of his mission. Right after he made Peter the rock on which the Church would be built, he predicted his Passion. "Jesus began to show his disciples that he must go to Jerusalem and suffer greatly from the elders, the chief priests and the scribes, and be killed, and on the third day be raised" (Mt 16:21). When Peter protested this possibility, Jesus rebuked him, "You are thinking, not as God does, but as human beings do" (Mt 16:23). Jesus predicted his Passion again after the Transfiguration (cf. Mt 17:22-23).

Not only would Jesus accept the Cross, he expected the same willingness from his disciples. "If anyone wishes to come after me, he must deny himself, take up his cross daily and follow me" (Lk 9:23). Jesus explained this truth further by means of an agricultural image. "Unless a grain of wheat falls to the ground and dies, it remains just a grain of wheat, but if it dies it produces much fruit" (Jn 12:24). Jesus noted that the greatest expression of love is to die for the beloved. "No one has greater love than this, to lay down one's life for one's friends" (Jn 15:13).

Because Christ's suffering and death was the instrument of salvation, from what did he save us? We needed to be saved from sin and its damaging effects. God's plan to save us involved having the Son of God enter into this world to be like us in all things except sin. Divine love made this possible.

Jesus, Son of God, was sent by the Father to restore the harmony between himself and humanity that had been disrupted by sin. He came to teach and show us love. Jesus was without sin, but in his human nature, he was subject to all that human beings suffer, including hatred from others, torture, and death itself. He proclaimed the coming of God's

Kingdom by his words and deeds in obedience to the will of his Father. He showed the full meaning of all that had been revealed in the Old Testament. But some did not want to hear his message. They opposed him and turned him over to the administration of the Roman Empire in Palestine to be put to death.

On the Cross, Jesus freely gave his life as a sacrifice. His sacrifice was an act of atonement, that is, it makes us one again with God by the power of divine mercy extending to us the Father's forgiveness of our sins. His sacrifice is also called an *act of satisfaction* or *reparation*[7] because he lives out fully the Father's call to human beings to be faithful to his plan for them, thus overcoming the power of sin. It is also an *expiation*[8] for our sins, which in the understanding of Scripture means that God takes the initiative in bringing about reconciliation to himself. In the words of Christian Tradition, Jesus' sacrifice merits salvation for us because it retains forever the power to draw us to him and to the Father.

Who is responsible for the death of Jesus? Every one of us from the dawn of history to the end of time who in pride and disobedience has sinned is in some way responsible. Historically, some Jewish leaders handed Jesus over to Pontius Pilate, the Roman governor who condemned Jesus to death on the Cross.

It is wrong to blame the Jewish people for the death of Christ in the manner that often has been done in history. "The Church does not hesitate to impute to Christians the gravest responsibility for the torments inflicted upon Jesus, a responsibility with which they have all too often burdened the Jews alone" (CCC, no. 598). At the Second Vatican Council, the Church made the following declaration regarding the Jewish people:

---

7 *Reparation* means "making amends for a wrong done or for an offense, especially for sin, which is an offense against God. By his death on the cross, the Son of God offered his life out of love for the Father to make reparation for our sinful disobedience" (CCC, Glossary).

8 *Expiation* is "the act of redemption and atonement for sin which Christ won for us by the pouring out of his blood on the cross, by his obedient love 'even to the end' (*Jn* 13:1)" (CCC, Glossary).

Neither all Jews indiscriminately at that time, nor Jews today, can be charged with the crimes committed during his Passion. . . . [T]he Jews should not be spoken of as rejected or accursed as if this followed from holy Scripture. (CCC, no. 597; citing Second Vatican Council, *Declaration on the Relation of the Church to Non-Christian Religions* [*Nostra Aetate*; NA], no. 4)

The Apostles' Creed professes that after his death and burial, Jesus descended into hell. In the language of the early Church, this meant that Jesus went into the realm of the dead, from which he called out all the just people who had lived before him to enter with him into the glory of the Kingdom of Heaven. A popular icon of the Eastern Churches pictures the risen Jesus with his hands reaching into the realm of the dead to draw out Adam and Eve.

In his human soul united to his divine person, the dead Christ went down into the realm of the dead. He opened Heaven's gates for the just who had gone before him. (CCC, no. 637)

CHRIST IS RISEN! ALLELUIA!

Christ's Resurrection is an object of faith in that it is a transcendent intervention of God himself in creation and history.

—CCC, no. 648

When we speak of the Paschal Mystery, we refer to Christ's death and Resurrection as one inseparable event. It is a mystery because it is a visible sign of an invisible act of God. It is paschal because it is Christ's passing through death into new life. For us it means that we can now die to sin and its domination of our lives, and we pass over into divine life already here on earth and more completely in heaven. Death is conquered in the sense that not only do our souls survive physical death, but even our bodies will rise again at the end of time at the Last Judgment and resurrection of the dead.

The Resurrection narratives in all four Gospels—though differing in details because of varying viewpoints of the different authors—maintain a similar structure in the narration of the events. At dawn on the Sunday after Christ's death, Mary Magdalene and a companion go to the tomb to anoint the dead body of Jesus. They find the tomb is empty. They meet an angel who proclaims the Resurrection of Jesus: "He is not here, for he has been raised" (Mt 28:6). They are told to bring the Good News to the Apostles. Mary Magdalene leads the way and is celebrated in the liturgy of the Church as the first witness to the Resurrection.

Next come the appearance narratives when Jesus appears to the Apostles and disciples in a number of instances. St. Paul summarizes these appearances in his first Letter to the Corinthians (cf. 1 Cor 15:3-8). Finally, the disciples are commissioned to bring the Gospel to the world.

While the empty tomb of itself does not prove the Resurrection, since the absence of Christ's body could have other explanations, it is an essential part of the proclamation of the Resurrection because it demonstrates the fact of what God has done in raising his Son from the dead in his own body. When St. John entered the empty tomb, "He saw and believed" (Jn 20:8).

HISTORICAL EVENT

The Resurrection is historical in that it actually took place at a specific time and place, and therefore there were witnesses to its impact. Mary Magdalene met the Risen Christ and embraced his feet. Thomas the Apostle saw Jesus and the wounds and said, "My Lord and my God" (Jn 20:28). Two disciples walked with Jesus on the road to Emmaus and recognized him in the Breaking of the Bread (Lk 24:13-35). All the Apostles saw him (cf. Jn 20:19-23). St. Paul tells us he met the Risen Lord on the Road to Damascus (cf. Acts 9:3-6). He also writes that five hundred people saw Jesus on a single occasion (cf. 1 Cor 15:3-8).

None of the witnesses to Jesus' Resurrection expected it. In fact, they were demoralized by the execution of Jesus. Even when they did see him, some had lingering doubts. "When they saw him, they worshiped him, but they doubted" (Mt 28:17). In other words, they were not easily convinced, nor were they caught up in some kind of mystical self-delusion or hysteria. Some of them even died as martyrs rather than deny what they had witnessed. In this light, their testimony that the Resurrection was a historical event is more convincing (cf. CCC, nos. 643-644).

A TRANSCENDENT EVENT

The reality of Christ's Resurrection is also something beyond the realm of history. No one saw the actual Resurrection. No evangelist describes it. No one can tell us how it physically happened. No one perceived how the earthly body of Christ passed over into a glorified form. Despite the fact that the risen Jesus could be seen, touched, heard, and dined with, the Resurrection remains a mystery of faith that transcends history.

Its transcendent quality can also be inferred from the state of Christ's risen body. He was not a ghost; Jesus invited them to touch him. He asked for a piece of fish to show them that he could eat. He spent time with them, often repeating teachings from the days before the Passion but now in the light of the Resurrection. Nor was it a body like that of Lazarus, which would die again. His risen body would never die. Christ's body was glorified; it is not confined by space or time. He could appear and disappear before the Apostles' eyes. Closed doors did not bar his entry. It is a real body, but glorified, not belonging to earth but to the Father's realm. It is a body transformed by the Holy Spirit (cf. 1 Cor 15:42-44). The Holy Spirit "gave life to Jesus' dead humanity and called it to the glorious state of Lordship" (CCC, no. 648).

What do we learn from Christ's Resurrection? If Jesus had not risen, our faith would mean nothing. St. Paul makes this clear in his first Letter to the Corinthians: "But if Christ is preached as raised from the dead, how can some among you say there is no resurrection of the dead? If there is no resurrection of the dead, then neither has Christ been raised. And if Christ has not been raised, then empty, too, is our preaching; empty, too, your faith" (1 Cor 15:12-14). We also learn that, by raising him from the dead, the Father has placed his seal upon the work accomplished by his only begotten Son through his Passion and death. We see now the fullness of Jesus' glory as Son of God and Savior.

FROM THE CATECHISM

1. How was Jesus able to save all of us?
No man, not even the holiest, was ever able to take on himself the sins of all men and offer himself as a sacrifice for all. The existence in Christ of the divine person of the Son, who at once surpasses and embraces all human persons and constitutes himself as Head of all mankind, makes possible his redemptive sacrifice for all. (CCC, no. 616)

2. Why did Jesus die on the Cross?
Jesus came "to give his life as a ransom for many" (Mt 20:28). By his loving obedience to the Father, he fulfilled the atoning mission of the suffering Servant, "he was pierced for our offenses, crushed for our sins . . . by his stripes we were healed" (Is 53:5) (cf. CCC, nos. 599-618).

3. How is Christ's Resurrection a work of the Trinity?
The three divine persons act together as one. . . . The Father's power "raised up" Christ his Son. . . . Jesus is conclusively revealed as "Son of God in power according to the Spirit of holiness by his Resurrection from the dead." (CCC, no. 648, citing Rom 1:3-4)

As for the Son, he effects his own Resurrection by virtue of his divine power. . . . he affirms explicitly: "I lay down my life, that I may take it again." (CCC, no. 649, citing Jn 10:17-18)

THE ASCENSION INTO HEAVEN

The Paschal Mystery culminates in the Ascension of Jesus. After his appearance here on earth in his risen body, and "after giving instructions through the holy Spirit to the apostles whom he had chosen" (Acts 1:2), Jesus "was lifted up and a cloud took him from their sight" (Acts 1:9):

Christ's ascension marks the definitive entrance of Jesus' humanity into God's heavenly domain, whence he will come again (cf. Acts 1:11). . . . Jesus Christ, the head of the Church, precedes us into the Father's glorious kingdom so that we, the members of his Body, may live in the hope of one day being with him for ever. Jesus Christ, having entered the sanctuary of heaven once and for all, intercedes constantly for us as the mediator who assures us of the permanent outpouring of the Holy Spirit. (CCC, nos. 665-667)

FROM DOUBT TO FAITH

When the women reported the Resurrection to the Apostles, "their story seemed like nonsense and they did not believe them" (Lk 24:11). The Apostles thought they were seeing a ghost when Jesus first appeared to them. Thomas refused to believe unless he could touch the nail marks.

Within a few decades, there arose heretics who denied the Resurrection because they did not think Jesus had a body at all. Greeks believed in the immortality only of the soul. Bodies did not endure beyond death. Resurrection was impossible. Nonetheless, the Apostles and other witnesses who came to faith in the Resurrection preached its reality and centrality to faith. Unless it happened, there would be no Church and no Eucharist. Early Christian believers died by the thousands for their faith in the Risen Christ and his salvation.

In our present culture, there are some who present new denials of the Resurrection. They distort the language of the New Testament to support their disbelief. Arbitrarily they "reinterpret away" what the authors of the text said and meant. In their view, the Resurrection "appearances" were either warm memories of Jesus, projections of their inner needs, or inward spiritual experiences—not real appearances, despite the concrete descriptions in the New Testament documents. Such skeptics seem to mean, "It was impossible, so it did not happen."

The Resurrection makes credible everything Jesus did and taught. It discloses how Jesus accomplished God's eternal plan for our salvation. Through it we taste heavenly gifts and the glory of the age to come. The power of the Resurrection reminds our culture that grace is always more powerful and effective than sin and evil.

FOR DISCUSSION

1. When Jesus says our discipleship involves the Cross, what does this mean for you? In what ways do you find yourself resisting this part of Christ's call? What is your "way of the Cross"?
2. How would you help people come to faith in the Resurrection of Christ? Why is it so central to your faith?
3. How could you come to understand or experience the need for a Savior? Why are the Cross and the Resurrection bound together in the Paschal Mystery?

DOCTRINAL STATEMENTS

- To many in Israel, Jesus seemed to be acting against the Law, the Temple, and their faith in the One God.
- Christ suffered because he was "rejected by the elders and chief priests and scribes" who handed "him over to the Gentiles to be mocked and scourged and crucified" (Mk 8:31; Mt 20:19).
- Jesus did not abolish the Law of Sinai. He fulfilled it and revealed its ultimate meaning (cf. Mt 5:17-19; 6:43-48).
- Jesus honored the Temple, to which he journeyed for the major feasts and which he loved as God's dwelling on earth.
- By forgiving sins, Jesus manifested himself to be the Savior (Jn 5:16-18). Those who did not accept him as the Savior saw him only as a man who claimed to be God, a blasphemer (Jn 10:33).
- Our salvation flows from God's love for us because "he loved us and sent his Son as expiation for our sins" (1 Jn 4:10). "Christ died for our sins in accordance with the scriptures" (1 Cor 15:3).
- Jesus came "to give his life as a ransom for many" (Mt 20:28). By his loving obedience to the Father, he fulfilled the atoning mission of the suffering Servant, "he was pierced for our offenses, / crushed for our sins, / . . . by his stripes we were healed" (Is 53:5).

- The Son of God who became man truly died and was buried, but his body underwent no corruption. In his human soul united to his divine person, the dead Christ went to the realm of the dead and opened heaven for the just who came before him (cf. CCC, no. 637).
- Christ's Resurrection is an event that is historically attested to by the Apostles who really met the Risen One. The Resurrection is also a transcendent mystery because God the Father raises his Son from the dead by the power of the Holy Spirit.
- The empty tomb helped the disciples accept the fact of the Resurrection. When St. John entered the tomb, "he saw and believed" (Jn 20:8).
- Christ is the "firstborn from the dead" (Col 1:18) and so is the principle of our own resurrection, now by the salvation of our souls, and at the end of time, when new life will be given to our bodies.
- Christ's Ascension marks the definitive entrance of his humanity into heaven. Christ precedes us there so that we, the members of his Body, may live in the hope of being with him forever. Jesus intercedes constantly for us as our mediator and assures the permanent outpouring of the Holy Spirit.
- At the end of time, Jesus Christ will come in glory to judge the living and the dead.

MEDITATION

Make Holy Week Holy

Let us stretch ourselves, going beyond our comfort zones to unite ourselves with Christ's redemptive work. We unite ourselves with Christ's redemptive work when we make peace, when we share the good news that God is in our lives, when we reflect to our brothers and sisters God's healing, God's forgiveness, God's unconditional love. Let us break bread together. Let us relive the holy and redemptive mystery. Let us do it in memory of him, acknowledging in faith his real presence on our altars.[9]

---

9   Thea Bowman, FSPA, *Mississippi Today* (April 1990). These words come from a column Sr. Thea wrote the week she died.

PRAYER

Now that we have seen the resurrection of Christ,
let us adore the all-holy Lord Jesus, the only Sinless One.
We bow in worship before your cross, O Christ,
and we praise and glorify your resurrection,
for You are God, and we have no other,
and we magnify your name.
All you faithful, come: let us adore the holy resurrection of Christ,
for behold, through the cross joy has come to the world!
Let us always bless the Lord, let us sing his resurrection,
for by enduring for us the pain of the cross, He has crushed
  death by his death.

—Hymn from Easter Sunday,
Byzantine Daily Worship

I know that my Redeemer lives.
What joy the blest assurance gives!
He lives, he lives who once was dead;
He lives my everlasting head!

—Samuel Medley

9 RECEIVE THE HOLY SPIRIT (Jn 20:22)

THE REVELATION OF THE SPIRIT, JOINT MISSION
OF SON AND SPIRIT
—CCC, NOS. 683-747

SHE WAS LED BY THE HOLY SPIRIT

 Kateri Tekakwitha was born in 1656 at Ossernenon, a Mohawk village in what is now Auriesville, New York. She was the daughter of a Mohawk chief and a Christian Algonquin woman who had come to live among the Mohawks after being captured at Trois Rivieres, Quebec. Kateri was four years old when her parents and little brother died of smallpox. Kateri also contracted the disease, which disfigured her face. Two aunts and an uncle adopted her. The family moved to Caughnawaga, now Fonda, New York. She proved to be an industrious young woman but showed no interest in getting married.

When she was in her teens, Jesuit missionaries came to her village. She was attracted to Catholicism but experienced the opposition of her family and the tribe. Fr. James de Lamberville began to meet with her regularly, teaching her the faith and how to pray and open her heart to God. In her twentieth year, she was baptized on Easter Sunday and was given the name Catherine, or *Kateri* in the Mohawk language.

Since the villagers showed so much hostility to her newfound faith, she decided to leave home and go to a Christian colony of Indians near Montreal. There she spent the remaining years of her life. She promised to remain a virgin. She dedicated her life to prayer, penance, and care for the aged and sick. Every morning at 4 a.m., she arrived at the local chapel for Mass and contemplation. She was devoted to the Eucharist and the mystery of the Cross.

She died on April 7, 1680. Witnesses said her last words were, "Jesus, I love you." They also testified that the smallpox scars on her face vanished. In death she was radiant and beautiful.

Blessed Kateri Tekakwitha is the first North American Indian to be declared Blessed. Her Feast Day is July 14. Along with St. Francis of Assisi, she is the patroness of the environment and ecology. She is popularly known as the "Lily of the Mohawks."

Pope John Paul II addressed six hundred Native Americans on the occasion of Kateri's beatification. Noting that Blessed Kateri is a witness to their faith, he said,

> You have come to rejoice in the beatification of Kateri Tekakwitha. It is a time to pause and give thanks to God for the unique culture and rich human tradition which you have inherited, and for the greatest gift anyone can receive, the gift of faith. (*L'Osservatore Romano* (June 30, 1980): 13)

The Holy Spirit works in the hearts of all who are baptized, but the power of his gifts is most evident in the lives of extraordinary witnesses to faith such as Blessed Kateri.[10]

JESUS GIVES US THE TRANSFORMING SPIRIT

Just before his Ascension, Jesus said these words to the Apostles: "You will receive power when the holy Spirit comes upon you, and you will be my witnesses in Jerusalem, [in all] Judea and Samaria, and to the ends of the earth" (Acts 1:8).

These words of Christ to the Apostles are also addressed to each believer. The Holy Spirit comes to us as a teacher of the meaning and depth of Revelation. He also fills us with power, the grace to understand the Church's teachings and the wisdom to see how they apply to our lives. Finally, the Spirit puts courage into our hearts so that we can witness what we believe to believer and unbeliever alike.

---

10   For more information about Blessed Kateri, see texts from the Tekakwitha Conference National Center reprinted online at *www.cin.org*.

The Acts of the Apostles shows how the Holy Spirit transformed the Apostles from being fearful disciples, huddling behind closed doors, into courageous witnesses for Christ.

> When the time for Pentecost was fulfilled, they were all in one place together. And suddenly there came from the sky a noise like a strong driving wind, and it filled the entire house in which they were. Then there appeared to them tongues as of fire, which parted and came to rest on each one of them. And they were all filled with the holy Spirit and began to speak in different tongues, as the Spirit enabled them to proclaim. (Acts 2:1-4)

Beginning with the gift of the Spirit at Pentecost, the disciples became dynamic missionaries. He filled those disciples with the gift of courage so that nothing stopped them from proclaiming the love of Christ for all people.

When we learn how to be open to the Holy Spirit, he shares with us the gift of understanding that contains the power to know Jesus and to give witness to him. At our Baptism, the Spirit works through the waters which take away Original Sin and actual sins and give us new life with the Triune God. At Confirmation, the Holy Spirit is conferred by the anointing with the Chrism, by which the bishop seals us so that the Holy Spirit can strengthen us to pursue the mission of Christ to transform the world. At every Mass, the Holy Spirit changes the bread and wine into the Body and Blood of Christ by the ministry of the priest.

The Holy Spirit is dynamic, transforming our bodies into temples of God and our souls into dwelling places for Christ. Sometimes called the *Paraclete*, a term that describes him as advocate and consoler, the Holy Spirit wants to fill us with inspiration and encouragement.

We may not have to do great things, but we are called to do everyday duties with great love. The Holy Spirit is essentially Love. Love can change those we meet and change ourselves in each encounter. Because of the Holy Spirit our whole being, mind, heart, soul, and body can be permeated with Love.

> "God is Love" and love is his first gift, containing all others. "God's love has been poured into our hearts through the Holy

Spirit who has been given to us." (CCC, no. 733, citing 1 Jn 4:8, 16 and Rom 5:5)

A rich example of the Holy Spirit's transforming power can be seen in the life of the Blessed Virgin Mary, the mother of Jesus. She is God's masterpiece, transformed by him into a luminous witness of grace from the moment of her conception. The angel Gabriel rightly addressed her as "full of grace." It is also by the power of the Holy Spirit that Mary conceived Jesus, the Son of God.

> Finally, through Mary, the Holy Spirit begins to bring men, the objects of God's merciful love, *into communion* with Christ. And the humble are always the first to accept him: shepherds, magi, Simeon and Anna, the bride and groom at Cana, and the first disciples. (CCC, no. 725)

THE HOLY SPIRIT IS REVEALED GRADUALLY

The Holy Spirit is the last of the Persons of the Trinity to be revealed. St. Gregory Nazianzus (AD 329-389) gives us an excellent picture of God's teaching method, slowly unfolding the truth about the Trinity. Scripture reveals the truth about the Trinity in three stages:

> The Old Testament proclaimed the Father clearly, but the Son more obscurely. The New Testament revealed the Son and gave us a glimpse of the divinity of the Spirit. Now the Spirit dwells among us and grants us a clearer vision of himself. (CCC, no. 684, citing St. Gregory Nazianzus, *Theological Orations*, 5, 26)

The fact that the Holy Spirit is God—equal in being with the Father and the Son, of the same divine nature as they are (*consubstantial* with them), the Third Person of the Holy Trinity—took time to be recognized and proclaimed. In the Old Testament, the Holy Spirit is hidden but is at work. "When the Church reads the Old Testament, she searches there for what the Spirit, 'who has spoken through the prophets,' wants to tell us about Christ" (CCC, no. 702). Both the Hebrew word and the Greek word for the *Spirit* originally meant a "breath," or "air," or "wind."

The Spirit was thus understood to be the source of inspiration, life, and movement within God's people.

Among these holy writings, the Church honors the promise that the Spirit of the Lord shall rest upon the Messiah and endow him with spiritual gifts (cf. Is 11:1-2), and the prophecy that the Messiah will be moved by him to "bring glad tidings to the lowly, / to heal the broken-hearted / . . . to announce a year of favor from the Lord" (Is 61:1-2).

The Gospels show us the dynamic action of the Holy Spirit. It is by the Spirit that Jesus is conceived in the womb of Mary. The Holy Spirit appears in the form of a dove over Jesus at his baptism in the Jordan. He leads Jesus into the desert before he starts his public mission. In the Last Supper discourse in John's Gospel, Chapter 16, Jesus speaks at length about the promised revelation and the sending of the Holy Spirit.

The Holy Spirit is again revealed at Pentecost, when the seven weeks after Easter have concluded. "Christ's Passover is fulfilled in the out-pouring of the Holy Spirit, manifested, given, and communicated as a divine person: of his fullness, Christ, the Lord, pours out the Spirit in abundance" (CCC, no. 731).

The Acts of the Apostles and the various epistles of the New Testament give us further evidence of the presence and action of the Holy Spirit in the first-century Church. Later, in response to a denial of the divinity of the Spirit, the First Council of Constantinople (AD 381) declared as the constant faith of the Church the divinity of the Holy Spirit.

Even though the Holy Spirit is the last Person of the Trinity to be revealed, we must understand that, from the beginning, he is a part of the loving plan of our salvation from sin and of the offer of divine life. He has the same mission as the Son in the cause of our salvation. When the Father sends the Son, he also sends the Holy Spirit:

> When the Father sends his Word, he always sends his Breath. In their joint mission, the Son and the Holy Spirit are distinct but inseparable. (CCC, no. 689)

The Holy Spirit continues to give us knowledge of God, living and active in the Church. The *Catechism* sets out eight ways in which the

Holy Spirit provides us with an experience of God's presence (cf. CCC, no. 688):

- When we pray and study the Scripture which the Holy Spirit inspired, we can sense his presence in the biblical words.
- When we read the lives of the saints, their teachings and witness, we can be motivated to holiness by their example which was shaped by the Holy Spirit.
- When we assent with obedience to the teachings of the Magisterium, we are guided by the Holy Spirit. His presence is uniquely experienced at Ecumenical Councils.
- When we actively participate in the liturgies and Sacraments of the Church, we enter into a sacred moment when the Holy Spirit opens us to experience God, especially in the Eucharist.
- When we give ourselves to prayer, whether that be the Rosary or the Liturgy of the Hours or meditation or other prayers, the Holy Spirit prays within us and intercedes for us.
- When we offer ourselves to the various missionary or apostolic efforts of the Church or see signs of those efforts, we can sense the Holy Spirit at work in the world.
- When we recognize the charisms and ministries which help build the Church, we also understand that it is the Holy Spirit providing us with the leadership we need.
- When we dwell on the great Tradition of the Church, its marvelous history and its host of saintly witnesses, we sense the Holy Spirit's sustaining power through it all.

THE SPIRIT IS THE IMMEDIACY OF GOD

Though we frequently reflect on the secular or worldly nature of our culture in the United States, we must also note that our country is one of the most religious of all industrialized nations. This is true in the sense that a large percentage of our people are active members of churches, synagogues, and mosques. In addition, there is a quality seemingly unique to our culture that moves millions of our people to seek an immediate experience of God. This is most evident in the focus on the Holy Spirit

FROM THE CATECHISM

1. What is our faith regarding the Holy Spirit?
To believe in the Holy Spirit is to profess that the Holy Spirit is one of the persons of the Holy Trinity, consubstantial with the Father and the Son: "with the Father and the Son he is worshiped and glorified." (CCC, no. 685, citing the Nicene Creed)

2. What are images of the Holy Spirit in Scripture?
In Scripture, some of the images of the Holy Spirit are fire, cloud and light, seal, hand, finger of God and dove (cf. CCC, nos. 696-701).

3. How are water and anointing, symbols of the Holy Spirit?
Water: . . . signifies the Holy Spirit's action in Baptism, since after the invocation of the Holy Spirit it becomes the efficacious sacramental sign of new birth. (CCC, no. 694)

Anointing: The . . . anointing with oil also signifies the Holy Spirit. . . . In Christian initiation, anointing is the sacramental sign of Confirmation, called "chrismation" in the Churches of the East. (CCC, no. 695)

across a wide spectrum of Christian believers. In the Catholic Church, a devotion to the Holy Spirit is evident in movements such as Charismatic Renewal, Marriage Encounter, Cursillo, TEC (Teens Encounter Christ), and similar outpourings of faith.

Catholic parishes regularly witness and celebrate the transformative power of the Holy Spirit at the conferral of the Sacrament of Confirmation and in the parishes' support for the journey of candidates in the Rite of Christian Initiation of Adults. In a special way, the immediacy of the Holy Spirit in the life of the Church is remembered on Pentecost Sunday

GIFTS AND FRUITS OF THE HOLY SPIRIT

Gifts of the Holy Spirit: Wisdom, Understanding, Counsel [Right Judgment*], Fortitude [Courage], Knowledge, Piety [Reverence], and Fear of the Lord [Wonder and Awe in God's Presence]. (cf. Is 11:1-2)

Fruits of the Holy Spirit: Charity, Joy, Peace, Patience, Kindness, Goodness, Generosity, Gentleness, Faithfulness, Modesty, Self-control, Chastity. (cf. Gal 5:22-23)

*Bracketed names are alternate names for the gifts as used in the Confirmation Rite.

as we hear of the Apostles and disciples gathered in the Upper Room and receiving the Holy Spirit.

FOR DISCUSSION

1. When in your life would you say you experienced God's presence? What were the occasions and the value of these experiences?
2. The Holy Spirit is the Sanctifier who calls us to holiness. When you hear about being called to be holy, what thoughts arise in your mind? What would you need to do to be more holy?
3. How do you see the gifts and fruits of the Holy Spirit at work in people you know?

DOCTRINAL STATEMENTS

- Before his Ascension, Jesus said to the Apostles, "You will receive power when the Holy Spirit has come upon you, and you will be my witnesses in Jerusalem, in all Judea and Samaria and to the ends of the earth" (Acts 1:8).
- Whenever the Father sends his Son, he always sends his Spirit: Their mission is inseparable.

- The life of the Blessed Virgin Mary shows us the power of the Holy Spirit. She was made by the Holy Spirit into a witness of grace from the moment of her conception. It is also by the power of the Holy Spirit that Mary conceived Jesus, the Son of God.
- By the anointing of the Holy Spirit at his Incarnation, the Son of God was consecrated as Christ (*Messiah*).
- At Pentecost, Peter said of Jesus that "God has made him both Lord and Messiah" (Acts 2:36). From this fullness of his glory, Jesus poured out the Holy Spirit on the Apostles and the Church.
- The Holy Spirit builds up, animates, and sanctifies the Church. He prepares us to go out and bring others to Christ. He opens our minds to understand Christ's death and Resurrection. He makes present for us the mystery of Christ, especially in the Eucharist, and brings us to communion with God that we may bear much fruit (cf. CCC, no. 737).

MEDITATION

In the life of faith there are always two movements: God in search of us and we in search of God. The poet Francis Thompson described God's attempts to reach us in terms of his being the "Hound of Heaven." Thompson said he felt God coming after him and yearning to give him love. But the poet was not ready:

I fled Him, down the labyrinthine ways
of my own mind. . . . I hid from him.

At the same time, God has stamped in our souls a longing for himself. We are born with a longing for the divine that cannot be satisfied by anyone or anything short of God. We are created to be seekers for the absolute love, which is God. Thompson not only experienced God as the hound pursuing him; he also felt his own hunger and thirst for God. One day he stopped running, turned, and rushed toward God:

Naked, I wait Thy love's uplifted stroke!
My harness, piece by piece, Thou hast hewn from me, . . .
I am defenseless, utterly.

And God, the other seeker, in this spiritual drama says:

"Rise, clasp my hand, and come!"

The Holy Spirit presided over this spiritual adventure. It is the mission of the Spirit to help us draw near to God. When the Holy Spirit is present and active in our lives, we can have an experience of his presence.

▮ PRAYER ▮

Come, Holy Spirit, fill the hearts of your faithful.
And kindle in them the fire of your love.
Send forth your Spirit and they shall be created.
And you shall renew the face of the earth.
Let us pray.
Lord, by the light of the Holy Spirit you have taught the hearts
    of your faithful.
In the same Spirit, help us to know what is truly right
and always to rejoice in your consolation.
We ask this through Christ, Our Lord. Amen.

When he comes, the Spirit of truth, he will guide you to
    all truth.

—Jn 16:13

10 THE CHURCH: REFLECTING THE LIGHT OF CHRIST

IMAGES AND MISSION OF THE CHURCH
—CCC, NOS. 748-810

PETER IS A ROCK AND A LOVING PASTOR

The account in Chapter 16 of Matthew begins with Jesus and the Apostles' arrival at Caesarea Philippi, a city that was twenty-five miles north of the Sea of Galilee. In this setting, Jesus asks the Apostles who people thought he was. They replied that some thought Jesus was John the Baptist, others that he was Elijah, or Jeremiah, or one of the prophets. They wondered if Jesus was one of the great prophets come back from the dead.

Jesus asked them, "Who do you say that I am?" Simon Peter alone replied, "You are the Messiah, the Son of the living God" (v. 16). Jesus praised Peter's reply, noting that he had not arrived at such an insight through his own human abilities. Peter had received a revelation from God and had spoken from his faith. "Blessed are you, Simon son of Jonah. For flesh and blood has not revealed this to you, but my heavenly Father" (v. 17).

Jesus then proceeded to make Peter the *rock* on which he would build the Church. Beneath the backdrop of a temple built on a rock and devoted to the idolatrous worship of an emperor, Peter, whose name means "rock," is chosen to lead God's Church. "You are Peter, and upon this rock I will build my Church" (v. 18). Jesus went further and promised to give Peter the "keys to the Kingdom of Heaven," that is, authority to shepherd the Church. Jesus also promised that the gates of hell will not prevail against the Church. These words are a reminder that, while disorder and chaos might threaten the Church, they will never prevail over the Church because of Christ's protection. This scene ends with Christ's prediction of his suffering and death.

John 21:15-17 recounts a Resurrection scene. The risen Jesus spoke to a repentant Peter, who is filled with sorrow because of his triple denial of Christ, "Simon, son of John, do you love me more than these?" Peter replied, "Yes Lord, you know that I love you." Jesus said to him, "Feed my lambs." Jesus repeated the question two more times, and Peter strongly professed his love. Each time Jesus commissioned him to feed his lambs and sheep, that is, the members of the Church.

This scene complements the one in Matthew. There, Jesus called Peter to be the rock of the Church. Here, Christ summoned Peter to be a shepherd who loves Jesus and the Church's people.

Peter was one of the Twelve Apostles, all chosen by Jesus to be the foundation of his Church. At the head of the Twelve, Jesus placed Peter. From Jesus, the Twelve received the mandate to preach the Gospel to all nations. Peter ultimately made his way to Rome, where he died as a martyr. In establishing the Twelve Apostles with Peter at their head, Jesus gave the Church the basic structure of its leadership.

<hr />

THE CHURCH AS MYSTERY

The Church is essentially both human and divine, visible but endowed with invisible realities, zealous in action and dedicated to contemplation.

—CCC, no. 771, citing Second Vatican Council,
Constitution on the Sacred Liturgy
(*Sacrosanctum Concilium*; SC), no. 2

The Church is a holy mystery because of her origin in the Holy Trinity and her mission to be the Sacrament of Salvation (the sign and instrument of God's plan to unite all under Christ).

The Holy Trinity brought the Church into being. The Father called the Church into existence. The Son established the Church. The Holy Spirit filled the Church with power and wisdom at Pentecost. The Holy

Trinity abides with the Church always, creatively and providentially. The Church, empowered by the Holy Spirit, brings Christ's salvation to the world. She is the instrument of God's universal call to holiness. At the same time, the Church is made up of a sinful people. Yet despite the personal sinfulness of her members, the Church remains holy by the presence of Jesus and the Holy Spirit who permeates her.

MEANINGS OF THE WORD *CHURCH*

The word *Church* is a translation of biblical words: the Hebrew word *qahal*, and the Greek word *ekklesia*, both of which mean "gathering of people or community" for worship. It was first applied to the people of Israel whom God called into existence. The Church is also called into existence by God. Responding to the proclamation of the Gospel begun by the Apostles, men and women embrace God's gift of faith and through Baptism become members of the community of the Church.

The word *Church* means the people gathered by God into one community, guided today by the bishops, who are the successors of the Apostles and whose head is the Bishop of Rome, the Pope. The term *Church* also applies to specific geographical communities called dioceses. It also applies to the buildings where the faithful gather for the Sacraments, especially the Eucharist, and to families, who are called domestic churches.

PLANNED BY THE FATHER

How did the Church come to be?

From the beginning, the Church was part of God's plan for sharing his divine life with all people. There was a gradual formation of God's family through a series of events described in the Old Testament: God's covenant with Abraham as the father of a great people, the liberation of ancient Israel from slavery in Egypt and their establishment in the Promised Land, and their solidification as a nation through the kingship of David.

FOUNDED BY JESUS CHRIST

Jesus brought about the fulfillment of the Father's plan for the Church first by his preaching and witnessing the Good News of the Kingdom, with its gifts of salvation from sin and participation in divine life. The seed and beginning of the Kingdom was the little flock whom Jesus shepherded as his family. Jesus established the beginnings of a visible structure of the Church that will remain until the Kingdom is fully achieved, through his choice of the Twelve Apostles, with Peter as the head.

By his Cross, Jesus gave birth to the Church:

> The Church is born primarily of Christ's total self-giving for our salvation, anticipated in the institution of the Eucharist and fulfilled on the cross. "The origin and growth of the Church are symbolized by the blood and water which flowed from the open side of the crucified Jesus." "For it was from the side of Christ as he slept the sleep of death upon the cross that there came forth the 'wondrous sacrament of the whole Church.'" As Eve was formed from the sleeping Adam's side, so the Church was born from the pierced heart of Christ hanging dead on the cross. (CCC, no. 766, citing LG, no. 3, and SC, no. 5)

REVEALED BY THE SPIRIT

The Holy Spirit revealed the Church at Pentecost, coming upon the Apostles and the disciples with a transforming fire, forming them into a visible community, and empowering them to proclaim the Gospel of Jesus Christ.

The early Church Fathers taught that there was an inseparable link between the Holy Spirit and the Church: "Where the Church is, there also is God's Spirit; where God's Spirit is, there is the Church" (St. Irenaeus, *Against Heresies*, III, 24.1). So forceful is the presence of the Spirit in the life of the early Church that the New Testament narrative of the Church's early growth, the Acts of the Apostles, is often called the "Gospel of the Holy Spirit."

The Acts of the Apostles and early Church history show how the Holy Spirit bestowed gifts on the community of believers for their roles and responsibilities in serving the Church. This was a dynamic process that illustrated the abiding presence and action of the Spirit along with the increased understanding of the Faith. From Pentecost onward, the Church began her earthly pilgrimage that will be fulfilled one day in glory. The Holy Spirit maintains the stability, durability, and continuity of the Church both in favorable and unfavorable historical circumstances.

THE CHURCH MANIFESTS THE HOLY TRINITY

The Church is the continuing manifestation of the Father, Son, and Holy Spirit. The Church exists by the will of God the Father and his plan to gather all people under the Lordship of his Son. As Head of the Church, Jesus Christ continues to fill her with his life and saving grace, pouring into her the Holy Spirit with his gifts of unity, peace, and love.

CHURCH AS THE SACRAMENT OF SALVATION

To say that the Church is a sacrament is to say that she is a mystery, being both visible and spiritual.

The visible Church is a public institution, with a hierarchical government, laws, and customs. She is visible in her worldwide membership of millions of believers who gather in Christian homes, parishes, dioceses, monasteries, convents, and shrines to praise God and then to go forth to witness Christ and serve the world in love, justice, and mercy.

This Church is also a spiritual reality, with interior bonds of faith and love forged by the Holy Spirit. The Church as both visible and spiritual is traditionally described as the Mystical Body of Christ. It is a living body, sustained by the hidden work of the Holy Spirit.

The complexity that characterizes the Church as a visible institution and, at the same time, a spiritual reality causes some to miss the basic unity of the Church. The Holy Spirit is the source of unity of all the aspects of the Church. The Holy Spirit integrates the visible aspects of the Church with the invisible aspects in such a way that the Church is always a unity of both aspects.

> In the unity of this Body [of which Christ is the head], there is a diversity of members and functions. All members are linked to one another, especially to those who are suffering, to the poor and persecuted. (CCC, no. 806)

The Church is the sacrament of salvation. "The Church is like a sacrament—a sign and instrument, that is, of communion with God and of unity among all men" (CCC, no. 775). The Church is a sacrament of the union of all people with God, and a sacrament of the unity of all peoples—for the Church gathers people "from every nation, race, people, and tongue" (Rev 7:9).

The Spirit communicates to us the salvation gained for us by Jesus Christ through the Church and her seven Sacraments. "The Church 'is the visible plan of God's love for humanity,' because God desires 'that the whole human race may become one People of God, form one Body of Christ, and be built up into one temple of the Holy Spirit'" (CCC, no. 776, citing Pope Paul VI [June, 22, 1973]).

THE CHURCH IS THE PEOPLE OF GOD

> [God] has . . . willed to make men holy and save them, not as individuals without any bond between them, but rather to make them into a people who might acknowledge him and serve him in holiness.
>
> —CCC, no. 781

Chapter two of the *Dogmatic Constitution on the Church* (*Lumen Gentium*) gives prominence to a scriptural and patristic image of the Church as the People of God. The Father began this formation process with the Israelites and brought it to fulfillment in the Church. A person is initiated into God's people not by physical birth, but by a spiritual birth through faith in Christ and Baptism. God's people include the popes, patriarchs, bishops, priests, deacons, the laity, religious men and women—each group with its special mission and responsibility.

Jesus Christ is the head of this people whose law is love of God and neighbor. Its mission is to be the salt of the earth and the light of the world and a seed of the possibility of unity, hope, salvation, and holiness for humanity. Its destiny is the Kingdom of God, already partially experienced on earth and fully known in heaven. All God's people, through their Baptism, participate in Christ's offices of priest, prophet, and king.

A PRIESTLY PEOPLE

All of the baptized share in Christ's priesthood. This participation is called the "common priesthood of all the faithful." Their works, prayers, activities of family and married life, apostolic endeavors, relaxation, and even the sufferings and setbacks of life can become spiritual offerings pleasing to God when united to the sacrifice of Christ. Such acts of God's people become forms of divine worship that by his design sanctify the world.

Based on the common priesthood of all the faithful and ordered to its service is the ordained, ministerial priesthood. This priesthood is conferred by the Sacrament of Holy Orders.

> The ministerial priesthood differs in essence from the common priesthood of the faithful because it confers a sacred power for the service of the faithful. (CCC, no. 1592)

In a later chapter, we will reflect on the unique role of those in Holy Orders and on the special service they provide the whole Body of Christ.

A PROPHETIC PEOPLE

God's people also share in Christ's role as prophet. This means both teaching and witnessing God's Word in the world. A real prophet, by teaching and good example, leads others to faith. St. Francis of Assisi once said, "Preach always. Sometimes use words." Priests, laity, and religious can all collaborate in the Church's missionary and evangelization activity, catechetical ministry, the teaching of theology, and the use of all forms of contemporary media. While witness is essential, we should be always aware of opportunities to share our faith verbally with each other and with all those who do not yet profess it. This prophetic role is exercised with the guidance of the bishops, who have a special teaching responsibility entrusted to them by Christ.

A ROYAL PEOPLE

God's people share in Christ's kingly mission, which is to lead others through loving service to them. Jesus came not "to be served but to serve and to give his life as a ransom for many" (Mt 20:28). We are called, in imitation of the Lord Jesus, to be people who offer ourselves willingly in service to others. Actions of such service can point to Christ's Kingdom of love, justice, mercy, and salvation to all persons, cultures, governments, and other structures of society. We are also called to a life of service to the Church herself. Servant leadership is a responsibility of all God's people within their differing roles and responsibilities. Bishops have a particular responsibility of leadership and governance in the Church.

> "Lay members of the Christian faithful can cooperate in the exercise of this power [of governance]." . . . The Church provides for their presence at particular councils, diocesan synods, pastoral councils; the exercise of the pastoral care of a parish, collaboration in finance committees, and participation in ecclesiastical tribunals, etc. (CCC, no. 911, citing *Code of Canon Law*, can. 129 §2)

THE CHURCH AS COMMUNION

The image of the Church as Communion has the value of connecting truths about the Church in a fruitful and harmonious manner. We begin with a definition of the Church as Communion.

The Church as Communion is our loving fellowship and union with Jesus and other baptized Christians in the Church, the Body of Christ, which has its source and summit in the celebration of the Eucharist by which we are joined in divine love to the communion of the Father, Son and Holy Spirit. (cf. CCC, Glossary)

The Church, the Body of Christ, is the assembly of people gathered into her by Baptism and their participation in the Sacraments, especially the Eucharist, which open their minds and hearts to the Trinity, a loving communion of divine persons. In this communion of the Church, the members are called to love God, others, and self, and so to be a communal witness of the love by which Christ saved the world. By divine love, we are joined to the communion of the Father, Son, and Holy Spirit.

At the center of the Gospel message is God's desire to share the communion of Trinitarian life with us. Jesus came to invite everyone to participate in the loving communion that Father, Son, and Spirit have with each other. All creation is meant to show us the Trinity's plan of love for us. Everything Jesus did pointed to this goal.

In the Church, the Holy Spirit works in us to achieve the same purpose. When we say God is love, we are doing more than applying an abstract quality to the Lord. We testify in faith that God as Trinity wants to relate to us and to be engaged in our world.

This truth in no way diminishes the mystery of God as totally other, unique, awesome, majestic, and pure holiness. But love within the Trinity makes possible a divine closeness to us. Love preserves the mystery and yet overcomes what might have been a gulf between us and God. Unity and communion with God in the Church also calls us to become a source of unity for all people.

UPON THIS ROCK—A COMMUNITY OF LOVE

In our culture, some have a resistance to institutions. Our history reminds us of the freedom of the frontier where the homestead was central and the fields endless—even though such traditions as wagon trains, communal barn-raising, and volunteer fire departments show us that even frontier freedom needed structure of some sort. But the sense of endless

FROM THE CATECHISM

1. How did the Second Vatican Council relate Christ as the light of humanity to the Church?

"Christ is the light of humanity. . . . By proclaiming his Gospel to every creature, it may bring to all . . . that light of Christ which shines out visibly from the Church." . . . By choosing this starting point the Council demonstrated that the article of faith about the Church depends entirely upon the articles concerning Jesus Christ. (CCC, no. 748, citing LG, no. 1)

2. What do we learn from the scriptural images of the Church, such as Body of Christ, sheepfold, cultivated field, and temple?

The images taken from the Old Testament are variations of a profound theme: the People of God. In the New Testament, all these images find a new center because Christ has become the head of his people, which henceforth is his Body. Around this center are grouped images taken "from the life of the shepherd or from cultivation of the land, from the art of building or from family life and marriage." (CCC, no. 753, citing LG, no. 6)

3. How is the Church the Temple of the Holy Spirit?

"What the soul is to the human body, the Holy Spirit is to the Body of Christ, which is the Church" (St. Augustine, Sermon 267, 4). . . . The Holy Spirit is "the principle of every vital and truly saving action in each part of the Body" (Pope Pius XII, *The Mystical Body* [*Mystici Corporis*]: DS 3808). (CCC, nos. 797-798)

freedom is sometimes in tension with belonging to the Church as a community of believers.

When it comes to the Church, some claim that its institutional needs take a toll on the values of community and relationships. Institutions require time, money, and effort for their maintenance. Since the Second Vatican Council highlighted the Church as the People of God, does this not mean that our energies should be focused on people, not buildings, committees, laws, and rules? Should we not recapture the simplicity of Christ's relationship with his disciples and the intimacy of the early Church as described in the Acts of the Apostles?

In response, we would say this is not an "either/or" situation. There is no doubt that the Church is called to be a community of love in the Father, the Son, and the Holy Spirit. The risen Jesus himself presented a model of Church leadership based in love when he solicited three affirmations of love from Peter (cf. Jn 21:15-17). At the same time, though, the Church has many structures that are needed to build up the bond of love.

Jesus himself established one of those structures of the Church when he named Peter as the rock of the Church, the head of the Apostles (Mt 16:18). While St. Paul taught us that love is the greatest gift of the Holy Spirit (1 Cor 13:1-13), he also listed administration as a gift of the Spirit (1 Cor 12:28).

The Church needs an institutional framework for its stability, continuity, and mission for serving the cause of the Gospel and opening people to God's call to holiness. Problems with the institution are not arguments for its removal, but for its renewal. Just as the Son of God took on our human flesh and just as a soul needs a body, so a community needs to be organized to serve and be served. The Church is a community that is served by a multiplicity of structures.

■ FOR DISCUSSION ■

1. How is the Church viewed as a mystery? What would you see as the link between the Church as mystery and your faith?
2. Why is the image of the Church as People of God important? What is meant by the description of the Church as a Sacrament of Salvation?
3. How does the understanding of the Church as Body of Christ shape your faith? Why is the link between the Holy Spirit and the Church so vital?

▬▬▬ DOCTRINAL STATEMENTS ▬▬▬

- The word *Church* is based on both the Greek word *ekklesia* and the Hebrew word *qahal*, which mean the gathering of the community. It was first applied to the people of Israel, whom God called into existence. The Church was planned and formed by God, who called together into one those who accepted the Gospel.

- The Father prepared for the Church through a series of covenant events described in the Old Testament. Jesus fulfilled the divine plan for the Church through his saving death and Resurrection. The Holy Spirit manifested the Church as a mystery of salvation.

- The Church is a visible society and a spiritual community; she is a hierarchical institution and the Body of Christ; she is an earthly Church and one filled with heavenly treasures. Hence the Church is a complex reality that has human and divine elements.

The reality of the mystery of the Church is expressed in a variety of ways as follows:

- The Church is the sacrament of salvation, the sign and instrument of our communion with God (cf. CCC, nos. 774-776).

- The Church is the People of God. "You are a chosen race, a royal priesthood, a holy nation. . . . Once you were 'no people,' / but now you are God's people" (1 Pt 2:9-10). We become members of God's People through faith and Baptism (cf. CCC, nos. 781-786).

- The Church is the Body of Christ. Christ is the head, and we are the members. In the unity of this Body, there is a diversity of members and roles, yet everyone is linked together by Christ's love and grace, especially the poor, the suffering, and the persecuted (cf. CCC, nos. 787-795).

- The Church is the Bride of Christ. "Christ loved the Church and handed himself over [to death] for her that he might sanctify her" (Eph 5:25-26; cf. CCC, no. 796).

- The Church is the Temple of the Holy Spirit. "We are the temple of the living God" (2 Cor 6:16; cf. 1 Cor 3:16-17, Eph 2:21; cf. CCC, nos. 797-801).

- The Church is a communion. The starting point of this communion is our union with Jesus Christ. This gives us a share in the communion of the Persons of the Trinity and also leads to a communion among men and women (cf. CCC, nos. 813, 948, 959).
- These truths about unity and communion in the Church call us to become a source of unity for all peoples.

MEDITATION

Christians do not make a house of God until they are one in charity. The timber and stone must fit together in an orderly plan, must be joined in perfect harmony, must give each other the support as if it were of love, or no one would enter the building. When you see the stones and beams of a building holding together securely, you enter the building with an easy mind. . . .

The work we see complete in this building is physical; it should find its spiritual counterpart in your hearts.

—St. Augustine, Sermon 336, 1, 6

PRAYER

Father, you called your people to be your Church.
As we gather together in your name, may we love,
honor and follow you to eternal life in the kingdom
    you promise.

—Prayer for the Dedication of a Church,
Liturgy of the Hours, vol. III, 1596

You are a chosen race, a royal priesthood,
a holy nation, God's own people.

—1 Pt 2:9

11 THE FOUR MARKS OF THE CHURCH

THE CHURCH IS ONE, HOLY, CATHOLIC, AND APOSTOLIC
—CCC, NOS. 811-962

I WANTED TO BE A MISSIONARY

 In 1749, Fr. Junipero Serra petitioned his Franciscan provincial for permission to become a missionary after having served as theology teacher for ten years on the island of Majorca, off the coast of Spain. He wrote, "All my life I have wanted to be a missionary. I have wanted to carry the Gospel teachings to those who have never heard of God and the kingdom he has prepared for them."

He received permission and sailed for Mexico, where he worked among the native populations for twenty years. When the Spanish government decided to complete the conquest of California, Fr. Serra and fifteen other Franciscan missionaries accompanied the army. In the ensuing years, Fr. Serra founded nine of the twenty-one California missions. Many of these later became cities such as San Diego, San Gabriel, San Luis Obispo, San Francisco, San Juan Capistrano, Santa Clara, San Buenaventura, and San Carlos (Monterey-Carmel).

During the fifteen years of his California apostolate, he had to confront the military and civil authorities concerning the mistreatment of the Native Americans. He presented a memorandum of thirty-two points to the Viceroy for the improvement of the situation, some of which were implemented and some not. Despite having a chronically ulcerated leg, Fr. Serra visited his numerous missions many times. He baptized and confirmed thousands of Native Americans. While he concentrated on their spiritual needs, he did not ignore their material ones. The new converts were taught methods of farming, raising cattle, and arts and crafts. In this way, they were helped to move from their nomadic past to a stable domestic way of life. His extensive factual reports of his missionary actions reveal a man who loved his people.

In 1987, when Pope John Paul II planned to beatify Fr. Serra, a protest was raised by some Native Americans, who argued that the Spanish soldiers and missionaries tried to eradicate the language, culture, and identity of their people in California. The Pope met with Native American leaders in Phoenix. He defended the legacy of the Franciscan missionaries.

He admitted that there had been some excesses. He also noted that the weight of the evidence indicated that Fr. Serra had never been guilty of mistreating the Native Americans. Actually, he had defended them from harm. The Pope then went to the San Carlos mission (Monterey-Carmel) and prayed at Fr. Serra's grave. He beatified Fr. Serra on September 25, 1988, in St. Peter's Square. He praised Fr. Serra as "an exemplary model of the selfless evangelizer, a shining example of Christian virtue and the missionary spirit."

A statue of Blessed Junipero Serra is in the National Statuary Hall in the U.S. Capitol building in Washington, D.C. A bronze statue of Serra is mounted in Golden Gate Park in San Francisco. His name has been adopted by the lay organization known as the Serra Club, which does much to foster vocations to the priesthood and religious life in the United States and other countries. Fr. Serra died in 1784.

Blessed Junipero Serra, now on his final step to sainthood, witnessed to the holiness of the Church. As an extraordinary missionary, Serra is an exceptional example of the Church's apostolic calling to preach and witness the Gospel to all peoples. He thus exhibited in an extraordinary way two of the four marks that characterize the Church.

THE FOUR MARKS OF THE CHURCH

It is Christ who, through the Holy Spirit, makes his Church one, holy, catholic and apostolic, and it is he who calls her to realize each of these qualities.

—CCC, no. 811

In the earliest professions of faith, the Catholic Church identified herself as "one, holy, catholic, and apostolic." We find these words in the Nicene Creed professed at Sunday Mass. Traditionally, they refer to what are known as the four marks of the Church, traits that identify the Church before the world.

Inseparably linked with one another, these four marks indicate the essential features of the Church and her mission on earth. Each mark is so joined with the others that they form one coherent and interrelated idea of what Christ's Church must be. They strengthen the faith of the believer and at the same time can attract non-Catholics to investigate the Church more fully. Because of the sinfulness of the Church's members, these marks are not always lived out fully, so we need to view them as both a reality and yet a challenge.

THE CHURCH IS ONE

The mark of oneness reflects the unity of the Trinity. The Holy Spirit, the bond of love between the Father and the Son, unites all the members of the Church as the one People of God. The Church professes one Lord, one faith, and one Baptism and forms one body (cf. CCC, no. 866) under the leadership of the Holy Father, successor to Peter the Apostle. Within the Church there is a diversity of races, nations, cultures, languages, and traditions, which are held together in one communion by the gift of love from the Holy Spirit. The unity that Christ bestowed on his Church is something she can never lose (cf. Second Vatican Council, *Decree on Ecumenism* [*Unitatis Redintegratio*; UR], no. 4; CCC, nos. 813, 815).

Tragically, members of the Church have offended against her unity, and throughout the centuries, there have developed divisions among Christians. Already in the fifth century, doctrinal disagreements led to the separation of some Christians in the eastern region of the Roman Empire from the main body of the Church. More damaging was the rupture between Rome and Constantinople in AD 1054. And in the sixteenth century Western Europe experienced the divisions that followed the Protestant Reformation.

The Catholic Church has always been committed to the restoration of unity among all Christians. This commitment was intensified by the

Second Vatican Council and led the Church to participate in what is called the ecumenical movement. The word *ecumenical* means "world-wide" and, in a Catholic understanding, describes efforts "for the reconciliation of all Christians in the unity of the one and only Church of Christ" (UR, no. 24; CCC, no. 822). This is to be a visible communion. "Full unity will come about when all share in the means of salvation entrusted by Christ to his Church" (Pope John Paul II, *On Commitment to Ecumenism* [*Ut Unum Sint*; UUS], no. 86). "Communion of the particular Churches with the Church of Rome, and of their Bishops with the Bishop of Rome, is—in God's plan—an essential requisite of full and visible communion" (UUS, no. 97). Ecumenism includes efforts to pray together, joint study of the Scripture and of one another's traditions, common action for social justice, and dialogue in which the leaders and theologians of the different churches and communities discuss in depth their doctrinal and theological positions for greater mutual understanding, and "to work for unity in truth" (UUS, nos. 18, 29). In dialogue the obligation to respect the truth is absolute. "The unity willed by God can be attained only by the adherence of all to the content of revealed faith in its entirety" (UUS, no. 18). On the worldwide level, these dialogues are sponsored on the Catholic side by the Pontifical Council for the Promotion of Christian Unity, a Vatican office directly accountable to the Pope.

The Catholic Church retains the structures of episcopal leadership and sacramental life that are the gift of Christ to his Church (cf. CCC, nos. 765, 766) and that date back to apostolic times. At the same time, the Catholic Church recognizes that the Holy Spirit uses other churches and ecclesial communities "as means of salvation, whose power derives from the fullness of grace and truth that Christ has entrusted to the Catholic Church" (CCC, no. 819; LG, no. 8). Depending on what and how much of the elements of sanctification and truth (UR, no. 3) these communities have retained, they have a certain though imperfect communion with the Catholic Church. There are also real differences. In some cases "there are very weighty differences not only of a historical, sociological, psychological and cultural character, but especially in the interpretation of revealed truth" (UR, no. 19). (The word *church* applies to those bodies of Christians who have a valid episcopal leadership or hierarchy, while the phrase *ecclesial communities* refers to those bodies of Christians that do not have an apostolic hierarchy.)

THE CHURCH IS HOLY

The Church has her origin in the Holy Trinity, and that is the source of her holiness. In his plan for the salvation of humanity, God the Father willed the existence of the Church. Jesus Christ, the Son of God, established a community of disciples and died on the Cross for the forgiveness of sins. The Holy Spirit, sent by the Father and the Son, works within the Church to keep her members faithful to the Gospel. The Church is holy in her Founder, in her saints, and in her means of salvation.

Through Baptism and Confirmation, Catholics have become a people consecrated by the Holy Spirit to the praise of God through Jesus Christ. Christians grow in holiness by working to live in conformity to the Gospel of Jesus and thus to become more like him, especially in the totality of his love for others shown by his sacrifice of himself on the Cross. But Christians also remain subject to temptation and sin, thus needing God's mercy and forgiveness. In teaching his disciples how to pray, Jesus included the following petition to the Father: "Forgive us our trespasses as we forgive those who trespass against us."

In the following parts of this catechism, the Sacraments, the Ten Commandments, the virtue of charity, and prayer will be presented as sources of holiness for the Church.

THE CHURCH IS CATHOLIC

The word *catholic* means "universal." The Catholic Church has lived and continues to live in a diversity of cultures and languages because she is led by the Spirit of Christ to bring the Gospel to all peoples. She has known how to accept what is true and good in all cultures and, at the same time, to infuse the truth and goodness of her tradition and life into them. The process of inculturation includes this dynamic.

The Church is also catholic because of her universal extension and her presence in local communities that are known as dioceses, or eparchies in the case of Eastern Churches, and are called "particular Churches."

> The Church of Christ is really present in all legitimately organized local groups of the faithful, which, in so far as they are united to their pastors, are also quite appropriately called Churches in the New Testament. . . . In them the faithful are gathered together through the preaching of the Gospel of Christ, and the mystery of the Lord's Supper is celebrated. . . . In these communities, though they may often be small and poor, or existing in the diaspora, Christ is present, through whose power and influence the One, Holy, Catholic, and Apostolic Church is constituted. (CCC, no. 832)

These local communities are linked together through their communion with the Church of Rome and her bishop, the Pope.

In the Catholic Church, the word *Church* is also used to refer to those communities which have their own "ecclesiastical disciplines, liturgical rites, and theological and spiritual heritages" (cf. CCC, no. 835). Thus we speak of the Latin Church and the Eastern Churches. Several of these Eastern Churches have formal structures in the United States. In this country, there are eparchies or dioceses for Armenian Catholics, Melkite-Greek Catholics, Syrian Catholics, Maronite Catholics, Byzantine Ruthenian Catholics, Ukrainian Catholics, Romanian Byzantine Catholics, Chaldean Catholics, and Syro-Malabar Catholics.

The Church is catholic also because of her relationship to all people. First of all, "the Church knows that she is joined in many ways to the baptized who are honored by the name of Christian, but do not profess the Catholic faith in its entirety or have not preserved unity or communion under the successor of Peter" (CCC, no. 838, citing LG, no. 15). Thus there exists an imperfect communion between the Catholic Church and other Christian churches and faith communions.

The Catholic Church also acknowledges her special relationship to the Jewish people. The Second Vatican Council declared that "this people remains most dear to God, for God does not repent of the gifts he makes nor of the calls he issues" (LG, no. 16). When God called

Abraham out of Ur, he promised to make of him a "great nation." This began the history of God's revealing his divine plan of salvation to a chosen people with whom he made enduring covenants. Thus the covenant that God made with the Jewish people through Moses remains eternally valid for them. At the same time, "remembering, then, her common heritage with the Jews and moved not by any political consideration, but solely by the religious motivation of Christian charity, she [the Church] deplores all hatreds, persecutions, displays of antisemitism leveled at any time or from any source against the Jews" (Second Vatican Council, *Declaration on the Relation of the Church to Non-Christian Religions* [*Nostra Aetate*; NA], no. 4).

The Church also recognizes that she has a unique relationship to Muslims. "The plan of salvation also includes those who acknowledge the Creator, in the first place amongst whom are the Muslims; these profess to hold the faith of Abraham, and together with us they adore the one, merciful God, mankind's judge on the last day" (CCC, no. 841, citing LG, no. 16).

The Church engages in dialogue not only with Muslims but also with Hindus and Buddhists. "She has a high regard for the manner of life and conduct, the precepts and doctrines which, although differing in many ways from her own teaching, nevertheless often reflect a ray of that truth which enlightens all men" (NA, no. 2). These dialogues are conducted on the local level and also on the international level through the Pontifical Council for Interreligious Dialogue.

Dialogue is a form of evangelization. It is a way of making Christ and his Gospel known to others, while at the same time respecting their freedom of conscience and adherence to their own religious tradition. The Church has received from Christ the mandate to make him known to all people. She does this in many ways. Dialogue is one way, but another way is the missionary activity of the Church. Through the work of missionaries (priests, consecrated men and women, and lay people) the Church makes Christ known as they teach the Gospel to others by word and deed, inviting them to respond to this proclamation by the commitment of faith.

"OUTSIDE THE CHURCH THERE IS NO SALVATION"

From the *Catechism*, nos. 846-847:

> How are we to understand this affirmation, often repeated by the Church Fathers? Re-formulated positively, it means that all salvation comes from Christ the Head through the Church which is his Body: "Basing itself on Scripture and Tradition, the Council teaches that the Church, a pilgrim now on earth, is necessary for salvation: the one Christ is the mediator and the way of salvation; he is present to us in his body which is the Church. He himself explicitly asserted the necessity of faith and Baptism, and thereby affirmed at the same time the necessity of the Church which men enter through Baptism as through a door. Hence they could not be saved who, knowing that the Catholic Church was founded as necessary by God through Christ, would refuse either to enter it or to remain in it" (LG, no. 14; cf. Mk 16:16; Jn 3:5).

> This affirmation is not aimed at those who, through no fault of their own, do not know Christ and his Church: "Those who, through no fault of their own, do not know the Gospel of Christ or his Church, but who nevertheless seek God with a sincere heart, and, moved by grace, try in their actions to do his will as they know it through the dictates of their conscience—those too may achieve eternal salvation" (LG, no. 16; cf. DS 3866-3872).

THE CHURCH IS APOSTOLIC

The Church is built upon the foundation of the Apostles, who were chosen by Christ himself, and at whose head he placed Peter. The entire community of Christians received the Apostles' proclamation of the Gospel, and so the Church in her entirety is called "apostolic." Under the guidance of the Holy Spirit, the Church as a whole remains and will always remain faithful to the teaching of the Apostles. This is called the indefectibility of the Church, because she will never fall away from the Gospel.

To further ensure the Church's fidelity to the Gospel, Christ has willed that the Apostles be succeeded by the bishops. The Apostles acted together as a body, with Peter at their head, in their leadership of the Church. Thus they are called by the Church a "college." The college of bishops has succeeded the college of the Apostles, and it is the Bishop of Rome, the Pope, who has succeeded the role of Peter as head of the college. Thus they are called by the Church a "college," and their essential unity as one body is understood as the principle of collegiality.

Each bishop works in his particular diocese in a priestly shepherding and teaching role. He possesses the fullness of the priesthood and so is the principal celebrant of the Sacraments, especially the Eucharist, by which the Church grows in holiness and union with Christ. He is also the chief shepherd of the diocese and so is responsible for compassionate and loving governance of the people entrusted to him. And he is the chief teacher of his diocese, responsible for authentic proclamation of the Gospel.

The teaching office of the college of bishops is called the "Magisterium." When all the bishops throughout the world, together with the Pope, in the fulfillment of their teaching office, proclaim a doctrine that has been divinely revealed, it must be accepted with the obedience of faith by the whole People of God. "The Church, through its magisterium, has been entrusted with the task of authoritatively interpreting what is contained in revelation, so that 'all that is proposed for belief, as being divinely revealed, is drawn from the one deposit of faith' (DV, no. 10). In some cases, these doctrines have been explicitly defined; in others, they are universally considered to be an essential and irreformable element of the one Catholic faith" (USCCB, *The Teaching Ministry of the Diocesan Bishop* [1992]).

However, at certain times, the bishops gather in an Ecumenical Council with the Pope, and they teach and proclaim a doctrine that must be accepted with faith because it is divinely revealed. The bishops of the world defined and proclaimed a divinely revealed doctrine at the First Vatican Council (1869-1870). This was when they taught that under certain conditions the Pope himself can proclaim a doctrine that is divinely revealed and must be believed by all. This is known as the dogma of papal infallibility.

The entire Church as a body is infallible because the Holy Spirit ensures that she will not err in matters of faith and morals. But this infallibility is exercised in a special way by the Pope and the bishops when together they teach what has been divinely revealed either in the ordinary way of their day-to-day teaching or the extraordinary way of an Ecumenical Council or the Pope himself.

The Pope and bishops also together teach truths that flow from Divine Revelation or that are closely related to it. Sometimes they teach these truths as being definitive, which means they must be firmly accepted and held. Sometimes they teach in a less than definitive way, which requires a religious submission of will and mind.

LAITY

By Baptism, every member of the Church participates in Christ's role as priest, prophet, and king (which is understood in terms of being the shepherd of his people). The laity do this in the context of their lives within families, parish communities, civic communities, and the workplace. The everyday gift of themselves in love and care for others, often done at great personal cost, is a priestly offering that is joined to the sacrifice of Christ in the Eucharist. By words and deeds faithful to the Gospel, they evangelize others, thus fulfilling their prophetic role. By seeking to build the common good of society on the basis of moral principles, they strengthen civic communities and thus fulfill their kingly or shepherding role.

The laity are in the unique position of being able directly to infuse culture and society with the Gospel. But they also contribute to the vitality of the life of the Church through ministry as catechists and many other ministries. Most are volunteers, but some have been called to serve as salaried ministers. Working with their pastors, they enable the Church to witness to Christian faith and love before the world.

In the post-conciliar period, a distinctly new and different group of lay ministers has emerged in the Church in the United States. This group consists of lay women and men performing roles that entail varying degrees of pastoral leadership and administration in parishes, church agencies, and organizations, and at diocesan and national levels. They are doing so in a public, stable, recognized, and authorized manner. Furthermore, when these lay ministers speak of their responsibilities, they emphasize ministering in ways that are distinguished from, yet complementary to, the roles of ordained ministers. Many of them also express a deep sense of vocation that is part of their personal identity and that motivates what they are doing. Many have sought academic credentials and diocesan certification in order to prepare for their ministry. (USCCB Subcommittee on Lay Ministry, *Lay Ecclesial Ministry: The State of the Questions* [Washington, DC: USCCB, 1999], 9)

CONSECRATED LIFE

From the beginning of the Church, there have been men and women who have chosen to live in a radical witness to Christ by imitating him as closely as possible in his poverty, chastity, and obedience. In the course of the centuries, this commitment became more and more visible through the establishment of monasteries, religious orders and congregations, and other types of institutes. Men and women professed publicly evangelical "counsels" (vows) of poverty, chastity, and obedience and committed themselves to stability of life within communities.

Blessed Junipero Serra was a Franciscan, the member of an order that goes back to St. Francis of Assisi (1181-1226). That is one form of consecrated life among the many that have developed in the course of the Church's history. They enrich the Church not only by the radicalness of their embrace of the evangelical counsels, but also by the many apostolates (e.g., education and health care) by which they follow Christ in his compassion and care for others.

MAKE DISCIPLES

This chapter has uncovered the richness of the Catholic Church, as she comes from her source in God himself. Catholics today are encouraged to share this life of the Church with others, thus enabling them to know

FROM THE CATECHISM

1. Are non-Catholic Christians guilty of separation from the Church?

One cannot charge with the sin of the separation those who at present are born into these communities [that resulted from such separation] and in them are brought up in the faith of Christ, and the Catholic Church accepts them with respect and affection as brothers. . . . All who have been justified by faith in Baptism are incorporated into Christ; they therefore have a right to be called Christians, and with good reason are accepted as brothers in the Lord by the children of the Catholic Church. (CCC, no. 818, citing UR, no. 3)

2. What does *particular Church* mean for Latin Catholics?

The phrase "particular church," which is first of all the diocese . . . refers to a community of the Christian faithful in communion of faith and sacraments with their bishop ordained in apostolic succession. These particular Churches "are constituted after the model of the universal Church; it is in these and formed out of them that the one and unique Catholic Church exists." (CCC, no. 833, citing LG, no. 23)

3. What is the principal vocation of the laity in the Church?

By reason of their special vocation it belongs to the laity to seek the kingdom of God by engaging in temporal affairs and directing them according to God's will. (CCC, no. 898, citing LG, no. 31)

Christ. This is evangelization. Fr. Alvin Illig (1926-1991), a Paulist priest, devoted his life to making evangelization a priority in the Church of the United States. He helped us recover the great Commission of Jesus Christ to evangelize the world. He composed some practical ways to evangelize in an American context. Here are a few of his thoughts:

1. Consider Christ's great Commission to evangelize (Mt 28:18-20) as a spiritual vocation contained in our baptismal commitment.
2. Be positive and hope-filled. As God's messengers and Easter people, we have Good News to share with others.
3. Include all major paths to evangelization: (a) interpersonal dialogue, (b) parish programs, (c) diocesan direction. The interpersonal approach is the most effective. Friends, relatives, and neighbors account for four out of five of those who become Catholics.
4. Begin with the human situation of the person. This might be people's four basic fears: failure, rejection, pain, death. Raise questions about existence and future life. Show how Jesus understands these fears and offers a salvation that is the best response.
5. Build on faith experiences. Empathize with people's love of beauty, music, and art. Note this in the popular religion of ethnics and immigrants—and the faith experiences in Cursillo, Marriage Encounter, charismatic renewal.
6. Evangelize yourself through daily spiritual renewal in union with Christ. Convinced people convince others. (*Catholic Evangelization* [June 1991]: 39-41)

FOR DISCUSSION

1. How do the Church's four marks strengthen your Catholic identity? How can we lessen mistrust and the misunderstandings that exist among the various Christian denominations in our community? What can we do to eliminate anti-Semitism?
2. How is the hierarchy—pope, bishops, priests, and deacons—valuable for your growth in faith? What sources of spiritual strength do you receive from the Church's structures: parish, diocese, universal Church?
3. Identify practical ways to evangelize others. What are some benefits the Church receives from those who have embraced consecrated life? What are ways that the laity can help spread the faith?

◼◼◼ DOCTRINAL STATEMENTS ◼◼◼

- The four Marks of the Church—that she is one, holy, catholic, and apostolic—are inseparably linked to each other, and all are essential to the Church's mission and pursuit of holiness.
- The Church is one. She professes "one Lord, one faith, one baptism" (Eph 4:5). This unity, sustained by the Holy Spirit, includes a diversity of gifts, talents, cultures, and rites.
- The Church is holy. Jesus, the founder, is holy and makes his holiness available through his death and Resurrection. The Holy Spirit imparts holiness to us, especially through the Sacraments. The Church's holiness shines in the saints, and most especially in the Blessed Virgin Mary.
- The Church is catholic. The word *catholic* means universal. All the means of salvation are found in the Church. The Church has the fullness of the faith, the Sacraments, and apostolic succession. Jesus commissions us to bring the Gospel to all peoples at all times; hence the Church is "by its very nature missionary" (Second Vatican Council, *Decree on the Church's Missionary Activity* [*Ad Gentes Divinitus*; AG], no. 2).
- The Church is apostolic. Jesus willed to build the Church on the foundation of the Apostles. The Church hands on the teaching of the Apostles through all generations. Christ shepherds the Church through Peter and the other Apostles, whose successors are the Pope and the college of bishops.
- Under the guidance of the Holy Spirit, the Apostles chose bishops to succeed them. Helped by the priests and deacons, the bishops teach the faith; celebrate the Sacraments, especially the Eucharist; and guide the Church. Their responsibility includes concern for all the Churches in union with the Pope.
- God calls lay people to witness and share their faith in the midst of the world. By their Baptism they share in Christ's priesthood and are sealed by the Spirit. They are thus called to holiness, to a prophetic witness in the world, and to a kingly resolve to sanctify the world by their words and deeds.

- Those who live a life consecrated to God profess the evangelical counsels of poverty, chastity, and obedience in a stable state of life recognized by the Church. They solemnly promise to surrender themselves to God with an undivided heart, thus liberating themselves to serve God, the Church, and the needs of others.

MEDITATION

God first called the Israelites to holiness: "You shall be holy because I am holy" (Lv 11:45). St. Peter repeated this command of the Lord for the Christian people. "As he who called you is holy, be holy yourselves in every aspect of your conduct, for it is written, 'Be holy because I [am] holy'" (1 Pt 1:15-16). God addresses this call to every member of the Church. He begins the life of holiness in us at our Baptism when we are made partakers of divine life through the gift of sanctifying grace. Holiness is a gift, which the Holy Spirit continually offers us. It should bear fruit in us as we live out our love of God, our neighbor, and ourselves; grow in virtue; and work for justice and mercy for all, especially the poor and defenseless.

PRAYER

Praised be to you, Lord, for your holy Church founded on
    the apostles,
where we are gathered together into your community.
Praise be to you, Lord, for the cleansing power of Baptism
    and Penance
that you have entrusted to your apostles,
through which we are cleansed of our sins.

—Intercessions from Common of the Apostles,
Liturgy of the Hours, vol. III, 1668

The Church is the Bride of Christ.
Come let us worship Christ, the Bridegroom of his Church.

12 MARY: THE CHURCH'S FIRST AND MOST PERFECT MEMBER

MARY, MOTHER OF JESUS, MOTHER OF GOD,
MOTHER OF THE CHURCH
—CCC, NOS. 484-507, 963-972, 2673-2677

ST. JUAN DIEGO SEES MARY

St. Juan Diego, a native of Mexico, was born in 1474 and given the name *Cuauhtlatoatzin*. At his Baptism, which took place around 1525, he received the Christian name Juan Diego. On December 9, 1531, while he was walking to Mass, Our Lady appeared to Juan Diego at Tepeyac Hill, northwest of what is now Mexico City. Her appearance was that of a *mestizo* woman in both features and dress, and she spoke to Juan Diego in his own language. Mary asked "Juanito" to go to the local bishop and request that he build a church on the site of her appearance. The bishop, reluctant to believe Juan Diego, asked for a sign.

Before Juan Diego could return to the hill, he learned that his uncle was dying. Concerned that he would die without the grace of the last Sacraments, Juan Diego hurried to bring a priest to his dying uncle's bedside. However, Mary met him on his route, told him that his uncle had been cured, and instructed Juan Diego to return to the hill to gather flowers as a sign for the bishop. Though it was out of season, he found roses, wrapped them in his cloak, or *tilma*, and returned to the bishop. When Juan Diego unfolded his tilma, the roses fell out, and both he and the bishop were astounded to discover the image of Mary on the cloak looking exactly as Juan Diego had described her.

The tilma that bore Mary's image soon became an object of veneration. In 1533 a small chapel was built on the site of the apparitions to house the cloak with its miraculous image. Today, just below Tepeyac Hill stands the Basilica of Our Lady of Guadalupe, where the tilma can be seen just as it was seen by the bishop in 1531. The church is a triumph of contemporary architecture incorporating many facets of Mexican culture and spirituality, and it creates a warm, prayerful, and welcoming environment. Pilgrims, on foot or on their knees, often bearing roses, slowly process to the enshrined image. They come to ask favors of the merciful Mother or to give thanks for her tender and compassionate response to their prayers. A moving walkway for pedestrians is set behind and beneath the sanctuary so that pilgrims can get a closer look at the image of Our Lady of Guadalupe displayed on the sanctuary wall. Despite the constant river of pilgrims, the shrine is quiet and meditative. The crowds are not a distraction to those who come to worship in the body of the basilica.

Pilgrims still climb to the top of Tepeyac Hill to visit the original chapel and the site of the apparitions. They can also visit the room where Juan Diego spent his last years in prayer and in propagating the account of the apparitions to his countrymen. Through Mary under the title of "Our Lady of Guadalupe" and through the evangelizer St. Juan Diego, many of the native peoples of Mexico were converted to Christianity and were baptized into the Church. As a place of pilgrimage, this shrine ranks among the most popular in the world, attracting over ten million pilgrims each year.

Mary appeared at Tepeyac as a young, pregnant woman of indigenous descent. She revealed herself as Mary, the true Mother of God, a merciful mother who listens to the suffering of her people and consoles them all. As her image was imprinted on Juan Diego's tilma, so Mary becomes imprinted in the deepest recesses of the hearts of all who come to her. Under the title of Our Lady of Guadalupe, Mary is the patroness of the Americas. There are millions of Catholics in the United States whose devotion to Our Lady of Guadalupe and regard for St. Juan Diego help keep our faith and commitment to evangelization alive. The feast of Our Lady of Guadalupe is celebrated on December 12.

Pope John Paul II beatified Juan Diego in 1990. In 2002 the same pope canonized him at the Basilica of Our Lady of Guadalupe. The Church celebrates the feast of St. Juan Diego on December 9.

St. Juan Diego is in the company of numerous others who have been privileged with a vision of the Virgin Mary, such as St. Bernadette of

Lourdes, France, and the three children, Jacinta, Francisco, and Lucia, of Fatima, Portugal. These visionaries loved the Virgin Mary. Their lives of faith and the gift of God's graces have drawn millions closer to Christ. Jacinta and Francisco were beatified by Pope John Paul II on May 13, 2000. Lucia, a nun in Coimbra, Portugal, attended the ceremony.

GOD'S PLAN FOR MARY

The Second Vatican Council reminds us that Mary is a member of the Church who "occupies a place in the Church which is the highest after Christ and also closest to us" (LG, no. 54). She is the first and the greatest of all the disciples of Christ.

When the Gospel of St. Luke (1:26-38) narrates God's call to Mary, the Virgin of Nazareth, to be the Mother of the Savior, his Son, from all eternity, she consents to this call with profound faith and trust. Thus, she "gave to the world the Life that renews all things, and who was enriched by God with gifts appropriate to such a role" (LG, no. 56).

"BLESSED ARE YOU AMONG WOMEN"

An essential part of God's plan for the mother of his Son was that she be conceived free from Original Sin. "Through the centuries the Church became ever more aware that Mary, 'full of grace' through God, was redeemed from the moment of her conception" (CCC, no. 491).

In anticipation that she was to bear the Son of God, Mary was preserved from the time of her conception from Original Sin. We call this the Immaculate Conception. No sin would touch her, so that she would be a fitting and worthy vessel of the Son of God. The Immaculate Conception does not refer to the virginal conception and birth of Christ, but rather to Mary's being conceived without inheriting Original Sin.

In the course of time, the doctrine of the Immaculate Conception became more precisely enunciated, as its truth—long supported by the universal popular devotion of the faithful—was better understood by deepening theological inquiry. In 1854, Pope Pius IX proclaimed this dogma infallibly: that is, in his role as supreme teacher of the Church, he declared that this doctrine is divinely revealed and must be accepted with faith by the entire Church.

It is also the faith of the Church that Mary is to be called the "Mother of God." "The One whom she conceived as man by the power of the Holy Spirit, who truly became her Son according to the flesh, was none other than the Father's eternal Son, the second person of the Holy Trinity. Hence, the Church confesses that Mary is truly the 'Mother of God'" (CCC, no. 495, citing Council of Ephesus: DS 251). In the Eastern Churches Mary is honored by use of the Greek expression *Theotokos* or "Birth-giver of God" (sometimes translated as "God-Bearer").

The Holy Spirit's power made possible the conception of Jesus in Mary's womb. There was no human father. The Gospels clearly present the virginal conception of Jesus as a divine work (cf. Mt 1:18-25; Lk 1:26-38).

Mary was always a virgin, both in conceiving Jesus, giving birth to him, and remaining virgin ever after. God granted her this privilege to emphasize that this was a unique moment in history—the birth of Jesus who is the Son of God and the Son of Mary. The liturgy of the Church speaks of Mary as "ever virgin." In the early Church some denied this, arguing that the Gospels speak of the brothers and sisters of Jesus, and thus maintained that Mary did not remain a virgin after the birth of Jesus. But already in the fourth century, theologians pointed out that the Greek word for brother used in the New Testament can refer also to cousin. A second explanation was that these brothers and sisters were children of Joseph by a previous marriage. However, it is the constant teaching of the Church that Mary remained a virgin even after the birth of Jesus. In her virginity, Mary lived a life dedicated exclusively to her Son and his mission. Her example has been followed by some of Christ's disciples who have lived lives of consecrated virginity and celibacy from apostolic times to the present.

In the mystery of her Assumption, Mary experiences immediately what we all will experience eventually, a bodily resurrection like Christ's own. "The Immaculate Virgin . . . when the course of her earthly life was

FROM THE CATECHISM

1. What is the role of Mary's faith in the plan of salvation?
The Virgin Mary "freely cooperat[ed] in the work of man's salvation through faith and obedience" (LG, no. 56). She uttered her yes "in the name of all human nature" (St. Thomas Aquinas, *Summa Theologiae*, III, 30, 1). By her obedience she became the new Eve, the mother of all the living. (CCC, no. 511)

2. Does Mary intercede on our behalf?
This motherhood of Mary in the order of grace continues uninterruptedly. . . . Taken up into heaven she did not lay aside this saving office, but by her manifold intercession continues to bring us the gifts of eternal salvation. (CCC, no. 969, citing LG, no. 62)

3. How does the Church honor Mary?
The Church rightly honors the Blessed Virgin with special devotion. "From the earliest times the Blessed Virgin is honored under the title Mother of God, whose protection the faithful take refuge together in all their perils and needs. . . . This cult . . . differs essentially from the cult of adoration, which is offered equally to the Incarnate Word and to the Father and the Holy Spirit, and it is most favorable to it" (LG, no. 66). The liturgical feasts dedicated to the Mother of God and Marian prayer, such as the rosary, an "epitome of the whole Gospel," express this devotion to the Virgin Mary. (CCC, no. 971)

finished, was taken up body and soul into heavenly glory, and exalted by the Lord as Queen over all things, so that she might be more fully conformed to her Son, the Lord of lords and conqueror of death" (CCC, no. 966, citing LG, no. 59).

Finally, in Mary we behold what the Church is already like during her pilgrimage of faith—and what the Church will become at the end of the journey. "Mary figured profoundly in the history of salvation and in a certain way unites and mirrors within herself the central truths of the faith" (LG, no. 66).

MARY AS MOTHER OF THE CHURCH

At the beginning of the third session of the Second Vatican Council, Pope Paul VI announced that Mary would be honored under the title "Mother of the Church."

From Christ's conception until his death, Mary was united to her Son in his work of salvation. From the Cross, Jesus entrusted his beloved disciple to Mary, telling him to see her as his own mother (Jn 19:27). When the Apostles and disciples gathered to pray after the Ascension of Jesus, Mary was with them praying for the coming of the Holy Spirit. Mary continues to pray before God for the Church and all humanity.

Like Mary, the Church has a maternal role, giving birth to people in Christ. The Church can never cease to look at Mary, who gave birth to Jesus Christ. The Church contemplates Mary's motherhood in order to fulfill her own calling to be mother of the members of Christ's Mystical Body, the Church. Also like Mary, the Church is virginal. The description of the Church as virginal is used here in the spiritual sense of the undivided heart and of fidelity in its most luminous form. God calls all the members of the Church to fidelity to the union with him begun at Baptism and continued in the other Sacraments.

MARY'S MATERNAL INTERCESSION

In our culture, there can be a discomfort with praying for Mary's intercession on our behalf. This seems to be a mediating role that crosses a line set out in the First Letter to Timothy: "For there is one God. / There is also one mediator between God and the human race, / Christ Jesus, himself human / who gave himself as a ransom for all" (1 Tm 2:5). So Jesus Christ is the one and only mediator. Jesus alone is the Savior.

But this does not deny the possibility that Christ would permit others to share in his mediating role. Here on earth we routinely ask others for prayers. Instinctively, we turn to holy people for their prayers because they seem nearer to God. Why would we stop asking saints for their prayers after they die? If we believe they are in heaven, would not their prayers be even more effective?

From the earliest times, Christians have sought Mary's prayers and help. There has been the basic sense on the part of the Church that Mary continues in heaven to be concerned for the growth of all members of the Church into holiness and an intimate relationship with her Son.

FOR DISCUSSION

1. How would you explain to others the connection between Mary as the Mother of God and all her special gifts: the Immaculate Conception, perpetual virginity, and the Assumption? Why is it important to understand that Mary, too, needed to be redeemed?
2. In what ways can you identify with Mary's "yes" to God at the Annunciation? If Mary's life serves as an example for us of an undivided heart in response to the love of God, how are you able to daily demonstrate your love for God?
3. Mary was the greatest disciple of her Son. How are you growing in your call to discipleship?

DOCTRINAL STATEMENTS

- "What the Catholic faith believes about Mary is based on what it believes about Christ, and what it teaches about Mary illumines in turn its faith in Christ" (CCC, no. 487).
- "When the fullness of time had come, God sent his Son, born of a woman" (Gal 4:4).
- An essential part of God's saving plan for the mother of his Son was that she be conceived free of Original Sin. "Through the centuries the Church became ever more aware that Mary, 'full of grace' through God, was redeemed from the moment of her conception" (CCC, no. 491). This is the doctrine of her Immaculate Conception.

- At the Annunciation, Mary responded to the angel Gabriel with these words: "Behold, I am the handmaid of the Lord. May it be done to me according to your word" (Lk 1:38). This was her consent to the Incarnation. From that moment onwards the Virgin Mary cooperated freely and in the obedience of faith with the plan of salvation. She uttered her yes to God "in the name of all human nature" (St. Thomas Aquinas, *Summa Theologiae*, III, 30, 1).

- The Gospels call Mary the "Mother of Jesus." Mary is truly the Mother of God since she is the mother of the Son of God made man. In the Eastern Churches Mary is honored as the *Theotokos*, or "Birth-giver of God."

- Mary was always a virgin, in conceiving Jesus, in giving birth to him, and for the rest of her life.

- "The Most Blessed Virgin Mary, when the course of her earthly life was completed, was taken up body and soul into the glory of heaven, where she already shares in the glory of her Son's Resurrection, anticipating the resurrection of all members of his Body" (CCC, no. 974). This is the doctrine of her Assumption into heaven.

- "We believe that the Holy Mother of God, the New Eve, Mother of the Church, continues in heaven to exercise her maternal role on behalf of the members of Christ" (Pope Paul VI, *Credo of the People of God*, no. 15).

MEDITATION

Magnificat (Lk 1:46-55)

After the Annunciation, the Virgin Mary went to stay with her cousin Elizabeth to assist Elizabeth in the forthcoming birth of her child. When Elizabeth saw Mary, she praised Mary's faith by saying, "Blessed are you who believed that what was spoken to you by the Lord would be fulfilled" (Lk 1:45). Mary responded with a canticle in which she praised God. We reflect here on her words, known to us today as the *Magnificat*, which is the first word of this canticle in Latin:

My soul proclaims the greatness of the Lord;
    my spirit rejoices in God my Savior.

for he has looked with favor on his lowly servant.
    From this day all generations will call me blessed:
the Almighty has done great things for me,
    and holy is his name.
He has mercy on those who fear him
    in every generation.
He has shown the strength of his arm,
    He has scattered the proud in their conceit.
He has cast down the mighty from their thrones
    and has lifted up the lowly.
He has filled the hungry with good things
    and the rich he has sent away empty.
He has come to the help of his servant, Israel,
for he has remembered his promise of mercy,
    the promise he made to our fathers,
    to Abraham and his children forever.

—*Liturgy of the Hours*; cf. Lk 1:46-55

PRAYER

Memorare

Remember, O most gracious Virgin Mary,
that never was it known that anyone
who fled to your protection,
implored your help or sought your
intercession was left unaided.
Inspired with this confidence, we fly unto you,
O Virgin of Virgins, our Mother.
To you we come. Before you we kneel, sinful and sorrowful.
O Mother of the Word Incarnate, despise not our petitions,
but in your clemency, hear and answer them. Amen.

—St. Bernard of Clairvaux

Hail Mary, full of grace!

13 OUR ETERNAL DESTINY

LAST THINGS: RESURRECTION OF THE BODY,
DEATH, PARTICULAR JUDGMENT, HEAVEN,
PURGATORY, HELL, LAST JUDGMENT,
NEW HEAVENS, AND NEW EARTH
—CCC, NOS. 988-1065

LOVE IS PROVED BY DEEDS

St. Katharine Drexel often said, "Love is proved by deeds." Her long life witnessed the wisdom of her faith-filled insight. Born in Philadelphia in 1858, Katharine was the daughter of a wealthy banker. Her parents taught Katharine to be generous with her money. Mr. Drexel trained his daughter to realize that one's money is meant to be shared with others.

Her father died in 1885. By the terms of his will, Katharine was one of the beneficiaries of his estate during her lifetime. That year, Katharine traveled throughout the country and became acquainted with the difficult living conditions of the Native Americans. She began to build schools for the children, supplying food, clothing, furnishings, and salaries for the teachers. She also found priests to serve the spiritual needs of the people. As she became aware of the suffering of the African Americans, she extended her charitable efforts to them. Throughout her lifetime, working with the government's Bureau of Colored and Indian Missions, she encouraged and financially supported missions throughout this country.

In 1891, with the sponsorship of her close family friend, Omaha's Bishop James O'Connor, Katharine Drexel founded the religious congregation the Sisters of the Blessed Sacrament. She and her sisters took the vows of poverty, chastity, and obedience—and she took a fourth vow "to be the mother and servant of the Indian and Negro races." Mother Katharine Drexel used the income from her father's trust—$350,000 a year in the 1900s—to build over sixty schools in the rural U.S. West and South. She also established Xavier University in New Orleans, the only Catholic African American college in the United States. She struggled for civil rights, taking on the Ku Klux Klan and financing some of the National Association for the Advancement of Colored People's investigations into exploitation of African American workers. Throughout her lifetime, Mother Katharine Drexel gave more than $21 million to help found churches, schools, and hospitals across the United States.

In 1935, Mother Katharine suffered a severe heart attack, and for the next twenty years, she lived in prayerful retirement. Her interest and love for the missions deepened until her death on March 3, 1955.

Pope John Paul II canonized Mother Katharine Drexel on October 1, 2000. She had lived the true meaning and virtue of the Gospel, with heart-felt generosity. She put her money and her life where her heart was—with her beloved African and Native Americans.

St. Katharine drew immense spiritual strength from her devotion to the Eucharist. In her adoration of the Blessed Sacrament, she discovered how to surrender herself totally to God. She wrote, "The Eucharist is a never-ending sacrifice. It is the Sacrament of love, the act of love." She often prayed to Christ in the Eucharist: "Help me each moment today and always to communicate myself to you by doing your will. Let the doing of your will each moment be a spiritual communion. In it you will give me yourself. I will give you myself."[11]

In her work for Native and African Americans, St. Katharine Drexel fol-lowed Christ's words describing his care as the Good Shepherd for the sheep: "I came that they may have life, and have it abundantly" (Jn 10:10). She wanted those whom she served to have a greater fullness of life now and to achieve the ultimate fullness of life in eternity.

As God's holy people, we, too, share in holy mysteries such as the Eucharist, but we are also related to all other members of the Church—those still living and those who have preceded us into the Kingdom of Heaven. We are, thus, part of the Communion of Saints. In this chapter, we consider our journey from life through death to the perfection of the Communion of Saints in eternity.

---

11   Quoted in Ellen Tarry, *Saint Katharine Drexel* (Boston: Pauline Books and Media, 2000), 149.

THE MEANING OF CHRISTIAN DEATH

Lord, for your faithful people, life is changed,
* not ended.*
When the body of our earthly dwelling lies in death,
we gain an everlasting dwelling place in heaven.

—Preface of Christian Death I,
Roman Missal; CCC, no. 1012

The final article of the Creed proclaims our belief in everlasting life. At Catholic funerals we sometimes hear this prayer: "Go forth, Christian soul, from this world. . . . May you live in peace this day, may your home be with God in Zion, may you see your redeemer face to face" (Prayer of Commendation). Death is the natural and inevitable end of life on earth. "[There is] a time to be born, and a time to die" (Eccl 3:2). We change, we grow old, and even death seems appropriate after a full life. "And the dust returns to earth as it once was, / and the life breath returns to God who gave it" (Eccl 12:7).

But the reality of death and its finality give an urgency to our lives. "Death puts an end to human life as the time open to either accepting or rejecting the divine grace manifested in Christ" (CCC, no. 1021). This teaching recognizes that the death of a person marks an end to our earthly journey with its sorrows and joys, its sinful failures, and the triumphs of Christ's saving grace and help.

The Church teaches that "each man receives his eternal retribution in his immortal soul at the very moment of his death, in a particular judgment" (CCC, no. 1022). St. John of the Cross (1542-1591) wrote, "At the evening of life, we shall be judged on our love" (*Dichos*, no. 64). Perfect love will make possible entrance into heaven, imperfect love will require purification, and a total lack of love will mean eternal separation from God.

"Heaven is the ultimate end and fulfillment of the deepest human longings, the state of supreme, definitive happiness" (CCC, no. 1024). This will be brought about by a perfect communion with the Holy Trinity, the Blessed Mother, the angels and saints. Jesus Christ opened heaven to us by his death and Resurrection.

What is heaven like? Scripture uses a variety of pictures to help us understand heaven, such as a wedding party, a banquet, the Father's house, a state of unending happiness. But the real heaven is beyond any picture we can paint of it. "What eye has not seen, and ear has not heard, / and what has not entered the human heart, / what God has prepared for those who love him" (1 Cor 2:9). Seeing God face to face in all his glory is the essential aspect of heaven. This is called the *beatific vision*. To make this possible God must reveal himself and give us the capacity to behold him.

> How great will your glory and happiness be, to be allowed to see God, to be honored with sharing the joy of salvation and eternal light with Christ your Lord and God, . . . to delight in the joy of immortality in the Kingdom of Heaven with the righteous and God's friends. (St. Cyprian, Letter 58, 10, 1)

"The Church gives the name *Purgatory* to [the] final purification of the elect, which is entirely different from the punishment of the damned" (CCC, no. 1031). Those who die in the state of friendship with God but who are not fully purified and perfected are assured of their eternal salvation. However, they must undergo a purification to obtain the perfection of love and holiness needed to enter heaven, where they have a heart that is totally open to him. This process is called Purgatory.

It is impossible for us to imagine what Purgatory is. Traditionally, it has been described as a purifying fire. Since the human soul cannot be touched by earthly flames, the image serves to recall that perfect love is achieved by a gradual and painful spiritual detachment from selfishness and self-centeredness. The Church assists those in Purgatory through prayer and especially the Eucharist in their final process of purification. Offering Masses for the deceased is a most powerful way of aiding them. November 2 of each year, the Commemoration of All the Faithful Departed (All Souls Day), is a day for special remembrance and prayer for the dead.

"The chief punishment of hell is eternal separation from God" (CCC, no. 1035). It is impossible for us to be united with God if we refuse to love him. When we sin seriously against God, neighbor, or self, we have failed to love God. Persistence in a state of serious sin reflects a choice to reject God's love and an intention to separate ourselves from him. Freely chosen eternal separation from communion with God is called *hell*. While images of fire have been used traditionally to picture hell, for example in the Scriptures, the reality exceeds our ability to describe the pain of isolation that comes from rejecting God's love.

Scripture and the teaching of the Church regarding heaven and hell emphasize a call to personal responsibility by which we use our freedom, aided by divine grace, to respond completely to God's love. There is always an urgent call to conversion and repentance. "God predestines no one to go to hell" (CCC, no. 1037).

THE RESURRECTION OF THE BODY

The profession of our faith in God, the Father, the Son, and the Holy Spirit . . . culminates in the proclamation of the resurrection of the dead on the last day and in life everlasting.

—CCC, no. 988

Faith in the resurrection of our bodies is inseparable from our faith in the Resurrection of Christ's body from the dead. He rose as our head, as the pattern of our rising, and as the life-giving source of our new life. "If the Spirit of the one who raised Jesus from the dead dwells in you, the one who raised Christ from the dead will give life to your mortal bodies also, through his Spirit that dwells in you" (Rom 8:11).

Belief in the resurrection of the body already existed in Christ's time among the Pharisees. Jesus performed miracles of raising the dead to life as symbols of his future Resurrection, and he associated these events with himself: "I am the resurrection and the life" (Jn 11:25).

> Christ, "the first-born from the dead" (Col 1:18), is the principle of our own resurrection, even now by the justification of our souls (cf. Rom 6:4), and one day by the new life he will impart to our bodies (cf. Rom 8:11). (CCC, no. 658)

All the dead will rise when Jesus comes again to judge the living and the dead. In the final resurrection, our bodies will be transformed, though we do not know precisely how. The manner of our resurrection exceeds our understanding and imagination and is accessible only to our faith.

> But someone may say, "How are the dead raised? With what kind of body will they come back?" You fool! What you sow is not brought to life unless it dies. And what you sow is not the body that is to be, but a bare kernel of wheat, perhaps or of some other kind. . . . It is sown corruptible, it is raised incorruptible. . . . The dead will be raised incorruptible. . . . For that which is corruptible must clothe itself with incorruptibility, and that which is mortal must clothe itself with immortality. (1 Cor 15:35-37, 42, 52, 53)

Every time we attend a funeral vigil or Mass, view a deceased body at a wake, or pass by a cemetery, we are reminded of this simple and profound article of the Creed, the belief in the resurrection of the body. It is a sobering belief, because it reminds us of the judgment yet to come, and at the same time it is a joyful belief that heralds life everlasting with God.

THE LAST JUDGMENT

The Last Judgment will come when Christ returns in glory.

—CCC, no. 1040

Immediately after death, each person comes before God and is judged individually (the particular judgment) and enters heaven, Purgatory, or hell. Yet at the end of time when Christ returns in glory, a final judgment will occur when all are raised from the dead and assembled before God; then their relationship to him is made public (the general judgment).

The judgment scene in the Gospel of Matthew is perhaps the most accessible way to appreciate the Last Judgment. "When the Son of Man comes in his glory, and all the angels with him, he will sit upon his glorious throne, and all the nations will be assembled before him. And he will separate them one from another, as a shepherd separates the sheep from the goats" (Mt 25:31-32). The sheep will inherit the Kingdom of God. The goats will be sent to the eternal fire prepared for the devil and his angels. In this parable, the criteria for being saved are described as whether one fed the hungry, gave water to the thirsty, welcomed the stranger, clothed the naked, cared for the sick, and visited the prisoners. In each of these cases, it is Jesus himself who is thus treated. "Whatever you did for these least brothers of mine, you did for me" (Mt 25:40). If we care for Jesus in these ways, we will receive the Kingdom. If we do not, we will be separated from him forever.

> The Last Judgment will come when Christ returns in glory. Only the Father knows the day and the hour. . . . Christ . . . will pronounce the final word on all history [making clear] the ultimate meaning of the whole work of creation and of the entire economy of salvation. . . . The Last Judgment will reveal that God's justice triumphs over all the injustices committed by his creatures and that God's love is stronger than death. (CCC, no. 1040)

THE NEW HEAVEN AND THE NEW EARTH

> *God is preparing a new dwelling and a new earth in which righteousness dwells.*
>
> —CCC, no. 1048, citing GS, no. 39

Once the Kingdom of God arrives in its fullness at the end of time there will be a renewal of the universe in Christ. Scripture uses many images to describe this mysterious reality. There will be a new heaven and a new earth:

> "Creation itself will be set free from its bondage to decay" (cf. Rom 8:19-23). The holy city of Jerusalem will descend from heaven to earth (cf. Rev 21:10). We do not know when or how

FROM THE CATECHISM

1. What happens when we die?

By death the soul is separated from the body, but in the resurrection God will give incorruptible life to our body, transformed by reunion with our soul. Just as Christ is risen and lives for ever, so all of us will rise at the last day. (CCC, no. 1016)

2. What is the beatific vision?

Because of his transcendence, God cannot be seen as he is, unless he himself opens up his mystery to man's immediate contemplation and gives him the capacity for it. The Church calls this contemplation of God in heavenly glory "the beatific vision." (CCC, no. 1028)

3. What does the Last Judgment call people to do?

The message of the Last Judgment calls men to conversion while God is still giving them the "acceptable time . . . the day of salvation." (CCC, no. 1041, citing 2 Cor 6:2)

this will happen. But we do know that God will make this happen. At the end of time, "The universe itself, which is so closely related to man and which attains its destiny through him, will be perfectly re-established in Christ." (LG, no. 48)

CHRISTIAN DEATH

We do not like to think about death. There is much in our culture that distracts us from reflection about our final destiny. We are encouraged to think only about the present moment and to fulfill today's needs. But the Christian embraces the total reality of life and God's call to the fullness of life after death. Thus, for example, Christians assist those whose earthly journey is coming to an end. "The dying should be given attention and care to help them live their last moments in dignity and peace. They will be helped by the prayer of their relatives, who must see to it that the sick receive at the proper time the sacraments that prepare them to meet the living God" (CCC, no. 2299).

Not only do we care for the dying to help them pass their final moments in dignity and peace, but we also maintain reverence for their bodies once they are deceased. "The bodies of the dead must be treated with respect and charity, in faith and in the hope of the Resurrection. The burial of the dead is a corporal work of mercy [cf. Tb 1:16-18]; it honors the children of God, who are temples of the Holy Spirit" (CCC, no. 2300). The rituals accompanying respect for the dead include the funeral vigil (wake), the funeral itself, and the burial of the body or the cremated remains of the deceased at the cemetery. Participation in these rites enables friends and others to demonstrate reverence for the deceased, to pray together for the eternal repose of the deceased, and to give the family of the deceased prayerful support.

CHRISTIAN FUNERALS

The Christian funeral liturgy tells us that life is changed, not ended. Funerals are acts of faith. In the dialogue between Martha and Jesus just before the raising of Lazarus, Jesus tells her, "Your brother will rise again." She replies, "I know that he will rise in the resurrection on the last day." Jesus then identifies himself as the Resurrection and the Life, and asks her, "Do you believe this?" She responds, "Yes, Lord, I have come to believe that you are the Messiah, the Son of God" (cf. Jn 11:17-27). We express this same belief at Christian funerals. Jesus, who walks with us through all our other events in life, is present at our funerals, the liturgy of the passage from death to eternal life. Arrangements for a funeral need to include a Mass and burial in a Catholic cemetery whenever possible.

It is preferable that the body be buried in a Catholic cemetery or columbarium (repository for cremated remains) consecrated for this purpose. We bury the body or the cremated remains of a person once washed with baptismal water, anointed with the oils of Confirmation and the Sacrament of the Sick, and nourished by the Eucharist.

The Church prefers the burial of the body but does allow cremation. "The Church permits cremation, provided that it does not demonstrate a denial of faith in the resurrection of the body" (CCC, no. 2301). In cases where cremation is planned, the Church urges that if at all possible, the body be present for the funeral Mass with cremation taking place afterwards. However, if for some reason cremation takes place before the funeral Mass, the diocesan bishop can permit the practice in his diocese of allowing cremated remains to be brought into the Church for the funeral rites.[12] Whenever a Catholic is cremated, the remains are to be buried, not scattered.

FOR DISCUSSION

1. What experiences have you had that bring you to think about death? How does the Church's teachings about eternal life help shape your thinking about death?
2. When you read the New Testament teachings about the Last Judgment, such as in the parable of the sheep and goats (Mt 25:31-46), what impact does this have on you? What does the Church teach about Purgatory? Why do we pray for the dead?
3. Why is the resurrection of our bodies important? In speaking of heaven or hell, why do we explain them in terms of our relationship with God?

DOCTRINAL STATEMENTS

• The Communion of Saints includes the faithful on earth, the souls in Purgatory, and the blessed in heaven. In this Communion, the

---

12 On March 21, 1997, in response to a request from the then-National Conference of Catholic Bishops, the Congregation for Divine Worship and the Discipline of the Sacraments published an indult (Prot. 1589/96/L) giving to each diocesan bishop in the United States the right to allow for the presence of the cremated remains of a body at the full course of Catholic funeral rites.

merciful love of God and his saints is always attentive to our prayers for one another here and for the souls of the faithful departed. The Communion of Saints also refers to "holy things," above all the Eucharist, by which the believers are formed into one Body of Christ.

- "The dying should be given attention and care to help them live their last moments in dignity and peace. They will be helped by the prayer of their relatives, who must see to it that the sick receive at the proper time the Sacraments that prepare them to meet the living God" (CCC, no. 2299).

- "The bodies of the dead must be treated with respect and charity, in faith and in the hope of the Resurrection. The burial of the dead is a corporal work of mercy [cf. Tb 1:16-18]; it honors the children of God, who are temples of the Holy Spirit" (CCC, no. 2300).

- Immediately after death, each person comes before God and is judged individually (the particular judgment) and enters heaven, Purgatory, or hell. Yet at the end of time, a final judgment will occur when all are assembled before God and their relationship to God is made public (the general judgment).

- The traditional designation of the four "Last Things" refers to death, judgment, heaven, and hell.

- The soul is immortal; it does not perish when it separates from the body at death. At the final resurrection, it will be reunited with the body.

- Those who die in the state of grace and friendship with God but who are not fully purified are assured of their eternal salvation. They must undergo a purification to attain the holiness needed to enter heaven. This process is called *Purgatory*. We pray for those in Purgatory, that they may soon be with God in heaven.

- Following the example of Christ, the Church warns the faithful of the sad reality of eternal death, also called hell, which is brought about by a person's free and permanent rejection of God and his love.

- "The Last Judgment will come when Christ returns in glory. . . . The Last Judgment will reveal that God's justice triumphs over all the injustices committed by his creatures and that God's love is stronger than death" (CCC, no. 1040).

MEDITATION

It is in regard to death that man's condition is most shrouded in doubt. Man is tormented not only by pain and by the gradual breaking-up of his body but also, and even more, by the dread of forever ceasing to be. But a deep instinct leads him rightly to shrink from and to reject the utter ruin and total loss of his personality. Because he bears in himself the seed of eternity, which cannot be reduced to mere matter, he rebels against death. All the aids made available by technology, however useful they may be, cannot set his anguished mind at rest. They may prolong his life-span; but this does not satisfy his heartfelt longing, one that can never be stifled, for a life to come. . . .

The Church, taught by divine Revelation, declares that God has created man in view of a blessed destiny that lies beyond the limits of his sad state on earth.

—GS, no. 18

PRAYER

May you live in peace this day, may your home be with God
    in Zion,
with Mary, the Virgin Mother of God, with Joseph and all the
    angels and saints . . .
May you return to [your Creator], who formed you from the
    dust of the earth . . .
May you see your Redeemer face to face.

—Prayer of Commendation,
Order of Christian Funerals

I am not dying. I am entering eternal life.

—St. Thérèse of Lisieux

PART II
THE SACRAMENTS:
THE FAITH CELEBRATED

14 THE CELEBRATION OF THE PASCHAL MYSTERY OF CHRIST

INTRODUCTION TO THE CELEBRATION OF THE
LITURGY IN THE SACRAMENTS
—CCC, NOS. 1076-1209

MARTIN LOVED LITURGY

"Today, Sunday, November 9, 1890, at 4 o'clock in the afternoon, the Lord blessed us with our first child. Next Sunday he will become a Christian and his name will be Martin Hellriegel." These words were written by Martin's mother in her prayerbook, and the Baptism took place at St. Peter Church in Heppenheim, Germany. The child flourished in a good Catholic home, and at age seventeen he received a scholarship to Kenrick Seminary in St. Louis, Missouri.

Ordained in 1914, he served first as an assistant in a parish, then as a chaplain to the Sisters of the Precious Blood at O'Fallon, Missouri, for twenty-two years. In 1940 he became pastor of Holy Cross Church in St. Louis where he served until his death forty years later. During his long years as a priest, he was a pioneer of the liturgical movement in the United States, always from the viewpoint of pastoral practice. This movement aimed to bring people closer to the meaning and effectiveness of Christian worship.

Following the teaching of Pope Pius XII's 1947 encyclical *On the Sacred Liturgy* (*Mediator Dei*), Msgr. Hellriegel sought to help his parishioners draw from the liturgy grace and strength for Christian living. He did this by showing them how the readings, ceremonies, and music can open their hearts to the presence of Jesus living and active in the liturgy. He drew his people into a loving participation in the Mass and the other

Sacraments. He believed that all the aspects of liturgical celebration should be understood.

Martin produced a small card that contained a record of days of grace in his life: Baptism, First Confession, First Communion, Confirmation, and his ordination (Holy Orders). On the respective days, he burned a candle before this framed card and spent an hour in prayer reflecting on the saving grace he had received from God. He frequently reminded his people to celebrate the anniversaries of their own sacred days, when they received their own first Sacraments.

He spent several Lenten sabbaticals in Rome. Each day he participated in Lenten liturgies at various ancient churches in Rome, studying their history and art. He incorporated this experience into his Lenten catechesis for his parishioners and others, helping them to sense Lent as a journey to Easter. He possessed an instinctive appreciation of the sacramental principle in which the visible elements of nature and history speak of the hidden but active presence of God in Christian worship.

Inspired by Pope Pius X's *motu proprio* on sacred music, he popularized Gregorian Chant to the point where his people could sing it easily and prayerfully. He taught them the prayer life of the Church by which they could enrich their lives in union with Jesus ever interceding for us before the Father.

Msgr. Hellriegel died in 1981.

The encyclical *On the Sacred Liturgy* by Pope Pius XII was a major statement about the Church's liturgy in the years prior to the Second Vatican Council. Pope Pius provided a vision for the Church's liturgical life that bore fruit in the Second Vatican Council's *Constitution on the Sacred Liturgy* (*Sacrosanctum Concilium*). Msgr. Hellriegel and others working in the liturgical movement drew inspiration from these developments.

LITURGY CELEBRATES THE PASCHAL MYSTERY

The Church celebrates in the liturgy above all the Paschal mystery by which Christ accomplished the work of our salvation.

—CCC, no. 1067

Part Two of the *Catechism*, containing two sections, deals with the liturgy of the Church. Section One presents the basic teachings about liturgy. Section Two presents the Seven Sacraments. The word *liturgy* comes from a Greek term meaning "public work or work done on behalf of the people." Liturgy always referred to an organized community. A work, then, done by an individual or a group was a liturgy on behalf of the larger community. All the worshipers are expected to participate actively in each liturgy, for this is holy "work," not entertainment or a spectator event. Every liturgical celebration is an action of Christ the High Priest and of his Mystical Body, which is the Church. It therefore requires the participation of the People of God in the work of God.

Liturgy is centered on the Holy Trinity. At every liturgy the action of worship is directed to the Father, from whom all blessings come, through the Son in the unity of the Holy Spirit. We praise the Father who first called us to be his people by sending us his Son as our Redeemer and giving us the Holy Spirit so that we can continue to gather, to remember what God has done for us, and to share in the blessings of salvation.

Through the liturgical celebrations of the Church, we participate in the Paschal Mystery of Christ, that is, his passing through death from this life into eternal glory, just as God enabled the people of ancient Israel to pass from slavery to freedom through the events narrated in the Book of Exodus (cf. Ex 11-13). The liturgies of the Church also help to teach us about Jesus Christ and the meaning of the mysteries we are celebrating.

A mystery is a reality that is both visible and hidden. Jesus Christ's death and Resurrection become present to us and effective for us in the liturgical life of the Church. His death and Resurrection are hidden now in the eternity of God, but as Risen Lord and Head of the Church, Jesus Christ calls us to share in them through the liturgy of the Church, that is, by the visible gathering of the community for worship and remembrance of what God has done for us. It is the Holy Spirit, the source of the Church's life, who draws us together through liturgical actions, the chief of which are the Sacraments. The term *liturgy* itself has a broader application than that of Sacrament, for it embraces all the official public prayer life of the Church, while the term *Sacrament* refers to a particular celebration of Christ's salvific work.

THE SACRAMENTS

The whole liturgical life of the Church revolves around the Eucharistic sacrifice and the sacraments.

—CCC, no. 1113

As we come to understand the Sacraments, it is important to recognize that the Sacraments have a visible and invisible reality, a reality open to all the human senses but grasped in its God-given depths with the eyes of faith. When parents hug their children, for example, the visible reality we see is the hug. The invisible reality the hug conveys is love. We cannot "see" the love the hug expresses, though sometimes we can see its nurturing effect in the child.

The visible reality we see in the Sacraments is their outward expression, the form they take, and the way in which they are administered and received. The invisible reality we cannot "see" is God's grace, his gracious initiative in redeeming us through the death and Resurrection of his Son. His initiative is called *grace* because it is the free and loving gift by which he offers people a share in his life, and shows us his favor and will for our salvation. Our response to the grace of God's initiative is itself a grace or gift from God by which we can imitate Christ in our daily lives.

The saving words and deeds of Jesus Christ are the foundation of what he would communicate in the Sacraments through the ministers of the Church. Guided by the Holy Spirit, the Church recognizes the existence of Seven Sacraments instituted by the Lord. They are grouped together in the following way:

- Sacraments of Initiation: Baptism, Confirmation (or Chrismation, as it is called in the Eastern Churches), and Eucharist
- Sacraments of Healing: Penance and Reconciliation and Anointing of the Sick

- Sacraments at the Service of Communion: Holy Orders and Matrimony

What are the Sacraments? "The sacraments are efficacious signs of grace, instituted by Christ and entrusted to the Church, by which divine life is dispensed to us" through the work of the Holy Spirit (CCC, nos. 1131; cf. no. 774).

First of all, Sacraments are efficacious signs: that is, they are effective. In human life, signs and symbols are found everywhere. Because we are both body and spirit, we express our inner selves through visible signs and symbols. We use them to communicate with each other in speech, gestures, and deeds. Sacramental signs are different in the sense that Christ uses them to confer his life and grace. When these sacramental signs are celebrated, they reveal and make present the reality they signify. They are efficacious, that is, effective, because Jesus Christ is at work in them. "It is he who baptizes, he who acts in the sacraments in order to communicate the grace that each sacrament signifies" (CCC, no. 1127). As we reflect on the individual Sacraments in later chapters of this *Catechism*, we will see that each Sacrament brings with it some particular grace.

Second, Christ instituted the Sacraments. "Adhering to the teaching of the Holy Scriptures, to the apostolic traditions, and to the consensus . . . of the Fathers," we profess that "the sacraments of the new law were . . . all instituted by Jesus Christ our Lord" (CCC, no. 1114, citing the Council of Trent: DS 1600-1601).

Third, Jesus entrusted the Sacraments to the Church. By Christ's will, the Church oversees and celebrates the Sacraments. Throughout his earthly life, Christ's words and deeds anticipated the power of his Paschal Mystery. Sacraments confer the grace that comes forth from Jesus Christ and that appears in the life of the Church by the power of the Holy Spirit.

Fourth, the Sacraments transmit divine life. Our share in this life is God's grace, his gift to us. In the Sacraments, we encounter Jesus Christ. The Spirit heals us and draws us closer to Christ and makes us partakers in the life of the Holy Trinity. Depending on our responsiveness to the grace of each Sacrament, our loving union with Jesus can increase throughout our journey of faith. Fruitful reception of the Sacraments presupposes the faith of the one who receives them. This faith is preceded by the faith of the Church (cf. CCC, no. 1124). We grow in holiness, which is both personal and communal—a matter of personal sanctity and of unity with the mission and holiness of the Church.

Jesus gave us the Sacraments to call us to worship God, to build up the Church, to deepen our faith, to show us how to pray, to connect us with the living Tradition of the Church, and to sanctify us. While God works primarily through the Sacraments, he also touches us through the community of the Church, through the lives of holy people, through prayer, spirituality, and acts of love. But "for believers, the sacraments of the New Covenant are necessary for salvation. . . . The fruit of the sacramental life is that the Spirit of adoption makes the faithful partakers of the divine nature" (CCC, no. 1129).

LITURGY IS THE BODY OF CHRIST AT PRAYER

Liturgy is an action of the whole Christ. . . . Liturgical services are not private functions but are celebrations of the Church.

—CCC, nos. 1136, 1140

When it comes to celebrating the Sacraments, there are four questions that need our attention: Who celebrates the liturgy? How is the liturgy celebrated? When is the liturgy celebrated? Where is the liturgy celebrated?

Who Celebrates?

The entire Body of Christ, animated by the Holy Spirit, celebrates the liturgy. The celebrating assembly is the community of the baptized. Liturgy is not a matter of private prayer, but a public act of worship by the faithful gathered together by the power of the Spirit under the authority of the bishop, their teacher and shepherd. "Mother Church earnestly desires that all the faithful should be led to that full, conscious and active participation in liturgical celebrations which is demanded by the very nature of the liturgy, and to which the Christian people . . . have a right and an obligation by reason of their Baptism" (CCC, no. 1141). The faithful are called to come to the liturgy consciously prepared to make their thoughts agree with what they say and hear, and to cooperate with divine grace.

Within the assembly, the ordained have a unique function of service. "These servants are chosen and consecrated by the sacrament of Holy Orders, by which the Holy Spirit enables them to act in the person of Christ the head, for the service of all the members of the Church" (CCC, no. 1142). Thus, for example, priests preside at the Eucharist, in which the elements of bread and wine are changed into the Body and Blood of Christ. Priests act in the person of Christ, the Head of the Church, and in the name of the Church when presenting to God the prayers and self-offering of the people and when offering the Eucharistic sacrifice, above all as they proclaim the Eucharistic Prayer.

How Do We Celebrate?

The Church celebrates the liturgy using an abundance of signs, symbols, and rituals. We celebrate the Sacraments with scriptural readings, homilies, music, processions, blessings, bread, wine, oil, arms outstretched in prayer, gestures of peace, bowed heads, kneeling, standing, sitting, incense, holy water, flowers, candles, colors, ritual vestments, choirs, and musical instruments.

We do this in a holy environment in which architecture, sculpture, paintings, icons, and stained glass lend an ambience that speaks of the mystery of God and divine transcendence on the one hand, and the unity of God with the worshiping community on the other. Since the Son of God honored us by becoming incarnate—the true visible image of the invisible God—we use these signs and symbols to help us experience God's invisible presence.

The Liturgy of the Word is part of all sacramental celebrations. The reading of Sacred Scripture is meant to awaken a response of faith in the listeners. When the word is proclaimed, Christ himself speaks. Having encountered Christ in the word, the people enter with a deeper appreciation into the heart of the celebration. The signs that accompany this reading emphasize its dignity: the use of a beautiful book, a procession with the Book of the Gospels including incense and candles, an effective reading of the Scripture, a homily that breaks open the word, silent reflection, and a prayerful response from the assembly. The combination of word and action helps make visible the invisible action of Christ and the Holy Spirit to open the hearts of the assembly to the grace of the particular sacramental celebration.

Liturgical Traditions and the Catholicity of the Church

> The liturgical traditions or rites presently in use in the Church are the Latin (principally the Roman rite, but also the rites of certain local churches such as the Ambrosian rite, centered in Milan, Italy, or those of certain religious orders) and the Byzantine, Alexandrian or Coptic, Syrian, Armenian, Maronite, and Chaldean rites. In "faithful obedience to tradition the sacred Council declares that Holy Mother Church holds all lawfully recognized rites to be of equal right and dignity, and that she wishes to preserve them in the future and to foster them in every way." (CCC, no. 1203, citing SC, no. 4)

> The rich variety of ecclesiastical disciplines, liturgical rites, and theological and spiritual heritages proper to the local churches, "unified in a common effort, shows all the more resplendently the catholicity of the undivided Church." (CCC, no. 835, citing LG, no. 23)

When Do We Celebrate?

The Lord's Day

Central to the Church's liturgical life is Sunday, the day of Christ's Resurrection. The observance begins with the evening of the preceding day. It is a day when all Catholics are obliged to take part in the Mass. "The Lord's Supper is its center, for there the whole community of the faithful encounters the risen Lord who invites them to his banquet"

(CCC, no. 1166). The Church encourages that Sunday, the "Lord's Day," also be a day for rest and recreation. It is also a day when the faithful can devote themselves to works of mercy and to the apostolate. This is discussed again in the chapter on the Third Commandment.

The Liturgical Year

In the Liturgical Year, the Church celebrates the whole mystery of Christ from the Incarnation until the day of Pentecost and the expectation of Christ's second coming. The summit of the Liturgical Year is the Easter Triduum—from the evening of Holy Thursday to the evening of Easter Sunday. Though chronologically three days, they are liturgically one day unfolding for us the unity of Christ's Paschal Mystery. The presence of the Risen Lord and his saving work permeates the entire Liturgical Year: Advent, the Christmas Season, Lent, the Easter Season, and Ordinary Time.

The Cycle of Saints

Besides the liturgical times just cited, the Church, with a special love, venerates Mary, the Mother of God, and also offers for the devotion of the faithful the memory of the martyrs and other saints. The veneration of Mary is evident in the number of feasts of the Blessed Virgin Mary. Mary is intimately linked to the saving work of her Son. Her feasts call us to admire and praise her as the outstanding fruit of Christ's redeeming work. Mary is the pure image of the kind of discipleship we hope to attain. She prays for us, loves us, and always brings us to Jesus. The feasts and memorials of the martyrs and other saints are occasions to praise God for their identification with Christ's Paschal Mystery. They are examples to us of love for God and others, of heroic courage in practicing faith, and of concern for the needs of others. We also rely on their intercession when we present our needs to God in prayer.

The Liturgy of the Hours

Closely tied to the Eucharist in the daily liturgical life of the Church is the Liturgy of the Hours, especially Morning and Evening Prayer. The

Liturgy of the Hours, in which the whole Church pours out her praise to God, prolongs the Eucharistic celebration, and leads us back to it. Besides offering praise to God, the Church in the Liturgy of the Hours expresses the prayers and desires of the Christian faithful. This is evident especially in the Intercessions at Morning and Evening Prayer, the praying of the Our Father, and the concluding prayer.

This public prayer of the Church is intended for the whole People of God. In this prayer Christ continues his priestly work and consecrates time. All God's people can participate in it according to their calling and circumstances. In this prayer, we harmonize our voices with praying hearts, and we come to a more profound understanding of the Psalms and other parts of Scripture that make up the largest part of the Liturgy of the Hours.

Even though the Liturgy of the Hours is celebrated in various ways in the Eastern and Latin Churches, the hymns, canticles, and readings from Church Fathers, other saints, and other Church writers offer us a rich meditation on God's Word. This public prayer prepares us for private prayer.

Where Do We Celebrate?

In one sense, worship is not confined to any one place, for the whole earth is entrusted to God's people. But practically, when religious freedom is not suppressed, it is customary to build churches for divine worship. A church is "a house of prayer in which the Eucharist is celebrated and reserved, where the faithful assemble, and where is worshiped the presence of the Son of God our Savior" (CCC, no. 1181, citing Second Vatican Council, *Decree on Priestly Life and Ministry* [*Presbyterorum Ordinis*; PO], no. 5). While the church building is important, the worshiping community, "living stones built into a spiritual house" (1 Pt 2:4-5), is of greater importance. Nevertheless, church buildings should be dignified enough to reflect the importance of what takes place there. They should be beautiful places that foster prayer and a sense of the sacred.

FROM THE CATECHISM

1. What does Sunday and its vigil mean for Catholics?

Sunday, the "Lord's Day," is the principal day for the celebration of the Eucharist because it is the day of the Resurrection. It is the pre-eminent day of the liturgical assembly, the day of the Christian family, and the day of joy and rest from work. Sunday is the "foundation and kernel of the whole liturgical year." (CCC, no. 1193, citing SC, no. 106)

2. What are the criteria for the use of songs and music in the Liturgy?

Songs and music fulfill their function as signs . . . when they are closely connected . . . with the liturgical action, according to three principal criteria: beauty expressive of prayer, the unanimous participation of the assembly at the designated moments, and the solemn character of the celebration. In this way they participate in the purpose of the liturgical words and actions: the glory of God and the sanctification of the faithful. (CCC, no. 1157)

3. What is the purpose of the Liturgy of the Word?

The Liturgy of the Word is an integral part of the celebration. The meaning of the celebration is expressed by the Word of God which is proclaimed and by the response of faith to it. (CCC, no. 1190)

THE LINK BETWEEN LITURGY AND LIFE

Our society favors being practical and tends to evaluate people and institutions in this light. Practicality has led to numerous inventions that have made life more humane. It also asks people to draw a closer link between theory and everyday life, urging them to be more down-to-earth.

But for some practical-minded people, religion appears to put too much emphasis on the next world rather than this one. Further, they claim that the time and effort devoted to ceremonies and otherworldly endeavors seems to have little value. They would want religion to confine itself to humanitarian deeds.

The Church has a vital role to play in shaping responsible citizens with moral character and with a willingness to contribute to the well-being of society. The liturgy and worship of the Church have much to do with these admirable goals. At divine worship, people receive the grace to help them to be formed ever more closely to Christ. The saving grace of the dying and rising of Christ are communicated to us in the Sacraments so that we might live more perfectly Christ's truth and virtues such as love, justice, mercy, and compassion.

Every Mass ends with the mission to go forth and serve the Lord. This sending means that the love of God and neighbor and the moral implications of the Beatitudes and the Ten Commandments should be witnessed by the participants in everyday life. People of faith know that their liturgical experience provides a unique spiritual vision and strength for making this a better world.

The lives of the saints provide ample evidence of this truth. Saints of every age have improved health care and education and fostered the human dignity of the poor, the oppressed, and the society at large. Saints attribute their remarkable energies to the power that comes from prayer and above all from the Sacraments, especially the Eucharist.

FOR DISCUSSION

1. How might you participate more fully, more consciously, and more actively in the Sunday Mass? In a culture that is centered on the "weekend," what can people do to observe Sunday as a day dedicated to God?

2. Review the definition of the Sacraments. How would you explain its elements to others? What can you learn from the sacred times in which liturgy is celebrated, such as Sunday, the Liturgical Year, and the feasts and memorials of the saints?

3. In what ways are you aware of the link between liturgy and your daily life? What are some stories about people you know or read about that illustrate the connection between liturgy and Christian witness?

◼ DOCTRINAL STATEMENTS ◼

- In liturgy, we praise and adore the Father as the source of all the blessings of creation, salvation, and divine adoption.
- "The liturgy is the work of the whole Christ, head and body" (CCC, no. 1187). In liturgy, Christ the Son of God made flesh acts in the Sacraments in which he communicates his saving power for his Body the Church.
- In liturgy, the Holy Spirit brings the assembly to meet Christ, to make Christ's saving work present, and to sanctify the members that they may witness Christ.
- "The Sacraments are efficacious signs of grace, instituted by Christ and entrusted to the Church, by which divine life is dispensed to us" (CCC, no. 1131).
- The Church celebrates the Sacraments as an assembly of all the baptized, led by the ordained, each having a special role to play in the sacramental celebrations.
- The Holy Spirit prepares the faithful for the Sacraments by helping them to welcome the Word of God in faith.
- The Sacraments communicate to each person a participation in God's life and a growth of love and witness in the Church. This is grace, the result of God's favor and initiative.
- A liturgical celebration uses signs and symbols drawn from creation, human life, and the history of salvation. Integrated into faith, the signs become bearers of the sanctifying action of Christ.
- The Liturgy of the Word is an important part of every liturgy because the proclamation of the Word of God and the response of faith to it help give meaning to the celebration.
- Sacred song and music, closely linked to the celebration, should lead to prayer, invite the participation of all in the assembly, and reflect the sacred character of the Sacrament.

- Sacred images nourish faith in the mystery of Christ. Through images of Christ we are moved to adore him and his saving works. In images of Mary and the saints we venerate the persons represented.
- Sunday and its vigil celebrate Christ's Resurrection, and it is the day that the faithful are obliged to attend Mass, rest from work, and engage in charitable works.
- In the course of the Liturgical Year, the Church unfolds the mystery of Christ's Incarnation, public ministry, death and Resurrection, Ascension, sending of the Holy Spirit, and the Church's expectation of his second coming.
- The feasts and memorials of the Mother of God and the saints call us to praise God for what he has accomplished in them and to imitate their virtues.
- The faithful who pray the Liturgy of the Hours are united with Christ in giving glory to the Father and imploring the gifts of the Holy Spirit for the world.
- Our parish churches are places where the faithful gather for public worship and personal prayer. These holy places are images of the heavenly kingdom to which we journey.
- "The diverse liturgical traditions or rites, legitimately recognized, manifest the catholicity of the Church, because they signify and communicate the same mystery of Christ" (CCC, no. 1208).

MEDITATION

For two thousand years, Christian time has been measured by the memory of that "first day of the week" (Mk 16:2, 9; Lk 24:1; Jn 20:1), when the Risen Christ gave the Apostles the gift of peace and of the Spirit (cf. Jn 20:19-23). The truth of Christ's Resurrection is the original fact upon which Christian faith is based (cf. 1 Cor 15:14), an event set at the center of the mystery of time, prefiguring the last day when Christ will return in glory. We do not know what the new millennium has in store for us, but we are certain that it is safe in the hands of Christ, the "King of kings and Lord of lords" (Rev 19:16); and precisely by celebrating his Passover not just once a year but every

Sunday, the Church will continue to show to every generation "the true fulcrum of history, to which the mystery of the world's origin and its final destiny leads."

—Pope John Paul II, *At the Close of the Great Jubilee of the Year 2000* (*Novo Millennio Ineunte*; NMI), no. 35

PRAYER

Sing to the LORD a new song,
    a hymn in the assembly of the faithful.
Let Israel be glad in their maker,
    the people of Zion rejoice in their king. . . .
Let the faithful rejoice in their glory,
    cry out for joy at their banquet,
With the praise of God in their mouths.

—Ps 149:1-2, 5-6

How I wept when I heard your hymns and canticles, being deeply moved by the sweet singing of your Church.

—St. Augustine, *The Confessions*, bk. 9, chap. 6;
Liturgy of the Hours, vol. IV, 1337

15 BAPTISM: BECOMING A CHRISTIAN

BAPTISM IS THE FIRST OF THE SACRAMENTS OF INITIATION
—CCC, NOS. 1210-1284

A BAPTISMAL WITNESS TO JUSTICE FOR MINORITIES

 In 1829, Bishop Benedict Joseph Fenwick of Boston founded a Catholic newspaper to explain, defend, and spread the teachings of the Catholic Church. By 1836 he decided it would be better to put the paper in the hands of the laity. He transferred the ownership to Patrick Donahue, who renamed the paper *The Boston Pilot*.

One of the *Pilot*'s editors, John Boyle O'Reilly, assumed that office in 1876. He was born to a family of educators in Ireland. As a young man, he enlisted in the British army, where he worked covertly to advance the cause of Irish independence. When he was discovered, he was arrested, given a twenty-year prison term, and sent to a penal colony in western Australia. Eventually he escaped and made his way to Boston, where he became a reporter and then the editor of the *Pilot*.

For the next twenty years, O'Reilly was the foremost influence in directing Irish immigrants through the process of cultural assimilation. For a time his literary talents and friendly attitude toward the Protestant establishment earned him a favorite place in society and an invitation to join the exclusive Papyrus Club.

But he never forgot his ethnic roots or his Catholic faith. He used his gifts as a public speaker, civil rights leader, poet, and novelist to bridge the gap between Catholics and Protestants in nineteenth-century Boston while enhancing Catholic identity in the process. He wrote a book of verse, *Songs from the Southern Seas*. He also wrote articles for *The Atlantic Monthly* and *Scribner's Monthly*.

He used the *Pilot* as a platform for defending an independent Ireland and addressing the rights of African Americans and Native Americans. He compared the oppression that these minorities were suffering to that which the Irish immigrants were experiencing. These oppressed groups had a friend in this man. He openly campaigned in the *Pilot* for political candidates who were for social reform. He joined several charitable organizations and was an outstanding proponent of Catholic education. He received honorary doctorates from Georgetown University, in Washington, D.C., and Notre Dame University, in South Bend, Indiana.

His unexpected death from a heart attack in 1890 was termed a "public calamity" by Cardinal Gibbons of Baltimore. "When he died," observes historian Mark Schneider, in *Boston Confronts Jim Crow*, "the opportunity slipped away for some kind of progressive association between Irish Catholics and members of Boston's small African American community. The light of 'green and black' unity flickered and died."[13]

Because of his forceful public presence and outstanding Catholic witness, the wake for O'Reilly was held in St. Mary's Church, in Charlestown, a neighborhood in Boston, where mourners by the thousands came to pay their respects.

The *Catechism* says that all who are reborn as children of God in Baptism "must profess before men the faith they have received from God through the Church and participate in the apostolic and missionary activity of the People of God" (CCC, no. 1270). God gave John Boyle O'Reilly the grace to live out, in a vigorous and inspiring manner, his baptismal commitment to the cause of Christ, the Church, and God's Kingdom. He showed how the laity can bring the Gospel to society and can make a difference.

---

13 Cited in Thomas H. O'Connor, *Boston Catholics* (Boston: Northeastern University Press, 1998), 145.

SACRAMENTS OF INITIATION

The Sacraments of Initiation—Baptism, Confirmation, and the Eucharist—are the foundations of the Christian life. "Baptism, the Eucharist, and the sacrament of Confirmation together constitute the 'sacraments of Christian initiation,' whose unity must be safeguarded" (CCC, no. 1285). We begin with our study of Baptism in this chapter and will treat the other two Sacraments in the following ones.

DYING AND RISING WITH CHRIST

Are you unaware that we who were baptized into Christ Jesus were baptized into his death? We were indeed buried with him through baptism into death, so that, just as Christ was raised from the dead by the glory of the Father, we too might live in newness of life.

—Rom 6:3-4

Baptism is birth into the new life in Christ. In accordance with the Lord's will, it is necessary for salvation, as is the Church herself, which we enter by Baptism.

—CCC, no. 1277

In his dialogue with Nicodemus, Jesus taught that Baptism was necessary for salvation. "No one can enter the Kingdom of God without being born of water and Spirit" (Jn 3:5). After his Resurrection, Jesus met with the eleven Apostles and gave them the commission to preach the Gospel and baptize, telling them, "Whoever believes and is baptized will be saved" (Mk 16:16). The word *baptism* in its origins is Greek and means "immersion" and "bath." Immersion in water is a sign of death, and emersion out of the water means new life. To bathe in water is also to undergo cleansing. St. Paul sums up this truth when he says, "You were buried with him in baptism, in which you were also raised with him through faith in the power of God, who raised him from the dead" (Col 2:12).

The origin and foundation of Christian Baptism is Jesus. Before starting his public ministry, Jesus submitted himself to the baptism given by John the Baptist. The waters did not purify him; he cleansed the waters. "He comes to sanctify the Jordan for our sake . . . to begin a new creation through the Spirit and water" (St. Gregory Nazianzen, *Liturgy of the Hours*, I, 634). Jesus' immersion in the water is a sign for all human beings of the need to die to themselves to do God's will. Jesus did not need to be baptized because he was totally faithful to the will of his Father and free from sin. However, he wanted to show his solidarity with human beings in order to reconcile them to the Father. By commanding his disciples to baptize all nations, he established the means by which people would die to sin—Original and actual—and begin to live a new life with God.

THE LITURGY OF BAPTISM

The meaning and grace of the sacrament of Baptism are clearly seen in the rites of its celebration.

—CCC, no. 1234

The eight major elements in the baptismal ceremony teach us the meaning of this Sacrament of Initiation and help us appreciate our life in Christ. Signs and symbols have their own capacity to communicate their meaning. Of course, the Sacrament is more than an instructive symbol; it accomplishes what it signifies.

The Sign of the Cross

At the beginning of the celebration, the celebrant traces the Sign of the Cross on the forehead of the one being baptized. This recalls Christ's saving death and the redemption it brought. Baptism is a Sacrament of salvation.

Readings from Scripture

Proclaiming the Word of God in the midst of the community sheds divine light on the celebration and is meant to build the faith of all the participants. One of the traditional names for Baptism is "Illumination." The Holy Spirit fills the heart and mind with the light of revealed truth and enables the response of faith.

Exorcism and Anointing

Baptism liberates us from sin. An exorcism prayer is recited over the one being baptized, preparing the person to renounce sin and be released from evil. The celebrant anoints the person to be baptized with the Oil of Catechumens (an oil that has been blessed by the bishop for the candidates for Baptism) or imposes hands on the person. In this way, the person is being called to renounce sin and to leave behind the domination of the power of evil.

Blessing the Baptismal Water

Baptismal water is blessed at the Easter Vigil. Outside the Easter Season, the water used for Baptism can also be blessed at each celebration of the Sacrament. The blessing prayer asks the Father "that through his Son the power of the Holy Spirit may be sent upon the water, so that those who will be baptized may be 'born of water and the Spirit'" (CCC, no. 1238).

Renunciation of Sin and Profession of Faith

Those being baptized are asked to reject sin and Satan, and to profess their faith in the Triune God. In the case of infants, parents, godparents, and the entire community present for the liturgy do this on behalf of those who cannot yet speak for themselves.

The Essential Rite of the Sacrament

The bishop, priest, or deacon either pours water three times on the person's head or immerses the candidate in water three times. In the Latin Church, he accompanies the act with the words, "[Name], I baptize you in the name of the Father, and of the Son, and of the Holy Spirit." The celebrant matches each pouring or immersion with the invocation of each of the Divine Persons. The ritual of immersion or washing helps us understand that our sins are buried and washed away as we die with Jesus, and we are filled with divine light and life as we rise from immersion in the water or are cleansed by the pouring.

> In the Eastern liturgies the catechumen turns toward the East and the priest says: "The servant of God, [Name], is baptized in the name of the Father, and of the Son, and of the Holy Spirit." At the invocation of each person of the Most Holy Trinity, the priest immerses the candidate in the water and raises him up again. (CCC, no. 1240)

"Today in all the rites, Latin and Eastern, the Christian initiation of adults begins with their entry into the catechumenate and reaches its culmination in a single celebration of the three Sacraments of Initiation: Baptism, Confirmation, and the Eucharist" (CCC, no. 1233). After the completion of initiation, the neophytes or new members begin the period of continued learning and formation in Christian life called *Mystagogy*.

With regard to infants, in the Latin Church, the Sacraments of Confirmation and Eucharist are received at a later time after Baptism. This is partly because of the emphasis on the bishop as the ordinary minister of Confirmation. Though the bishop cannot baptize everyone, he has a role in everyone's initiation into the Church by confirming them. In the Eastern Churches, the Baptism of infants is followed in the same ceremony by Confirmation (Chrismation) and Eucharist.

The Anointing with Sacred Chrism

The celebrant anoints the newly baptized with the sacred Chrism (a perfumed oil signifying the gift of the Holy Spirit), so that united with

God's people the person may remain forever a member of Christ, who is Priest, Prophet, and King. In the liturgy of the Eastern Churches, this anointing is the Chrismation, or the Sacrament of Confirmation, and is done immediately after Baptism. At the initiation of adults into the Church at the Easter Vigil, Confirmation follows Baptism.

Reception of the White Garment and the Candle

Following the Anointing with Chrism, the minister of Baptism presents the newly baptized with a white garment and a candle. The white garment shows that the newly baptized have put on Christ and have risen with him. To be clothed in the baptismal white garment is to be clothed in Christ's protective love. Included in this ceremony is the admonition to keep the garment unstained by sin. The Book of Revelation describes the significance of the white robe: "They have washed their robes and made them white in the blood of the Lamb" (Rev 7:14).

The candle is lit from the Paschal Candle, which represents the Risen Christ. The lighted candle reminds the newly baptized of the light of Christ they have received. It also reminds us that all those baptized in Christ are to be lights for the world.

These two symbols used at Baptism appear again in the Latin Church's funeral liturgy in the forms of the white pall covering the casket and the lighted Paschal Candle, which ordinarily stands near the casket. This is to remind us that the salvation and new life promised at Baptism can now be experienced fully by the one who has gone to God.

THE NECESSITY OF BAPTISM

As mentioned earlier in this chapter, the Lord himself affirms that Baptism is necessary for salvation. "No one can enter the Kingdom of God without being born of water and the Spirit" (Jn 3:5). Christ commanded his disciples to preach the Gospel, draw people to faith in him, and baptize those who come to conversion. The Church does not neglect the mission she has received from Christ to ensure that all be baptized and reborn of water and the Spirit.

Who Can Baptize?

The ordinary ministers of Baptism are the bishop and priest and, in the Latin Church, also the deacon. In case of necessity, anyone, even a non-baptized person, with the required intention, can baptize, by using water and the Trinitarian baptismal formula. The intention required is to will to do what the Church does when she baptizes. The Church finds the reason for this possibility in the universal saving will of God and the necessity of Baptism for salvation. (CCC, no. 1256)

WHO CAN RECEIVE BAPTISM?

The Baptism of Adults

For adults today, the Church, after the Second Vatican Council, has restored the order of the Catechumenate in the Rite of Christian Initiation of Adults (RCIA). It outlines the steps for the formation of catechumens, bringing their conversion to the faith to a greater maturity. It helps them respond more deeply to God's gracious initiative in their lives and prepares them for union with the Church community. This process is meant to form them into the fullness of the Christian life and to become disciples of Jesus, their teacher. This includes an initiation into the mystery of salvation, the practice of faith, hope, and love, and other virtues in a succession of liturgical rites.

Persons baptized into another Christian church and now seeking full communion with the Catholic Church are also welcomed to participate along with catechumens in the RCIA in the process of learning about the Catholic faith and being formed in that faith. They bring to the process of preparation their prior experience of Christian life and prayer. For a baptized Christian, reception into full communion with the Catholic Church involves reception of the Sacrament of Penance and Reconciliation and then a Profession of Faith followed by the celebration of Confirmation and the Eucharist.

SPONSORS FOR BAPTISM

Whenever a person is baptized, as an infant, as a child, or as an adult, there should be at least one person present who will act as sponsor for the one being baptized. The sponsor, commonly referred to as one's godmother or godfather, accepts the responsibility of helping the person grow in the Catholic faith. One who acts as a sponsor for an infant or child agrees to help the parents teach their child about the faith and how to live as a practicing Catholic. One who acts as sponsor for an adult agrees to encourage and support the person, pray with and for the person, and offer whatever help, information, or support is needed while the person is preparing to enter the Church and then is living out the rest of his or her life as a practicing Catholic.

For a person to act as a sponsor for Baptism, he or she must be at least sixteen years old, must have already received all the Sacraments of Initiation (Baptism, Confirmation, and Holy Eucharist), and must be living in a way that demonstrates that one's faith is strong enough to be able to fulfill the responsibilities involved with being a sponsor. A sponsor who is married must be married in accord with the laws of the Church (cf. CIC, can. 874).

The Baptism of Infants

Infant Baptism has been practiced since apostolic times. Infants need to be baptized because through this Sacrament, they are freed from Original Sin and are welcomed into the community of the Church, where they have access to the fullness of the means of salvation. Their parents, godparents, and the parish community commit themselves to their ongoing formation in faith and knowledge of the tradition of the Church. The best gift that parents can give their children is a life in the Church. "The Church and the parents would deny a child the priceless grace of becoming a child of God were they not to confer Baptism shortly after birth

RCIA STEPS

For adults who have not yet been baptized, the RCIA has three major liturgical rites: Acceptance into the Order of Catechumens; Election or Enrollment of Names, and Celebration of the Sacraments of Initiation. The celebration of initiation is followed by a postbaptismal catechesis, or *Mystagogy*. (For those already baptized, there are rites appropriate for their journey into full communion in the Catholic Church. These are sometimes celebrated separately from the catechumens, and sometimes in a combined rite with the catechumens.)

The process begins with the **Precatechumenate**, in which the person shows initial faith in Jesus Christ and the Church. This is a time for inquiry and the exploration of the beginnings of faith.

After the person has been given a fundamental understanding of the Gospel and has decided to take the first step to become a member of the Church, the person is brought into the Catechumenate at the Rite of Acceptance.

The period of the **Catechumenate** is a time for exploring the teachings of the faith in a deeper and more systematic manner within the context of worship and prayer. At Sunday Mass, the catechumens with their catechists are often dismissed after the homily for further, prayerful study of the Scripture readings for the day.

This period concludes with the **Rite of Election or Enrollment of Names**, which takes place on the First Sunday of Lent. This rite is celebrated by the bishop or his delegate, usually at the cathedral of the diocese. The catechumens' suitability and resolve to be initiated into the sacramental life of the Church is supported by the testimony of their sponsors and catechists. After this, the catechumens become known as the Elect.

The Elect enter the stage of **Purification and Enlightenment** that occurs during the season of Lent. They prepare themselves for the reception of the Sacraments of Initiation by prayerful reflection. On the third, fourth, and fifth Sundays of Lent, the Scrutinies are celebrated. These rites, which take place during Mass, offer opportunities for the Elect to reflect on the full meaning of the step they are preparing to take. They are meant to bring God's illuminating Word to the Elect so that whatever is weak or sinful in their hearts can be healed and so that whatever is good in them can be strengthened. The parish community joins them by examining their own lives and interceding with God for the Elect. This period concludes at the Easter Vigil, when the Elect receive the Sacraments of Initiation and become full members of the Church and are called neophytes.

From Easter to Pentecost, there is a period of postbaptismal catechesis, or **Mystagogy**. This is a time for the neophytes, or newly initiated, along with the members of the parish to come closer together as a faith community to examine more deeply the Gospel, to share in the Eucharist, and to do works of charity. During this joyful time, the neophytes' enthusiasm can inspire the faithful of the parish, who in turn can share their experiences of the faith with them.

(CCC, no. 1250; cf. *Code of Canon Law* [*Codex Iuris Canonici*; CIC], can. 867). However, the Church also teaches that the Baptism of an infant may be postponed if there is not a "founded hope" that the child will be brought up in the Catholic Faith (CIC, can. 868 §2).

There are the children—born and unborn—who die without Baptism. The Church entrusts them to the mercy of God, who wills that all people be saved. We recall Christ's tender welcome of children saying, "Let the children come to me and do not hinder them" (Mk 10:14). Because of this the Church confidently hopes for the salvation of children who die without Baptism.

Baptism of Blood, Baptism of Desire

Often the question is raised about those who die without Baptism. The *Catechism* offers this principle: "God has bound salvation to the sacrament of baptism, but he himself is not bound by the sacraments" (CCC, no. 1257). The Church holds that those who suffer and die for their faith in Christ before they could be baptized are saved by Baptism of Blood.

Candidates for Baptism who die before they receive the Sacrament but have repented their sins and have embraced Christ's love are saved by what is called Baptism of Desire. What about those people who have never had the Gospel presented to them, who do not know Jesus or the Church, yet seek the truth and try to do God's will as they understand it? "It is may be supposed that such persons would have desired baptism explicitly had they known its necessity" (CCC, no. 1260).

EFFECTS OF BAPTISM

Sins Forgiven

By Baptism all sins are forgiven, Original Sin and all personal sins, and temporal punishment due to sin is removed. After one has been reborn in Christ, there is nothing to prevent one's entry into God's Kingdom.

However, though all sins are removed, there remains, as an effect of Original Sin, the inclination to sin that is called *concupiscence*. This inclination to sin shows itself in what is sometimes referred to as a darkening of the mind and a weakening of the will, that is, the inability to know clearly the right or wrong of an action and/or the lack of strength to resist temptation and always to do the right thing no matter how hard this is. The effects of Original Sin need not harm us so long as we seek strength to resist them through the Sacrament of Penance, the Sacrament of the Eucharist, prayer, a deepening spirituality, growth in virtue, and a wholehearted dependence on God.

Adopted Children of God

Baptism also gives us new life as adopted children of God. We become sharers of divine life and temples of the Holy Spirit. We are now made righteous by God and live in a state of grace, that is, we live in union with God because of his gracious and loving initiative. Our permanence in the state of grace is called *sanctifying grace* because God "sanctifies" us, that is, makes us his holy people by giving us his life. God continues to assist us by many helps that are called *actual graces*. Thus, we have the ability to live and act under the guidance and light of the gifts of the Holy Spirit. This helps us mature in goodness through the practice of virtues, such as the Cardinal Virtues: prudence, justice, temperance, and fortitude.

Initiated into the Church

By Baptism we become members of the Church, the Body of Christ. We share in the priesthood of Christ as well as his prophetic and royal mission. "You are 'a chosen race, a royal priesthood, a holy nation, a people of his own, so that you may announce the praises' of him who called you out of darkness into his marvelous light" (1 Pt 2:9). We enjoy the community we find in the Church, share our talents and gifts with its members, respond willingly to its teachings and requirements, and assume the responsibilities that our membership implies.

Bonded to Other Christians

Baptism provides a common foundation among all Christians, including those not yet in full communion with the Catholic Church. The Church recognizes the validity of Baptism in other Christian Churches as long as the rite involved the pouring of or immersion in water, a Trinitarian formula, and the intention to baptize. Those who have been baptized have been saved by their faith in Christ and the grace of Baptism. "They therefore have a right to be called Christians and with good reason are accepted as brothers [and sisters] by the children of the Catholic Church" (CCC, no. 1271, citing UR, no. 3).

FROM THE CATECHISM

1. Why are the rites of Baptism so helpful for understanding this Sacrament?

The meaning and grace of the Sacrament of Baptism are clearly seen in the rites of its celebration. By following the gestures and words of this celebration with attentive participation, the faithful are initiated into the riches this sacrament signifies and actually brings about in each newly baptized person. (CCC, no. 1234)

2. Why is sin possible after Baptism?

Certain temporal consequences of sin remain in the baptized, such as suffering, illness, death, and such frailties inherent in life as weaknesses of character ... as well as an inclination to sin that Tradition calls *concupiscence*. (CCC, no. 1264)

God also gave us free will. While he gives us Baptism and the other Sacraments to help us make the correct choices, these Sacraments do not force a person to do good and to avoid sin.

3. What helps the growth of faith after Baptism?

For all the baptized, children or adults, faith must grow after Baptism. . . . For the grace of Baptism to unfold, the parents' help is important. So too is the role of the godfather and godmother who must be firm believers and ready to help the newly baptized—child or adult—on the road of Christian life. (CCC, nos. 1254-1255)

Baptismal Character

"Incorporated into Christ by Baptism, the person baptized is configured to Christ. Baptism seals the Christian with the indelible spiritual mark

ARE CATHOLICS BORN-AGAIN?

A number of non-Catholic Christians call themselves "born-again." Catholics, for the most part, do not use this term. A "born-again" Christian is one who has experienced a particularly intense moment of conversion that leads him or her to want to dedicate his or her life to God. It is a one-time action that is not necessarily tied to any type of baptismal rite. While we Catholics are born again as children of God in the Sacrament of Baptism, our rebirth happens in and through the grace of the Sacrament. Our rebirth in Baptism is also not a one-time event but a lifelong process through which we continually strive to die to sin and rise to new life in Christ. Catholics are indeed born again.

(character) of his belonging to Christ. No sin can erase this mark, even if sin prevents Baptism from bearing the fruits of salvation. Given once for all Baptism cannot be repeated" (CCC, no. 1272). This spiritual mark is also called a character, which St. Augustine likened to distinctive brandings impressed upon soldiers and slaves during Roman times to signify the commander or owner to whom they belonged. Baptism marks us permanently as belonging to Christ, whose image we bear.

BAPTISM IS A CALL TO HOLINESS

Reborn . . . [the baptized] . . . must participate in the apostolic and missionary activity of the People of God.

—CCC, no. 1270

"Baptism is the door to life and to the Kingdom of God. Christ offered the first sacrament of the new law to all that they may have eternal life. Baptism is, above all, the sacrament of that faith by which men and women, enlightened by the Spirit's grace, respond to the Gospel of Christ" ("Christian Initiation, General Instruction," in *The Rites of the Catholic Church* [1976], no. 3).

In Baptism, the Holy Spirit moves us to answer Christ's call to holiness. In Baptism, we are asked to walk by the light of Christ and to trust in his wisdom. We are invited to submit our hearts to Christ with ever deeper love. What is this light, this wisdom, this holiness? Jesus is clear about the high ideals to which he invites us:

> Be perfect, just as your heavenly Father is perfect. (Mt 5:48)
> Be merciful as your Father is merciful. (Lk 6:36)
> Love one another as I love you. (Jn 15:12)

The Lord Jesus, our divine teacher and model of all virtue, preached holiness of life to everyone without exception. Through Baptism, we are cleansed of all sin, are made partakers of the divine nature, and are truly sanctified. Our goal now is to hold onto this gracious act of sanctification that we have received from Christ. St. Paul lays out a practical plan for holiness:

> Put on, then, as God's chosen ones, holy and beloved, heartfelt compassion, humility, gentleness and patience, bearing with one another. If one has a grievance against another, as the Lord has forgiven you, so must you also do. And over all these put on love, that is, the bond of perfection. (Col 3:12-13)

This is a strong challenge that we cannot meet by human strength alone. "Accordingly, all Christians in the conditions, duties and circumstances of their life and through all these, will sanctify themselves more and more if they receive all things with faith from the hand of the heavenly Father and cooperate with the divine will, thus showing forth in the temporal service the love with which God has loved the world" (LG, no. 41). The baptized are called to transform the world with the light and power of the Gospel.

Living out one's Baptism is a lifelong responsibility. Growing in holiness and discipleship involves a willingness to continue to learn throughout one's whole life about the faith and how to live it. It also involves a willingness to support and encourage others who share the faith and who have committed themselves to the ongoing process of conversion of heart and mind to God, which results in the holiness to which we are called.

FOR DISCUSSION

1. St. Paul tells us that in Baptism we die and rise with Christ. Why is it necessary to remember the "dying" part? If you were to do a survey of what Baptism means to people, what answers do you think you would hear?
2. What differences do you see between some "cradle Catholics" and those who have entered the Church through the RCIA? What are the responsibilities of godparents in looking after the growth in faith of the baptized they sponsor?
3. What is an effective way of attracting others to Christ?

DOCTRINAL STATEMENTS

- The Sacraments of Initiation are Baptism, Confirmation, and Eucharist.
- The Risen Jesus commissioned the Apostles to baptize when he said, "Go, therefore, and make disciples of all nations, baptizing them in the name of the Father, and of the Son, and of the Holy Spirit" (Mt 28:19-20).
- Baptism gives a person birth into new life. It is necessary for salvation and for entry into the Church.
- The rite of Baptism consists in immersing the person in water three times or pouring water on his or her head three times while invoking the Holy Trinity: the Father, the Son, and the Holy Spirit.
- The effects of Baptism are delivery from all sins (Original and personal), reception of the grace of divine adoption, being made a member of Christ and a temple of the Holy Spirit, initiation into the Church, and being made a sharer in Christ's mission as priest, prophet, and king.

- Baptism seals the person's soul with a permanent spiritual mark or character identifying one as belonging to Christ. Because of this character, Baptism cannot be repeated.
- People who die for the faith, catechumens who died before being baptized, and those who do not know Christ or the Church through no fault of their own but who, by the action of grace, seek God sincerely and do his will can be saved even without being baptized.
- Infants have been baptized since apostolic times, for this is a gift from God and does not presuppose human merit. Children are baptized in the faith of the Church.
- Trusting in God's mercy, we confidently hope for the salvation of children who die without Baptism.
- In time of necessity such as the danger of death, all persons can baptize. The person baptizing must intend to do what the Church does, by pouring water three times on the candidate's head while saying, "I baptize you in the name of the Father and of the Son and of the Holy Spirit."

MEDITATION

By three immersions and as many invocations, the great mystery of Baptism is performed. So the appearance of death is conveyed, and through the handing over of divine knowledge the baptized are enlightened. Therefore, if there is any grace in the water, it is not because of any power the water may possess, but because it derives from the power of the Spirit. . . . The Lord, to prepare us for the risen life, lays before us all the gospel precepts. We must avoid anger, endure evil, be free from the love of pleasure and the love of money. So by our own choice we shall achieve those things which are the natural endowments of the world to come.

—St. Basil the Great, *On the Holy Spirit*, XV, nos. 35-36

PRAYER

God the Father of our Lord Jesus Christ has freed you from sin,
given you a new birth by water and the Holy Spirit,
and welcomed you into his holy people.

He now anoints you with the chrism of salvation.
As Christ was anointed Priest, Prophet and King,
so may you live always as members of his body,
sharing everlasting life. Amen.

—Prayer for Anointing with Chrism,
Rite of Baptism

You were buried with him [Christ] in baptism,
in which you were also raised with him through
faith in the power of God, who raised him from the dead.

—Col 2:12

16 CONFIRMATION: CONSECRATED FOR MISSION

CONFIRMATION IS THE SECOND SACRAMENT
OF INITIATION
—CCC, NOS. 1285-1321

FRANCES CABRINI, "GO TO AMERICA"

 When Frances Cabrini received the Sacrament of Confirmation, she was more perfectly bound to the Church as a true witness to Christ and more urgently called to spread and defend the faith in word and deed. She heard that call and responded with extraordinary generosity. This is her story.

This spirited woman was born in Italy in 1850. Early on, she felt the call to religious life, but no congregation accepted her because of her poor health.

At age twenty-seven, her missionary zeal led her to found a new congregation, the Missionary Sisters of the Sacred Heart. Within a few years, she and her sisters had opened six orphanages.

In 1889, she obtained an audience with Pope Leo XIII, asking him to support her desire to open a mission in China. Pope Leo directed her elsewhere. He told her to go to America and work among the Italian immigrants there.

A short time later, she was in New York City opening a Catholic school at St. Gioacchino's parish church. Within a year, she had begged enough money to buy a 450-acre Jesuit property across the Hudson River to house her first American orphanage. Soon after, she realized that Italian immigrants and others needed a hospital. Her skills at fundraising and getting people to give of themselves led her to found the first Columbus Hospital, where she relied on the donated services of the doctors, Catholic as well as Jewish and Protestant. The hospital had free wards for the poor and private rooms for the rich, whose fees helped finance the care of the poor. She built other Columbus hospitals in Denver, Los Angeles, Philadelphia, Seattle, New Orleans, and Chicago.

She continued to visit the various convents and institutions she founded in Europe. She also sailed to Brazil and Argentina to expand the work of her community. Her thirty-seven years of apostolic service saw her almost constantly on the move. She could be found deep in a Denver mine encouraging Italian American miners or, on another occasion, at a scaffold holding hands and praying with Italian American prisoners who were about to be hanged.

When she died in 1917, she left behind sixty-seven convents in Europe, the United States, and South America and 1,500 Missionary Sisters of the Sacred Heart. She had become a citizen of the United States in 1909 and was the first American citizen to be canonized a saint. At her canonization in 1946, Pius XII said this in his homily:

> Where did she acquire all that strength and the inexhaustible energy by which she was able to perform so many good works and to surmount so many difficulties? She accomplished all this through the faith that was always so vibrant in her heart; through the divine love that burned within her; and, finally, through the constant prayer by which she was so closely united to God. . . . She never let anything turn her aside from striving to please God and to work for his glory for which nothing, aided by grace, seemed too difficult or beyond human strength. (*Liturgy of the Hours*, vol. IV, 2022)

Mother Cabrini lived deeply the mission of the Church to bring Christ's compassion and care to all people. She responded generously to the grace of the Sacrament of Confirmation that binds Christians to such a deeper identification with the Church and her mission.

THE SACRAMENT OF THE HOLY SPIRIT

The reception of the sacrament of Confirmation is necessary for the completion of baptismal grace. . . . "By the sacrament of Confirmation [the baptized] are more perfectly bound to the Church and are enriched with a special strength of the Holy Spirit."

—CCC, no. 1285, citing LG, no. 11

Confirmation, together with Baptism and Eucharist, form the Sacraments of Initiation that are all intimately connected. In the Sacrament of Confirmation, the baptized person is "sealed with the gift of the Holy Spirit" and is strengthened for service to the Body of Christ.

The prophets of the Old Testament foretold that God's Spirit would rest upon the Messiah to sustain his mission. Their prophecy was fulfilled when Jesus the Messiah was conceived by the Spirit and born of the Virgin Mary. The Holy Spirit descended on Jesus on the occasion of his baptism by John. Jesus' entire mission occurred in communion with the Spirit. Before he died, Jesus promised that the Spirit would be given to the Apostles and to the entire Church. After his death, he was raised by the Father in the power of the Spirit.

The New Testament reports many manifestations of the Holy Spirit, two of which we note here. St. John's Gospel describes an outpouring of the Spirit on Easter night when Jesus breathed on the Apostles and said, "Receive the holy Spirit" (Jn 20:22). St. Luke's Acts of the Apostles gives another account of the sending of the Holy Spirit at Pentecost, fifty days after the Resurrection of Christ (cf. Acts 2). Filled with the Holy Spirit, the Apostles proclaimed God's mighty deeds. Peter preached that this coming of the Spirit fulfilled the prophecy of Joel: "In the last days . . . I will pour out a portion of my spirit / upon all flesh" (Acts 2:17; cf. Jl 3:1).

Those who believed in the Apostles' preaching were baptized and received the Holy Spirit through the laying on of hands. The Apostles baptized believers in water and the Spirit. Then they imparted the special gift of the Spirit through the laying on of hands. "The imposition of hands is rightly recognized by the Catholic tradition as the origin of the sacrament of Confirmation, which in a certain way perpetuates the grace of Pentecost in the Church" (CCC, no. 1288, citing Pope Paul VI, *Divinae Consortium Naturae*, no. 659).

By the second century, Confirmation was also conferred by anointing with holy oil, which came to be called sacred Chrism. "This anointing highlights the name 'Christian,' which means 'anointed' and derives from that of Christ himself whom God 'anointed with the Holy Spirit'" (CCC, no. 1289, citing Acts 10:38).

THE LITURGY OF CONFIRMATION

The signs, symbols, ritual acts, and words of the liturgy speak to us of the meaning of a Sacrament and of what Christ enacts in the event through his ministers and the disposition of the candidate. With this in mind, we reflect on the following elements of Confirmation: the anointing with sacred Chrism, the recipient, the essential rite, the ministers, and the effects of the Sacrament.

The Anointing with Sacred Chrism

The post-baptismal anointing with sacred chrism in Confirmation . . . is the sign of consecration. . . . those who are anointed, share more completely in the mission of Jesus Christ.

—CCC, no. 1294

In or near Holy Week, the bishop consecrates the sacred Chrism during the course of the Chrism Mass. It is used to anoint the newly baptized, to confer the Sacrament of Confirmation, and to anoint bishops and priests during the celebration of the Sacrament of Holy Orders.

Anointing with oil has many meanings such as cleansing as part of a bath, limbering up the muscles of athletes, and healing the wounds of the sick. Two other sacramental celebrations make use of blessed oil: "The pre-baptismal anointing with the oil of catechumens signifies cleansing and strengthening; the anointing of the sick expresses healing and comfort" (CCC, no. 1294). The Oil of Catechumens is used in Baptism. The Oil of the Sick is used for the Sacrament of the Anointing of the Sick.

The Recipient of Confirmation

Each baptized person not yet confirmed can and should receive the Sacrament of Confirmation. In the Latin Church, it is customary to confirm candidates between the age of discretion, also called the age of reason, and about sixteen years of age. It is not uncommon that Catholics not confirmed during this period of their lives for a variety of reasons are confirmed as adults, often on Pentecost Sunday. The candidate should be in the state of grace (that is, without serious sin), be well prepared by prayer and catechesis, and be committed to the responsibilities entailed by the Sacrament.

The Essential Rite of Confirmation

In continuity with the New Testament custom of laying hands on those who would receive the gift of the Spirit, the bishop extends his two hands over all those to be confirmed. He recites a prayer that begs the Father of our Lord Jesus Christ for the outpouring of the Holy Spirit and for the seven gifts traditionally associated with the Spirit. These gifts are permanent dispositions that move us to respond to the guidance of the Spirit. The traditional list of the gifts is based on Isaiah 11:1-3: wisdom, understanding, knowledge, counsel, fortitude, piety (reverence), and fear of the Lord (wonder and awe in God's presence).

The essential rite then follows. In the Latin Rite, "the Sacrament of Confirmation is conferred through the anointing with Chrism on the forehead, which is done by the laying on of hands, and through the words, 'Be sealed with the gift of the Holy Spirit'" (Introduction to the *Rite of Confirmation*, no. 9). In the Eastern Churches, after a prayer for the presence and action of the Holy Spirit, the priest anoints the forehead, eyes, nose, ears, lips, chest, back, hands, and feet of the candidate with *Myron* (holy oil). With each anointing he says, "The seal of the gift of the Holy Spirit." The Eastern Churches call Confirmation "Chrismation."

When Confirmation is celebrated separately from Baptism, its connection with Baptism is expressed, among other ways, by the renewal of baptismal promises. The celebration of Confirmation during the Eucharist helps underline the unity of the sacraments of Christian initiation. (CCC, no. 1321)

The connection between Confirmation and Baptism is also reflected in the choosing of a name by which the candidate will be confirmed, especially when the chosen name is one of the names by which the candidate was baptized.

The Minister of Confirmation

In the early Church, sacramental initiation always involved the bishop; the bishop was the ordinary minister of both Baptism and Confirmation. However, pastoral practice changed as the Church expanded rapidly. When bishops could no longer be present at all celebrations of Baptism, they chose to retain a role in the process of initiation by continuing to be the ordinary minister of Confirmation.

In the Latin Church, with the bishop as the minister of Confirmation, it is evident how this Sacrament can serve to strengthen the person's bond with the Church and her apostolic origins. However, there are also times when the bishop entrusts the celebration of the rite of Confirmation to a priest, such as in the case of the Baptism of an adult or the reception of an adult from another Christian community into full communion with the Church. Bishops may also give this permission in other cases.

In the Eastern Churches, Confirmation is conferred by a priest at the time of Baptism, and in some of these Churches, it is followed by the reception of the Eucharist. This practice underlines the unity of the three Sacraments of Initiation. The priest confirms with the *Myron* or oil consecrated by the bishop. This expresses the apostolic unity of the Church.

The Effects of Confirmation

Confirmation brings an increase and deepening of baptismal grace:
—it roots us more deeply in the divine filiation [becoming adopted sons and daughters of God] which makes us cry, "Abba! Father!";
—it unites us more firmly to Christ;
—it increases the gifts of the Holy Spirit in us;
—it renders our bond with the Church more perfect;
—it gives us a special strength of the Holy Spirit to spread and defend the faith by word and action as true witnesses of Christ, to confess the name of Christ boldly, and never to be ashamed of the Cross.

—CCC, no. 1303

As the words of the liturgy indicate, the person being confirmed is sealed with the Holy Spirit. This seal is called a *character*, marking the person forever as called to fulfill the Church's mission in all the circumstances of life.

The one who gives us security with you in Christ and who anointed us is God; he has also put his seal upon us and given the Spirit in our hearts as a first installment. (2 Cor 1:21-22)

THE MISSION AND WITNESS OF THE CONFIRMED

Confirmation deepens our baptismal life that calls us to be missionary witnesses of Jesus Christ in our families, neighborhoods, society, and the world. Through Confirmation, our personal relationship with Christ is strengthened. We receive the message of faith in a deeper and more intensive manner with great emphasis given to the person of Jesus Christ, who asked the Father to give the Holy Spirit to the Church for building up the community in loving service.

The Holy Spirit bestows seven gifts—wisdom, understanding, knowledge, fortitude, counsel, piety, and fear of the Lord—to assist us

FROM THE CATECHISM

1. Who may receive Confirmation?
Every baptized person not yet confirmed can and should
receive the Sacrament of Confirmation. Since Baptism,
Confirmation, and Eucharist form a unity, it follows that
"the faithful are obliged to receive this sacrament at the
appropriate time." (CCC, no. 1306, citing CIC, can. 890)

2. How should candidates for Confirmation be prepared?
Preparation for Confirmation should aim at leading the
Christian toward a more intimate union with Christ and
a more lively familiarity with the Holy Spirit—his actions,
his gifts, and his biddings—in order to be more capable
of assuming the apostolic responsibilities of Christian
life. To this end catechesis for Confirmation should strive
to awaken a sense of belonging to the Church of Jesus
Christ, the universal Church as well as the parish community. The latter bears special responsibility for the preparation of confirmands. (CCC, no. 1309)

3. Why do we not receive Confirmation more than once?
Confirmation, like Baptism, imprints a spiritual mark, or
indelible character on the Christian's soul; for this reason
one can receive this Sacrament only once in one's life.
(CCC, no. 1317)

in our mission and witness. The impact of these gifts accompanies us in
the various stages of our spiritual development.

As the confirmed, we walk with the seven gifts of the Holy Spirit.
Wisdom enables us to see the world from God's viewpoint, which can
help us come to grasp the purpose and plan of God. It grants us the long-
range view of history, examining the present in the light of the past and
the mystery of the future. It saves us from the illusion that the spirit of
the times is our only guide. The Spirit's gift of knowledge directs us to a

contemplation, or thoughtful reflection, of the mystery of God—Father, Son, and Holy Spirit—as well as of the mysteries of the Catholic faith. We are drawn to meditative prayer, where we allow God to lead us while we rest patiently in the divine presence.

The gift of understanding stimulates us to work on knowing ourselves as part of our growth in knowing God. It is what St. Augustine meant when he prayed, "That I may know You, may I know myself." When the Spirit pours fortitude or courage into our hearts, we can trust that we will be prepared to stand up for Christ and the Gospel when challenged. As the gift of counsel or right judgment grows in us, we can sense the quiet teaching that the Spirit gives us about our moral lives and the training of our consciences.

The gift of piety or reverence is an act of respect for the Father who created us, for Jesus who saved us, and for the Spirit who is sanctifying us. We learn reverence for God and people from our parents and others who train us in virtue. The Spirit fills us with this gift at liturgy, which is a masterful school of reverence, as well as through popular devotions and piety.

Finally, the gift of fear of the Lord or wonder and awe in God's presence can infuse honesty into our relationship with God, a frankness that places us in awe before the majesty of God. Yet the gift also imparts an attitude of grateful wonder that God loves us and that we can share in his life.

When we are responsive to the grace of Confirmation and the seven gifts of the Holy Spirit, we begin to bear the fruits of the Spirit. The tradition of the Church names twelve fruits of the Holy Spirit: love, joy, peace, patience, kindness, goodness, generosity, gentleness, faithfulness, modesty, self-control, and chastity (cf. CCC, no. 1832; Gal 5:22).

FOR DISCUSSION

1. If you have been confirmed, describe what the experience was like. When did it happen? Who confirmed you? How were you prepared?
2. How are the healing and cleansing qualities of anointing with oil symbols of what happens in the Sacraments of Baptism and Confirmation?

3. What are the consequences of the deeper identification with the mission of the Church that comes from Confirmation?

◼◼◼ DOCTRINAL STATEMENTS ◼◼◼

- Jesus promised the Apostles that he would send the Holy Spirit to them. At Pentecost that promise of Christ was fulfilled (cf. Jn 16:12-15; Acts 2:1-47).
- The effects of Confirmation include a permanent character, a perfection of baptismal grace, an increase in the gifts and fruits of the Holy Spirit, a deepening of our identity as adopted sons and daughters of God, a closer bond to the Church and her mission, and helps for bearing witness.
- In the Eastern Churches, Chrismation (Confirmation) is administered immediately after Baptism, followed by participation in the Eucharist. This tradition emphasizes the unity of these three Sacraments of Initiation.
- In the Western or Latin Church, Confirmation is administered after the age of reason is attained and is normally conferred by the bishop, signifying one's bond with the Church and its apostolic origins.
- The candidate for Confirmation in the Latin Church should be in the state of grace, be well prepared by prayer and catechesis, and be committed to the responsibilities entailed by the Sacrament.
- This is the essential rite of Confirmation in the Western Church: The bishop confers Confirmation through the anointing with Chrism on the recipient's forehead, which is done by the laying on of the hand, while saying the words "Be sealed with the gift of the Holy Spirit."
- In the Eastern Churches, after a prayer for the presence and action of the Holy Spirit, the priest anoints the forehead, eyes, nose, ears, lips, chest, back, hands, and feet of the candidate with *Myron* (holy oil). With each anointing, he says, "The seal of the gift of the Holy Spirit."
- The spiritual, indelible marks (or characters) received in the Sacraments of Baptism, Confirmation, and Holy Orders affirm a

permanent relationship with God and indicate that these Sacraments may be received only once.

- "When Confirmation is celebrated separately from Baptism, its connection with Baptism is expressed, among other ways, by the renewal of baptismal promises. The celebration of Confirmation during the Eucharist helps underline the unity of the Sacraments of Christian Initiation" (CCC, no. 1321).

MEDITATION

There are those who have said that courage in witnessing our faith is one of the best proofs for the existence of God. Confirmation is the Sacrament that makes possible courageous witness. The never-ending stories of martyrs and other Christian heroes and heroines throughout the centuries to the present provide ample evidence of the Holy Spirit's gift of courage. Today, there are plenty of opportunities to act courageously on behalf of the teachings of Christ and the Church, to promote the stability of marriage, to support the ideals of family life, to be brave in defending human life from conception to death, to be steadfast in seeking justice for the oppressed, and to be determined that the light of Christ's compassion and peace will shine everywhere on earth.

PRAYER

Come, Holy Ghost (A Hymn to the Holy Spirit)
Come, Holy Ghost, Creator blest,
and in our hearts take up thy rest.
Come with thy grace, and heavenly aid
to fill the hearts which thou hast made.

Breathe on me breath of God, my soul with grace refine,
Until this earthly part of me, glows with your fire divine.

—Edwin Hatch

17 THE EUCHARIST: SOURCE AND SUMMIT OF THE CHRISTIAN LIFE

THE HOLY EUCHARIST COMPLETES CHRISTIAN INITIATION
—CCC, NOS. 1322-1419

AN APOSTLE OF THE EUCHARIST

In 1946, a bright young man named Carlos Manuel Rodriguez enrolled at the University of Puerto Rico. But despite excellent grades and his love of learning, he fell ill with ulcerated colitis, which prevented him from completing his second year. Nevertheless, he continued to study on his own. He read widely in science, philosophy, arts, and religion. He learned to play the organ for the sacred music that he was enthusiastically promoting.

Born in 1918 to parents who valued education, he showed signs of great intelligence early on. When a fire destroyed the family store and home, his family moved in with Carlos' maternal grandparents. His grandmother, Alejandrina Esteras, imparted her devout faith in the Eucharist to Carlos. Under her influence, he began his devotion to the liturgy and decided to commit his life to Jesus Christ.

Though he was unable to finish his university education, he experienced a call to do whatever he could to help the university students respond to God's call to holiness through the liturgy. Carlos became an unofficial campus minister. He wanted to open up the riches of the Mass to them, to show them how to participate actively in the Eucharistic celebration. He urged them to build their spirituality from the wealth of God's grace given in the Sacraments, especially the Eucharist.

Carlos obtained a job as an office worker at the University Agriculture Experiment station. He spent his salary to promote an appreciation of the spiritual wealth of the liturgy. He started a magazine, *Liturgy and Christian Culture*, in which he published articles on liturgy that he translated into Spanish from English and French journals.

He gradually gathered a number of students and professors together in a Liturgy Circle that met at the University Center. He taught them how to live out the liturgy and the Easter mystery of Christ's dying and rising, especially at the Easter Vigil.

He organized Christian Life days for the students to renew their spirituality through the liturgy. He promoted the active participation of the laity in the Mass and the use of the vernacular. Carlos anticipated a number of the teachings of the Second Vatican Council, especially those found in the *Constitution on the Sacred Liturgy (Sacrosanctum Concilium)*.

Carlos did not let his deteriorating physical condition get in the way of his calling. He knew he was rising with Christ even as his body was dying. He kept reminding his disciples at the university that they should be joyful because they are called to live the joy and hope that Jesus brings with his Resurrection. He frequently said, "*Vivimos para esa noche de la Resurrección*" (We live for the night of the Resurrection). He entered eternal life on July 13, 1963, at age forty-four.

A crowd that traveled to Rome from Puerto Rico cheered and waved their island's flag in St. Peter's Square on April 29, 2001, when Pope John Paul II beatified Carlos Manuel Rodriguez. The pope pointed out that this lay activist witnessed the fact that all Christians are called to pursue holiness "in a conscious and responsible way."

Blessed Carlos loved the Eucharist, which is the center of the liturgy. Remarkably, in the twenty years before the Second Vatican Council when the voices for liturgical renewal were being heard from Benedictine monks, scholarly theologians, and visionary priests, this alert Puerto Rican layman showed university students how to base their faith life on the liturgy, especially the Eucharist.

THE REVELATION OF THE EUCHARIST

The holy Eucharist completes Christian initiation. . . .
The Eucharist is the efficacious sign and sublime cause
of that communion in the divine life and that unity of the
People of God by which the Church is kept in being.

—CCC, nos. 1322 and 1325, citing Sacred Congregation of Rites,
Instruction on the Worship of the Eucharistic Mystery
(Eucharisticum Mysterium), no. 6

The origins of the Eucharist are found in the Last Supper that Jesus shared with his Apostles. "In order to leave them a pledge of this love, in order never to depart from his own and to make them sharers in his Passover, he instituted the Eucharist as the memorial of his death and Resurrection and commanded his apostles to celebrate it until his return; 'thereby he constituted them priests of the New Testament'" (CCC, no. 1337, citing Council of Trent: DS 1740).

So rich is this mystery that we have a number of terms to illumine its saving grace: the Breaking of the Bread; the Lord's Supper; the Eucharistic Assembly; the Memorial of Christ's Passion, Death, and Resurrection; the Holy Sacrifice of the Mass, the Holy and Divine Liturgy; the Eucharistic Liturgy; Holy Communion; and Holy Mass (cf. CCC, nos. 1328-1332).

The use of bread and wine in worship is already found in the early history of God's people. In the Old Testament, bread and wine are seen as gifts from God, to whom praise and thanks are given in return for these blessings and for other manifestations of his care and grace. The story of the priest Melchizedek's offering a sacrifice of bread and wine for Abraham's victory is an example of this (cf. Gn 14:18). The harvest of new lambs was also a time for the sacrifice of a lamb to show gratitude to God for the new flock and its contribution to the well-being of the family and tribe.

These ancient rituals were given historical meaning at the Exodus of God's people. They were united into the Passover Meal as a sign of God's delivering the Israelites from slavery in Egypt, a pledge of his fidelity to his promises and eventually a sign of the coming of the

Messiah and messianic times. Each family shared the lamb that had been sacrificed and the bread over which a blessing had been proclaimed. They also drank from a cup of wine over which a similar blessing had been proclaimed.

When Jesus instituted the Eucharist he gave a final meaning to the blessing of the bread and the wine and the sacrifice of the lamb. The Gospels narrate events that anticipated the Eucharist. The miracle of the loaves and fish, reported in all four Gospels, prefigured the unique abundance of the Eucharist. The miracle of changing water into wine at the wedding feast in Cana manifested the divine glory of Jesus and the heavenly wedding feast in which we share at every Eucharist.

In his dialogue with the people at Capernaum, Christ used his miracle of multiplying the loaves of bread as the occasion to describe himself as the Bread of Life: "I am the living bread that came down from heaven. . . . Unless you eat the flesh of the Son of Man and drink his blood, you do not have life within you" (Jn 6:51, 53).

THE LAST SUPPER

The account of the institution of the Eucharist may be found in the Gospels of Matthew, Mark, and Luke as well as in Paul's First Letter to the Corinthians (see Mt 26:17-29; Mk 14:12-25; Lk 22:7-20; 1 Cor 11:23-26). Jesus chose the Passover feast as the time in which he would institute the Eucharist and would undergo his dying and rising (cf. CCC, nos. 1339-1340). With the institution of the Eucharist, Jesus gave the Passover its new and definitive meaning. He showed himself to be the High Priest of the New Covenant, offering himself as a perfect sacrifice to the Father. Jesus changed the bread and wine into his Body and Blood, given now as an offering for the salvation of all people.

> For I received from the Lord what I also handed on to you, that the Lord Jesus, on the night he was handed over, took bread, and, after he had given thanks, broke it and said, "This is my body that is for you. Do this in remembrance of me." In the same way also the cup, after supper, saying, "This cup is the new covenant in my blood. Do this, as often as you drink it, in remembrance

of me." For as often as you eat this bread and drink the cup, you proclaim the death of the Lord until he comes. (1 Cor 11:23-26)

By the words "Do this in memory of me," Jesus commanded the Apostles and their successors to repeat his actions and words "until he comes again." From earliest times, the Church has remained faithful to this command. Particularly on Sunday, the day of Christ's Resurrection, the faithful has gathered for the Breaking of the Bread. This practice has continued unbroken for two thousand years right up to the present day.

In the Gospel of John, instead of an account of the institution of the Eucharist, there is the narrative of the foot washing (Jn 13:1-20) at the beginning of the Last Supper, which sets the tone of humble service, exemplified by Christ and fulfilled in his death on the Cross. The Church has selected this Gospel for the Holy Thursday liturgy, highlighting Christ's teaching: "If I, therefore, the master and teacher, have washed your feet, you ought to wash one another's feet. I have given you a model to follow, so that as I have done for you, you should also do" (Jn 13:14-15).

Christ's Last Supper Discourse (Jn 14:1–17:26) reflects Eucharistic themes of divine love, a union with Christ as intimate as a branch is to a vine, and a priestly prayer for the Apostles and those who would believe through them.

THE MASS FOR THE ROMAN RITE

Since the second century, the Mass (or the Eucharistic Liturgy) has had a structure that is common to all Catholics. While there can be different emphases during the celebration of Mass in Eastern Churches, they maintain the fundamental twofold structure with which members of the Latin Church are familiar. Thus, the Mass unfolds in two major parts that form a single act of worship. First, there is the Liturgy of the Word, with Scripture readings, homily, Profession of Faith, and General Intercessions. Second, there is the Liturgy of the Eucharist, with the presentation of the bread and wine, the Eucharistic Prayer, and the reception of Holy Communion. The essential elements of Eucharistic celebrations may be summarized in the following four points.

1. The Introductory Rites

The Christian community, united by the Holy Spirit, gathers for worship in response to God's call. Jesus, our High Priest, is the principal agent of our celebration. The bishop or priest acts in the person of Christ, the Head of the Church. All the worshipers participate actively with interior devout attention and with external reverence shown by singing the hymns and giving the responses and, when appropriate, observing silence. There are also the deacon, the lectors, those who present the offerings, the extraordinary ministers of Holy Communion, the altar servers, the musicians, and other ministers. This first movement contains the Introductory Rites, which begin the celebration of the Mass. These include the Penitential Rite, the *Gloria*, and the Opening Prayer.

> Mother Church earnestly desires that all the faithful should be led to that full, conscious and active participation in liturgical celebrations which is demanded by the very nature of the liturgy, and to which the Christian people, "a chosen race, a royal priesthood, a holy nation, a redeemed people" (1 Pt 2:9, 4-5) have a right and obligation by reason of their baptism. (SC, no. 14)

2. Liturgy of the Word

Over the course of the liturgical year, readings from Scripture, especially the Gospels, provide the heart of this part of the celebration. The proclamation of God's Word and its explanation are meant to arouse our faith and prepare us for an ever deeper participation in the mystery of the Eucharist. The readings are followed by a homily from a bishop, priest, or deacon; the Profession of Faith in the recitation of the Creed; and intercessory prayers.

3. Liturgy of the Eucharist

a. *The Preparation of the Gifts* (Jesus took bread and wine). The offerings of bread and wine are received by the priest, who may be assisted by a deacon. "They will be offered by the priest in the name of Christ in the Eucharistic sacrifice in which they will become his Body

THE CHURCH AND THE EUCHARIST

The Church draws her life from the Eucharist. This truth does not simply express a daily experience of faith, but recapitulates the heart of the mystery of the Church. In a variety of ways, she joyfully experiences the constant fulfillment of the promise, "Lo, I am with you always, to the close of the age" (Mt 28:20), but in the Holy Eucharist, through the changing of the bread and wine into the Body and Blood of the Lord, she rejoices in this presence with unique intensity. Ever since Pentecost, when the Church, the People of the New Covenant, began her pilgrim Journey towards her heavenly homeland, the Divine Sacrament has continued to mark the passing of her days, filling them with confident hope. (Pope John Paul II, *On the Eucharist* [*Ecclesia de Eucharistia*; EE], no. 1)

and Blood" (CCC, no. 1350). From the earliest days of the Church, there was also an offering of gifts for the poor and needy. This has become the customary place and time for the parish collection.

b. *The Eucharistic Prayer* (Jesus blessed and gave thanks). This is the heart of the Eucharistic Liturgy, which unfolds in the following manner.

- *Thanksgiving* (expressed especially in the Preface): In this prayer, we thank God the Father, through Christ in the Spirit, for the gifts of creation, salvation, and sanctification.
- *Acclamation*: The whole congregation joins with the angels and saints in singing or saying the *Sanctus* (Holy, Holy).
- *Epiclesis* (Invocation): The Church implores the power of the Holy Spirit to change the bread and wine offered by human hands into Christ's Body and Blood.
- *Institution Narrative and Consecration*: The priest proclaims Jesus' words at the Last Supper over the bread and wine. "The power of the words and the action of Christ, and the power of

the Holy Spirit, make sacramentally present, under the species of bread and wine, Christ's Body and Blood, his sacrifice offered on the cross for all" (CCC, no. 1353).

- *Anamnesis* (The Remembrance): We recall the death and Resurrection of Christ and look forward to his glorious return.
- *Second Epiclesis*: The Holy Spirit is invoked upon the gathered community, to bring unity to the worshippers who will receive Holy Communion.
- *Intercessions*: With the whole Communion of Saints and all God's people on earth, we pray for the needs of all the members of the Church, living and dead.
- *Doxology and Great Amen*: We conclude the Eucharistic Prayer with praise of God the Father, through his Son Jesus Christ, in the Holy Spirit. This glorification is confirmed and concluded by the people's acclamation "Amen."

c. *Communion Rite* (Jesus broke the bread and gave his Body and Blood). After the Lord's Prayer, the Lamb of God is sung or said during the breaking of the Body of Christ, or fraction, then we receive the Body and Blood of Christ in Holy Communion. The Communion Rite concludes with a closing prayer.

4. Concluding Rite

Following the prayer after Holy Communion, the priest blesses the people and dismisses the assembly.

Centuries of reflection on the Eucharist have left us a spiritual heritage that continues to deepen and grow. Three key truths about the Eucharist draw our attention: it is a Sacrifice, a Holy Meal, and the Real Presence of Christ.

THE MASS IS A SACRIFICE

The Mass is a sacrifice in the sense that when it takes place, Jesus Christ, through the bishop or priest celebrating the Mass, makes present sacramentally his saving, sacrificial death on the Cross by which he redeemed us from our sins. This Eucharistic sacrifice is the memorial of Christ's redeeming death. The term *memorial* in this context is not simply a remembrance of past events; it is a making present in a sacramental manner the sacrifice of the Cross of Christ and his victory. "When the Church celebrates the Eucharist, the memorial of her Lord's death and resurrection, this central event of salvation becomes really present and 'the work of our redemption is carried out'" (EE, no. 11). The Eucharistic sacrifice is offered to adore and thank God, to pray for all our needs, and to gain pardon for our sins.

In this divine sacrifice which is made present in the Mass, especially in the Eucharistic Prayer, the same Christ who offered himself once in a bloody manner on the altar of the Cross offers himself in an unbloody manner. Present and effective, Christ's sacrifice is applied to our lives. "If the blood of goats . . . can sanctify those who are defiled . . . how much more will the blood of Christ . . . cleanse our consciences from dead works to worship the living God" (Heb 9:14).

The Mass is also the sacrifice of the Church. The ordained priest in the Mass links the Eucharistic consecration to the sacrifice of the Cross and to the Last Supper (cf. EE, no. 29), thus making it possible that the sacrifice of Christ becomes the sacrifice of all the members of the Church. "The lives of the faithful, their praise, sufferings, prayer, and work, are united with those of Christ and with his total offering, and so acquire a new value" (CCC, no. 1368). This also reminds us of the importance of sacrifice in each individual's life. In a self-centered culture where people are taught to extend themselves only for something in return, the sacrifices each of us make, following the example of Jesus, who freely sacrificed his life in love for all, point to the reality and power of God's love for us.

The offering of Christ unites the members here on earth and those in heaven. The Pope, as chief shepherd of the People of God, is named at every Mass for the sake of the unity of the whole Church. The bishop of a diocese is named because he is the shepherd of the local Church and the instrument of its unity. The text of the Eucharistic Prayer also recalls the presence of the Blessed Virgin Mary and all the saints as they join us in this act of worship. Drawing from the benefits of Christ's sacrifice, the Mass is also offered for the faithful departed—who have died in Christ but may not yet be totally purified—so they may enter the glory of heaven.

THE MASS IS A HOLY MEAL

"Unless you eat the flesh of the Son of Man and drink his blood, you do not have life within you" (Jn 6:53). Jesus Christ shares with us his Body and Blood under the form of bread and wine. Thus the Mass is a sacred banquet that culminates in the reception of Holy Communion. The Church urges us to prepare conscientiously for this moment. We should be in the state of grace, and if we are conscious of a grave or serious sin, we must receive the Sacrament of Penance before receiving Holy Communion. We are also expected to fast from food or drink for at least one hour prior to the reception of Holy Communion. "Like every Catholic generation before us, we must be guided by the words of St. Paul, 'Whoever therefore eats the bread or drinks the cup of the Lord in an unworthy manner will be guilty of profaning the Body and Blood of the Lord' (1 Cor 11:27). That means that all must examine their consciences as to their worthiness to receive the Body and Blood of our Lord. This examination includes fidelity to the moral teaching of the Church in personal and public life" (United States Conference of Catholic Bishops, *Catholics in Political Life*, 2004). The Church gives us the humble words of a Roman centurion to say as we prepare to receive Communion: "Lord, I am not worthy to receive you, but only say the word and I shall be healed" (cf. Mt 8:8).

Although the Church urges us to receive Communion at each Mass, there is an obligation for everyone to receive Communion at least once a year some time during the interval between the First Sunday of Lent and Trinity Sunday. Since Christ is fully present under each form of the Eucharist (that is, both the consecrated Bread and Wine), it is sufficient to receive him under the species (form) of bread or wine alone. However, the "sign of communion is more complete when given under both kinds, since in that form the sign of the Eucharistic meal appears more clearly" (CCC, no. 1390).

Holy Communion increases our union with Christ. Just as bodily food sustains our physical life, so Holy Communion nourishes our spiritual life. This Communion moves us away from sin, strengthening our moral resolve to avoid evil and turn ever more powerfully toward God. "The more we share the life of Christ and progress in his friendship, the more difficult it is to break away from him by mortal sin" (CCC, no. 1395).

THE REAL PRESENCE OF CHRIST

By the power of the Holy Spirit, Christ is present in the proclamation of God's Word, in the Eucharistic assembly, in the person of the priest, but above all and in a wholly unique manner in the Eucharist. "This presence is called 'real'—by which is not intended to exclude the other types of presence as if they could not be 'real' too, but because it is presence in the fullest sense: that is to say, it is a *substantial* presence by which Christ, God and man, makes himself wholly and entirely present" (CCC, no. 1374, citing Pope Paul VI, *Mystery of Faith*, no. 39).

Since the Middle Ages, the change of bread and wine into the Body and Blood of Christ has been called "transubstantiation." This means that the substance of the bread and wine is changed into the substance of the Body and Blood of Christ. The appearances of bread and wine remain (color, shape, weight, chemical composition), but the underlying reality—that is, the substance—is now the Body and Blood of Christ.

The Real Presence of Jesus Christ endures in the consecrated elements even after the Mass is ended. Once Communion has been distributed, any remaining hosts are placed in the tabernacle. If any of the Precious Blood remains, it is reverently consumed. The hosts are reserved to provide Communion for the sick, *Viaticum* (Communion for the dying), and to allow the faithful to worship Christ in the reserved Sacrament and to pray in his presence. As a sign of adoration, Latin Catholics genuflect to the Real Presence of Jesus Christ in the tabernacle or genuflect or kneel when the Blessed Sacrament is exposed for prayer. Eastern Catholics show their reverence by a profound bow rather than a genuflection: "It is for this reason the tabernacle should be located in an especially worthy place in the Church and should be constructed in such a way that it emphasizes and manifests the truth of the real presence of Christ in the Blessed Sacrament" (CCC, no. 1379).

With the passage of time, reverent reflection led the Church to enrich its Eucharistic devotion. Faith that Jesus is truly present in the Sacrament led believers to worship Christ dwelling with us permanently in the Sacrament. Wherever the Sacrament is, there is Christ, who is our Lord and our God. Such worship is expressed in many ways: in genuflection, in adoration of the Eucharist, and in the many forms of Eucharistic devotion that faith has nourished.

The Eucharistic Liturgy contains the entire treasure of the Church since it makes present the Paschal Mystery, the central event of salvation. Eucharistic adoration and devotion flow from and lead to the Eucharistic Liturgy, the Mass.

WAYS OF PARTICIPATING IN THE PASCHAL MYSTERY

Through participation in the Eucharist, we also participate in the Paschal Mystery of Christ, that is, in his dying and rising, which is made present for us in the Eucharistic sacrifice. This participation in the Paschal Mystery of Christ reaches its consummation when we receive his Body and Blood in Holy Communion. Christ's victory and triumph over death is then made present in the lives of those who participate in the Eucharist.

Holy Communion increases our union with Christ. "Whoever eats my flesh and drinks my blood remains in me and I in him" (Jn 6:56). Communion with the Body of Christ preserves, increases, and renews the life of grace received at Baptism.

Holy Communion separates us from sin. We receive the Body of Christ "given up for us" to save us from sin. We receive the Blood of Christ "shed for many for the forgiveness of sins." Our love of God is intensified and therefore our disordered attachments are weakened and even broken. Divine love wipes away venial sins.

Holy Communion offers us strength, called grace, to preserve us from mortal sin. By deepening our friendship with Christ, this Sacrament makes it more difficult for us to break our union with him by mortal sin.

Holy Communion expands the life of the Church. The Church as a communion is bound ever more closely together through the celebration of the Eucharist. As an ancient axiom states, the Church makes the Eucharist, and the Eucharist makes the Church. In receiving Communion, we are more fully united to the Church.

Holy Communion commits us to care for the poor. St. Paul reminded the Corinthians that in sharing the Body of Christ in the Eucharist, they were also called to care for the poorer members of the community (cf. 1 Cor 11:17-34).

Participation in the celebration of the Eucharistic sacrifice is a source and means of grace even apart from the actual reception of Holy Communion. It has also been long understood that when circumstances prevent one from receiving Holy Communion during Mass, it is possible to make a spiritual communion that is also a source of grace. Spiritual communion means uniting one's self in prayer with Christ's sacrifice and worshiping him present in his Body and Blood.

THE EUCHARIST TRANSFORMS THE RECIPIENT

To participate actively in the Mass, we need to resist a tendency to passivity when gathered in an audience-like setting. At Mass, we are an assembly of believers called to be a community joined in the praise and worship of God. We do this in the singing of hymns, psalms, recitation of prayers and responses, especially in our "Yes" to God in the Great Amen. Active participation also requires an interior attention and a profound inner offering, as St. Paul urges in Romans 12:1: "I urge you therefore, brothers, by the mercies of God to offer your bodies as a living sacrifice, holy and pleasing to God, your spiritual worship."

When the assembly of the faithful, from the hands of the priest, offers the sacrifice of Christ to the Father, the members of the assembly are called to offer their bodies as a living sacrifice, holy and pleasing to God. In using the word *body*, St. Paul does not mean simply our flesh

FROM THE CATECHISM

1. What happens at the consecration in the Mass?

By the consecration, the transubstantiation of the bread and wine into the Body and Blood of Christ is brought about. Under the consecrated species of bread and wine, Christ himself, living and glorious, is present in a true, real and substantial manner: His Body and Blood, with his soul and divinity. (CCC, no. 1413; Council of Trent: DS 1640, 1651)

2. What are the effects of Holy Communion?

Communion with the Body and Blood of Christ increases the communicant's union with the Lord, forgives his venial sins, and preserves him from grave sins. Since receiving this sacrament strengthens the bonds of charity between the communicant and Christ, it also reinforces the unity of the Church as the Mystical Body of Christ. (CCC, no. 1416)

3. Why is it valuable to visit the Blessed Sacrament?

Because Christ himself is present in the sacrament of the altar, he is to be honored with the worship of adoration. "To visit the Blessed Sacrament is . . . a proof of gratitude, an expression of love, and a duty of adoration toward Christ our Lord." (CCC, no. 1418; Pope Paul VI, *Mystery of Faith*, no. 66)

and bones, but rather our very selves. This, then, is a spiritual sacrifice. How can we do this?

In the Eucharistic Prayer, we hear that Jesus took the bread, blessed it, broke it, made it his Body, and gave it for our salvation. One way of identifying with this is to pray, "Lord, take me. Bless me. Break me. Make me a part of your saving, sacrificial gift for the world's bodily and spiritual needs." Having offered ourselves to the Father in union with Christ, we practice active participation in the Mass in its highest form.

This inner drama at each Mass contributes to the process of our spiritual transformation into Christ. It all takes time. When we receive Communion, we need to remember that we are not changing Christ into ourselves. Jesus is transforming us into himself. This requires a proper understanding of the Real Presence of Jesus under the appearance of bread and wine. It is not simply a symbol that merely points to Jesus. Nor is Christ's presence just a projection on our part in the sense that we make him present when we receive him. As Pope Benedict XVI told the young people gathered for the Twentieth World Youth Day:

> The Body and Blood of Christ are given to us so that we our-selves will be transformed in our turn. We are to become the Body of Christ, his own Flesh and Blood.
>
> We all eat the one bread, and this means that we ourselves become one. In this way, adoration, as we said earlier, becomes union. God no longer simply stands before us as the One who is totally Other. He is within us, and we are in him. His dynamic enters into us and then seeks to spread outwards to others until it fills the world, so that his love can truly become the dominant measure of the world. (Benedict XVI, Homily at Marienfeld, Twentieth World Youth Day [August 21, 2005])

The consecrated bread has become Christ's Body. The consecrated wine has become Christ's Blood. Jesus Christ is substantially present in a way that is entirely unique. This happens by the power of the Holy Spirit through the ministry of the priest's or bishop's acting in the person of Christ during the Eucharistic Prayer. At Mass, when we are offered the Host and hear the statement "The Body of Christ," we answer, "Amen," that is, "Yes, I believe."

Only Jesus can transform us into himself. Our inner receptivity is critical. To receive love, we need to be open to it. The sacrificial gift of self at every Mass is the best way to be continuously transformed into Christ. Then in Christ we become bread for the world's bodily and spiritual hungers.

FOR DISCUSSION

1. What has been your experience of Mass at various times in your life? What has helped you to become a more active participant in the celebration of the Eucharist?

2. Who are the people who have influenced your appreciation of the Eucharist? What do we mean when we speak of the Real Presence of Jesus? What can draw you to visit the Blessed Sacrament more frequently and spend time there in the adoration of Christ?

3. The *Catechism* reminds us that the Eucharist commits us to care for the poor (see CCC, no. 1397). How do you live this commitment during the week? How are you the "Body of Christ" at work, at home, at school?

DOCTRINAL STATEMENTS

- Jesus instituted the Eucharistic sacrifice, the banquet of divine life, at the Last Supper.

- We need to remember that the Eucharist is the summit and source of our Christian life. Why? Because in the Eucharist is found the entire treasure of the Church—Jesus Christ.

- The Eucharistic celebration begins with the Introductory Rites and the Liturgy of the Word, followed by the Liturgy of the Eucharist— the preparation of the gifts, the Eucharistic Prayer (the prayer of thanksgiving and praise, including the consecration of the bread and wine), and the reception of Holy Communion. The celebration concludes with the sending forth to serve the Lord.

- The Eucharist is the memorial of Christ's saving life, death, and Resurrection, made present for our salvation by the action of the liturgy.

- Christ, acting through the ministry of his priests, is both the priest offering the sacrifice and the victim being sacrificed.

- "Only validly ordained priests can preside at the Eucharist and consecrate the bread and wine so that they become the Body and Blood of the Lord" (CCC, no. 1411).

- The essential signs of the Eucharist for the Latin Church are unleavened wheat bread and grape wine.

- At Mass, the consecrated bread is Christ's Body. The consecrated wine is Christ's Blood. Jesus Christ, whole and entire, is fully present under each form of the Eucharist. He is substantially present in a way that is entirely unique. This happens by the power of the Holy Spirit through the ministry of the priest's acting in the person of Christ during the Eucharistic Prayer.

- "As sacrifice, the Eucharist is also offered in reparation for the sins of the living and the dead and to obtain spiritual and temporal benefits from God" (CCC, no. 1414).

- To receive Communion, one should be in the state of grace. A person conscious of mortal sin may not receive Communion until absolved from the sin in the Sacrament of Penance (see 1 Cor 11:27-29).

- A person who is conscious of grave sin but has no opportunity for sacramental confession may receive Communion for a serious reason; in such a case, the person must first make an act of perfect contrition and have the intention of confessing as soon as possible (cf. CIC, can. 916).

- The fruits of Holy Communion include a deeper union with Christ, a closer identity with all the faithful, a commitment to the poor, and a pledge of future glory.

- The faithful are urged to receive Communion at Mass. The Church obliges them to do so at least once a year during the Easter season.

- Once Communion has been distributed, the remaining hosts are placed in the tabernacle to provide Communion for the sick and *Viaticum* for the dying and also to provide opportunity for prayer and worship before Christ in his Real Presence.

MEDITATION

O Jesus, joy of loving hearts,
the fount of life and my true light,
We seek the peace your love imparts
and stand rejoicing in your sight.

We taste in you my living bread
and long to feast upon you still.
We drink of you my fountain head,
my thirsting soul to quench and fill.

For you my thirsting spirit yearns,
where'er our changing lot is cast;
Glad when your presence we discern,
blest when our faith can hold you fast.

O Jesus ever with us stay;
make all our moments calm and bright.
O chase the night of sin away;
shed o'er the world your holy light.

—Attributed to St. Bernard of Clairvaux,
Jesu Dulcedo Cordium
(*Jesus Joy of Loving Hearts*),
trans. Ray Palmer, *Worship Hymnal*, Third Edition, 605

PRAYER

Anima Christi

Soul of Christ, be my sanctification.
Body of Christ, be my salvation.
Blood of Christ, fill all my veins.
Water of Christ's side, wash out my stains.
Passion of Christ, my comfort be.
O good Jesu, listen to me.
In Thy wounds I fain would hide,
N'er to be parted from Thy side,
Guard me, should the foe assail me.
Call me when my life shall fail me.
Bid me come to Thee above,
With Thy saints to sing Thy love,
World without end. Amen.

Guidelines for the Reception of Communion

On November 14, 1996, the National Conference of Catholic Bishops (now the United States Conference of Catholic Bishops) approved the following guidelines on the reception of Communion. The guidelines seek to remind all those who may attend Catholic liturgies of the present discipline of the Church with regard to the sharing of Eucharistic communion.

For Catholics

As Catholics, we fully participate in the celebration of the Eucharist when we receive Holy Communion. We are encouraged to receive Communion devoutly and frequently. In order to be properly disposed to receive Communion, participants should be conscious of no grave sin and normally should have fasted for one hour. A person who is conscious of grave sin is not to receive the Body and Blood of the Lord without prior sacramental confession except for a grave reason where there is no opportunity for confession. In this case the person is to be mindful of the obligation to make an act of perfect contrition, including the intention of confessing as soon as possible (CIC, can. 916). A frequent reception of the Sacrament of Penance is encouraged for all.

For Our Fellow Christians

We welcome our fellow Christians to this celebration of the Eucharist as our brothers and sisters. We pray that our common baptism and the action of the Holy Spirit in this Eucharist will draw us closer to one another and begin to dispel the sad divisions which separate us. We pray that these will lessen and finally disappear, in keeping with Christ's prayer for us "that they all may be one" (Jn 17:21).

Because Catholics believe that the celebration of the Eucharist is a sign of the reality of the oneness of faith, life and worship, members of those churches with whom we are not yet fully united are ordinarily not admitted to Holy Communion. Eucharistic sharing in exceptional circumstances by other Christians requires permission according to the directives of the diocesan bishop and the provisions of canon law (CIC, can. 844

§4). Members of the Orthodox Churches, the Assyrian Church of the East, and the Polish National Catholic Church are urged to respect the discipline of their own Churches. According to Roman Catholic discipline, the Code of Canon Law does not object to the reception of communion by Christians of these Churches (CIC, can. 844 §3).

For Those Not Receiving Holy Communion
All who are not receiving Holy Communion are encouraged to express in their hearts a prayerful desire for unity with the Lord Jesus and with one another.

For Non-Christians
We also welcome to this celebration those who do not share our faith in Jesus Christ. While we cannot admit them to Holy Communion, we ask them to offer their prayers for the peace and unity of the human family.

All my other senses, cannot now perceive,
But my hearing, taught by faith, always will believe:
I accept whatever God the Son has said:
Those who hear the Word of God, by the truth are fed.

—St. Thomas Aquinas, *Adoro Te Devote*
(*God with Hidden Majesty*),
trans. Anthony G. Petti

18 SACRAMENT OF PENANCE AND RECONCILIATION: GOD IS RICH IN MERCY

IN THIS SACRAMENT OF HEALING WE ARE
RECONCILED TO GOD AND THE CHURCH
—CCC, NOS. 1420-1498

AUGUSTINE: THE SINNER WHO BECAME A SAINT

Very few men have had such an impact on Christianity as St. Augustine. He was born in AD 354 in North Africa, at that time a strong and dynamic Christian region. His father was a prominent pagan, but his mother, Monica, was a devout Christian. She intended that Augustine be baptized, but in his adolescence he distanced himself from the Church and did not want to be baptized. He studied Latin literature and became a follower of an esoteric philosophy known as Manichaeism.

He had a mistress with whom he lived for fifteen years. She bore him a son, but he later broke off with her while living in Milan, where they had gone because he had been given a teaching position there. He found himself gradually more attracted to Christianity as he listened to the preaching of St. Ambrose, the bishop of Milan. But he resisted conversion, though his mother prayed persistently for him.

In a book entitled *The Confessions*, written in his later years as a spiritual and theological reflection on his life, Augustine describes the final steps to his conversion. He had felt the tension between attachment to his sinful ways and attraction to Christ and the Gospel. One day in the year 386, he went crying into the garden of the house where he was staying with friends. He was weeping because of his inability to make a decision for conversion. But then he heard the voice of a child from a neighboring house singing the refrain, "Take it and read, take it and read." He picked up the Letters of St. Paul and read the first passage his eyes fell upon: "not in orgies and drunkenness, not in promiscuity and licentiousness, not in rivalry and jealousy. But put on the Lord Jesus Christ, and make no provision for the desires of the flesh" (Rom 13:13-14). Augustine recognized the grace of God in this reading and embraced conversion.

He was baptized by St. Ambrose in 387 and returned to North Africa in 388. In 391, while visiting the town of Hippo, he was urged by the Christian population to become a priest; he accepted, though reluctantly. In 395 he became bishop of Hippo. As a Christian, priest, and bishop, he wrote numerous books to explain and defend Christian doctrine. His homilies and sermons were written down, and they witness to the depth and power of his preaching. He died in 430.

Augustine knew the damaging effects of sin. In *The Confessions*, he admits his own sinfulness even as a boy: "Many and many a time I lied to my tutor, my masters, and my parents, because I wanted to play games or watch some futile show or was impatient to imitate what I saw on the stage." But he also experienced the greater power of grace, of God's enabling us to overcome sin and accept the Gospel of his Son. St. Augustine knew God's mercy in the forgiveness of sins gained for us by Jesus Christ. Today Catholics encounter this same mercy and forgiveness in the Sacrament of Penance.

THE FORGIVENESS OF SINS

The Lord Jesus Christ, physician of our souls and our bodies . . . has willed that his Church continue, in the power of the Holy Spirit, his work of healing and salvation.

—CCC, no. 1421

Because of human weakness, the new life in Christ, which we receive in the Sacraments of Initiation, is often threatened by sin. Moreover, we all face sickness and death. God constantly reaches out to us to reconcile ourselves to him. Through the gifts of the Church, Jesus, our divine physician, has given us the Sacraments of Healing—Penance and Reconciliation and Anointing of the Sick—for the forgiveness of sins and the ministry to the sick and the dying.

Sins committed after Baptism are forgiven in the Sacrament of Penance and Reconciliation, also called the Sacrament of Forgiveness, Confession, and Conversion. We will refer to the Sacrament both as Penance and as Reconciliation, using the terms interchangeably.

Divine mercy and conversion from sin are constant themes in Scripture. God's mercy makes possible the repentance of the sinner and the forgiveness of sin. Time and again in the Old Testament, the sins of the people are met with God's outreach of mercy and the invitation to be healed and return to a covenant relationship. Even when the beloved King David lied, committed adultery, and caused the death of an innocent man, he was not beyond God's mercy, to which he had a humble recourse. Psalm 51 gives us words to express the kind of contrition and to trust in God's forgiveness that David felt after committing these sins.

JESUS FORGAVE SINS

The Gospels provide numerous examples of Christ's mission to forgive sins. When a paralytic was lowered through the roof of a house and placed at his feet, Christ first forgave the man's sins and then cured his affliction (cf. Lk 5:17-26). When a sinful woman knelt at his feet in the house of Simon the Pharisee, Jesus forgave her sins because she had "loved much," unlike the Pharisee, who had little insight into his own sinfulness (cf. Lk 7:36-50). Christ's parable of the prodigal son illustrates the sublime meaning of his earthly ministry, which is to forgive sins, reconcile people to God, and lead us to true happiness (cf. Lk 15:11-32).

Jesus died on the Cross and rose from the dead to reconcile sinful people with God through the forgiveness of sins and the gift of new life with the Triune God. Even on the Cross, he forgave those who were killing him and had mercy on the repentant thief.

Only God can forgive our sins. But Jesus willed that the Church should be his instrument of forgiveness on earth. On Easter night the Risen Christ imparted to his Apostles his own power to forgive sins. He breathed on them, imparting the promised Holy Spirit, and said, "Peace be with you." Jesus was actually filling them with peace that is rooted in friendship with God. But he did more. He shared with them his own merciful mission. He breathed on them a second time and said,

> As the Father has sent me, so I send you. . . . Receive the holy Spirit. Whose sins you forgive are forgiven them, and whose sins you retain are retained. (Jn 20:21-23)

That night Jesus gave the Church the ministry of the forgiveness of sins through the Apostles (cf. CCC, no. 1461). By the Sacrament of Holy Orders, bishops and priests continue this ministry to forgive sins "in the name of the Father, and of the Son, and of the Holy Spirit." In this Sacrament, the priest acts in the person of Christ, the Head of the Church, to reconcile the sinner to both God and the Church. "When he celebrates the Sacrament of Penance, the priest is fulfilling the ministry of the Good Shepherd who seeks the lost sheep. . . . The priest is the sign and instrument of God's merciful love for the sinner" (CCC, no. 1465).

The Sacrament of Penance involves a conversion of our hearts to God, a confession of sins to a priest, the forgiveness of our sins, a penance to make some amends for sin, and reconciliation with God and the Church. For those who commit mortal sin after Baptism, this Sacrament is necessary for being reconciled to God and the Church.

CONVERSION, CONFESSION, FORGIVENESS

The Sacrament of Penance must be seen within the context of conversion from sin and a turn to God. Peter wept bitterly over his triple denial of Christ but received the grace of conversion and expressed it with a three-fold confession of love for Jesus (cf. Lk 22:54-62; Jn 21:15-19). Paul was converted from persecuting Christians to becoming one of the greatest disciples of Christ who ever lived (cf. Acts 9:1-31). These moments of conversion were only the beginning of their lifelong commitment to living in fidelity to the Gospel of Jesus Christ.

Sin harms our relationship with God and damages our communion with the Church. Conversion of heart is the beginning of our journey back to God. Liturgically this happens in the Sacrament of Penance. In the history of the Church, this Sacrament has been celebrated in different ways. Beneath the changes, there have always been two essentials: the acts of the penitent and the acts of Christ through the ministry of the Church. Both go hand in hand. Conversion must involve a change of heart as well as a change of actions. Neither is possible without God's grace.

THE LITURGY OF THE SACRAMENT OF PENANCE

In the Liturgy of Penance, the elements are ordinarily these: a greeting and blessing from the priest, a reading from Scripture, the confession of sins, the giving and accepting of a penance, an act of contrition, the priest's absolution, a proclamation of praise of God, and a dismissal. We offer here a description of the acts of the penitent and that of the priest.

Contrition

In order to be forgiven, we need to have sorrow for our sins. This means turning away from evil and turning to God. It includes the determination to avoid such sins in the future. Such sins may either be mortal or venial.

> Sins are rightly evaluated according to their gravity. The distinction between mortal and venial sin, already evident in Scripture (cf. 1 Jn 5:16-17), became part of the tradition of the Church. It is corroborated by human experience. (CCC, no. 1854)

> Mortal sin destroys charity in the heart of man by a grave violation of God's law; it turns man away from God, who is his ultimate end and beatitude, by preferring an inferior good to him. Venial sin allows charity to subsist, even though it offends and wounds it. (CCC, no. 1855)

Contrition that arises from the love of God above all else is called "perfect contrition." This loving sorrow remits venial sins and even mortal sins so long as we resolve to confess them as soon as possible. When other motives, such as the ugliness of sin or fear of damnation, bring us to confession, this is called "imperfect contrition," which is sufficient for forgiveness in the Sacrament. The Holy Spirit moves us in either case and initiates the conversion.

Confession

Confession liberates us from sins that trouble our hearts and makes it possible to be reconciled to God and others. We are asked to look into our souls and, with an honest and unblinking gaze, identify our sins. This opens our minds and hearts to God, moves us toward communion with the Church, and offers us a new future.

In confession, by naming our sins before the priest, who represents Christ, we face our failings more honestly and accept responsibility for our sins. It is also in confession that a priest and penitent can work together to find the direction needed for the penitent to grow spiritually and to avoid sin in the future (cf. CCC, nos. 1455, 1456).

When we have examined our consciences and have taken responsibility for our sins, we then confess them to the priest. We must confess all our mortal sins in kind and number. The Church strongly recommends confessing venial sins, though this is not strictly necessary. In the Latin Church, children must go to confession before making their First Communion.

There are three rites of Reconciliation: the rite for the Reconciliation of individual penitents; the rite for the Reconciliation of several penitents with individual confession and absolution; and the rite of Reconciliation of penitents with general confession and absolution.

In the first rite, which is the most familiar, the penitent goes to a reconciliation room or a traditional confessional and either confesses face to face with the priest or kneels behind a screen to confess the sins. In the second rite, which usually happens in Advent or Lent, there is a communal service during which the Scripture is read and a homily is given. This is followed by individual confession and individual absolution.

General confession and absolution is the third rite and is used only in extraordinary situations, danger of death, or an insufficient number of confessors so that "penitents would be deprived of sacramental grace

WHAT IS THIS SACRAMENT CALLED?

It is called the Sacrament of Conversion because it makes sacramentally present Jesus' call to conversion, the first step in returning to the Father from whom one has strayed by sin. It is called the Sacrament of Penance, since it consecrates the Christian sinner's personal and ecclesial steps of conversion, penance, and satisfaction. It is called the Sacrament of Confession since the disclosure or confession of sins is an essential element of this Sacrament. In a profound sense, it is also a "confession"—acknowledgment and praise—of the holiness of God and of his mercy toward sinful man. It is called the Sacrament of Forgiveness, since by the priest's sacramental absolution, God grants the penitent "pardon and peace." It is called the Sacrament of Reconciliation because it imparts to the sinner the love of God who reconciles: "Be reconciled to God" (2 Cor 5:20). He who lives by God's merciful love is ready to respond to the Lord's call: "Go, first be reconciled to your brother." (CCC, nos. 1423-1424, citing Mt 5:24)

or holy communion for a long period of time through no fault of their own" (cf. CIC, can. 961). General absolution involves one priest's giving absolution to a group of people, who do not make individual confessions to a priest. Those penitents guilty of serious or grave sin are expected to make an individual confession as soon as possible but certainly within a year of receiving general absolution. Judgment as to whether the conditions for general absolution are present is a matter not for the confessor, but for the diocesan bishop to determine under the guidance of norms established by the Holy See.

Absolution from the Priest

After we confess our sins to the priest, we are given some encouragement from the priest for our moral and spiritual growth. The priest then gives us a penance and asks us to say an Act of Contrition. Then the priest grants absolution, that is, he sets us free from our sins, using the power that Christ entrusted to the Church and by which he pardons the sins of the penitent (cf. CCC, no. 1424). In the Latin Church, the priest, representing Christ and bringing us his forgiveness, absolves us from our sins with these words:

> God the Father of mercies, through the death and resurrection of his Son, has reconciled the world to himself, and sent the Holy Spirit among us for the forgiveness of sins; through the ministry of the Church may God give you pardon and peace, and I absolve you from your sins in the name of the Father and of the Son and of the Holy Spirit.

Satisfaction

"Absolution takes away sin, but does not remedy all the disorders sin has caused" (CCC, no. 1459). It is obvious that we need to repair certain damages that our sins have caused, such as restoring the reputation of someone we have injured, returning money that we have stolen, or rectifying an injustice. Sin also weakens the relationship we have with God and others. Our inner life is harmed by sin and needs restoration.

This is the reason for acts of penance and satisfaction for sins. The penance given by the priest helps us to begin making satisfaction for our sins. Just as when we get physically out of shape, we need to take up some exercise, so also when the soul is morally out of shape, there is the challenge to adopt spiritual exercises that will restore it. Obviously, this is always done in cooperation with God's graces, which are essential for the healing.

> Absolution takes away sin, but it does not remedy all the disorders that sin has caused. Raised up from sin, the sinner must still recover his full spiritual health by doing something more to make amends for sin: he must "make satisfaction for" or "expiate" his sins. This satisfaction is called "penance." (CCC, no. 1459)

FROM THE CATECHISM

1. How can we prepare for the Sacrament of Penance?
The reception of this sacrament ought to be prepared for by an examination of conscience made in the light of the Word of God. The passages best suited to this can be found in the Ten Commandments, the moral catechesis of the Gospels and the apostolic Letters, such as the Sermon on the Mount and apostolic teaching. (CCC, no. 1454)

2. What is the seal of Confession?
The Church declares that every priest who hears confessions is bound under very severe penalties to keep absolute secrecy regarding the sins that his penitents have confessed to him. He can make no use of knowledge that confession gives him about penitents' lives. This secret, which admits of no exceptions, is called the "sacramental seal," because what the penitent has made known to the priest remains "sealed" by the sacrament. (CCC, no. 1467)

3. How does reception of the Sacrament of Reconciliation anticipate a person's judgment before God?
In this sacrament, the sinner, placing himself before the merciful judgment of God, anticipates in a certain way the judgment to which he will be subjected at the end of his earthly life. For it is now, in this life, that we are offered the choice between life and death, and it is only by the road of conversion that we can enter the Kingdom, from which one is excluded by grave sin. In converting to Christ through penance and faith, the sinner passes from death to life and "does not come into judgment." (CCC, no. 1470, citing Jn 5:24)

EFFECTS OF THE SACRAMENT

The Sacrament of Penance reconciles us with God. "The whole power of the sacrament of Penance consists in restoring us to God's grace and joining us with him in an intimate friendship" (CCC, no. 1468).

This Sacrament also reconciles us with the Church. Sin should never be understood as a private or personal matter, because it harms our relationship with others and may even break our loving communion with the Church. The Sacrament of Penance repairs this break and has a renewing effect on the vitality of the Church itself.

In this Sacrament, the penitent receives the merciful judgment of God and is engaged on the journey of conversion that leads to future life with God. The Church also recommends that a person go regularly to confession, even if only for venial sins. This is because "the regular confession of our venial sins helps us form our consciences, fight against evil tendencies, let ourselves be healed by Christ and progress in the life of the Spirit" (CCC, no. 1458).

RECOGNIZE SIN—PRAISE GOD'S MERCY

The Sacrament of Penance is an experience of the gift of God's boundless mercy. Not only does it free us from our sins but it also challenges us to have the same kind of compassion and forgiveness for those who sin against us. We are liberated to be forgivers. We obtain new insight into the words of the Prayer of St. Francis: "It is in pardoning that we are pardoned."

By the help of God's grace, our call to holiness will be clearer when we recover an awareness of the reality of sin and evil in the world and in our own souls. Scripture will be enormously helpful in this since it reveals sin and evil clearly and fearlessly. Scriptural realism does not hesitate to pronounce judgment on the good and evil that affects our lives. The New Testament is filled with calls to conversion and repentance, which need to be heard in our culture today.

If we say, "We are without sin," we deceive ourselves, and the truth is not in us. If we acknowledge our sins, he is faithful and just and will forgive our sins and cleanse us from every wrong-doing. (1 Jn 1:8-9)

In our churches, we behold Jesus nailed to the Cross, an image that reminds us of his painful sacrifice to bring about the forgiveness of all our sins and guilt. If there were no sin, Jesus would not have suffered for our redemption. Each time we see the crucifix, we can reflect on the infinite mercy of God, who saves us through the reconciling act of Jesus.

Despite society's efforts to downplay the reality of sin, there is an instinctive recognition of its existence. Children generally know, even when not told, when they have done something morally wrong. Adults readily admit the evil of terrorism, unjust war, lies, unfair treatment of people, and similar matters. Society as a whole must also learn to admit the evil of abortion, physician-assisted suicide, and obtaining stem cells from embryos, which results in the death of embryonic human life. Denying evil corrupts us spiritually and psychologically. Rationalizing our own evil is even more destructive.

Jesus laid the foundation for the Sacrament of Penance during his ministry and confirmed it after his Resurrection. When Peter asked the number of times a person should forgive, Jesus told him that there should be no limit to forgiving. Jesus forgave Peter his triple denial, showed mercy to the woman taken in adultery, forgave the thief on the cross, and continually witnessed the mercy of God.

Jesus entrusted the ministry of reconciliation to the Church. The Sacrament of Penance is God's gift to us so that any sin committed after Baptism can be forgiven. In confession we have the opportunity to repent and recover the grace of friendship with God. It is a holy moment in which we place ourselves in his presence and honestly acknowledge our sins, especially mortal sins. With absolution, we are reconciled to God and the Church. The Sacrament helps us stay close to the truth that we cannot live without God. "In him we live and move and have our being" (Acts 17:28). While all the Sacraments bring us an experience of the mercy that comes from Christ's dying and rising, it is the Sacrament of Reconciliation that is the unique Sacrament of mercy.

INDULGENCES

Every sin has consequences. It disrupts our communion with God and the Church, weakens our ability to resist temptation, and hurts others. The necessity of healing these consequences, once the sin itself has been forgiven, is called temporal punishment. Prayer, fasting, almsgiving, and other works of charity can take away entirely or diminish this temporal punishment. Because of the fullness of redemption obtained for us by Christ, the Church attaches to certain prayers and actions an *indulgence* or pardon, that is, the full or partial remission of temporal punishment due to sin. Christ, acting through the Church, brings about the healing of the consequences of sin when an individual uses such a prayer or engages in such an action.

FOR DISCUSSION

1. What is your attitude to confession today? How would you explain the Sacrament of Reconciliation to people of other faiths?
2. How can Scripture help you discern the reality of sin in the world? Why do we confess our sins to a priest? Why is it necessary to be reconciled to the Church as well as to God?
3. Why do you think that people need to have the burden of sin and guilt lifted from their hearts? Why is it essential to understand the mission of Jesus Christ as the Savior? How can you commit yourself to a lifelong process of moral and spiritual conversion?

DOCTRINAL STATEMENTS

- On Easter night Jesus appeared to the Apostles, greeted them with peace, and breathed on them, saying, "Receive the holy Spirit. Whose sins you forgive are forgiven, and whose sins you retain are retained" (Jn 20:22-23).
- "The Creed links 'the forgiveness of sins' with its profession of faith in the Holy Spirit, for the risen Christ entrusted to the apostles the

power to forgive sins when he gave them the Holy Spirit" (CCC, no. 984).

- Sins committed before Baptism are forgiven by Baptism. Sins committed after Baptism are forgiven in the Sacrament of Penance and Reconciliation, also called the Sacrament of Forgiveness, Confession, and Conversion.
- Sin wounds our relationship with God and others and our human dignity. Faith reveals to us the destructive force of sin in our lives and the world.
- The path back to God after sin is a process of conversion initiated by his grace. The return to God includes sorrow for sin and the resolve to sin no more.
- In the Sacrament of Penance and Reconciliation, the acts of the penitent are contrition, confession, and satisfaction. The act of the priest is absolution for the sins of the penitent.
- Perfect contrition arises from love for God; imperfect contrition results from other motives.
- The penitent, after an examination of conscience, needs to confess all mortal sins. While it is not necessary to confess venial sins, the Church strongly recommends this practice.
- The priest proposes a penance to the penitent to repair the harm due to sin and to restore the penitent's commitment to be a disciple of Christ.
- Individual confession of grave sins according to kind and number is the only ordinary way of receiving absolution and reconciliation with God and the Church.
- The effects of the Sacrament of Penance and Reconciliation include reconciliation with God and the Church, peace of conscience and spiritual consolation, the remission of eternal punishment due to mortal sin as well as some degree of temporal punishments, and a greater power to face spiritual challenges (cf. CCC, no. 1496).
- "Through indulgences the faithful can obtain the remission of temporal punishment resulting from sin, for themselves and also for the souls in Purgatory" (CCC, no. 1498).

MEDITATION

A Paraphrasing of the Parable of the Prodigal Son
(Also Known as the Parable of the Forgiving Father:
Lk 15:11-22)

A man had two sons. The younger son said to his father, "Father, give me my inheritance now." The father agreed, giving his son the inheritance that was due to him. Upon receiving it, the son traveled to a foreign country, where he wasted his money on sinful pleasures. Totally broke, he found himself in a land facing its own financial woes because of a famine. A swineherd gave him a job taking care of the pigs. So small were his wages that he could not buy enough food to feed himself. He yearned to eat the food given to the pigs but was not allowed to.

Hitting rock bottom, he came to his senses, realizing that his father's workers had plenty to eat while he was starving. He decided to go home, apologize to his father and to God for his sins, declare that he was unworthy to be called his father's son, and ask for a job on the estate.

Meanwhile, the father sorely missed his young son. Each day he stood on a hill, peering into the distance, aching to see his son and hoping he would come home. Then one day he saw his son coming toward him. He ran to his son, hugged and kissed him, and praised God for his son's return. With tears of joy and much embracing, the father smothered the repentant words of his son.

The father jubilantly called out to his servants to clothe his son in the best robe and to put a ring on his finger and sandals on his feet. He ordered the fattened calf to be slain and roasted for a feast. Why? "Because this son of mine was dead and has come to life again; he was lost and has been found" (Lk 15:24).

The older son heard the excitement and asked what it was about. When he heard the reason, he was furious. Pouting, he refused even to enter the house. The father came out and pleaded with him to come inside and celebrate the homecoming of his younger brother. The older son argued that his younger brother did not deserve this party. He had wasted his inheritance. Why should he who had been the good and faithful son—and never had a party like this given in his honor—be humiliated by experiencing the festive meal, joyous music, and enthusiastic welcome for such a good-for-nothing brother?

The father replied that the older son had absolute security and the utmost love and regard of his father. Everything the father owned belonged to him. "My son, be forgiving and generous of heart. Your brother was dead and is now alive. We must celebrate. Rejoice in his return to us and this home of love."

Usually this story is named after the prodigal son who wasted his inheritance. But it could just as well be entitled "The Forgiving Father," as he has a heart of sheer generosity and spends his love lavishly on forgiving and welcoming his son back home. In scriptural terms, the son represents a sinner in need of forgiveness who is moved to repent, confess his sin, and humble himself before God.

The father in the story represents God's immense compassion, rich in mercy and ever willing to search out sinners and offer them the forgiveness that brings them home. The story encourages us to trust in God the Father's love and forgiveness, which we receive in the Sacrament of Reconciliation.

PRAYER

An Act of Contrition (a traditional version)
> O my God, I am heartily sorry for having offended thee
> and I detest all my sins, because of thy just punishments,
> but most of all because they offend thee, my God,
> who are all good and worthy of all my love.
> I firmly resolve, with the help of thy grace,
> to sin no more and to avoid the near occasions of sin. Amen.

Prayer of the Penitent (Rite of Penance)
> Lord Jesus, Son of God
> Have mercy on me, a sinner.

A clean heart create for me, God.

—Ps 51:12

19 ANOINTING THE SICK AND THE DYING

THE SACRAMENT OF ANOINTING OF THE SICK IS THE
SECOND OF THE SACRAMENTS OF HEALING
—CCC, NOS. 1499-1532

I CAN SAY IN ALL SINCERITY
THAT I AM AT PEACE

In 1996, Cardinal Joseph Bernardin, Archbishop of Chicago, was told by his doctors that he had pancreatic cancer and did not have long to live. He did in fact die in November of that year. He was born in South Carolina in 1928, the son of Italian immigrants. His father was a stonecutter; his mother, a seamstress. At age thirty-eight, he became the youngest bishop in the United States. He served as president of the National Conference of Catholic Bishops from 1974 to 1977 and was elevated by Pope John Paul II to the College of Cardinals in 1983. He is remembered for a significant number of achievements, but the manner in which he faced his forthcoming death remains one of his most memorable gifts to all people.

At an earlier stage of his illness while he was undergoing treatments, Cardinal Bernardin reached out to other patients, especially those who were terminally ill. He met many of them at the hospital waiting room, took down their names and addresses and phone numbers, and stayed in touch with them by phone and mail. He offered them his love, his prayers, and his encouragement and in some instances was able to give them the Sacrament of Anointing of the Sick.

He called death "a friend": "While I know that humanly speaking I will have to deal with difficult moments, and there will be tears, I can say in all sincerity, that I am at peace. I consider this as God's special gift to me at this particular moment in my life."

In his last book, *The Gift of Peace*, he wrote of embracing suffering and finding new life. In a general way, he constructed the book around the Stations of the Cross, testifying that our search for peace on our life's journey is nothing less than embracing the Christ of Calvary. "In an age like our own, marked in part by the quest for instant relief from suffering, it takes special courage to stand on Calvary. Uniting our suffering with that of Jesus, we receive strength and courage, a new lease on life, and undaunted hope for the future."

In his last week on earth, he wrote a letter to the Supreme Court of the United States. He begged the justices not to approve of physician-assisted suicide. "As one who is dying, I have come to appreciate in a special way the gift of life," he wrote. He added that to approve a new right to assisted suicide would endanger America and send the false signal that a less than "perfect" life was not worth living.

A few weeks before he died, eight hundred archdiocesan and religious priests joined him for a prayer service at Holy Name Cathedral in Chicago. He concluded his homily with these words, which he had originally spoken to the priests on the evening before his installation as Archbishop of Chicago in 1982:

> As our lives and ministries are mingled together through the breaking of the Bread and the blessing of the Cup, I hope that long before my name falls from the Eucharistic prayer in the silence of death you will know well who I am. You will know because we will work and play together, fast and pray together, mourn and rejoice together, despair and hope together, dispute and be reconciled together. You will know me as a friend, fellow priest and bishop. You will also know that I love you. For I am Joseph, your brother! (Cardinal Joseph Bernardin, *Gift of Peace* (Chicago: Loyola Press, 1997), 141-142)

The Sacrament of the Anointing of the Sick brings the compassionate presence of Christ into the midst of the sufferings of those who are ill. Cardinal Bernardin was both a minister of that Sacrament and a recipient during his own illness.

CHRIST'S COMPASSION FOR THE SICK

Christ's compassion toward the sick and his healings of almost every kind of infirmity are a resplendent sign that "God has visited his people."

—CCC, no. 1503, citing Lk 7:16

Jesus came to heal the whole person, body and soul. Mark's Gospel, chapter 2:1-12, relates the following event that illustrates this teaching. Jesus was in a house in Capernaum teaching an overflow crowd. The house was probably a stone dwelling whose walls were coated with plaster. The rooms surrounded an inner courtyard. A roof of reeds and sticks packed with thick clay would have kept out the rain. Opening a hole in the roof would have been relatively easy. Since they could not enter by the door because of the crowd, four men, carrying a paralytic, climbed the stairway that led to the roof. They opened a hole in it and lowered their friend into the area where Jesus was preaching.

Jesus said to the paralyzed man, "Your sins are forgiven" (Mk 2:5). Scripture makes no comment on the man's reaction. But into that spiritual moment a discordant note emerged. Some religious scholars in the group complained inwardly that Jesus was blasphemous because, according to them, only God could forgive sins. Jesus, knowing their thoughts, challenged them: "Which is easier to say to the paralytic, 'Your sins are forgiven,' or to say, 'Rise, pick up your mat and walk'? But that you may know that the Son of Man has authority to forgive sins on earth"—he said to the paralytic, "I say to you, rise, pick up your mat, and go home" (Mk 2:9-11). The man rose and went home. The people glorified God for Christ's healing of soul and body.

The Gospels narrate many other occasions when Jesus healed the sick. While Jesus sometimes simply spoke some words to accomplish a healing, he often touched the afflicted person to bring about the cure. In the Church's Sacrament of the Anointing of the Sick, through the ministry of the priest, it is Jesus who touches the sick to heal them from sin—and sometimes even from physical ailment. His cures were signs of the arrival of the Kingdom of God. The core message of his healings tells us of his plan to conquer sin and death by his dying and rising.

On the Cross, Jesus bore the full weight of evil and removed its power over us. He provided a new meaning for suffering by giving it redemptive power. By his grace we are able to unite our pain to his redemptive passion. St. Paul witnessed this when he wrote, "I rejoice in my sufferings for your sake, and in my flesh I complete what is lacking in the afflictions of Christ on behalf of his body, that is, the church" (Col 1:24).

THE CHURCH CONTINUES CHRIST'S MINISTRY OF HEALING

The Church carries forward Christ's healing ministry in a variety of approaches. Catholic families in countless ways care for family members who are ill. There are numerous inspiring stories of an aging spouse who personally ministers to an ailing spouse in cases of Alzheimer's and other illnesses. Caregivers find that faith and prayer mean a great deal to them in these situations.

A multitude of religious orders and congregations have established Catholic hospitals to take care of the physical and spiritual needs of the sick. Church-sponsored hospice care is another form of this ministry of healing. Besides the doctors, nurses, and chaplains, there are occasional instances of individuals with the charism (gift) of healing. "The Holy Spirit gives to some a special charism of healing, so as to make manifest the power of grace of the risen Lord" (CCC, no. 1508).

Millions of believers journey to shrines like the one at Lourdes, often in search of physical cures but always to experience a deepening of faith. The Church requires healing miracles as part of the canonization process, the procedure for declaring the sainthood of a given person.

Above all, the Church continues Christ's healing ministry in the Sacrament of Anointing of the Sick. St. James describes its celebration in apostolic times: "Is anyone among you sick? He should summon the presbyters [priests] of the church, and they should pray over him and anoint [him] with oil in the name of the Lord, and the prayer of faith will save the sick person, and the Lord will raise him up. If he has committed any sins, he will be forgiven" (Jas 5:14-15).

A SACRAMENT OF HEALING

The Anointing of the Sick "is not a sacrament for those only who are at the point of death. Hence as soon as anyone of the faithful begins to be in danger of death from sickness or old age, the fitting time to receive this sacrament has certainly already arrived."

—CCC, no. 1514, citing SC, no. 73

The Rite of Anointing tells us there is no need to wait until a person is at the point of death to receive the Sacrament. A careful judgment about the serious nature of the illness is sufficient. The Sacrament may be repeated if the sick person recovers after the anointing but becomes ill once again, or if, during the same illness, the person's condition becomes more serious. A person should be anointed before surgery when a dangerous illness is the reason for the intervention (cf. Rite of Anointing, Introduction, nos. 8-10).

Moreover, "old people may be anointed if they are in weak condition even though no dangerous illness is present. Sick children may be anointed if they have sufficient use of reason to be comforted by this sacrament. . . . [The faithful] should be encouraged to ask for the anointing, and, as soon as the time for the anointing comes, to receive it with faith and devotion, not misusing the sacrament by putting it off" (Rite of Anointing, nos. 11, 12, 13).

Only bishops and priests may be ministers of the Sacrament of the Anointing of the Sick. A penitential rite followed by the Liturgy of the Word opens the celebration. Scripture awakens the faith of the sick and family members and friends to pray to Christ for the strength of his Holy Spirit. The priest lays his hands on the head of the sick person. He then proceeds to anoint, with the blessed Oil of the Sick, the forehead and hands of the sick person (in the Roman Rite). He accompanies these acts with the words "Through this holy anointing may the Lord in his love and mercy help you with the grace of the Holy Spirit. May the Lord who frees you from sin save you and raise you up" (CCC, no. 1513).

For those who are about to depart from this life, the Church offers the person Penance, Anointing of the Sick, and the Eucharist as *Viaticum* (food for the journey) given at the end of life. These are "the sacraments that prepare for our heavenly homeland" (cf. CCC, no. 1525). These rites are highly valued by Catholics as powerful aids to a good death. Since Holy Communion is the effective sign of Christ's Paschal Mystery, it becomes for the recipient the opportunity to unite one's own suffering and dying to that of Christ with the hope of life eternal with him. The special words proper to *Viaticum* are added: "May the Lord Jesus protect you and lead you to everlasting life. Amen."

EFFECTS OF THE SACRAMENT

When the Sacrament of Anointing of the Sick is given, the hoped-for effect is that, if it be God's will, the person be physically healed of illness. But even if there is no physical healing, the primary effect of the Sacrament is a spiritual healing by which the sick person receives the Holy Spirit's gift of peace and courage to deal with the difficulties that accompany serious illness or the frailty of old age. The Holy Spirit renews our faith in God and helps us withstand the temptations of the Evil One to be discouraged and despairing in the face of suffering and death. Also, a sick person's sins are forgiven if he or she was not able to go to Confession prior to the celebration of the Sacrament of the Anointing of the Sick.

Another effect of this Sacrament is union with the Passion of Christ. By uniting ourselves more closely with the sufferings of Our Lord, we receive the grace of sharing in the saving work of Christ. In this way, our suffering, joined to the Cross of Christ, contributes to building up the People of God.

This Sacrament also prepares us for our final journey when we depart from this life. The Anointing of the Sick completes our identification with Jesus Christ that was begun at our Baptism. Its grace and power fortify us in our final struggles before we go to the Father's house.

FROM THE CATECHISM

1. When should we receive the Sacrament of the Anointing of the Sick?

The proper time for receiving this holy anointing has certainly arrived when the believer begins to be in danger of death because of illness or old age. Each time a Christian falls seriously ill, he may receive the Anointing of the Sick, and also when, after he has received it, the illness worsens. (CCC, nos. 1528, 1529)

2. Who are the ministers of the Sacrament of the Anointing of the Sick?

Only priests . . . and bishops can give the sacrament of the Anointing of the Sick, using oil blessed by the bishop, or if necessary by the celebrating presbyter [priest or celebrant] himself. (CCC, no. 1530)

3. What are the effects of the Sacrament of the Anointing of the Sick?

The special grace of the Sacrament of the Anointing of the Sick has as its effects:

—the uniting of the sick person to the passion of Christ, for his own good and that of the whole Church;
—[giving the sick person the strength], peace, and courage to endure in a Christian manner the sufferings of illness or old age;
—[imparting] the forgiveness of sins, if the sick person was not able to obtain it through the sacrament of Penance;
—[providing for] the restoration of health, if it is conducive to the salvation of his soul;
—[helping the sick person in] the preparation for passing over to eternal life. (CCC, no. 1532)

THE IMPORTANCE OF THE SACRAMENT FOR THE COMMUNITY

For some, there is nothing more frustrating than being sick. Sickness runs from annoying inconvenience—like a headache or a common cold—to grave, life-threatening cases involving major surgery or incurable disease. In each case, sickness reminds us of our limitations.

Our reaction to infirmity is to seek alleviation. With a perfect understanding of the human person, Christ has provided the Church from its beginning with a spiritual as well as a corporeal remedy for our illness. We are not just flesh and bone. We are spirit, mind, and body.

In a very real sense, the Sacrament of the Anointing of the Sick has a very important community dimension. In any illness, particularly one as we near the end of our lives, we should never have to stand alone. We should not have to face infirmity without the consolation of others. In the New Testament's Letter of St. James, the sick person is instructed to call for the presbyters (priests) of the Church for an anointing and prayers.

These presbyters represented the Christian community and its concern for the sick person. Such concern is further highlighted in the "prayer of faith" that St. James said will reclaim the one who is ill—the prayer arising from the community of faith, the Church, gathered around the sick person precisely to invoke the "name of the Lord."

The *Catechism of the Catholic Church* reminds us that "the Anointing of the Sick is a liturgical and communal celebration, whether it takes place in a family home, a hospital or church, for a single sick person or a whole group of sick persons" (CCC, no. 1517).

Increasingly today, there is an effort to bring people together for a communal celebration of this Sacrament, usually in a parish church. Since infirmity and old age constitute legitimate reasons for receiving this Sacrament, a parish can easily provide a setting for a number of parishioners to receive the Sacrament of the Anointing of the Sick regularly. It can serve the purpose of the Sacrament and, at the same time, build up the faith of the community itself.

FOR DISCUSSION

1. How would you describe your reaction to illnesses you have had? What do you expect of caregivers? How have you been moved to pray and seek the spiritual resources of the Church?
2. If you have been present at the Sacrament of Anointing of the Sick, what were your impressions? Why is it important to be aware of the proper time to call the priest?
3. From a faith perspective, what value does an experience of illness have for an individual and for the parish community to which he or she belongs? Why is it important to acknowledge and incorporate those who are sick and dying into the faith community?

DOCTRINAL STATEMENTS

- "Is anyone among you sick? He should summon the presbyters [priests] of the church, and they should pray over him and anoint [him] with oil in the name of the Lord, and the prayer of faith will save the sick person, and the Lord will raise him up. If he has committed any sins, he will be forgiven" (Jas 5:14-15).
- The Sacrament of the Anointing of the Sick is for those who are seriously ill or in danger of death or suffering the difficulties of old age. The Sacrament may be received each time the believer falls seriously ill or an illness worsens (cf. CCC, no. 1529).
- Only priests and bishops may administer the Sacrament of the Anointing of the Sick. This is because one effect of this Sacrament can be the forgiveness of sin. They use Oil of the Sick blessed by the bishop or, in necessity, an oil blessed by the priest.
- The rite of the Anointing of the Sick includes the anointing of the forehead and hands of the sick or other parts of the body accompanied by the liturgical prayer that asks for the grace of the Sacrament.
- The gifts of this Sacrament include uniting the sick person with Christ's Passion, for the person's well-being and that of the Church; strength to endure patiently the sufferings of illness and old age; the

forgiveness of sins if the person was unable to receive the Sacrament of Penance; and preparation for the passage to eternal life.

MEDITATION

Good Shepherd Psalm

The sick and the dying of every age have been consoled by the verses of the Shepherd Psalm (Ps 23). They are further inspired by Christ's words, "I am the good shepherd, and I know mine and mine known me. . . . I have come so that they may have life and have it more abundantly" (Jn 10:14, 10). It is not hard for them to see Jesus as the shepherd of the twenty-third Psalm. The Psalm expresses trust in the divine shepherd so needed when one is ill. "The LORD is my shepherd; / there is nothing I lack" (v. 1).

"In green pastures, you let me graze" (v. 2). A shepherd leads his sheep to the rough herbage, then to the smoother grass, and then to the sweet grass of the green pastures where they rest. Jesus abides with the sick throughout their rough moments and guides them to peaceful acceptance and an experience of a soul at rest.

"To safe waters you lead me" (v. 2). Sheep are nervous about drinking from running streams. The shepherd often constructs pools of still waters to ease their thirst. Illness breaks the running pace of life, but there is still the need of calming down. Jesus brings the patients an inner stillness that permits the believers to drink of the renewing fountains of his love.

"Even when I walk through a dark valley, / I fear no harm, for you are at my side; / your rod and staff give me courage" (v. 4). In search of better pastures, the shepherd sometimes leads the sheep through dangerous valleys. The sheep may fall into a hole. The shepherd uses the curved part at the top of his staff to gently pull the sheep to safety. Wild dogs and wolves may come to threaten the flock. The shepherd uses the pointed end of his staff to kill them or drive them away. Jesus knows that suffering people are in their own dark valley. Jesus is with them to remove their fears and awaken their hope. There are times that Jesus drives away life-threatening ills through his ministers in the Sacrament of the Anointing of the Sick.

"You set a table before me. / . . . You anoint my head with oil; my cup overflows" (v. 5). In some pastures there is so much rough herbage that the shepherd must harvest the edible grasses and place these on table-like stones from which the sheep may dine. Jesus himself is the Bread of Life who comes to his friends in pain. Communion for the sick is one of Christ's most consoling gifts. When the sheep have wounds caused by thorns, the shepherd anoints them with oil. When they have a fever, the shepherd bathes their heads in cool water. With holy oil Jesus anoints the sick.

"I will dwell in the house of the LORD / for years to come" (v. 6). The shepherd knows the sheep need him to guard their home. Jesus says he is the gate of the sheepfold (the enclosure where they live). In biblical times the shepherd served as the gate to the sheepfold. He was the living gate, guarding them with his body. To enter the community of Christ the beloved, both the sick and the healthy must enter through his body that will guard them. People in suffering and pain are disposed to the faith that sees these truths. Christ is their guardian.

PRAYER

Lord Jesus Christ, you chose to share our human nature,
to redeem all people, and to heal the sick.
Look with compassion upon your servants whom we have
    anointed in your name with this holy oil for the healing of
    their body and spirit.
Support them with your power, comfort them with
    your protection,
and give them the strength to fight against evil.
Since you have given them a share in your own passion,
help them to find hope in suffering,
for you are Lord for ever and ever. Amen.

—From *Pastoral Care of the Sick*

[I was] ill and you cared for me.

—Mt 25:36

20 HOLY ORDERS

THE SACRAMENT OF HOLY ORDERS IS AT THE SERVICE OF THE COMMUNION OF THE CHURCH
—CCC, NOS. 1533-1600

A SAINTLY BISHOP AND A HOLY PRIEST

In just eight years as bishop of Philadelphia (1852-1860), John Nepomucene Neumann increased the number of parochial schools from two to nearly one hundred. He oversaw the building of fifty new churches and founded a preparatory seminary. To staff the schools, he enlisted the aid of a number of religious congregations. He was the first bishop in the United States to encourage the Forty Hours Devotion to the Blessed Sacrament. He wrote two catechisms, a Bible history, and a number of pastoral letters.

He preached frequently, heard confessions, went on sick calls, and followed an extensive schedule for the Sacrament of Confirmation. He could speak eight languages and several Slavic dialects, a gift he used to bring Christ and the Church to the multi-ethnic members of his diocese. He even learned Gaelic so he could minister to the immigrants from western Ireland who were escaping the potato famine.

Born in Bohemia (now the Czech Republic) in 1811, John Neumann studied at the seminary at Budweis and the University of Prague. He graduated with honors from the university in 1835, at the age of twenty-four. While he was at the seminary, he acquired an interest in the United States. After his graduation, he emigrated to New York, where Bishop John Dubois accepted him for ordination to the priesthood in 1836. He was then sent to the missions of upper and western New York State.

Four years later, he entered the Redemptorist Order. In 1847 he became a citizen of the United States. He became the superior of the Redemptorist house in Pittsburgh, Pennsylvania, and then provincial of the congregation. In 1852 he was named the fourth bishop of Philadelphia. His entire life as a priest and as a bishop was dedicated to the service of others. While on his way to minister to the sick at a hospital, he collapsed from sheer exhaustion on the street and died in 1860. He was canonized a saint in 1977. His feast day is January 5.

When John Neumann was pastor of the Redemptorist parish of St. Philomena's in Pittsburgh, he had a young assistant named Francis Xavier Seelos. After serving at the parish for nine years, Fr. Seelos became the pastor of St. Alphonsus parish in Baltimore. Three years later, he became the rector of the Redemptorist seminary, which he relocated from Cumberland to Annapolis, Maryland. He instilled in the seminarians a sense of dedication to God and to God's people, as well as a love of the priesthood and the desire to live a holy and virtuous life.

In 1863 he joined the mission band, the order's prime apostolate. He conducted missions in countless parishes in over a dozen states. In 1867 he was transferred to New Orleans, Louisiana. Soon after his arrival, a yellow fever epidemic broke out. The sick calls came frequently. The funerals were many. Fr. Seelos was stricken with the virus and died from it. He was forty-eight. He was much loved as a confessor who brought spiritual healing to people. The Holy Spirit chose to work through Fr. Seelos to bring physical healings to a number of people. Such healings, attributed to his intercession, have been reported for many years since his death. Fr. Seelos was beatified (the last step before sainthood) on April 9, 2000.

St. John Neumann and Blessed Francis Seelos exemplified what the Sacrament of Holy Orders calls priests to do. They were outstanding shepherds of God's people, bringing them the Sacraments of salvation, inspiring them to conversion, and witnessing in their own lives the holiness that drew their people to follow Christ more deeply.

SACRAMENTS AT THE SERVICE OF COMMUNION

Holy Orders and Matrimony belong to the Sacraments at the Service of Communion. This means they are primarily directed toward the salvation of others. The recipients of these Sacraments grow in holiness through their service to others. We reflect on Holy Orders in this chapter and Matrimony in the next one.

LOOK AT CHRIST, OUR HIGH PRIEST

The eyes of all . . . looked intently at him.

—Lk 4:20

Luke's Gospel reports the appearance of Jesus at a synagogue service in Nazareth early in his public ministry, his first visit since the beginning of his public ministry. The synagogue was a simple, unadorned meeting space for prayer and religious instruction. After a prayer, Jesus was handed a scroll on which was written Chapter 61 of Isaiah the prophet. He read these words: "The Spirit of the Lord is upon me, / because he has anointed me / to bring glad tidings to the poor. / He has sent me to proclaim liberty to captives, / and recovery of sight to the blind, / to let the oppressed go free / and to proclaim a year acceptable to the Lord" (Lk 4:18-19).

He rolled up the scroll and sat down. There was a quiet pause as the eyes of all looked intently at Jesus. He said, "Today, this scripture passage is fulfilled in your hearing" (Lk 4:21). Jesus presented himself to them as filled with the Spirit, consecrated and anointed to bring the Good News to the poor. From the moment of Jesus' conception in the womb of Mary until his Resurrection, he was filled with the Holy Spirit. In biblical language, he was anointed by the Holy Spirit and thus established by God the Father as our high priest.

As Risen Lord, he remains our high priest. "He is always able to save those who approach God through him, since he lives forever to make intercession for them. It was fitting that we should have such a high priest, innocent, undefiled, separated from sinners" (Heb 7:25-26). While all the baptized share in Christ's priesthood, the ministerial priesthood shares this through the Sacrament of Holy Orders in a special way.

HOLY ORDERS: BISHOP, PRIEST, DEACON

The Church adopted the term *order* from its use in the Roman Empire, where it referred to a governing group. In the Sacrament of Holy Orders, there are three degrees or "orders": bishop, priest, and deacon. The rite of ordination is the sacramental act that makes this possible. Ordination "confers a gift of the Holy Spirit that permits the exercise of a 'sacred power' . . . which can come only from Christ himself through the Church" (CCC, no. 1538).

The first priest figure to appear in the Old Testament is Melchizedek, who offered a sacrifice of bread and wine on behalf of the patriarch Abraham (Gn 14:18-20). He symbolized the permanence of priesthood: "Like Melchizedek you are a priest forever" (Ps 110:4). God also chose Aaron and his sons to be priests (Ex 28:1ff.) and designated the tribe of Levi for liturgical service. They acted on behalf of the people and offered gifts and sacrifices for sins. They proclaimed God's Word and led people to communion with him through sacrifices and prayers.

But these priests were unable to provide the fullness of salvation or definitive sanctification for the people. Only the sacrifice of Jesus Christ could bring this about. The priesthood of Melchizedek, Aaron, and the Levites prefigured the priesthood of Christ, as is seen in consecration prayers for the ordination of bishops, priests, and deacons.

The priesthood of the Old Testament found its perfect fulfillment in the priesthood of Jesus Christ, who is the one mediator between God and us. Jesus' sacrifice of himself on the Cross was a priestly act of perfect self-offering accepted by the Father and culminating in his Resurrection from the dead so that, as Risen Lord and High Priest, he continues to offer salvation to all.

By Baptism, all the members of the Church share in Christ's holy priesthood. It is called "the common priesthood of the faithful" because the entire Church shares in it. To build up this priesthood, Christ gives to his Church the ordained ministries of bishops, priests, and deacons through the Sacrament of Holy Orders. Only the ordained bishop and priest may be ministers of Confirmation (or Chrismation), the Eucharist, the Sacrament of Penance and Reconciliation, and the Sacrament of the Anointing of the Sick. Only bishops may ordain deacons, priests, and other bishops. "The ministerial priesthood differs in essence from the common priesthood of the faithful because it confers a sacred power for the service of the faithful. The ordained ministers exercise their service for the People of God by teaching (*munus docendi*), divine worship (*munus liturgicum*) and pastoral governance (*munus regendi*)" (CCC, no. 1592). Deacons in the Latin Church can baptize and witness the Sacrament of Marriage, as do priests and bishops.

The ordained bishop and priest serve the Church in the person of Christ as head of the Body. "Through the ordained ministry, especially that of bishops and priests, the presence of Christ as head of the Church is made visible in the midst of the community of believers" (CCC, no. 1549). The Sacrament does not preserve the ordained from weakness and sin, but the Holy Spirit guarantees that the minister's sin does not impede the effectiveness of the Sacrament and its graces. The ordained are called to a holiness of life and an attitude of humility that conforms them to Christ whose priesthood they share. The priest acts not only in the person of Christ, the Head of the Church, but also in the name of the Church when presenting to God the prayer of the Church, especially in the Eucharist.

ORDINATION

Let everyone revere the deacons as Jesus Christ, the bishop as image of the Father, and the presbyters as the senate of God and the assembly of the apostles. For without them, one cannot speak of the Church.

—CCC, no. 1554, citing St. Ignatius of Antioch, *Ad. Trall.* 3, 1

Bishops

By ordination to the episcopacy, bishops receive the fullness of the Sacrament of Holy Orders and become successors of the Apostles. Through this Sacrament, a bishop belongs to the college of bishops and serves as the visible head or pastor of the local church entrusted to his care. As a college, the bishops have care and concern for the apostolic mission of all the churches in union with and under the authority of the Pope—the head of the college of bishops, the Bishop of Rome, and the successor of St. Peter.

Priests

By ordination, "priests are united with the bishops in [priestly] dignity and at the same time depend on them in the exercise of their pastoral functions; they are called to be the bishops' prudent co-workers" (CCC, no. 1595). With the bishop, priests form a *presbyteral* (priestly) community and assume with him the pastoral mission for a particular parish. The bishop appoints priests to the pastoral care of parishes and to other diocesan ministries. The priest promises obedience to the bishop in service to God's people.

Deacons

The title *deacon* comes from the Greek word *diakonia* meaning "servant." A deacon has a special attachment to the bishop in the tasks of service and is configured to Christ, the Deacon—or Servant—of all (cf. CCC, nos. 1569-1570).

"There are two degrees of ministerial participation in the priesthood of Christ: the episcopacy and the presbyterate. The diaconate is intended to help and serve them" (CCC, no. 1554). The three degrees of the Sacrament of Holy Orders—bishop, priest, and deacon—are all conferred by ordination.

Deacons receive the Sacrament of Holy Orders from a bishop and are ordained not to the ministerial priesthood but to the ministry of service. Through ordination the deacon is conformed to Christ, who came to serve, not to be served. In the Latin Church, deacons may baptize, proclaim the Gospel, preach the homily, assist the bishop or priest in the celebration of the Eucharist, assist at and bless marriages, and preside at funerals. They dedicate themselves to charitable endeavors, which was their ministerial role in New Testament times.

Whether they are involved in the Church's liturgical or pastoral life or in her social and charitable endeavors, deacons are "strengthened by the imposition of hands that has come down from the apostles. They would be more closely bound to the altar and their ministry would be made more fruitful through the sacramental grace of the diaconate" (AG, 16, no. 6).

Since the Second Vatican Council, the Latin Church has restored the diaconate as a permanent rank of the hierarchy. Now, diaconate as a permanent office may also be conferred on both married and unmarried men. The Eastern Churches have always retained it. Seminarians preparing for priesthood have always been ordained to the diaconate before ordination to priesthood.

THE ESSENTIAL RITE OF HOLY ORDERS

The essential rite of the sacrament of Holy Orders for all three degrees consists in the bishop's imposition of hands on the head of the ordinand and in the bishop's specific consecratory prayer asking God for the outpouring of the Holy Spirit and his gifts proper to the ministry to which the candidate is being ordained.

—CCC, no. 1573

The additional rites surrounding this core ordination rite vary greatly among differing liturgical traditions, but all have in common the expression of aspects of sacramental grace. The only valid minister of ordination is a bishop. Now ascended to the Father, Christ continues to guide the Church through the bishops, who confer this Sacrament of apostolic ministry and hand on the gift of the Holy Spirit.

WHO MAY BE ORDAINED?

Only a baptized man may be ordained in the Sacrament of Holy Orders. Jesus Christ chose men to become part of the Twelve. Throughout his ministry, his attitude toward women was different from the culture, and he courageously broke with it. For example, he did not hesitate to speak with the Samaritan woman even though custom forbade it (cf. Jn 4:4-

42). But it was only men whom he chose to be the Twelve Apostles and the foundation of the ministerial priesthood.

Although after the Ascension, Mary occupied a privileged place in the little circle gathered in the Upper Room, she was not called to enter the college of the Twelve at the time of the election of Matthias. The Apostles continued Christ's practice and so, too, did their successors through the centuries.

The Church has the power to determine the way in which the Sacraments are to be celebrated, but she has no ability to change the essential aspects established by the Lord Jesus. Sacramental signs are natural, but they also carry a divine meaning. Just as the Eucharist is not only a communal meal, but also makes present the saving sacrifice of the Lord Jesus, so too ministerial priesthood is more than pastoral service: it ensures the continuity of the ministry Christ entrusted to the Apostles.

The priesthood has a sacramental nature. The priest is a sign of what is happening. Sacramental signs represent what they signify by a natural resemblance. This resemblance is as true for persons as for things. When the priest acts in the person of Christ, he takes on the role of Christ, to the point of being his representative. He is a sign of what is happening and must be a sign that is recognizable, which the faithful can see with ease.

An image used to explain this reality talks of a priest as an "icon" of Christ. An icon is a religious painting that is considered to make present the mystery of salvation or the saint it depicts. To say a priest is an icon of Christ means, then, that a priest is not just a reminder or image of Christ but is also a real means by which a person can be touched by Christ. Because Christ is a man, it is fitting that a priest as the icon of Christ should also be a man.

Another reason why the Church understands that ordination is reserved to men is the recognition of the priest's responsibility to reflect Christ as the Bridegroom of the Church. This image and understanding can be reflected most truly only when the priest is a man.

The teaching that priestly ordination is to be reserved to men alone has been preserved by the constant and universal Tradition of the Church (cf. Sacred Congregation for the Doctrine of the Faith, *Declaration on the*

Admission of Women to the Ministerial Priesthood [*Inter Insigniores*], nos. 9-10, 13, 20-21, 26-27). Pope John Paul II reaffirmed this teaching in these words: "In order that all doubt may be removed, I declare that the Church has no authority whatsoever to confer priestly ordination on women and that this judgment is to be definitively held by all the Church's faithful" (*On Reserving Priestly Ordination to Men Alone* [*Ordinatio Sacerdotalis*], no. 4). In that same document, the Pope underlined the incomparable achievements of women for the benefit of the People of God:

> The New Testament and the whole history of the Church give ample evidence of the presence in the Church of women, true disciples, witnesses to Christ in the family and in society, as well as in total consecration to the service of God and of the Gospel. "By defending the dignity of women and their vocation, the Church has shown honor and gratitude for those women who, faithful to the Gospel, have shared in every age in the apostolic mission of the whole People of God. They are the holy martyrs, virgins and mothers of families, who bravely bore witness to their faith and passed on the Church's faith and tradition by bringing up their children in the spirit of the Gospel." (*On Reserving Priestly Ordination to Men Alone*, no. 3, citing *On the Dignity and Vocation of Women* [*Mulieris Dignitatem*], no. 27)

Ordination to the priesthood is always a call and a gift from God. Christ reminded his Apostles that they needed to ask the Lord of the harvest to send laborers into the harvest. Those who seek priesthood respond generously to God's call using the words of the prophet, "Here I am, send me" (Is 6:8). This call from God can be recognized and understood from the daily signs that disclose his will to those in charge of discerning the vocation of the candidate.

When God chooses men to share in the ordained priesthood of Christ, he moves and helps them by his grace. At the same time, he entrusts the bishop with the task of calling suitable and approved candidates and of consecrating them by a special seal of the Holy Spirit to the ministry of God and of the Church (*Admission to Candidacy for Priesthood*, 5).

FROM THE CATECHISM

1. What does the prayer from the Byzantine Rite say about the spiritual gift a priest receives at ordination?

The prayer reads: Lord, fill with the gift of the Holy Spirit, him whom you have deigned to raise to the rank of the priesthood, that he may be worthy to stand without reproach before your altar, to proclaim the Gospel of your kingdom, to fulfill the ministry of your word of truth, to offer you spiritual gifts and sacrifices, to renew your people by the bath of rebirth. (CCC, no. 1587)

2. What is the essential rite of ordination?

The sacrament of Holy Orders is conferred by the laying on of hands by the bishop followed by a solemn prayer of consecration asking God to grant the man being ordained the graces of the Holy Spirit required for his ministry. (CCC, no. 1597)

3. What does it mean to say that the priest acts "in the person of Christ"?

In the ecclesial service of the ordained minister, it is Christ himself who is present to his Church as Head of the Body, Shepherd of his flock, high priest of the redemptive sacrifice, Teacher of Truth. This is what the Church means by saying that the priest, by virtue of the sacrament of Holy Orders, acts *in persona Christi capitis* (in the person of Christ the head). (CCC, no. 1548)

All candidates for ordination in the Latin Church—with the exception of permanent deacons, who can be married at the time of their ordination—are chosen from among those who intend to remain celibate "for the sake of the kingdom of heaven" (Mt 19:12). Their celibacy is a sign of their intention to imitate Christ's own celibacy and to serve God in the Church's ministry with an undivided heart. In some cases, married clergy of other Christian churches who convert to Catholicism have been admitted to Holy Orders. In the Eastern Churches, only the bishops must be celibate. Priests and deacons may be married; however, in the United States, priests in Eastern Churches are normally celibate.

EFFECTS OF THE SACRAMENT

This Sacrament configures the bishop and priest to Christ as the Head of the Church in Christ's threefold office of priest, prophet, and king. This Sacrament configures the deacon to Christ as servant.

The Sacrament of Holy Orders, like that of Baptism and Confirmation, confers an indelible or permanent character on the recipient. This means that this Sacrament cannot be received again. The indelible character is a reminder to the bishop, priest, or deacon that the vocation and mission he received on the day of his ordination marks him permanently. Like Baptism and Confirmation, which also confer a permanent character, Holy Orders is never repeated.

A bishop is given the grace to teach in the name of Christ; to sanctify the Church through the celebration of the Sacraments; to guide, govern, and defend the Church; and to be a sign of the unity of the Church.

A priest is given the grace to proclaim the Gospel and preach, to celebrate the Sacraments (except Holy Orders), and to shepherd the people entrusted to him.

A deacon in the Latin Church is ordained to proclaim the Gospel and preach, to baptize, to assist the bishop or priest in the celebration of the Eucharist, to assist at and bless marriages, to preside at funerals, and to serve the community through works of charity.

THE SPIRITUALITY OF THE PRIEST

[Priests] should be taught to seek Christ. This along with the *quaerere Deum* [the search for God] is a classical theme of Christian spirituality. It has a specific application in the context of the calling of the Apostles. When John tells the story of the way the first two disciples followed Christ, he highlights this "search." It is Jesus himself who asks the question: "What do you seek?" And the two reply, "Rabbi, where are you staying?" He said to them, "Come and see." They came and saw where he was staying; and they stayed with him that day" (Jn 1:37-39). In a certain sense, the spiritual life of the person who is preparing for priesthood is dominated by this search; by it and by the "finding" of the Master, to follow him, to be in communion with him. So inexhaustible is the mystery of the imitation of Christ and the sharing in his life that this "seeking" will have to continue throughout the priest's life and ministry. Likewise this "finding" the Master will have to continue in order to bring him to others, or rather in order to excite in others the desire to seek out the Master. But all this becomes possible if it is proposed to others as a living "experience," an experience that is worthwhile sharing. This was the path followed by Andrew to lead his brother Simon to Jesus. The evangelist John writes that Andrew "first found his brother Simon, and said to him, "We have found the Messiah (which means Christ)" and brought him to Jesus (Jn 1:41-42). And so Simon too will be called, as an apostle, to follow the Messiah: "Jesus looked at him and said, 'So you are Simon the son of John? You shall be called Cephas' (which means Peter)" (Jn 1:42). . . . An essential element of spiritual formation is the prayerful and meditated reading of the Word of God, a humble and loving listening to him who speaks. . . . Familiarity with the Word of God will make conversion easy, not only in the sense of detaching us from evil, so as to adhere to the good, but also in the sense of nourishing our heart with the thoughts of God, so that faith (as a response to the word) becomes our new basis for judging and evaluating persons and things, events and problems. (Pope John Paul II, *I Will Give You Shepherds* [*Pastores Dabo Vobis*], nos. 46-47)

FOR DISCUSSION

1. What qualities of a priest serve to draw people to them? What are a number of ways that the lay faithful and priests support each other for the good of families and the mission of the Church?

2. How can faith be strengthened by the effective preaching of priests and deacons? How can faith be strengthened through the ministry of priests as confessors?
3. What could you do to foster vocations to the priesthood? How could you also foster vocations to the permanent diaconate?

■ DOCTRINAL STATEMENTS ■

- Through Baptism all the members of the Church share in the priesthood of Christ. This is known as the "common priesthood of the faithful."
- Through Holy Orders there is another participation in Christ's priesthood, the ministerial priesthood of bishop and priest. This differs in essence from the common priesthood because it confers a sacred power for the service of the faithful.
- The ordained ministry occurs in three degrees or orders: bishop, priest, and deacon. These ministries are essential for the life of the Church.
- Bishops receive the fullness of the Sacrament of Holy Orders. They are the chief teachers, sanctifiers, and shepherds in their dioceses.
- "Priests are united with the bishops in priestly dignity and at the same time depend on them in the exercise of their pastoral functions; they are called to be the bishops' prudent co-workers" (CCC, no. 1595). With the bishop, priests form a presbyteral (priestly) community and assume with him the pastoral mission for a particular parish.
- Deacons receive the Sacrament of Holy Orders, but not the ministerial priesthood. Through ordination, the deacon is conformed to Christ, who came to serve, not to be served. Deacons in the Latin Church may baptize, read the Gospel, preach the homily, assist the bishop or priest in the celebration of the Eucharist, assist at and bless marriages, and preside at funerals. They dedicate themselves to charitable endeavors, which was their ministerial role in New Testament times.
- "The *essential rite* of the Sacrament of Holy Orders for all three degrees consists in the bishop's imposition of hands on the head of

the ordinand [man to be ordained] and in the bishop's specific consecratory prayer" (CCC, no. 1573). Ordination confers a permanent
sacramental character.

- Only men may be ordained.
- Normally in the Western Church, ordination to priesthood is conferred only on those men who freely promise lifelong celibacy.
- Only bishops may confer the Sacrament of Holy Orders in the
  three degrees.

MEDITATION

Priests should, therefore, occupy their position of leadership
as men who do not seek the things that are their own but the
things that are Jesus Christ's (cf. 1 Jn 4:1). They should unite
their efforts with those of the lay faithful and conduct themselves among them after the example of the Master, who came
. . . "not to be served but to serve, and to give his life as a ransom
for many" (Mt 20:28). Priests are to be sincere in their appreciation and promotion of lay people's dignity and of the special
role the laity have to play in the Church's mission. They should
also have an unfailing respect for the just liberty which belongs
to everyone in civil society. They should be willing to listen to
lay people, give brotherly consideration to their wishes, and recognize their experience and competence in the different fields of
human activity. In this way they will be able to recognize along
with them the signs of the times. (PO, no. 9)

The ministerial priesthood of bishops and priests and the common
priesthood of all the faithful participate in the one priesthood of Christ,
each in its own proper way. The two priesthoods complement each other
and are ordered to each other while differing essentially. In what sense?
The common priesthood of the faithful is exercised by the unfolding of
baptismal grace through a life of faith, hope, and charity, a life according to the Holy Spirit. The ministerial priesthood is at the service of the
common priesthood by unfolding the baptismal grace of all Christians
(cf. CCC, no. 1547).

The members of the common priesthood, among other things, are encouraged "to share their priests' anxieties and help them as far as possible by prayer and active work so that they may be better able to overcome difficulties and carry out their duties with greater success" (PO, no. 9).

████████████ **PRAYER** ████████████

May the tribute of my humble ministry be pleasing to you,
    Holy Trinity.
Grant that the sacrifice which I—unworthy as I am—
have offered in the presence of your majesty may be acceptable
    to you.
Through your mercy may it bring forgiveness to me
and to all for whom I have offered it, through Christ our Lord
Amen.

—*Placeat*—from Priests' Prayers After Mass

Like Melchizedek you are a priest forever.

—Ps 110:4

21 THE SACRAMENT OF MARRIAGE

MARRIAGE IS A SACRAMENT AT THE SERVICE OF COMMUNION
—CCC, NOS. 1601-1666

A MARRIED MAN: GOD'S SERVANT ABOVE ALL

St. Thomas More was born in London on February 7, 1478, to a middle-class family. His father, John More, was a knight and local judge. As a young boy, Thomas was placed in the service of the Archbishop of Canterbury John Morton—who was also Chancellor of England. More went on to study at Oxford University and then to study law in London. He mastered Greek and enjoyed the company of important figures of the Renaissance culture such as Desiderius Erasmus.

His attraction to a deeper spirituality led him to a close relationship with the Franciscans at Greenwich and with the London Carthusians, another religious community with whom he lived for a time. Called to marriage, More wed Jane Colt in 1505. They had four children before Jane died in 1511. After her death, Thomas married Alice Middleton, a widow. Their home was open to their entire family, friends, and many acquaintances. More continued his quest for virtue and union with Christ while fostering the faith of his family.

He was elected to Parliament in 1504. This began a political career that saw him knighted in 1521, elected Speaker of the House of Commons in 1523, and finally made Lord Chancellor of England on October 25, 1529, the first layman to hold the position. King Henry VIII, reigning at that time, was desperate to bear a male heir to the throne. Blaming his wife, Queen Catherine of Aragon, for their lack of a son, Henry VIII sought an annulment so that he might marry Anne Boleyn instead, whom he had fancied for quite some time. Unable to receive the declaration from Pope Clement VII, the king formally broke from the Catholic Church and declared himself the Supreme Head of the Church of England. If Rome would not grant him an annulment, his own church would. On May 15, 1532, all the English bishops (save St. John Fisher) submitted to the king as their new head. The following day, St. Thomas More resigned as Chancellor.

In 1534, the English Parliament passed the Act of Succession, which acknowledged the offspring of King Henry VIII and Anne Boleyn, rather than the daughter born to Queen Catherine, as the true heir to the English throne. The nobility and clergy were called to ascribe to an oath upholding the act, and as one of the most respected laymen in the country, so was More. However, More chose to uphold the indissolubility of marriage and refused to take the oath. Even faced with death, St. Thomas More would not act against his conscience. As a result, on July 1, 1535, St. Thomas More was tried in Westminster Hall and convicted of high treason. On July 6, he was led to execution outside the Tower of London. In his final words before being beheaded, he referred to himself as "the king's good servant, but God's first." As a martyr who died for his faith, St. Thomas More was beatified by Pope Leo XIII in 1886. He was later canonized by Pope Pius XI in 1935.

In this text we cite the stories of other married people—such as Elizabeth Seton, Pierre Toussaint, Rose Hawthorne Lathrop, Orestes Brownson, Cesar Chavez, John Boyle O'Reilly, and Luigi and Maria Quattrocchi—from the viewpoint of various teachings witnessed in their lives. God's grace blessed them with the faith and virtues that flourished in the marital state. In turn, married people have enriched the life of the Church by their faith and love and by the children whom they have raised and formed in the Christian tradition. Marriage is a Sacrament at the Service of Communion.

GOD IS THE AUTHOR OF MARRIAGE

The vocation to marriage is written in the very nature of man and woman as they came from the hand of the Creator. Marriage is not a purely human institution despite the many variations it may have undergone through the centuries in different cultures, social structures and spiritual attitudes.

—CCC, no. 1603

Sacred Scripture begins with the creation and union of man and woman and ends with "the wedding feast of the Lamb" (Rev 19:7, 9). Scripture often refers to marriage, its origin and purpose, the meaning God gave to it, and its renewal in the covenant made by Jesus with his Church.

God created man and woman out of love and commanded them to imitate his love in their relations with each other. Man and woman were created for each other. "It is not good for the man to be alone. I will make a suitable partner for him. . . . The two of them become one body" (Gn 2:18; 24). Woman and man are equal in human dignity, and in marriage both are united in an unbreakable bond.

But fidelity to God's plan for the unity and indissolubility of marriage developed gradually among the people of ancient Israel under God's providential guidance. The patriarchs and kings practiced polygamy, and Moses permitted divorce. Jesus later cited this case as a toleration of human hardness of heart and taught God's plan for marriage from the beginning (cf. Mt 19:8). It was the prophets of ancient Israel who prepared for Jesus' renewal of God's plan for marriage in their insistence that the permanent and exclusive fidelity of marriage illustrates the unending fidelity of God to his covenant with Israel and his will that Israel be faithful to him alone (cf., e.g., Hos 3 and Ez 16:59-63).

The books of Ruth and Tobit witness the ideals of marriage. They describe the fidelity and tenderness that should exist between the spouses. The Song of Solomon pictures a human love that mirrors God's love, which "many waters cannot quench" (cf. Sg 8:6-7).

THE UNDERSTANDING OF MARRIAGE IN CONTEMPORARY SOCIETY

There are attempts by some in contemporary society to change the definition or understanding of what exactly constitutes marriage. Efforts to gain approval for and acceptance of same-sex unions as marriages are examples. While the Church clearly teaches that discrimination against any group of people is wrong, efforts to make cohabitation, domestic partnerships, same-sex unions, and polygamous unions equal to marriage are misguided and also wrong. The Church and her members need to continue to be a strong and clear voice in protecting an understanding of marriage, which is rooted in natural law and revealed in God's law.

CHRIST'S TEACHING ON MARRIAGE

Jesus brought to full awareness the divine plan for marriage. In John's Gospel, Christ's first miracle occurs at the wedding in Cana. "The Church attaches great importance to Jesus' presence at the wedding at Cana. She sees in it the confirmation of the goodness of marriage and the proclamation that thenceforth marriage will be an efficacious sign of Christ's presence" (CCC, no. 1613).

Jesus unequivocally taught the indissolubility of marriage:

Some Pharisees approached him, and tested him, saying, "Is it lawful for a man to divorce his wife for any cause whatever?" He said in reply, "Have you not read that from the beginning the Creator 'made them male and female' and said, 'For this reason a man shall leave his father and mother and be joined to his wife, and the two shall become one flesh'? So they are no longer two, but one flesh. Therefore, what God has joined together, no human being must separate. (Mt 19:3-6)

St. Paul reinforces Christ's teaching on marriage. "A wife should not separate from her husband and a husband should not divorce his wife" (1 Cor 7:10-11). In the Letter to the Ephesians, we read, "'For this reason a man shall leave [his] father and [his] mother / and be joined to his wife, / and the two shall become one flesh.' / This is a great mystery, but I speak in reference to Christ and the church" (Eph 5:31-32). Thus the love of husband and wife reflects the love between Christ and the Church. By Christ's will, Marriage is one of the Seven Sacraments.

COVENANT AND LITURGICAL ACT

By their marriage, the couple witnesses Christ's spousal love for the Church. One of the Nuptial Blessings in the liturgical celebration of marriage refers to this in saying, "Father, you have made the union of man and wife so holy a mystery that it symbolizes the marriage of Christ and his Church." Through the liturgical celebration of marriage, husband and wife enter into a covenant which is also a Sacrament:

> The matrimonial covenant by which a man and a woman establish between themselves a partnership of the whole of life, is by its nature ordered toward the good of the spouses and the procreation and education of offspring; this covenant between baptized persons has been raised by Christ the Lord to the dignity of a sacrament. (CCC, no. 1601, citing CIC, can. 1055, and *Code of Canons of the Eastern Churches* [CCEO], can. 776)

The Sacrament of Marriage is a covenant, which is more than a contract. Covenant always expresses a relationship between persons. The marriage covenant refers to the relationship between the husband and wife, a permanent union of persons capable of knowing and loving each other and God. The celebration of marriage is also a liturgical act, appropriately held in a public liturgy at church. Catholics are urged to celebrate their marriage within the Eucharistic Liturgy.

THE CELEBRATION OF MARRIAGE

According to the Latin tradition, the spouses as ministers of Christ's grace mutually confer upon each other the sacrament of Matrimony by expressing their consent before the Church. In the traditions of the Eastern Churches, the priest (bishops or presbyters) are witnesses to the mutual consent given by the spouses, but for the validity of the sacrament their blessing is also necessary.

—CCC, no. 1623

In the Latin Church, the free consent of the couple is at the heart of the marriage celebration. By Church law, when two Catholics marry they must exchange this consent in the presence of the Church's minister, two witnesses, and the congregation. The priest or deacon calls forth this consent, but the marriage itself takes place through the public consent of the couple. The priest invites the couple to do so in these words: "Since it is your intention to enter into marriage, join your right hands and declare your consent before God and his Church." There are various formulas for this consent. One that may be used is as follows: "I, [Name], take you, [Name], to be my [wife/husband]. I promise to be true to you in good times and in bad, in sickness and in health. I will love you and honor you all the days of my life." In the Eastern Churches, the Sacrament is conferred by the blessing of the priest after receiving the couple's consent.

The consent is further symbolized in the Latin Church by the blessing and exchange of rings with the words: "Take this ring as a sign of my love and fidelity, in the name of the Father, and of the Son, and of the Holy Spirit."

THE PURPOSES OF MARRIAGE

The marriage covenant, by which a man and woman form with each other an intimate communion of life and love, has been founded and endowed with its own special laws by the Creator. By its very nature it is ordered to the good of the couple, as well as to the generation and education of children. Christ the Lord raised marriage between the baptized to the dignity of a sacrament.

—CCC, no. 1660

The *Catechism* teaches that Christ's grace in the Sacrament of Marriage protects the essential purposes of marriage: the good of the couple and the generation and education of children. These purposes are protected and fostered by the permanence of the marriage bond and the mutual fidelity of the spouses.

"What God has joined together, no human being must separate" (Mk 10:9). We have already noted that God's plan for marriage involves a permanent covenant embraced by the couple. The Church declares every valid sacramental consummated marriage to be indissoluble, that is, no one can dissolve the marriage bond.

The Sacrament obliges marital fidelity between the spouses. Love has a definitive quality about it. It is more than a practical arrangement or a temporary contract. Marital intimacy and the good of the children require total fidelity to conjugal love. This flows from Christ's own fidelity to the Church, which he loved so much that he died for her. By their mutual fidelity, the spouses continue to make present to each other the love of Christ and lead each other to greater holiness through the grace they receive from the Sacrament.

Married love is ordered to the good of the spouses and to the procreation and education of children. These are the unitive and procreative purposes of marriage. "By its very nature the institution of marriage and married love is ordered to the procreation and education of the offspring and it is in them that it finds its crowning glory" (CCC, no. 1652; GS, no. 48). The fruitfulness of married love includes the moral, spiritual,

FROM THE CATECHISM

1. Why is the family called "the domestic Church"?
The Christian home is the place where the children receive the first proclamation of the faith. For this reason the family is rightly called "the domestic church," a community of grace and prayer, a school of human virtues and of Christian charity. (CCC, no. 1666)

2. What is essential in the consent of those to be married?
The parties to a marriage covenant are a baptized man and woman, free to contract marriage, who freely express their consent; "to be free" means:
—not being under constraint;
—not impeded by any natural or ecclesiastical law. (CCC, no. 1625)

3. Why should the couples be prepared for marriage?
So that the "I do" of the spouses may be a free and responsible act, and so that the marriage covenant may have solid and lasting human and Christian foundations, preparation is of prime importance. . . . It is imperative to give suitable and timely instruction to young people, above all in the heart of their own families, about the dignity of married love, its role and exercise, so that, having learned the value of chastity, they will be able at a suitable age to engage in honorable courtship and enter upon a marriage of their own. (CCC, no. 1632)

and faith life the parents hand on to their children. Parents, as principal educators of their children, are at the service of life.

Together with their children, parents form what the Second Vatican Council called the domestic church. The Church lives in the daily life of families, in their faith and love, in their prayers and mutual care. The

Catechism notes that "All the members of the family exercise the priest-hood of the baptized in a privileged way" (CCC, no. 1657).

Not all married couples are able to have children. "Spouses to whom God has not granted children can nevertheless have a conjugal life full of meaning. . . . [and] can radiate a fruitfulness of charity, of hospitality and of sacrifice" (CCC, no. 1654).

EFFECTS OF THE SACRAMENT

The first effect of the Sacrament of Matrimony is the gift of the bond between the spouses. "The consent by which the spouses mutually give and receive one another is sealed by God himself" (CCC, no. 1639). "The marriage bond has been established by God himself in such a way that a marriage concluded and consummated between baptized persons can never be dissolved" (CCC, no. 1640).

The grace of this Sacrament perfects the love of husband and wife, binds them together in fidelity, and helps them welcome and care for children. Christ is the source of this grace and he dwells with the spouses to strengthen their covenant promises, to bear each other's burdens with forgiveness and kindness, and to experience ahead of time the "wedding feast of the Lamb" (Rev 19:9).

DO ALL YOU CAN TO STRENGTHEN MARRIAGE

The pastoral care of the Church for the support of marriage is shown by a variety of programs to help men and women to know God's plan for marriage and the Church's teaching. Remote preparation, which can begin in the family, takes on a more organized character in the form of courses in high school and college years. As engaged couples draw closer to the celebration of marriage, there are more intense programs of preparation (frequently called "pre-Cana programs").

These programs are all the more necessary because cultural changes in recent times have undermined God's will for marriage. The so-called sexual revolution, aided by artificial contraception, has made it more culturally acceptable for men and women to have sexual relations without having to marry each other. The legalization of abortion has reduced the pressure on men and women to worry about the consequences of unwanted pregnancies. The casual acceptance of unmarried cohabitation—and of couples' entering marriage without a permanent commitment—contradicts the very nature of marriage. The political pressure for the legalization of same-sex unions is yet another step in the erosion of God's plan for marriage and the understanding of marriage in the natural moral order of creation.

In her teaching, the Church gives us a picture of family life that begins with the total gift of love between the spouses evidenced in their resolve to remain exclusively faithful until death. This promise, made before God in the midst of family and friends before an authorized priest or deacon, is supported by the continuing presence of Christ in the life of the spouses as he pours into their hearts the gift of love through the Holy Spirit. The couple does not walk alone and possesses the graced freedom to respond to all natural and supernatural help.

The couple's joyful acceptance of children includes the responsibility to serve as models of Christian commitment for their children and helps them grow in wisdom and grace. In this way, their family becomes a "domestic church." The family honors the home as a place of prayer that conveys a sense of the sacred where so much of Christian life occurs.

The couple needs to remember they have entered a relationship between persons. They come to one another with two loves, the one commanded by Jesus and the one caused by their attraction to each other. They are challenged to unite their personal love with Christ's love. Their human love will survive more effectively the cultural challenges they face, as well as the psychological and economic ones, when it is merged with the powerful love of Christ, who wants them to succeed and whose divine grace is ever at their service.

The New Testament shows that Christ's command to love is the door to the whole supernatural order. At the same time, it encourages the couple to know that Jesus affirms the human good of each person. Together the couple must seek the same goals of mutual love united to Christ's love, the raising of a family and the continued growth of their own relationship.

It can seem difficult, or even impossible, to bind oneself for life to another human being. This makes it all the more important to proclaim the Good News that God loves us with a definitive and irrevocable love, that married couple share in this love, that it supports and sustains them, and that by their own faithfulness they can be witnesses to God's faithful love. Spouses who with God's grace give this witness, often in very difficult conditions, deserve the gratitude and support of the ecclesial community. (CCC, no. 1648)

DIVORCE AND PASTORAL CARE

Married couples have always experienced problems that threaten their union: jealousy, infidelity, conflicts, and quarrels. Lust and arbitrary domination can ruin a marriage. These issues arise from the impact of sin, both Original and actual. The first sin disrupted the original communion of man and woman. Despite this, God's plan for marriage persisted. He never failed to provide mercy and healing grace to help couples sustain their marriages. Sadly, some spouses fail to benefit from the Lord's help and from the many professional resources and support offered to them.

The Church's fidelity to Christ's teaching on marriage and against divorce does not imply insensitivity to the pain of the persons facing these unhappy situations. When divorce is the only possible recourse, the Church offers her support to those involved and encourages them to remain close to the Lord through frequent reception of the Sacraments, especially the Holy Eucharist. In the case of those who have divorced civilly and remarried, even though the Church considers the second marriage invalid, she does not want these Catholics to be alienated from her.

> Toward Christians who live in this situation, and who often keep the faith and desire to bring up their children in a Christian manner, priests and the whole community must manifest an attentive solicitude, so that they do not consider themselves separated from the Church, in whose life they can and must participate as baptized persons. (CCC, no. 1651)

DECLARATION OF NULLITY OF A MARRIAGE

The consent of the spouses must be an act of the will, free of coercion or external threats. If this freedom is absent, the marriage is invalid. For this reason (or other reasons that render the marriage null and void), the Church, after an examination of the situation by a competent Church court, can declare the nullity of a marriage, that is, that the sacramental marriage never existed. In this case, the contracting parties are free to marry, provided the natural obligations of the previous union are discharged (cf. CCC, nos. 1628-1629; CIC, can. 1095-1107).

Thus they are encouraged to participate in the life of their parish communities and to attend the Sunday Eucharist, even though they cannot receive Holy Communion.

A DECLARATION OF NULLITY (ANNULMENT)

The marriage of two baptized persons celebrated according to the norms of Church law is always presumed to be valid. When a marriage has broken down, this presumption remains in effect until the contrary is proven. The examination of the validity of a marriage is undertaken by a Church tribunal or court. When a Church court issues a declaration of nullity, it does not mean there was no civil, sexual, or emotional marital relationship, nor does it mean that the children of the union are illegitimate. The declaration means that no sacramental bond—or, in the case of one party's being unbaptized, no natural bond—took place because at the time of the wedding, the standards for a valid marriage were not met. Grounds for a declaration of nullity (annulment) include flaws in the rite itself, in the legal capacity of the parties to marry (i.e., an "impediment"), or in the consent they gave—whether they were lacking in discretion or maturity of judgment or were marrying due to force or fear or with an intent to exclude fidelity or the commitment to a lifelong union or were placing unacceptable conditions on the marriage (cf. CCC, nos. 1628-1629). Once a declaration of nullity has been granted, if there are no other restrictions, one or both of the parties are free to enter a sacramental marriage in the Catholic Church.

MIXED AND INTERFAITH MARRIAGES

The term *mixed marriage* refers to a union between a Catholic and a baptized non-Catholic. With appropriate permission, a Catholic can marry a baptized non-Catholic either in the Catholic Church or a non-Catholic church. In the first case, a non-Catholic minister can be present for the ceremony just as the Catholic priest can be present in the non-Catholic church with the permission of the bishop.

It is clear that there are differences because of diverse religious traditions, but these differences can be lessened when the spouses share what they have received from their respective traditions and learn from each other how they fulfill their fidelity to Christ. "But the difficulties of mixed marriages must not be underestimated. They arise from the fact that the separation of Christians has not yet been overcome. The spouses risk experiencing the tragedy of Christian disunity even in the heart of their own home" (CCC, no. 1634).

A marriage between a Catholic and a non-baptized person, which is an *interfaith* marriage and is not a sacramental marriage, can present even greater problems for a marriage. Nevertheless, the very differences regarding faith can be enriching for both spouses and, through God's grace, can lead them closer to him.

▬▬▬▬▬ FOR DISCUSSION ▬▬▬▬▬

1. How does the modern, secular view of marriage and the family affect your own family relationships? How do you resist forces that can weaken marriage?
2. What support for your family are you receiving from relatives, friends and your local parish? In what ways is your family a "domestic church"? How and when do you pray with your spouse? How

and when do you pray as a family? What is your practice concerning participation in Sunday Mass?

3. What help can you or your parish provide for other couples, especially those with troubled marriages in your neighborhood and parish? What do you think will turn the tide back to a society that does everything it can to sustain the ideal of a monogamous, permanent marriage?

■■■ DOCTRINAL STATEMENTS ■■■

-   God is the author of marriage.
-   "The matrimonial covenant by which a man and a woman establish between themselves a partnership of the whole of life, is by its nature ordered toward the good of the spouses and the procreation and education of offspring; this covenant between baptized persons has been raised by Christ the Lord to the dignity of a sacrament" (CCC, no. 1601; see CIC, can. 1055; CCEO, can. 776).
-   Marriage is a liturgical act, appropriately held in a public liturgy at church. By their marriage, the couple witnesses Christ's spousal love for the Church.
-   In the Latin Church, the spouses, as ministers of Christ's grace, mutually confer upon each other the Sacrament of Matrimony by expressing their consent before the Church. The free consent of the couple is at the heart of the marriage celebration.
-   Unity, permanent lifelong commitment, and openness to having and caring for children are essential to marriage.
-   The remarriage of persons divorced from a living, lawful spouse is not permitted by God's law as taught by Christ. They remain members of the Church but cannot receive Holy Communion. They are called and encouraged to lead Christian lives by attending Sunday Mass and participating as far as possible in the life of the parish and to bring up their children in the faith.
-   "The Christian home is the place where the children receive the first proclamation of the faith. For this reason the family is rightly called 'the domestic church,' a community of grace and prayer, a school of human virtues and of Christian charity" (CCC, no. 1666).

▬▬ MEDITATION ▬▬

Exhortation Before the Sacrament of Marriage

Dear Friends in Christ,

As you know, you are about to enter into a union which is most sacred and most serious, a union which was established by God himself. In this way he sanctified human love and enabled man and woman to help each other live as children of God, by sharing a common life under his fatherly care.

Because God himself is thus its author, marriage is of its very nature a holy institution, requiring of those who enter into it a complete and unreserved giving of self. This union then is most serious, because it will bind you together for life in a relationship so close and so intimate that it will profoundly influence your whole future. That future—with its hopes and disappointments, its successes and its failures, its pleasures and its pains, its joys and its sorrows—is hidden from your eyes. You know well that these elements are mingled in every life and are to be expected in your own. And so, not knowing what is before you, you take each other for better or for worse, for richer or poorer, in sickness and in health, until death.

These words, then, are most serious. It is a beautiful tribute to your undoubted faith in each other, that recognizing their full import, you are nevertheless so willing and so ready to pronounce them. And because these words involve such solemn obligations, it is most fitting that you rest the security of your wedded life on the great principle of self sacrifice. And so today you begin your married life by the voluntary and complete surrender of your individual lives in the interest of that deeper and wider life which you two are to have in common.

Henceforth you belong entirely to each other; you will be one in mind, one in heart, one in affections. And whatever sacrifices you may hereafter be required to make to preserve this common life, always make them generously. There will be problems which might be difficult, but genuine love can make them easy, and perfect love can make them a joy. We are willing to give in proportion as we love. And when love is perfect, the sacrifice is complete. God so loved the world that he gave his only begotten Son, and the Son so loved us that he gave himself for our salvation. "Greater love than this no one has, that one lay down his life for his friends."

No greater blessing can come to your married life than pure conjugal love, loyal and true to the end. May this love, then, with which you join your hands and hearts today, never fail, but grow deeper and stronger as the years go on. And if true love and the unselfish spirit of perfect sacrifice guide all your actions, you two can expect the greatest measure of earthly happiness that may be allotted on this earth. The rest is in the hands of God. Nor will God be wanting to your needs; he will pledge you the lifelong support of his graces in the holy sacrament which you are now going to receive.

> — Msgr. Charles Ramm,
> "Exhortation Before the Sacrament of Marriage," in
> *Liturgikon* (Huntington, IN: Our Sunday Visitor, 1977)

PRAYER

Almighty and eternal God,
your fatherly tenderness never ceases to provide for our needs.
We ask you to bestow on this family and this home
the riches of your blessing.
With the gift of grace, sanctify those who live here,
so that, faithful to your commandments,
they will care for each other, ennoble this world by their lives,
and reach the home you have prepared for them in heaven.
We ask this through Christ our Lord. Amen.

> —Blessing of Families, *Book of Blessings*

I will espouse you to me forever.

> —Hos 2:21

22 SACRAMENTALS AND POPULAR DEVOTIONS

FORMS OF POPULAR PIETY
—CCC, NOS. 1667-1679

THE ROSARY PRIEST

For a half century, from 1940 to 1990, Fr. Patrick Peyton, CSC, was "the Rosary priest" to millions of people around the world. To Catholics and other believers around the United States, he was the force behind the familiar slogan, "The family that prays together stays together."

He was born on January 9, 1909, in County Mayo, Ireland. In 1928, Patrick and his brother Tom left home to seek work in America. They went to Scranton, Pennsylvania. Patrick became a janitor at St. Peter's Cathedral. Eventually, he and Tom finished high school. Patrick then entered the seminary at the University of Notre Dame, staffed by the Holy Cross Fathers. Before he finished his theological studies, Patrick contracted tuberculosis. He wrote of this as his "darkest hour."

> God made my worst and darkest hour the start of a new life full of meaning. In the middle of the night, my right lung began to hemorrhage. A doctor came and told me he thought I would die that night. I had been strong, vigorous, independent. Now ambulance attendants placed me on a stretcher, maneuvered me down a narrow, winding stairway and raced me to the hospital. I deteriorated until the doctors said, "Try prayer. Our remedies are useless."

One of my teachers hurried to visit me. He saw me at my worst—discouraged, depressed, hopeless. "Mary is alive," he said, "She will be as good to you as you think she can be. It all depends on you and your faith." He activated my dormant faith. I asked Mary with all my heart and soul to pray to her Son for my cure. "If I survive, I will serve you and Christ for the rest of my life."

Shortly thereafter, Patrick asked the doctors to examine him again. They took X-rays and made tests. Amazingly, they found no trace of disease in his lungs. In reporting his healing, he wrote, "I am not describing a miracle. I'm giving witness to the power of Mary's intercession and the quiet unsensational way she works. When I heard the good news I said, 'Mary, I hope I will never disgrace you.'"

He went on to be ordained a priest in 1941. He wondered how he could pay back his spiritual debts to Christ, Mary, and the prayers of his family. Seven months later, during a retreat, God gave him the answer: The Family Rosary Crusade. During his illness, he had learned three lessons: solidarity with people and dependence upon others, appreciation of the gift of Christ's Mother, and total dependence upon God.

For the next fifty years, he traveled the globe as an apostle of prayer and family solidarity. From pulpits, in classrooms, in the media, in rallies, and in house-to-house visitations, he helped people to come to know the Virgin Mary and the spiritual power of the Rosary, which opened hearts to Jesus Christ and his unifying love. He often enlisted bishops and Catholic media stars to help the cause.

Fr. Peyton died on June 3, 1992. He is buried on the grounds of the Congregation of Holy Cross in Easton, Massachusetts. Since his death, Holy Cross Family Ministries, a ministry founded by Fr. Peyton and sponsored by the Congregation of Holy Cross, has built the Father Patrick Peyton Center, a place of pilgrimage and the international headquarters for the continuation of Fr. Peyton's ministry.

At the end of his life, Fr. Peyton mused about his past and his ministry: "In the summer-times of my childhood, the Ox Mountains in Ireland were a blanket of purple flowers. From the other direction, I heard the moaning of the gigantic waves of the Atlantic coming to their death on the shores. No matter how mighty and powerful, all things, even mountains and oceans come to an end. I gave my life to extol the beauty of the Family Rosary."[14]

Fr. Peyton's fervor in promoting the praying of the Rosary to strengthen family life remains an inspiring context for considering popular devotion and sacramentals. This dimension of Church life has proven to be a perennial source for discovering and relating God's active presence and for applying it to the details of daily Christian life.

SACRAMENTALS

Sacramentals are sacred signs instituted by the Church.
They are sacred signs that bear a resemblance to the
sacraments.

—CCC, no. 1667

Sacramentals dispose believers to receive the chief effects of the Sacraments. They are sacred signs that resemble the Sacraments in the sense that they signify spiritual effects that are obtained through the intercession of the Church. Sacramentals include blessings, actions such as processions, prayers such as the Rosary, and objects such as holy water, palms, ashes, candles, and medals.

The Church instituted sacramentals to sanctify certain ministries, states of life, and the variety of situations in which Christians are involved. Their use has been guided by bishops' pastoral decisions in responding to specific needs that are particular to a given period of history or locality. They include a prayer, usually with a gesture such as the Sign of the Cross or the sprinkling of holy water.

---

14 Quoted by Holy Cross Family Ministries, http://www.familyrosary.org/main/about-father-priesthood.php.

BLESSINGS

Among the sacramentals, blessings hold a major place. There are blessings for persons, meals, objects, places, and special occasions. All blessings praise God for his gifts. Most blessings invoke the Holy Trinity as expressed in the Sign of the Cross—sometimes accompanied by the sprinkling of holy water.

There are blessings that consecrate persons to God: leaders of religious orders or congregations, religious men and women, virgins and widows, and others, such as readers, acolytes, and catechists. There are blessings for vessels such as chalices or ciboria, bells, medals, rosaries, and similar objects for religious use. The text for these and other blessings may be found in the *Book of Blessings*. Making the Sign of the Cross at the beginning and the end of each day, saying morning and evening prayers, and offering a prayer before and after meals are among the most common ways to invoke God's blessing on our lives.

EXORCISMS

The Gospels report that Jesus performed exorcisms that removed a person from the power of evil as personified in the fallen angels—Satan and the devils. For example, when a man with an unclean spirit entered the synagogue where Jesus was preaching, and the unclean spirit challenged him, Jesus said to the demon, "Quiet! Come out of him" (Mk 1:25). The unclean spirit convulsed the man and left him. Christ's exorcisms were both a compassionate act of healing as well as a sign of his power over evil.

From Christ the Church has received the power and office of exorcism. At each Baptism, there is a simple form of exorcism, accompanied by the renunciation of Satan and sin. Within the Rite of Christian Initiation of Adults, minor exorcisms are celebrated as we are freed from sin and its effects. The elect receive new strength in the midst of their spiritual journey, and they open their hearts to receive the gifts of the Savior (cf. *Rite of Christian Initiation of Adults*, no. 144). A major exorcism can only be performed by a priest with a bishop's permission. The priest is to act prudently and follow the Church's rules for exorcism strictly. "Exorcism is directed at the expulsion of demons or to the liberation from demonic possession through the spiritual authority which Jesus entrusted to his Church" (CCC, no. 1673). One needs to distinguish psychological illness from demonic possession. Illness is the domain of psychological and medical care, whereas demonic possession requires the pastoral care of the Church through exorcism.

POPULAR DEVOTIONS

The faith of the Christian people has developed numerous forms of popular piety and devotions. The religious instincts of the Christian people have always found ways to surround sacramental life with helps to benefit more effectively from them. Popular devotions have proven to be powerful forms of prayer and to be of spiritual benefit to many.

These forms of piety include praying at the Stations of the Cross; making pilgrimages to the Holy Land, Rome, Marian shrines, and shrines of other saints; lighting candles in church; having throats blessed on the feast of St. Blaise; joining in Corpus Christi processions; wearing medals of the Blessed Virgin and the saints; and honoring sacred relics. Some materials that form part of the Church's liturgical rites, such as the ashes received on Ash Wednesday and the palms distributed on Palm Sunday, are also sacramentals.

Devotions to the Sacred Heart of Jesus, the Divine Mercy of Jesus, and the Blessed Mother are frequently part of parish life and often include a *novena*, nine days of prayer associated with the devotion. Prayer groups such as those sponsored by Charismatic Renewal, Cursillo, Marriage Encounter, and Teens for Christ have both a strong liturgical foundation as well as a vibrant devotional component.

The praying of litanies (a series of invocations of the Blessed Mother or the saints) and the use of icons, holy pictures, and statues as supports for prayer are also forms of popular devotion. The faithful do not worship pictures and statues; they venerate or honor the Virgin Mary and the saints and worship and adore only God. The veneration of Mary and the saints ultimately leads to God. Among the forms of popular devotion, the rosary holds a unique position because of its relationship to the mysteries of Christ and the faith of the Blessed Virgin Mary.

THE ROSARY

The Rosary takes its inspiration from the Gospel to suggest the attitude with which the faithful should recite it.

—Pope Paul VI, *For the Right Ordering and Development of Devotion to the Blessed Virgin Mary (Marialis Cultus)*, no. 44

Many of the appearances of Mary, especially at Lourdes and Fatima, have been associated with the praying of the Rosary. Numerous popes and saints have urged the faithful to pray the Rosary. Opening the Marian Year in 1987, the Rosary was a global prayer for peace offered by large groups at Marian shrines such as those in Washington, D.C., Lourdes, Frankfurt, Manila, Bombay, Rio de Janeiro, and Dakar.

The popularity of the Rosary has been attributed to St. Dominic and the Dominican Order. It grew out of the laity's desire to have 150 prayers to match the 150 psalms chanted by the monks in monasteries. In 1569, St. Pius V officially recommended the praying "of 150 angelic salutations . . . with the Lord's prayer at each decade . . . while meditating on the mysteries which recall the entire life of our Lord Jesus Christ."

The Rosary is a Scripture-based prayer. It begins with the Apostles' Creed, which is itself a summary of the great mysteries of Catholic faith, based on Scripture, from creation through redemption and up to the Resurrection of the body and everlasting life. The Our Father, which introduces each mystery, is taken from the Gospels. The first part of the Hail Mary is composed from verses from the Gospel of Luke (1:29 and 1:42), the angel's words announcing Christ's birth and Elizabeth's greeting to Mary. St. Pius V officially added the second part to the Hail Mary.

The Mysteries of the Rosary center on the events of Christ's life. The Joyful Mysteries, which recall aspects of the Incarnation, are the Annunciation, the Visitation, the Nativity, the Presentation of Jesus in the Temple, and the Finding of the Child Jesus after Three Days in the

FROM THE CATECHISM

1. What are sacramentals?

Sacramentals are sacred signs instituted by the Church. These are sacred signs that bear a resemblance to the sacraments. They signify effects, especially of a spiritual nature, which are obtained through the intercession of the Church. (CCC, no. 1667)

2. What is the first among the sacramentals?

Among sacramentals, blessings (of persons, meals, objects, and places) come first. Every blessing praises God and prays for his gifts. In Christ, Christians are blessed by God the Father "with every spiritual blessing" (Eph 1:3). This is why the Church imparts blessings by invoking the name of Jesus, usually while making the holy sign of the cross of Christ. (CCC, no. 1671)

3. What is the relationship of popular piety to the liturgy?

These expressions of piety extend the liturgical life of the Church but do not replace it. They "should be so drawn up that they harmonize with the liturgical seasons, accord with the sacred liturgy, are in some way derived from it and lead the people to it, since in fact the liturgy by its very nature is superior to any of them." (CCC, no. 1675, citing SC, no. 13, §3)

Temple. The Sorrowful Mysteries, which focus on Christ's suffering and death, are the Agony in the Garden, the Scourging at the Pillar, the Crowning with Thorns, the Carrying of the Cross, and the Crucifixion and Death of Jesus. The Glorious Mysteries are the Resurrection, the Ascension into Heaven, the Sending of the Holy Spirit upon the Apostles at Pentecost, the Assumption of Mary, and the Crowning of Mary as the Queen of Heaven and Earth. In October of 2002, Pope John Paul II issued the apostolic letter *On the Most Holy Rosary* (*Rosarium Virginis*

Mariae; RVM). In the letter, the Holy Father added the five additional mysteries that he called the Luminous Mysteries: the Baptism of the Lord, the Miracle at Cana, the Proclamation of the Kingdom of God, the Transfiguration, and the Institution of the Eucharist.

The repetition of the ten Hail Mary's with each Mystery is meant to lead us to restful and contemplative prayer related to the Mystery. Many who say the Rosary think of the words as background music that leads them to rest in the divine presence. The gentle repetition of the words helps us to enter the silence of our hearts, where Christ's Spirit dwells.

EXCERPT: POPULAR DEVOTIONAL PRACTICES: BASIC QUESTIONS AND ANSWERS

While the liturgy is "the summit toward which the activity of the Church is directed" and "the font from which all her power flows" (SC, no. 10), it is not possible for us to fill up all of our day with participation in the liturgy. The Council pointed out that the spiritual life "is not limited solely to participation in the liturgy. . . . according to the teaching of the apostle, [the Christian] must pray without ceasing" (SC, no. 12). Popular devotional practices play a crucial role in helping to foster this ceaseless prayer. The faithful have always used a variety of practices as a means of permeating everyday life with prayer to God. Examples include pilgrimages, novenas, processions and celebrations in honor of Mary and the other saints, the rosary, the *Angelus*, the Stations of the Cross, the veneration of relics, and the use of sacramentals. Properly used, popular devotional practices do not replace the liturgical life of the Church; rather, they extend it into daily life.

The Fathers of the Second Vatican Council recognized the importance of popular devotions in the life of the Church and encouraged pastors and teachers to promote sound popular devotions. They wrote, "Popular devotions of the Christian people are to be highly commended, provided they accord with the laws and norms of the Church" (SC, no. 13). More recently, Pope John Paul II has devoted an entire apostolic letter to a popular devotion—the rosary—calling on bishops, priests, and deacons "to promote it with conviction" and recommending to all the faithful, "Confidently take up the Rosary once again. Rediscover the Rosary in the light of Scripture, in harmony with the Liturgy, and in the context of your daily lives" (RVM, no. 43).

Because popular devotional practices have such an important role in the spiritual life of Catholics, we, the bishops of the United States, . . . hope to encourage the faithful to make use of sound devotional practices, so that their lives might be filled in various ways with praise and worship of God. Faithful practice of popular devotions can help us experience God in our everyday lives and conform us more closely to Jesus Christ. As Pope Pius XII pointed out, the purpose of popular devotional practices is "to attract and direct our souls to God, purifying them from their sins, encouraging them to practice virtue and, finally, stimulating them to advance along the path of sincere piety by accustoming them to meditate on the eternal truths and disposing them better to contemplate the mysteries of the human and divine natures of Christ" (*On the Sacred Liturgy* [*Mediator Dei*], no. 175). Referring to the many forms of popular piety found in America, Pope John Paul II declared, "These and other forms of popular piety are an opportunity for the faithful to encounter the living Christ" (*The Church in America*, no. 16). (USCCB, *Popular Devotional Practices: Basic Questions and Answers* [Washington, DC: USCCB, 2003])

FOR DISCUSSION

1. What kind of popular devotions have you experienced? If you have made a pilgrimage, what was the impact on your faith life?
2. Have you witnessed the blessings of homes, persons, or special objects used for liturgy? How might praying as a family, such as saying Grace Before Meals or Grace After Meals, strengthen family life as well as faith in God?
3. What are some benefits of praying the Rosary? Why do some people have sacred art such as crucifixes, statues, and holy images in prominent places in their homes?

DOCTRINAL STATEMENTS

- Sacramentals are sacred signs instituted by the Church. "These are sacred signs which bear resemblance to the sacraments. They signify effects, particularly of a spiritual nature, which are obtained through the intercession of the Church" (CCC, no. 1667, citing SC, no. 60).

- Among the sacramentals, blessings hold a major place. There are blessings for persons, meals, objects, places and ceremonial occasions such as graduations, testimonial honors, welcomes, and farewell. All blessings praise God for his gifts. Most blessings invoke the Holy Trinity as expressed in the Sign of the Cross, sometimes accompanied by the sprinkling of holy water.

- "Exorcism is directed at the expulsion of demons or to the liberation from demonic possession through the spiritual authority which Jesus entrusted to his Church" (CCC, no. 1673).

- "Expressions of piety extend the liturgical life of the Church, but do not replace it. They 'should be so drawn up that they harmonize with the liturgical seasons, accord with the sacred liturgy, are in some way derived from it and lead the people to it, since in fact the liturgy by its very nature is far superior to any of them'" (CCC, no. 1675, citing SC, no. 13 §3).

MEDITATION

A number of historical circumstances also make a revival of the Rosary quite timely. First of all, the need to implore from God the gift of peace. The Rosary has many times been proposed by my predecessors and myself as a prayer for peace. At the start of a millennium which began with the terrifying attacks of September 11, 2001, a millennium which witnesses every day in numerous parts of the world fresh scenes of bloodshed and violence, to rediscover the Rosary means to immerse oneself in contemplation of the mystery of Christ who "is our peace," since he made "the two of us one, and broke down the dividing wall of hostility" (Eph 2:14). Consequently, one cannot recite the Rosary without feeling caught up in a clear commitment to advancing peace, especially in the land of Jesus, still so sorely afflicted and so close to the heart of every Christian.

—RVM, no. 6

PRAYER

Grace Before Meals
Bless us, O Lord, and these thy gifts,
which we are about to receive from thy bounty
through Christ our Lord. Amen.

Grace After Meals
We give thee thanks, for all thy benefits, Almighty God,
who live and reign for ever. Amen.

Miraculous Medal Prayer
O, Mary, conceived without sin, pray for us who have recourse to you.

PART III

CHRISTIAN MORALITY:
THE FAITH LIVED

23 LIFE IN CHRIST— PART ONE

THE FOUNDATIONS OF THE CHRISTIAN MORAL LIFE
—CCC, NOS. 1691-2082

JESUS THE TEACHER

Jesus was frequently called a teacher (in Hebrew, *Rabbi*). Jesus taught about God as his Father and the Father of all human beings. He taught about his Father's mercy and forgiveness of sin. He taught about the Kingdom that his Father was establishing, a Kingdom where justice and love conquer injustice and hatred. He taught about himself as the Servant of God, sent by the Father to bring about conversion, even by the sacrifice of his own life.

Jesus also taught his disciples how they were to live in order to achieve the fullness of life and happiness that is God's will for all people. He did this by his own way of life and by his words. His teaching flowed from the tradition of ancient Israel but he also deepened that teaching and perfected it. A good illustration of this is his dialogue with a young man narrated in the Gospel of St. Matthew.

Now someone approached him and said, "Teacher, what good must I do to gain eternal life?" He answered him, "Why do you ask me about the good? There is only One who is good. If you wish to enter into life, keep the commandments." He asked him, "Which ones?" And Jesus replied, "'You shall not kill; you shall not commit adultery; you shall not steal; you shall not bear false witness; honor your father and your mother'; and 'you shall love your neighbor as yourself.'" The young man said to him, "All of these I have observed. What do I still lack?" Jesus said to him, "If you wish to be perfect, go, sell what you have and give to (the) poor, and you will have treasure in heaven. Then come, follow me." When the young man heard this statement, he went away sad, for he had many possessions. (Mt 19:16-22)

In this dialogue, Jesus reiterates the fundamental importance of the Ten Commandments for a moral life. He also goes beyond them and calls for a radical detachment from material goods and their distribution to the poor. Jesus himself lived as a poor man. The attainment of fullness of life and happiness requires fundamental attitudes and virtues such as the one that Jesus recommends to the young man and others that Jesus teaches throughout his public ministry as underlying the keeping of the Commandments.

These attitudes and virtues were proclaimed by Jesus in his Sermon on the Mount.

Blessed are the poor in spirit,
　　for theirs is the kingdom of heaven.
Blessed are they who mourn,
　　for they will be comforted.
Blessed are the meek,
　　for they will inherit the land.
Blessed are they who hunger and thirst
　　for righteousness, for they will be satisfied.
Blessed are the merciful,
　　for they will be shown mercy.
Blessed are the clean of heart (or pure of heart),
　　for they will see God.
Blessed are the peacemakers,
　　for they will be called children of God.
Blessed are they who are persecuted for the sake of righteousness,
　　for theirs is the kingdom of heaven.
Blessed are you when they insult you and persecute you and utter every kind of evil against you (falsely) because of me. Rejoice and be glad, for your reward will be great in heaven. (Mt 5:3-12)

These are called Beatitudes. The word *Beatitude* refers to a state of deep happiness or joy. These Beatitudes are taught by Jesus as the foundations for a life of authentic Christian discipleship and the attainment of ultimate happiness. They give spirit to the Law of the Ten Commandments and bring perfection to moral life. That spirit is ultimately the spirit of love. In response to a question from the leader of the people, Jesus taught that love is at the heart of all law.

> You shall love the Lord, your God, with all your heart, with all your soul, and with all your mind. This is the greatest and the first commandment. The second is like it: You shall love your neighbor as yourself. (Mt 22:37-39)

Jesus is the teacher sent by the Father to bring us to perfect happiness in God. Jesus teaches us the way to the Father.

LIFE IN CHRIST—PART ONE: THE FOUNDATIONS OF CHRISTIAN MORALITY

Part One of the *Catechism of the Catholic Church* presents the Creed—the revealed truths of the divine plan of salvation and the invitation to faith in this Revelation.

Part Two presents the Seven Sacraments by which the saving grace of God is made available to us. We receive this gift of divine love by our participation in the Christian mysteries.

Part Three explores our life in Christ and the Holy Spirit, which we have received through Revelation and the Sacraments. It unfolds the various ways we respond to divine love through our personal and social moral behavior.

In Section One of Part Three, the *Catechism* explores the various elements, principles, and foundations of Christian morality by addressing the dignity of the human person, the human community, and God's salvation through God's law and grace. In Section Two, it applies these principles to each of the Ten Commandments.

We will follow this order, beginning in this chapter with who we are as human beings called to live a moral life.

WE ARE MORAL BEINGS: FUNDAMENTAL ELEMENTS OF CHRISTIAN MORALITY

Made in the Image of God

The most basic principle of the Christian moral life is the awareness that every person bears the dignity of being made in the image of God. He has given us an immortal soul and through the gifts of intelligence and reason enables us to understand the order of things established in his creation. God has also given us a free will to seek and love what is true, good, and beautiful. Sadly, because of the Fall, we also suffer the impact of Original Sin, which darkens our minds, weakens our wills, and inclines us to sin. Baptism delivers us from Original Sin but not from its effects—especially the inclination to sin, concupiscence. Within us, then, is both the powerful surge toward the good because we are made in the image of God, and the darker impulses toward evil because of the effects of Original Sin.

But we should always remember that Christ's dying and rising offers us new life in the Spirit, whose saving grace delivers us from sin and heals sin's damage within us. Thus we speak of the value, dignity, and goal of human life, even with its imperfections and struggles. Human life, as a profound unity of physical and spiritual dimensions, is sacred. It is distinct from all other forms of life, since it alone is imprinted with the very image of its Creator.

The Responsible Practice of Freedom

The second element of life in Christ is the responsible practice of freedom. Without freedom, we cannot speak meaningfully about morality or moral responsibility. Human freedom is more than a capacity to choose between this and that. It is the God-given power to become who he created us to be and so to share eternal union with him. This happens when we consistently choose ways that are in harmony with God's plan. Christian morality and God's law are not arbitrary, but are specifically given to us for our happiness. God gave us intelligence and the capacity to act freely. Ultimately, human freedom lies in our free decision to say "yes" to God. In contrast, many people today understand human freedom merely as the ability to make a choice, with no objective norm or good as the goal.

An opposite tendency to one that makes the act of choosing the core of human freedom is one that denies that we are free at all. Some believe that due to outside forces, inner compulsions, social pressures, childhood experiences, or genetic makeup, our behavior is already determined and we are not truly free. Though we do recognize that "the imputability or responsibility for an action can be diminished or nullified by ignorance, duress, fear, and other psychological or social factors" (CCC, no. 1746), normally we are still free and responsible for our actions. Our freedom may be limited but it is real nonetheless.

The best way to grow in freedom is to perform good acts. Good deeds help to make us free and develop good habits. The road to loss of freedom is through evil acts. Sin makes us slaves of evil and reduces our capacity to be free. Freedom comes from being moral. Slavery to sin arises from being immoral.

The Understanding of Moral Acts

Another important foundation of Christian morality is the understanding of moral acts. Every moral act consists of three elements: the objective act (what we do), the subjective goal or intention (why we do the act), and the concrete situation or circumstances in which we perform the act (where, when, how, with whom, the consequences, etc.).

For an individual act to be morally good, the object, or what we are doing, must be objectively good. Some acts, apart from the intention or reason for doing them, are always wrong because they go against a fundamental or basic human good that ought never to be compromised. Direct killing of the innocent, torture, and rape are examples of acts that are always wrong. Such acts are referred to as intrinsically evil acts, meaning that they are wrong in themselves, apart from the reason they are done or the circumstances surrounding them.

The goal, end, or intention is the part of the moral act that lies within the person. For this reason, we say that the intention is the subjective element of the moral act. For an act to be morally good, one's intention must be good. If we are motivated to do something by a bad intention—even something that is objectively good—our action is morally evil. It must also be recognized that a good intention cannot make a bad action (something intrinsically evil) good. We can never do something wrong or evil in order to bring about a good. This is the meaning of the saying, "the end does not justify the means" (cf. CCC, nos. 1749-1761).

The circumstances and the consequences of the act make up the third element of moral action. These are secondary to the evaluation of a moral act in that they contribute to increasing or decreasing the goodness or badness of the act. In addition, the circumstances may affect one's personal moral responsibility for the act. All three aspects must be good—the objective act, the subjective intention, and the circumstances—in order to have a morally good act.

This teaching, which recognizes both the objective and subjective dimension of morality, is often at odds with a perspective that views morality as a completely personal or merely subjective reality. In such a view, held by some in our culture, there are no objective norms capable of demanding our moral compliance. Such a denial of an objective and unchanging moral order established by God results in a vision of morality and moral norms as being a matter of personal opinion or as established only through the consent of the individual members of society.

The Reality of Sin and Trust in God's Mercy

We cannot speak about life in Christ or the moral life without acknowledging the reality of sin, our own sinfulness, and our need for God's mercy. When the existence of sin is denied it can result in spiritual and psychological damage because it is ultimately a denial of the truth about ourselves. Admitting the reality of sin helps us to be truthful and opens us to the healing that comes from Christ's redemptive act.

> Sin is an offense against reason, truth, and right conscience; it is failure in genuine love for God and neighbor caused by a perverse attachment to certain goods. It wounds the nature of man and injures human solidarity. It has been defined as "an utterance, a deed, or a desire contrary to the eternal law." (CCC, no. 1849, citing St. Augustine, *Contra Faustum*, no. 22)

Thus, by its very definition, sin is understood as an offense against God as well as neighbor and therefore wrong. Sins are evaluated according to their gravity or seriousness. We commit mortal sin when we consciously and freely choose to do something grave against the divine law and contrary to our final destiny.

There are three conditions for a sin to be a mortal sin: grave matter, full knowledge, and deliberate consent (freedom). Mortal sin destroys the loving relationship with God that we need for eternal happiness. If not repented, it results in a loss of love and God's grace and merits eternal punishment in hell, that is, exclusion from the Kingdom of God and thus eternal death.

A venial sin is a departure from the moral order in a less serious matter. "All wrongdoing is sin, but there is sin that is not deadly" (1 Jn 5:17). Though venial sin does not completely destroy the love we need for eternal happiness, it weakens that love and impedes our progress in the practice of virtue and the moral good. Thus, over time, it can have serious consequences. "Deliberate and unrepented venial sin disposes us little by little to commit mortal sin" (CCC, no. 1863).

In considering sin we must always remember that God is rich in mercy. "Where sin increased, grace overflowed all the more" (Rom 5:20). God's mercy is greater than sin. The very heart of the Gospel is the revelation of the mercy of God in Jesus Christ. "For God did not send his Son into the world to condemn the world, but that the world might be saved through him" (Jn 3:17).

To receive this mercy, we must be willing to admit our sinfulness. Sorrow for sin and confession of sin are signs of conversion of heart that open us to God's mercy. Though we can judge a given offense to be the occasion for mortal sin, and thus an act of objective wrongdoing, we must always entrust the judgment of the person to the mercy and justice of God. This is because one person cannot know the extent of another individual's knowledge and freedom, which are integral factors determining when an occasion for mortal sin becomes an actual sin for which we are morally responsible.

The Formation of Conscience

The formation of a good conscience is another fundamental element of Christian moral teaching. "Conscience is a judgment of reason by which the human person recognizes the moral quality of a concrete act" (CCC, no. 1796). "Man has in his heart a law inscribed by God. . . . His conscience is man's most secret core, and his sanctuary" (GS, no. 16).

Conscience represents both the more general ability we have as human beings to know what is good and right and the concrete judgments we make in particular situations concerning what we should do or about what we have already done. Moral choices confront us with the decision to follow or depart from reason and the divine law. A good conscience makes judgments that conform to reason and the good that is willed by the Wisdom of God. A good conscience requires lifelong formation. Each baptized follower of Christ is obliged to form his or her conscience according to objective moral standards. The Word of God is a principal tool in the formation of conscience when it is assimilated by study, prayer, and practice. The prudent advice and good example of others support and enlighten our conscience. The authoritative teaching of the Church is an essential element in our conscience formation. Finally, the gifts of the Holy Spirit, combined with regular examination of our conscience, will help us develop a morally sensitive conscience.

Because our conscience is that inner sanctuary in which we listen to the voice of God, we must remember to distinguish between our subjective self and what is objectively true outside ourselves. We can be subjectively in error about something that is objectively true. On the objective level, if our conscience is "correct," then there is no error between what is internally perceived to be true and truth itself. If there is an incorrect conscience, that means that the conscience is erroneous in its view of truth.

On the subjective level we can have a "certain" conscience, which means we believe that our conscience is in conformity with what is objectively true. A person can have a "certain" conscience on the subjective level but an "incorrect" one on the objective level. For example, a person thinks that Ash Wednesday is a Holy Day of Obligation and chooses to miss Mass anyway. The person thinks it is a Holy Day (certain subjectively but incorrect objectively) and acts on it. This person has a certain but incorrect conscience. But because the conscience acted against what it perceived to be objectively the good, the conscience chooses to sin.

There are some rules to follow in obeying one's conscience. First, always follow a certain conscience. Second, an incorrect conscience must be changed if possible. Third, do not act with a doubtful conscience. We must always obey the certain judgments of our conscience, realizing that our conscience can be incorrect, that it can make a mistake about what is truly the good or the right thing to do. This can be due to ignorance in which, through no fault of our own, we did not have all we needed to make a correct judgment.

However, we must also recognize that ignorance and errors are not always free from guilt, for example, when we did not earnestly seek what we needed in order to form our conscience correctly. Since we have the obligation to obey our conscience, we also have the great responsibility to see that it is formed in a way that reflects the true moral good.

> Through loyalty to conscience Christians are joined to other men in the search for truth and the right solution to many moral problems which arise both in the life of individuals and from social relationships. Hence, the more a correct conscience prevails, the more do persons and groups turn aside from blind choice and try to be guided by the objective standards of moral conduct. (GS, no. 16)

The Excellence of Virtues

The Christian moral life is one that seeks to cultivate and practice virtue. "A virtue is an habitual and firm disposition to do the good. It allows the person not only to perform good acts, but to give the best of himself" (CCC, no. 1803). An effective moral life demands the practice of both human and theological virtues.

Human virtues form the soul with the habits of mind and will that support moral behavior, control passions, and avoid sin. Virtues guide our conduct according to the dictates of faith and reason, leading us toward freedom based on self-control and toward joy in living a good

FROM THE CATECHISM

1. How are we created in the image of God?

It is in Christ, "the image of the invisible God" (Col 1:15) that man has been created "in the image and likeness" of the Creator.... By virtue of his soul and his spiritual powers of intellect and will, man is endowed with freedom, an "outstanding manifestation of the divine image" (GS, no. 17). (CCC, nos. 1701, 1705)

2. What is freedom?

Freedom is the power to act or not to act, and so to perform deliberate acts of one's own. Freedom attains perfection in its acts when directed toward God, the sovereign Good.... The right to the exercise of freedom, especially in religious and moral matters, is an inalienable requirement of the dignity of man. But the exercise of freedom does not entail the putative right to say or do anything. (CCC, nos. 1744, 1747)

3. What are virtues?

Virtue is a habitual and firm disposition to do good.... The human virtues are stable dispositions of the intellect and will that govern our acts, order our passions, and guide our conduct in accordance with reason and faith. They can be grouped around the four cardinal virtues: prudence, justice, fortitude, and temperance.... There are three theological virtues: faith, hope, and charity. They inform all the moral virtues and give life to them. (CCC, nos. 1833, 1834, 1841)

moral life. Compassion, responsibility, a sense of duty, self-discipline and restraint, honesty, loyalty, friendship, courage, and persistence are examples of desirable virtues for sustaining a moral life. Historically, we group the human virtues around what are called the Cardinal Virtues.

This term comes from the Latin word *cardo* meaning "hinge." All the virtues are related to or hinged to one of the Cardinal Virtues. The four Cardinal Virtues are prudence, justice, fortitude, and temperance.

There are a number of ways in which we acquire human virtues. They are acquired by frequent repetition of virtuous acts that establish a pattern of virtuous behavior. There is a reciprocal relationship between virtue and acts because virtue, as an internal reality, disposes us to act externally in morally good ways. Yet it is through doing good acts in the concrete that the virtue within us is strengthened and grows.

The human virtues are also acquired through seeing them in the good example of others and through education in their value and methods to acquire them. Stories that inspire us to want such virtues help contribute to their growth within us. They are gained by a strong will to achieve such ideals. In addition, God's grace is offered to us to purify and strengthen our human virtues, for our growth in virtue can be hampered by the reality of sin. Especially through prayer and the Sacraments, we open ourselves to the gifts of the Holy Spirit and God's grace as another way in which we grow in virtue.

The Theological Virtues of faith, hope, and charity (love) are those virtues that relate directly to God. These are not acquired through human effort but, beginning with Baptism, they are infused within us as gifts from God. They dispose us to live in relationship with the Holy Trinity. Faith, hope, and charity influence human virtues by increasing their stability and strength for our lives.

Each of the Ten Commandments forbids certain sins, but each also points to virtues that will help us avoid such sins. Virtues such as generosity, poverty of spirit, gentleness, purity of heart, temperance, and fortitude assist us in overcoming and avoiding what are called the seven deadly or Capital Sins—pride, avarice or greed, envy, anger, lust, gluttony, and sloth or laziness—which are those sins that engender other sins and vices.

Growth in virtue is an important goal for every Christian, for the virtues play a valuable role in living a Christian moral life.

LOVE, RULES, AND GRACE

Our culture frequently exalts individual autonomy against community and tradition. This can lead to a suspicion of rules and norms that come from a tradition. This can also be a cause of a healthy criticism of a legalism that can arise from concentrating on rules and norms.

Advocates of Christian morality can sometimes lapse into a legalism that leads to an unproductive moralizing. There is no doubt that love has to be the essential foundation of the moral life. But just as essential in this earthly realm are rules and laws that show how love may be applied in real life. In heaven, love alone will suffice. In this world, we need moral guidance from the Commandments, the Sermon on the Mount, the Precepts of the Church, and other rules to see how love works.

Love alone, set adrift from moral direction, can easily descend into sentimentality that puts us at the mercy of our feelings. Popular entertainment romanticizes love and tends to omit the difficult demands of the moral order.

In our permissive culture, love is sometimes so romanticized that it is separated from sacrifice. Because of this, tough moral choices cannot be faced. The absence of sacrificial love dooms the possibility of an authentic moral life.

Scripturally and theologically, the Christian moral life begins with a loving relationship with God, a covenant love made possible by the sacrifice of Christ. The Commandments and other moral rules are given to us as ways of protecting the values that foster love of God and others. They provide us with ways to express love, sometimes by forbidding whatever contradicts love.

The moral life requires grace. The *Catechism* speaks of this in terms of life in Christ and the inner presence of the Holy Spirit, actively enlightening our moral compass and supplying the spiritual strength to do the right thing. The grace that comes to us from Christ in the Spirit is as essential as love and rules and, in fact, makes love and keeping the rules possible.

■ FOR DISCUSSION ■

1. What is the source of the love needed for moral life? Some current understandings of the word *love* refer to behavior that is actually contrary to the true meaning of love. What are some examples of this?

2. Why are the Ten Commandments, the Beatitudes, and other rules needed for us to be moral? What happens when we rely on the Ten Commandments and other rules without love? Can you name someone who models living the Ten Commandments, the Beatitudes, and other rules in real life in a loving way?

3. What are ways or means by which a person forms his or her conscience? What is the role of the Church in conscience formation?

■ DOCTRINAL STATEMENTS ■

- Every person bears the dignity of being made in the image of God. The Creator has given us an immortal soul and enables us to understand the order of things established by him. God has given us a free will to seek and love what is true, good, and beautiful.

- Because of the Fall, we also suffer the impact of Original Sin, which darkens our minds, weakens our wills, and inclines us to sin. Baptism delivers us from Original Sin, but not from its effects—especially the inclination to sin, concupiscence.

- Jesus calls us to be happy and shows us how to attain this. The desire for happiness is a principal motivation for the moral life. Our sinful inclinations, attitudes, and actions prevent us from being totally happy on earth. In heaven, we will have perfect joy.

- God gives us intelligence and the capacity to act freely. We can initiate and control our acts. Social pressures and inner drives may affect our acts and limit our freedom. Normally we are free in our actions.

- "The imputability or responsibility for an action can be diminished or nullified by ignorance, duress, fear, and other psychological and social factors" (CCC, no. 1746).

- The best way to have more freedom is to perform good acts. Good deeds make us free. The road to loss of freedom is through evil acts. Sin makes us slaves of evil and reduces our capacity to be free.
- Every moral act consists of three elements: the objective act (what we do), the subjective goal or intention (why we do the act), and the concrete situation or circumstances in which we perform the act (where, when, how, with whom, the consequences, etc.). All three elements must be good for the act to be morally acceptable.
- Moral laws assist us in determining what is good or bad. Some acts are always wrong—that is, intrinsically evil—and may never be done, no matter what the intention or the circumstances.
- "Conscience is a judgment of reason by which the human person recognizes the moral quality of a concrete act" (CCC, no. 1796).
- A good conscience requires lifelong formation. The Word of God is a principal shaper of conscience when assimilated by study, prayer, and practice. The prudent advice and good example of others support and enlighten our consciences. The authoritative teaching of the Church is an essential element in our conscience formation.
- A good conscience makes judgments that conform to reason and the good that is willed by the wisdom of God.
- We "must always obey the certain judgment of [our] conscience. Conscience can remain in ignorance or make erroneous judgments. Such ignorance and errors are not always free of guilt" (CCC, nos. 1800, 1801).
- An effective moral life demands the practice of human and Theological Virtues. Such virtues train the soul with the habits of mind and will that support moral behavior, control passions, and avoid sin.
- Virtues guide our conduct according to the dictates of faith and reason. We group these virtues around the Cardinal Virtues of prudence, justice, fortitude, and temperance.
- We will benefit greatly from practicing the Theological Virtues of faith, hope, and charity. We receive these virtues from God. They are called theological because they dispose us to live in relationship with the Holy Trinity. Faith, hope, and love influence our human virtues by increasing their stability and strength for our lives.

MEDITATION

Jesus Christ is the ultimate Teacher of morality. He indeed ratified the Ten Commandments, and he also pointed out that every Commandment in the Law and the Prophets is rooted in the two fundamental precepts of love of God and love of neighbor. Though the Old Testament also taught love of God and neighbor, the Lord's precepts were new because he taught us the right measure of love, which includes the love of enemies. We are to love one another "as I have loved you," that is, with a measure of love never seen before on earth. He taught by words and by his life that love essentially involves self-giving and self-sacrifice. We are never deliberately to do evil to anyone to achieve any objective whatsoever.

PRAYER

May the God of peace,
who brought up from the dead the great shepherd of the sheep
by the blood of the eternal covenant, Jesus our Lord,
furnish you with all that is good, that you may do his will.
May he carry out in you what is pleasing to him through
Jesus Christ, to whom be glory forever [and ever]. Amen.

—Heb 13:20-21

Return to me, says the LORD of hosts, and I will return to you.

—Zec 1:3

24 LIFE IN CHRIST— PART TWO

THE PRINCIPLES OF THE CHRISTIAN MORAL LIFE
—CCC, NOS. 1691-2082

HE IS A GOD-FEARING, CHRISTIAN GENTLEMAN

His Catholic faith led Cesar Chavez to improve the lives and livelihood of America's farm workers. Chavez was born on March 31, 1927. Raised in the grinding poverty of the Great Depression, he was trained by his parents to remember that there was always room for one more needy person at their dinner table. He served in the Navy for two years during World War II.

After the war, Chavez met a priest who ministered to the Mexican American migrant workers. The priest told Chavez about Catholic teachings concerning the rights of workers. Chavez said, "I would do anything to get Father to tell me more about labor history. I began going to the *bracero* (guest worker) camps with him to help with the Mass, to the city jail to talk to the prisoners, anything to be with him."

Chavez soon became active in drives for voter registration and in countering abuses against Mexican immigrants and Mexican American immigrants. During the 1960s, his organizing efforts gave birth to the United Farm Workers. But federal laws exempted the agriculture industry from the requirement of allowing free exercise of the right of farm workers to organize a union. Chavez had to find a unique way to get the growers to recognize his union. He resorted to the strategy of consumer boycotts. In 1968, he led the nation's first grape boycott. At one point, 17 million Americans honored the boycott. Chavez went further and asked the American bishops to support the boycott. In response, they intervened to mediate the conflict.

An owner of a large vineyard who fiercely opposed Chavez's United Farm Workers decided to ask Catholic bishops to help with the negotiations. They responded positively. Subsequent meetings with Chavez helped change the owner's mind about him.

Chavez gradually won many concessions. He operated from the perspective of faith, prayer, fasting, and the Church's teachings on justice. He linked the economy with morality. He aroused deep sentiments of self-respect and pride among his people.

He lived simply. While other union leaders received a six-figure salary, he lived on $5 a week and expenses, just like any other member of his union. Nothing tempted him away from *La Causa* (The Cause).

Cesar Chavez was enlightened by the Gospel and Jesus Christ. He knew that God loved the world and wanted to save it. He focused on one segment of the world, the poor who work in the fields. He was guided by Catholic teachings about respect for the dignity of each human person, the nobility of work, and the responsibility of all people to contribute to the common good and to be wise stewards of the goods of the earth.

He died on April 23, 1993. California has honored Cesar Chavez with a holiday in his honor on March 31.

Chavez once said, "I am convinced that the truest act of courage is to sacrifice ourselves for others in a totally non-violent struggle for justice." He sought a life in Christ both in his personal life and in his vision of social justice. This commitment to life in Christ is the theme of Part Three of the *Catechism*.

***

LIFE IN CHRIST—PART TWO

"Do to others whatever you would have them do to you. This is the law and the prophets" (Mt 7:12). This "Golden Rule" taught by Jesus in his Sermon on the Mount is a golden thread that weaves its way through the moral life of the Christian. It is a behavior that flows from life in Christ and in the Holy Spirit. Our journey in the moral life begins by looking at the person of Jesus, listening to his voice, and responding to the strong yet gentle movement of the Holy Spirit.

The *Catechism of the Catholic Church* presents to us the elements, foundations, and principles that serve as a sturdy point of departure for reflecting on Christian morality. This guidance from Christ brought to us through the Church is designed to help us answer his invitation to be holy, to be moral, to be fulfilled exactly in the way that God intended. The previous chapter focused on the individual human being as called to act morally. This chapter discusses morality as it pertains to the individual as situated within a community.

HUMAN COMMUNITY AND DIVINE ASSISTANCE: FURTHER FUNDAMENTAL ELEMENTS OF CHRISTIAN MORALITY

Consciousness of Solidarity and Social Justice

An awareness of the social dimension of human life is an important principle in understanding Christian morality, especially in light of the great emphasis on individualism in our society. The social aspect of what it means to be human is revealed in the natural inclination we have to seek social interaction and establish community. This awareness serves as a moral foundation for an attitude of solidarity with each other and leads to a dedication to social justice for everyone. Our Gospel commitment to Christ's Kingdom of love, justice, and mercy always includes advocating and supporting fairness for all. God calls us to form community and to correct both the symptoms and causes of injustice that rip apart the solidarity of a community.

Before God gave the Commandments at Sinai, he entered into a covenant of love with the community of Israel (cf. Ex 19:3-6). Once the covenant was established, God gave the people the Ten Commandments in order to teach them the way to live the covenant of love.

In Christ we have been called to a New Covenant and a New Law that fulfills and perfects the Old Law. We also are invited to experience God's love for us and to return that love to God and to our neighbor. Our love of neighbor includes our solidarity with the human community and a commitment to social justice for all.

We need to respect the human dignity of every person. Governments and all other social institutions should serve and enhance the dignity of people. Society has the responsibility to create the conditions that favor the growth of virtues and of authentic spiritual and material values.

People need to live in a human community where the authority is based on human nature and recognized and understood as having its origin in God (cf. CCC, nos. 1898, 1899). Political authority should be used for the common good. "The common good comprises 'the sum total of social conditions which allow people, either as groups or as individuals, to reach their fulfillment more fully and easily'" (CCC, no. 1924, citing GS, no. 26 §1). Governments ought to use morally acceptable means to foster the common good of all and establish the conditions that assure citizens of the proper exercise of their freedom. In fostering this common good excessive intervention by the government in the lives of individuals is to be avoided. The principle of subsidiarity teaches that governments should help and support individuals and groups for whom they are responsible without controlling their freedom and initiative (cf. CCC, no. 1883).

Just as governments and social institutions need to respect the unique human dignity of every individual, it is also the responsibility of every individual to do the same. Attitudes of prejudice and bias against any individual for any reason, as well as actions or judgments based on prejudiced or biased views, violate God's will and law.

Social justice is both an attitude and a practical response based on the principle that everyone should look at another person as another self. It is also a virtue that directs all the other virtues of individuals toward the common good. Civil laws can partially help to eliminate fears, prejudices, and attitudes of pride and selfishness that cause injustice, but an inner spiritual conversion is also needed.

Solidarity with others at every level is a way of accomplishing this. Solidarity takes many forms: "solidarity of the poor among themselves, between rich and poor, of workers among themselves, between employers and employees in a business, solidarity among nations and peoples" (CCC, no. 1941).

Examples of offenses against human solidarity are slavery and racism. Slavery reduces a human being to an object to be bought and sold. It is a failure to recognize the God-given dignity and rights of a human being. Racism is an attitude that rejects the fundamental equality of all human beings. It shows itself in discrimination and unjust actions against people of other races. Both slavery and racism are gravely immoral.

God's Law as Our Guide

We are assisted to know God's plan for our salvation through his law written in our human nature and revealed to us in his word. All things come to be and find their purpose and goal in God's plan. Thus we can speak of the eternal law as the wisdom of God ordering all things rightly.

It is God who brings creation into being; thus the physical world acts according to his plan found in the physical laws of nature. He also made man and woman in his own image and likeness. Human beings, then, are also directed according to God's created plan, written in their hearts and implanted in their human nature. "Man participates in the wisdom and goodness of the Creator who gives him mastery over his acts and the ability to govern himself with a view to the true and the good. The natural law expresses the original moral sense which enables man to discern by reason the good and the evil, the truth and the lie" (CCC, no. 1954). We come to know it through our human reason and through its confirmation in Divine Revelation.

Through our human reason, we can come to understand the true purpose of the created order. The natural law is thus our rational apprehension of the divine plan. It expresses our human dignity and is the foundation of our basic human rights and duties. This law within us leads us to choose the good that it reveals. Its most pronounced expression is found in the Ten Commandments, described as "the privileged expression of the natural law" (CCC, no. 2070).

Because the natural law is rooted in God's plan found in human nature, it applies to all people in all places and at all times. While situations may vary greatly, the natural law is unchangeable. It abides at the core of what makes us human and thus is not affected by the flow and currents from cultural ideas and customs. While a given person, region, culture, or era of time may attempt to suppress it, the fundamental principles of the natural law never die and soon reappear, even where they were once rejected.

We come to know God's plan for us not only through an understanding of our human nature and his created order but also because he speaks directly to us. In the Old Testament, God communicated to Moses the Ten Commandments. This Law prepared the world for the Gospel. Christian tradition reveres this Law as holy but in need of God's grace for its fulfillment. It is like a teacher who can tell us what to do but is not able to give us the strength to perform it. Nonetheless, we honor this Law as an aid to God's people on the way to the Kingdom. It prepared people to receive Christ.

In Jesus, Revelation comes to us in its fullness. His words shed light on the human condition in a way that transcends and fulfills the law written in our heart and God's plan revealed in the Old Testament.

In the Sermon on the Mount, Jesus revealed the full meaning of the Old Testament Law. "Do not think I have come to abolish the law and the prophets. I have come not to abolish but to fulfill" (Mt 5:17). Christ's teaching releases the hidden meaning of the Old Law and reveals its Divine Truth and human truth. Jesus established the law of love because love is poured into our hearts by the Holy Spirit. It is a law of grace, as we note in the next section.

Grace and Justification

God also directly assists us in living our moral life through the divine gift of grace and justification, first bestowed upon us in Baptism when we become members of the Church. We are justified—cleansed from our sins and reconciled to God—through the power of the Holy Spirit. Justification is both the Spirit's work in bringing us forgiveness of sins and our acceptance or reception of the holiness of God, which we call sanctification through participation in divine life. Christ's Passion merited justification for us. We receive justification in Baptism and become friends of God. We are thus conformed to the righteousness of God who justifies us. Justification's goal is God's glory and the glory of Christ and the gift of eternal life. It is a work of God's mercy (cf. CCC, no. 2020).

Grace is the free and undeserved assistance God offers us so that we might respond to his call to share in his divine life and attain eternal life. God's grace, as divinely offered gift, does not take away or restrict our freedom; rather, it perfects our freedom by helping us overcome the restricting power of sin, the true obstacle to our freedom. We call the grace of the Holy Spirit that we receive through faith in Jesus Christ the New Law. Significant expressions of this Law are found in Christ's Sermon on the Mount and his Last Supper discourse, where he emphasizes union with him in love as the substance and motivation for his law of grace.

> Grace is the help God gives us to respond to our vocation of becoming his adopted sons. It introduces us into the intimacy of the Trinitarian life. The divine initiative in the work of grace precedes, prepares, and elicits the free response of man. Grace responds to the deepest yearnings of human freedom, calls freedom to cooperate with it, and perfects freedom. Sanctifying grace is the gratuitous gift of his life that God makes to us; it is infused by the Holy Spirit into the soul to heal it of sin and to sanctify it. (CCC, nos. 2021-2023)

In addition to speaking about sanctifying grace, we also speak of actual graces. These refer to the particular interventions God offers us to aid us in the course of the work of sanctification. We recognize that many times and in many ways God's special love is such that he offers us help to live in a way that leads to sharing his life. Finally, there are sacramental graces, which are proper to the celebration of the Seven Sacraments, and special graces or charisms, which, while given to individuals, are meant for the common good of the Church (cf. CCC, no. 2003).

In this recognition of the reality and important role of grace in the Christian moral life, we face a struggle prompted by our culture's understanding that everything is within our human power. "My power is sufficient." Compare this with our understanding that we are indeed blessed and gifted, but much of what we fight to achieve—while written in our hearts—still needs God's grace because of the presence of sin and our inherent human weakness. The New Law is truly Good News, for not only does God give us the moral law that leads us to salvation, but through grace we receive divine assistance to follow it. We should always take heart from the words Our Lord spoke to St. Paul: "My grace is sufficient for you, for power is made perfect in weakness" (2 Cor 12:9).

The Church as Mother and Teacher

God assists us in living the moral life through the Church, who is our mother and teacher. The faith of the Church is found in its Creed and in its ordinary teaching, as articulated by its shepherds, the pope, and the bishops in communion with him.

Jesus said to the Apostles, "Whoever listens to you listens to me" (Lk 10:16). In the Church, when we deal with matters of faith and morals, the authoritative voice of Christ is exercised by the pope and bishops, successors of Peter and the Apostles who form the Magisterium. They are guided by the Holy Spirit, who abides with the Church to lead us into all truth.

The Church hears the perennial questions that each person asks at some point: "How shall I live?" "What values or principles shall I accept?" "What norms shall I make my own?" "What gives meaning to my life?" To answer questions such as these, we turn to a wise teacher. Christ is the ultimate teacher, and he continues to be heard in and through the Church today. The *Catechism* notes that "the *Magisterium of the Pastors of the Church* in moral matters is ordinarily exercised in catechesis and preaching, with the help of the works of theologians and spiritual authors" (CCC, no. 2033). In the task of teaching and applying the vision and practice of Christian morality, the Church relies on the dedication of pastors and the studies of theologians, as well as the contributions of all people of goodwill (cf. CCC, no. 2038).

The response based on faith that Catholics must give to the Church's teaching authority—the Magisterium—extends also to moral principles:

> The Church, the "pillar and bulwark of the truth," "has received this solemn command of Christ from the apostles to announce

FROM THE CATECHISM

1. Why is happiness a motivation to be moral?

The Beatitudes respond to the natural desire for happiness. This desire is of divine origin: God has placed it in the human heart in order to draw man to the One who alone can fulfill it. (CCC, no. 1718)

2. What is social sin?

Sin makes men accomplices of one another and causes concupiscence, violence, and injustice to reign among them. Sins give rise to social situations and institutions that are contrary to the divine goodness. "Structures of sin" are the expression and effect of personal sins. They lead their victims to do evil in their turn. In an analogous sense, they constitute a "social sin." (CCC, no. 1869)

3. What is the New Law?

The New Law or the Law of the Gospel is the perfection here on earth of the divine law, natural and revealed. It is the work of Christ and is expressed particularly in the Sermon on the Mount. It is also the work of the Holy Spirit, and through him it becomes the interior law of charity: "I will establish a New Covenant with the house of Israel. . . . I will put my laws into their minds, and write them on their hearts, and I will be their God, and they shall be my people." (CCC, no. 1965, citing Heb 8:8, 10)

the saving truth." "To the Church belongs the right always and everywhere to announce moral principles, including those pertaining to the social order, and to make judgments on any human affairs to the extent that they are required by the fundamental rights of the human person or the salvation of souls." (CCC, no. 2032, citing 1 Tm 3:15; LG, no. 17; CIC, can. 747 §2)

LIVING WITH FAITH AND HOPE
AFTER SEPTEMBER 11, 2001

This reflection is from the bishops of the United States on the tragedy of September 11, 2001. It was an event that dramatized the issues of good and evil and the need to draw moral guidance from the teachings of Christ and the Church.

After September 11, 2001, we are a wounded people. We share loss, pain, anger and fear, shock, and determination in the face of these attacks on our nation and all humanity. We also honor the selflessness of firefighters, police, chaplains, and other brave individuals who gave their lives in the service of others. They are true heroes and heroines.

Our nation has turned to God in prayer and in faith with a new intensity. This was evident in the prayers on the cell phones on hijacked airliners, on stairways in doomed towers, in cathedrals and parish churches, at ecumenical and interfaith services, in our homes and hearts.

Our faith teaches us about good and evil, free will, and responsibility. Jesus' life, teaching, death, and Resurrection show us the meaning of love and justice in a broken world. Sacred Scripture and traditional ethical principles define what it means to make peace. They provide moral guidance on how the world should respond justly to terrorism in order to reestablish peace and order.

The Role of Religion

We are particularly troubled that some who engage in and support this new form of terror seek to justify it, in part, as a religious act. Regrettably, the terrorists' notion of a religious war is inadvertently reinforced by those who would attribute the extremism of a few to Islam as a whole or who suggest that religion, by its nature, is a source of conflict. . . .

It is wrong to use religion as a cover for political, economic, or ideological causes. It compounds the wrong when extremists of any religious tradition distort their professed faith in order to justify violence and hatred. Whatever the motivation, there can be no religious or moral justification for what happened on September 11. People of all faiths must be united in the conviction that terrorism in the name of religion profanes religion. The most effective counter to terrorist claims of religious justification comes from within the world's rich religious traditions and from the witness of so many people of faith who have been a powerful force for nonviolent human liberation around the world.

A Time for Teaching

Many Catholics know the Church's teaching on war and peace. Many do not. This is a time to share our principles and values, to invite discussion and continuing dialogue within our Catholic community. Catholic universities and colleges, schools, and parishes should seek opportunities to share the Sacred Scripture and Church teaching on human life, justice, and peace more broadly and completely. In a special way, we should seek to help our children feel secure and safe in these difficult days. [Note: the Church's teaching on war appears in Chapter 29.]

A Time for Hope

Above all, we need to turn to God and to one another in hope. Hope assures us that, with God's grace, we will see our way through what now seems such a daunting challenge. For believers, hope is not a matter of optimism, but a source for strength and action in demanding times. For peacemakers, hope is the indispensable virtue. This hope, together with our response to the call for conversion, must be rooted in God's promise and nourished by prayer, penance, and acts of charity and solidarity. (United States Conference of Catholic Bishops, *A Pastoral Message: Living with Faith and Hope after September 11* [Washington, DC: USCCB, 2001])

THE PRECEPTS OF THE CHURCH
(SEE CCC, NOS. 2041-2043)

In addition to presenting the foundations for Christian morality, the *Catechism of the Catholic Church* includes a section on the Precepts of the Church. These are rules set in the context of a moral life, bound to and nourished by liturgical life. The obligatory character of these positive laws decreed by the pastoral authorities is meant to encourage on the part of the faithful the indispensable foundations for their lives as Catholics. The precepts are as follows:

- You shall attend Mass on Sundays and Holy Days of Obligation. Sunday, the day of the Resurrection, should be treated differently from the other days of the week. We do that in making the day holy by attending Mass and refraining from doing unnecessary work. Holy Days of Obligation, when we celebrate special feasts of Jesus, the Blessed Mother, and the saints, should be marked in the same way.
- You shall confess your sins at least once a year. This obliges in particular those who are conscious of serious sin. Regular reception of the Sacrament of Penance and Reconciliation helps to prepare us not only to receive the Eucharist but also to continue the process of conversion begun in Baptism.
- You shall receive the Sacrament of the Eucharist at least during the Easter season. In the United States, this extends from the First Sunday of Lent to Trinity Sunday. Because the Holy Eucharist is both the source and summit of life for all in the Church, the Church teaches that every member for his or her own good must receive Communion minimally at least once a year.
- You shall observe the prescribed days of fasting and abstinence. *Fasting* is refraining from food or drink to some

degree. *Abstinence* is refraining from eating meat. The Church identifies specific days and times of fasting and abstinence to prepare the faithful for certain special feasts; such actions of sacrifice can also help us to grow in self-discipline and in holiness.

- You shall help to provide for the needs of the Church. This means contributing to the support of the activities of the Church with time, talent, and financial resources, each according to their ability.

FOR DISCUSSION

1. As you review fundamental elements of Christian moral living, which ones gave you a new perspective on Christian moral life? How can all of them become a regular part of the growth of your life in Christ and the Spirit?

2. Moral life based on the teaching of Scripture flows from God's loving plan for us. How does this correspond to your view of what the moral life is about? How would you live out such a plan?

3. You are called to faithful assent to the Church's teachings on faith and morals. What challenges do you experience? How do you handle them? What motivates you to be a morally good person?

DOCTRINAL STATEMENTS

- God's divine law establishes our final destiny and the path to reach it. God has planted within each of us the natural law that is a reflection of his divine law.

- The natural law is our rational apprehension of the created moral order, an ability we have because we are made in God's image. It expresses our human dignity and forms the basis of our basic rights and duties.

- Divine wisdom leads us through various types of law (divine law, natural law, civil law, ecclesiastical [Church] law) designed to guide us to the very goals that will answer our deepest human aspirations.

- Revealed law is seen in the Old Testament when God communicated the Ten Commandments to Moses. The Commandments, along with the teaching of the Prophets and other revealed law, prepared the world for the Gospel.

- Christ's teachings release the hidden meaning of the Old Law and reveal its Divine Truth and human truth. The Gospel is a law of love because of the love poured into our hearts by the Holy Spirit.

- "Justification is the most excellent work of God's love made manifest in Christ Jesus and granted by the Holy Spirit" (CCC, no. 1994). Justification is both the Spirit's work in bringing us forgiveness of sins and our acceptance or reception of the holiness of God, which we call sanctification through participation in divine life.

- "Sanctifying grace is a habitual gift, a stable and supernatural disposition that perfects the soul itself to enable it to live with God, to act by his love. Habitual grace, the permanent disposition to live and act in keeping with God's call, is distinguished from actual graces, which refer to God's interventions, whether at the beginning of conversion or in the course of the work of sanctification" (CCC, no. 2000).

- "Sanctifying grace is the gratuitous gift of his life that God makes to us; it is infused by the Holy Spirit into the soul to heal it of sin and to sanctify it" (CCC, no. 2023).

- Christ's Passion merited justification for us. We receive justification in Baptism and become friends of God. We are thus conformed to the righteousness of God who justifies us.

- God called Israel to be holy. "You shall be holy, because I am holy" (Lv 11:45). St. Peter extended this invitation from God to Christians. "As he who called you is holy, be holy yourselves in every aspect of your conduct, for it is written, 'Be holy because I [am] holy'" (1 Pt 1:15-16).

- Jesus said to the Apostles, "Whoever listens to you listens to me" (Lk 10:16). In the Church, when we deal with matters of faith and morals, the authoritative voice of Christ is exercised by the pope and bishops who, as the successors of Peter and the Apostles, form the Magisterium. They are guided by the Holy Spirit, who abides with the Church to lead us into all truth.

- "The Magisterium of the Pastors of the Church in moral matters is ordinarily exercised in catechesis and preaching, with the help of the works of theologians and spiritual authors" (CCC, no. 2033).

- "Society ensures social justice by providing the conditions that allow associations and individuals to obtain their due" (CCC, no. 1943). Social justice deals with the essential needs of people who are called to live together in community with respect for each other's dignity. These needs include food, clothing, shelter, and an income that supports the family.

- "The principle of solidarity, also articulated in terms of 'friendship' or 'social charity,' is a direct demand of human and Christian brotherhood" (CCC, no. 1939). This involves a love for all peoples that transcends national, racial, ethnic, economic, and ideological differences. It respects the needs of others and the common good in an interdependent world.

MEDITATION

The Story of America has been the story of long and difficult struggles to overcome the prejudices which excluded certain categories of people from a full share in the country's life: first, the struggle against religious intolerance, then the struggle against racial discrimination and in favor of civil rights for everyone. Sadly, today a new class of people is being excluded. When the unborn child—"the stranger in the womb"—is declared beyond the protection of society, not only are America's deepest traditions radically undermined and endangered, but a moral blight is brought upon society. I am also thinking of threats to the elderly, the severely handicapped and all those who do not seem to have any social usefulness. When innocent human beings are declared inconvenient or burdensome, and thus unworthy of legal and social protection, grievous damage is done to the moral foundations of the democratic community.

—Pope John Paul II, Homily delivered at Giants Stadium
during pastoral visit to the United Nations and the
United States (October 5, 1995), no. 6

PRAYER

Act of Hope
O my God,
Relying on your infinite goodness and promises,
I hope to obtain pardon of my sins,
The help of your grace, and life everlasting,
through the merits of Jesus Christ, my Lord and Redeemer.

Now that you have been freed from sin and have
become slaves of God, the benefit that you have
leads to sanctification, and its end is eternal life.

—Rom 6:22

25 THE FIRST COMMANDMENT: BELIEVE IN THE TRUE GOD

"I, THE Lord, AM YOUR GOD. . . . YOU SHALL NOT HAVE
OTHER GODS BESIDES ME" (EX 20:2-3)
—CCC, NOS. 2083-2141

CATHERINE DE HUECK DOHERTY: LAY APOSTLE OF THE TWENTIETH CENTURY

In 1896, a daughter Catherine was born to Theodore and Emma Kolychkine, a wealthy couple who were deeply religious members of the Russian Orthodox Church. From her earliest years, Catherine accompanied her mother in bringing food, medicine, and clothing to less fortunate neighbors. Her mother wanted Catherine to learn to see the face of God in every human being.

Shortly after Catherine's marriage to the wealthy aristocrat Boris de Hueck, the Russian Revolution forced the couple to flee to England, where Catherine embraced Roman Catholicism, and then to Canada, where their son George was born. After the financial crisis of 1929, Boris's business failed. Soon after, the marriage also failed and was ultimately annulled by the Catholic Church in 1943.

Catherine had witnessed the inroads that Communism was making in the world. She warned people that atheism would destroy their human dignity, but few listened. Catherine became totally convinced that only Christ's Gospel would bring the justice and peace so needed by the world, and she determined to dedicate her life uncompromisingly to Jesus Christ as a layperson.

In 1931, with the blessing of Archbishop Neil McNeil of Toronto—and after making arrangements for her son—Catherine sold all her possessions, moved to the slums of Toronto, and embraced a life according to the Gospel. She lived a life of prayer and service to the poor. She rented a storefront and called it "Friendship House." Here she provided food, clothing, and shelter to the poor and homeless. A small group of like-minded people joined her, and together they lived the spirituality of St. Francis of Assisi.

In 1938, at the request of Fr. John LaFarge, SJ, a civil rights pioneer, Catherine established another Friendship House in Harlem in New York City. As in Toronto, a small group of followers joined her. During this time, Catherine met the American journalist Eddie.Doherty, and they were married in the Catholic Church in 1943. Eddie joined in the life of the Chicago Friendship House. As a result of controversy and criticism, Catherine and Eddie left the United States to live on a small piece of land that Eddie owned in Combermere, Ontario, and entered the most fruitful and enduring phase of their lives.

At their home, Madonna House, Catherine and Eddie started a training center for the Catholic lay apostolate. Former Friendship House staffers and others came to join the work. At the urging of Msgr. Giovanni Battista Montini—later Pope Paul VI—Catherine, Eddie, and their followers professed simple vows of poverty, chastity, and obedience as a sign of permanent commitment to their apostolate. Catherine and Eddie lived celibate lives from that point on.

Madonna House grew. Priests, laymen, and laywomen came from all over the world to live the gospel spirituality that Catherine taught and a lifestyle modeled after the Holy Family of Nazareth. Because of her reputation as a contemplative prayerful woman and her renown as a spiritual writer, many came to be counseled by Catherine, who directed individuals away from herself and to Christ instead. At the request of many bishops, Madonna House established apostolic centers throughout the world.

In 1985, ten years after Eddie's death, Catherine died, leaving behind a spiritual heritage. Reflective of what she learned from her mother and how she had lived her own life, Catherine urged her followers to be *cruciform*: to stretch out one hand to God and the other to the neighbor, to see God everywhere and in everyone, and to pour out their lives in service. The scope of Catherine's apostolate has spread to more than twenty houses on five continents.

Catherine's life illustrates the First Commandment in that she lived her life loving the Lord with all her heart, soul, and mind above all else and, because of that, respected and worked for the dignity of every human being.

THE ROLE OF THE COMMANDMENTS

God helps us in many different ways to live a moral life. He gives us grace, which awakens in us the desire to say no to temptation and sin and to choose only that which is good. He gives us the Theological and Cardinal Virtues and the grace to practice human virtues so that we can grow stronger in them. God gives us help and grace through the Church and through our reception of the Sacraments. He also teaches us how we should live. One way he does this is by giving us laws to guide our actions. The Ten Commandments are laws that God has revealed to us. Heeding the guidance God gives us in the Commandments will help us know how to serve God and how we should live with each other. It also helps us to be open to the grace of the Holy Spirit and what God can accomplish in us and through us by that grace.

THE FIRST COMMANDMENT

The first three Commandments treat our relationship to God. The last seven concern our relationship with each other. The First Commandment calls us to have faith in the true God, to hope in him, and to love him fully with mind, heart, and will. We respond to God, who has created and redeemed us and extends his providential care to us every minute of each day. The First Commandment fosters the virtue of religion that moves us to adore God alone because he alone is holy and worthy of our praise.

Adoring God, praying to him, offering him the worship that belongs to him, fulfilling the promises and vows made to him are acts of the virtue of religion which fall under obedience to the first commandment. (CCC, no. 2135)

All the Commandments call us to practice certain virtues and forbid a number of immoral behaviors. The positive invitation of the First Commandment calls us to practice the Theological Virtues of faith, hope, and charity by believing in the three Persons of the Holy Trinity, placing all our hope in them, and loving them with our whole heart and mind.

Faith

God has given us the virtue of faith, which is a personal response to the Lord's Revelation of his holiness, love, beauty, and transcendence. We experience hints of his majesty in creation, traces of his love in the human love we receive, and impulses of his concern for us in our inner life, especially in the movements of conscience. Our faith is also communal, coming to us from our families and parish community. Above all, our faith in God is a gift of grace and is constantly nourished by the Holy Spirit from the moment of our Baptism, through our prayer life, our participation in the Eucharist and the Sacraments, and our Christian witness.

While it is the duty of all to worship and serve God, regrettably, there are some who do not believe in him and others who seriously doubt his existence. Some hesitate to believe because they cannot overcome their objections to faith, or are puzzled by the mystery of God. Some of the baptized later lapse into heresy. "*Heresy* is the obstinate post-baptismal denial of some truth which must be believed with divine and catholic faith, or it is likewise an obstinate doubt concerning the same" (CCC, no. 2089).

Apostasy is a total repudiation of the faith (cf. CCC, no. 2089). *Schism* is the refusal to submit to the pope's authority as head of the Church. Christ calls us to have a prayerful, reconciling attitude toward people with difficulties in their faith, to help them toward assent to the truth of faith.

Hope

God has given us the virtue of hope. Hope fills us with the confidence that God accompanies us on our journey through life and guides us to eternal life with him. If we refuse this gift of hope, we stray into presumption or its opposite, despair. In the sin of presumption, we think we will be saved without any personal commitment to the moral life. In the sin of despair, we lose hope in God's mercy and believe we cannot be saved.

Love

Finally, God has given us the virtue of love, the very love that he has for us. Our Lord asks us to accept this love and respond to him with it. Jesus made the love of God the first of the two greatest Commandments: "You shall love the Lord, your God, with all your heart, with all your soul, and with all your mind" (Mt 22:37). We sin against this call to love by indifference, ingratitude, lukewarmness, spiritual sloth, and hatred of God (cf. CCC, no. 2094).

ISSUES RELATED TO THE FIRST COMMANDMENT

Idolatry

The First Commandment prohibits idolatry, the worship of false gods. In ancient times, people worshiped created things such as the sun, moon, stars, trees, bulls, eagles, and serpents. In some cases, emperors and kings were considered divine, and worship of them was expected.

Israel was forbidden to make images of God: Do not "degrade yourselves by fashioning an idol to represent any figure" (Dt 4:16). This injunction against "graven images" was based on the conviction that God is greater and more mysterious than any artistic representation of him. It also restrained Israel from carving idols like the pagans and lapsing into idolatry. But the people of Israel could make images that symbolically pointed toward salvation by the Messiah, such as the bronze serpent, the Ark of the Covenant, and the cherubim (cf. CCC, no. 2130).

Christians, however, have been permitted to fashion religious art. The veneration of icons—religious images of Christ, Mary, the angels, and the saints—was upheld by the seventh Ecumenical Council at Nicea (AD 787), in opposition to the iconoclasts—those who rejected the use of religious images such as statues, paintings, and mosaics. The fact that, in the Incarnation, Christ took on human nature provided the foundation for the Church's tradition that artistic images such as icons can portray mysteries of salvation. Whoever venerates a holy image venerates the person portrayed. This veneration of Mary and the saints—and images of them—differs from the adoration that belongs to God alone.

Today idolatry has emerged in new forms, whenever something created is given absolute value. Examples of where this happens include power, money, materialism, and sports. Also, those who resort to astrology, palm reading, and interpretation of omens by mediums, clairvoyants, and others who claim to control time and history weaken their faith in God, lapse into superstition, and sometimes fall into sin. Those who get involved with cults or the occult (e.g., magic, witchcraft, Satanism) open themselves to evil influence, undermine their faith in the true God, and commit sin.

Some contemporary individuals turn to a New Age spirituality. This spirituality does not have a doctrinal basis but reflects many religious strands from the non-Christian East, various occult practices like astrology, and some insights from psychology. Practitioners tend to abandon doctrinal teaching on the Trinity, Jesus Christ, the Church, and the sacraments. They also ignore the moral teaching of God and the Church.

Atheism

In the context of our culture, atheism often wears the face of secularism in its extreme form. Atheists or radical secularists deny God's existence. Some are strict materialists, believing that ultimately there is nothing spiritual whatsoever. Some are secular humanists, who claim that humans should control history and the world with no reference to God. Christians must always examine their own behavior because lack of consistency with the Gospel in their lives can encourage others in atheism.

FROM THE CATECHISM

1. Why should we adore the true God alone?
We adore God because he is God and deserving of our adoration. Human life finds its unity in the adoration of the one God. "Idolatry is a perversion of man's innate religious sense" (CCC, no. 2114). The Commandment to worship God alone integrates man and saves him from an endless disintegration.

2. What is the link between God's love and the Commandments?
God has loved us first. The love of the One God is recalled in the first of the "ten words." The commandments then make explicit the response of love that man is called to give to his God. (CCC, no. 2083)

3. How is it possible to obey God's commands?
What God commands he makes possible by his grace. (CCC, no. 2082)

Believers . . . have more than a little to do with the rise of atheism. To the extent that they are careless about their instruction in the faith, or present its teaching falsely, or even fail in their religious, moral, or social life, they must be said to conceal rather than reveal the true nature of God and of religion. (GS, no. 19)

Agnosticism

This is another way to evade the call of the First Commandment. The term *agnostic* means "I don't know." It comes in different forms. Some agnostics admit God's existence but claim nothing can be known about him. Others say it is impossible to know whether there is a God. Some agnostics are searching for God; others do not try. Many are practical atheists, who may not consciously deny God's existence, but live as if he does not exist.

THE HOLINESS OF GOD IN DAILY LIFE

When God appeared to Moses on Mount Horeb, he said, "The place where you stand is holy ground" (Ex 3:5). The sixth chapter of Isaiah describes the prophet's vision of God and hearing the angels sing, "Holy, holy, holy is the Lord" (Is 6:3). Moses reacts to God's holiness with awe, a deep reverence for the all-embracing majesty of God. Isaiah responds to God's holiness with an awareness of the profound and infinite purity of God. Both men undergo a spiritual transformation that they attribute to their experience of God's holiness.

The First Commandment is more than a reference to an abstract idea of God. It is an announcement of the presence of the most holy God, both in outward creation and within the human soul. His existence does call for our faith.

Our surrounding culture is filled with many distractions that shut out the majestic voice of our holy and glorious God. St. Augustine, commenting on his troubled youth, speaks of this experience with these words, "You were with me, but I was not with you. Created things kept me from you; yet if they had not been in you they would not have been at all." But God was not simply a passive presence to Augustine, a diffident lover wondering what to do. Augustine tells us that God spoke with a vigorous voice. "You called, you shouted, and you broke through my deafness. You breathed your fragrance on me. . . . I have tasted you, now I hunger and thirst for more" (*The Confessions*, bk. 10, no. 27).

This is the best context for appreciating the importance of the First Commandment. As God did with Augustine, he does for us again—calling, shouting, trying to break through our deafness, breathing his fragrance upon us.

Many, indeed, are listening. Numerous Catholics are seeking a deeper relationship with God through daily Mass, frequent reception of the Sacraments, the prayerful reading of Scripture, retreats, spiritual direction, diverse forms of prayer, and devotional practices. With Augustine, they can say, "You touched me, and I burned for your peace."

FOR DISCUSSION

1. Most people in our culture say they believe in the existence of God. What causes the disconnection between that belief and the behavior of many?
2. How do you find that acts of faith, hope, and love bring you closer to God and make your behavior an act of praise to the Lord?
3. How can we discover the presence of God in our lives? How can we share an awareness of this reality with others?

DOCTRINAL STATEMENTS

- "I, the LORD am your God. . . . You shall not have other gods besides me. . . . You shall love the LORD, your God, with all your heart, and with all your soul, and with all your strength" (Ex 20:2-3; Dt 6:5).
- The positive invitation of the First Commandment calls us to practice the Theological Virtues of faith, hope, and charity by believing in, hoping in, and loving God, and by our willingness to adore the Holy Trinity. The Theological Virtues relate directly to the living God.
- "Adoring God, praying to him, offering him the worship that belongs to him, fulfilling the promises and vows made to him are acts of the virtue of religion which fall under obedience to the first commandment" (CCC, no. 2135).
- Based on our faith in the Incarnation of Christ, we venerate images of Christ, Mary, the angels, and the saints. We do not worship the images themselves, but in venerating the image, we venerate whoever is portrayed—Jesus Christ, Mary, a saint, or an angel. This in turn can lead us to a deeper contemplation of God himself.
- The First Commandment forbids idolatry, which is the worship of a creature or an object.
- Other sins against the First Commandment include tempting God, which means that we put his power to the test as Satan did with

Jesus in the temptations in the desert; sacrilege, which means treating with disrespect persons, places, or things consecrated to God—above all the Eucharist; and simony, which is the buying or selling of spiritual things.

- "Since it rejects or denies the existence of God, atheism is a sin against the first commandment" (CCC, no. 2140).

- At the heart of our faith is our assent of mind and will to all that God reveals, all that the Church defines, and all that is presented by the Church in her ordinary and universal Magisterium as Christ's way to salvation.

MEDITATION

Prayer of the Heart

Prayer and converse with God is a supreme good: it is a partnership and union with God. As the eyes of the body are enlightened when they see light, so our spirit, when it is intent on God, is illumined by his infinite light. I do not mean the prayer of outward observance but prayer from the heart, not confined to fixed times or periods but continuous throughout the day and night.

Our spirit should be quick to reach out toward God, not only when it is engaged in meditation; at other times also, when it is carrying out its duties, caring for the needy, performing works of charity, giving generously in the service of others, our spirit should long for God and call him to mind, so that these works may be seasoned with the salt of God's love, and so make a palatable offering to the Lord of the universe.

—St. John Chrysostom, Homily 6, "On Procreation," in the *Liturgy of the Hours*, vol. II, 68-69

PRAYER

Act of Love

O my God, I love you above all things,
with my whole heart and soul,
because you are all good and worthy of all my love.
I love my neighbor as myself for the love of you.
I forgive all who have injured me,
and ask pardon of all whom I have injured.

"Your way, O God, is holy; / what god is as great as our God?"
Grant us, that without fear we might worship you
in holiness all our days.

—Ps 77:14; cf. Lk 1:73

26 THE SECOND COMMANDMENT: REVERENCE GOD'S NAME

"YOU SHALL NOT TAKE THE NAME OF THE Lord
YOUR GOD IN VAIN" (EX 20:7)
—CCC, NOS. 2142-2167

JOB: THE POOR MAN PRAISES GOD

Why do the innocent suffer? This has been an age-old question that is addressed in Scripture as well, perhaps most extensively in the Book of Job. Written probably in the sixth century BC, it tells the story of a prosperous and prestigious man named Job, father of a large family and deeply devoted to God. In a series of calamities provoked by Satan, Job loses everything—family, wealth, and even his own health. In the midst of all this loss, he cries out,

Naked I came forth from my mother's womb,
   and naked shall I go back again.
The Lord gave and the Lord has taken away;
   blessed be the name of the Lord! (Jb 1:21)

Nothing could shake his faith in God. His wife, seeing his pitiable state, tells him, "Curse God and die" (2:9). He responds, "We accept good things from God; and should we not accept evil?" (2:10). Three friends come to see Job and argue with him, telling him that he must have sinned against God and so is being punished. But Job insists that he has done nothing to offend God and is not deserving of such punishment. No matter how deep his anguish, he maintains his confidence in God:

> But as for me, I know that my Vindicator lives,
>> and that he will at last stand forth upon the dust;
> Whom I myself shall see:
>> my own eyes, not another's shall behold him,
> And from my flesh I shall see God;
>> my inmost being is consumed with longing. (19:25-27)

Job does question why God has afflicted him in this way, and he wants to plead his cause before God. He narrates all the good things he has done and wants God to respond to his questioning. A young man joins the conversation between Job and his friends. He is severe in his condemnation of Job's questioning of God. But then God suddenly appears to Job and says to him,

> Who is this that obscures divine plans
>> with words of ignorance?
> Gird up your loins now, like a man;
>> I will question you, and you tell me the answers!
> Where were you when I founded the earth?
>> Tell me, if you have understanding.
> Who determined its size; do you know? (38:2-5)

God then discloses to Job the majesty and order of creation, revealing himself as the Creator of all and as always mysterious in his workings. Job, the innocent man who has suffered, is privileged with an extraordinary revelation of God's wisdom and hiddenness. He is awed and overwhelmed by God's coming to him. He repents of his questioning and responds to God by acknowledging his greatness:

> I know that you can do all things,
>> and that no purpose of yours can be hindered.
> I have dealt with great things that I do not understand;
>> things too wonderful for me, which I cannot know.
> I had heard of you by word of mouth,
>> but now my eye has seen you.
> Therefore I disown what I have said,
>> and repent in dust and ashes. (42:2-5)

God then corrects the three friends because "you have not spoken rightly concerning me, as has my servant Job" (42:8). God then restores Job to health, grants him a family, and makes him prosperous once again.

Even in the midst of great suffering, Job praised God and, because of his fidelity, experienced the awesomeness, majesty, and holiness of God. In every circumstance of his life, he kept holy God's name.

⚜

THE NAME OF GOD IS HOLY

The second commandment [requires] respect for the Lord's name. Like the first commandment, it belongs to the virtue of religion and more particularly it governs our use of speech in sacred matters.

—CCC, no. 2142

At the burning bush, Moses asked God for his name. God replied, "I am who am. . . . This is what you shall tell the Israelites: I AM sent me to you" (Ex 3:14). The Hebrews treated this name for God with such respect that they did not speak it. It was honored in silence. Only the high priest, once a year at the feast of atonement, pronounced this name at the incense offering in the Holy of Holies in the temple. Out of reverence for the revealed holy name, the people substituted the name *Adonai*, which means "Lord." Modern Jews adapt this custom by writing "*G-d*" instead of the customary spelling.

The Second Commandment calls us to the virtue of reverence for God, which trains us to know and to preserve the difference between the Creator and the creature. Respect for God's name keeps us from reducing him to a mere fact, or even a thing that we can control or manipulate. At the same time, a gracious God desires to be intimate with us, even becoming incarnate in Jesus Christ and dwelling in us through the Holy Spirit. In John's Gospel, Jesus applies to himself the expression "I AM" (cf. Jn 8:58), thus identifying himself with God. He distinguishes himself from his Father and from the Holy Spirit, whom he will send to the world after his Resurrection. This was one way Jesus opened us to understanding God as Trinity.

A name in some way conveys the reality of a person—the origin, the history, the very being of the person. That is why people are protective about their names and expect them to be treated with honor. The name of God obviously deserves the highest honor and respect. The Lord gives us a Commandment that asks us to reverence his name and not to use it in a disrespectful or manipulative way. When Jesus taught the Our Father, his first petition was "Hallowed be thy name." We also praise God's holy name in every Mass at the beginning of the Eucharistic Prayer when we recite or sing the Holy, Holy, Holy.

We also draw strength from recalling our Baptism, which initiated us into the Church "in the name of the Father and of the Son and of the Holy Spirit." To be baptized in the name of the Trinity means to be immersed into the very life of the Father, Son, and Spirit. God's name sanctifies us. In Baptism, we also commonly receive the name of a saint, a disciple of Christ who has led an exemplary life, to remind us of our call to holiness. Patron saints—that is, the saint or saints whose name we have been given—serve as examples of the way to holiness by their witness to faith, hope, and love. They also intercede with God for our benefit. God calls us by name. Our name is sacred. We need to honor God's name and the names of others to make our world a center of dignity and respect.

THE WRONG USE OF GOD'S NAME

The Second Commandment forbids the wrong use or misuse of God's name. There are a number of ways in which this happens. Blasphemy uses the name of God and of Jesus Christ as well as those of the Blessed Mother and the saints in an offensive manner. The *Catechism* teaches that blasphemy consists "in uttering against God—inwardly or outwardly—words of hatred, reproach, or defiance" (CCC, no. 2148). This is gravely sinful. Habitual disrespect for God, displayed in cursing and even in the use of vulgar language, can create an attitude that erodes our relationship with the Lord.

FROM THE CATECHISM

1. What does the Second Commandment ask of us?
The second commandment *prescribes respect for the Lord's name*. Like the first commandment, it belongs to the virtue of religion and more particularly it governs our use of speech in sacred matters. (CCC, no. 2142)

2. Name one act forbidden by the Second Commandment.
The second commandment forbids every improper use of God's name. Blasphemy is the use of the name of God, of Jesus Christ, of the Virgin Mary, and of the saints in an offensive way. (CCC, no. 2162)

3. Why is our baptismal name important?
In Baptism, the Christian receives his name in the Church. Parents, godparents and the pastor are to see that he be given a Christian name. The patron saint provides a model of charity and the assurance of his prayer. (CCC, no. 2165)

At the same time, we recognize diminished culpability when the name of God is used because of an outburst of undisciplined speech due to passion or unexpected incitement to anger. We need to cultivate a persistent reverence for sacred names; if we do not, we can end up giving bad example and also fall into the sin of blasphemy. It should also be noted that in Scripture, the sometimes passionate language of the Prophets, in which they lament the troubles of their times and utter loud complaints to God, is not blasphemy or the taking of God's name in vain. It is actually prayer addressed to God.

We are forbidden to use God's name to witness a perjury or false oath, thereby using him to approve our lie.

God's name has been invoked to justify unjust wars and terrorism, slaughter enemies, and impose unwarranted power over others. Many have used the God of love to promote hatred, the God of trust to facilitate betrayal, and the God of mercy to validate acts of cruelty. Critics of religion cite the suffering and cruelty caused by the excesses by some of those who participated in the Crusades, the wars of religion during the Reformation, and the Salem witch trials as examples of using God's name to justify such acts. The sins of Christians do indeed undermine the credibility of faith. The name of God must never be used to support immoral acts.

O LORD, HOW GLORIOUS IS YOUR NAME OVER ALL THE EARTH (CF. PS 8:2)

When we bring to our culture this experience of the holiness of God's name, we arrive with a gift for society that can be all the better when the sacred is accepted as beneficial for the culture. It is no secret that irreverence for God and sacred matters is present in certain sectors of our society. For believers this is embarrassing, painful, and inappropriate. Public discourse at times routinely displays little sensitivity to the revered values of people of faith. Of course, this is not universally true. There are many people who show respect for matters religious. People of goodwill can be as dismayed as men and women of faith at the departures from decency in speech and the disregard for the holiness of God's name.

Everyone's name is important. We honor the dignity of persons by using their names with respect. Surely we will honor each other's names if we acquire a habitual reverence for God's name. Reverencing the name of God honors him. This is the beginning of treating each other with the respect for a dignity that is based on our being created as an image of God.

Scripture highlights numerous ways in which God's name is vital for our faith life. When Job was in the midst of his worst sufferings, he said, "The LORD gave and the LORD has taken away; / blessed be the name of the LORD" (Jb 1:21). God's name sustained him in his suffering. When the psalmist wanted to express exultant praise of God and thanksgiving for favors received, the holy name was invoked, "Bless the LORD, my soul; / all my being, bless his holy name" (Ps 103:1).

Jesus taught that he would be present to those who come together in his name. "Where two or three are gathered together in my name, there am I in the midst of them" (Mt 18:20). St. Peter staked his entire ministry on the utter uniqueness of Jesus, the only Savior, by employing the power of his name: "There is no salvation through anyone else, nor is there any other name under heaven given to the human race by which we are to be saved" (Acts 4:12). St. Paul proclaimed that the name of Christ is an occasion for the adoration of the Son of God:

> God greatly exalted him / and bestowed on him the name / that is above every name, / that at the name of Jesus / every knee should bend, / of those in heaven and on earth and under the earth. (Phil 2:9-10)

When the Blessed Virgin Mary praised God for calling her to be the Mother of his Son, she chanted, "Holy is his name" (Lk 1:49). All of these sublime tributes to God's name enliven our faith and love for God. They provide us with the context to understand the meaning of the Second Commandment.

This is a good time for people of faith to witness their love for God's name by appealing to those who err in this regard to reconsider what they say and appreciate how it affects others. Those who are involved in preaching and catechizing should always remember to model and encourage adoration. In order to be examples to society, believers themselves need to be temperate in the use of their tongues.

FOR DISCUSSION

1. In your family or workplace, what means do you take to eliminate the wrong use of God's name? What have you found to be the most effective approaches?
2. How do you help young people to address the use of coarse language in films, TV, and music? What has proven to be the most successful method?

3. Why is it correct to say that blasphemous talk and similar types of language corrupt the user? What are some new ways to elevate public taste and the moral quality of public entertainment?

■ DOCTRINAL STATEMENTS ■

- The Second Commandment requires *respect for the Lord's name.* Like the First Commandment, it belongs to the virtue of religion, and more particularly it governs our use of speech in sacred matters (cf. CCC, no. 2142).
- The Second Commandment forbids the wrong use of God's name. There are a number of ways in which it happens. Blasphemy uses the name of God and of Jesus Christ and the names of the Blessed Virgin and the saints in an offensive manner.
- In Baptism, the Christian receives a name in the Church. Parents, godparents, and the pastor are to see that he or she be given a Christian name. The patron saint provides a model of charity and the assurance of prayer (cf. CCC, no. 2165).
- We are forbidden to use God's name to witness a perjury or false oath, thereby using him to approve our lie.

■ MEDITATION ■

The Letter of James in the New Testament contains a reminder of the power of human speech:

If anyone does not fall short in speech, he is a perfect man, able to bridle his whole body also. If we put bits into the mouths of horses to make them obey us, we also guide their whole bodies. It is the same with ships: even though they are so large and driven by fierce winds, they are steered by a very small rudder wherever the pilot's inclination wishes. In the same way the tongue is a small member and yet has great pretensions. Consider how small a fire can set a huge forest ablaze. The tongue is also a fire. It exists among our members as a world of malice, defiling the whole body and setting the entire course of our lives on fire, itself set on fire by Gehenna. For every kind of beast and bird, of reptile and sea creature, can be tamed and has been tamed by the human species, but no human being can tame the tongue. It is a restless evil, full of deadly poison. With it we bless the Lord and Father, and with it we curse human beings who are made in the likeness of God. From the same mouth come blessing and cursing. This need not be so, my brothers. Does a spring gush forth from the same opening both pure and brackish water? Can a fig tree, my brothers, produce olives, or a grapevine figs? Neither can salt water yield fresh.

—Jas 3:2-12

PRAYER

The Divine Praises

Blessed be God.
Blessed be his holy Name.
Blessed be Jesus Christ, true God and true Man.
Blessed be the name of Jesus.
Blessed be his most Sacred Heart.
Blessed be his most Precious Blood.
Blessed be Jesus in the most holy Sacrament of the altar.
Blessed be the Holy Spirit, the Paraclete.
Blessed be the great Mother of God, Mary most holy.
Blessed be her holy and Immaculate Conception.
Blessed be her glorious Assumption.
Blessed be the name of Mary, Virgin and Mother.
Blessed be Saint Joseph, her most chaste spouse.
Blessed be God in his angels and in his saints.

Bless the LORD, my soul;
   and all my being, bless his holy name!

—Ps 103:1

27 THE THIRD COMMANDMENT: LOVE THE LORD'S DAY

REMEMBER TO KEEP HOLY THE LORD'S DAY
—CCC, NOS. 2168-2195

IT'S THE MASS THAT MATTERS

The history of the Church in the United States includes missionaries and priest circuit-riders who traveled widely in their territories to bring the Mass and the other Sacraments to the Catholic people. Fr. Junipero Serra planted mission stations in California from San Diego to Sonoma. Fr. Jacques Marquette did the same in the early days of Michigan and Wisconsin. Fr. Eusebio Kino rode the trails of Arizona to bring the Eucharist to the dispersed pioneers settling the new lands. Fr. Pierre DeSmet served the North American Indians in parts of the upper Midwest. Briefly sketched here are stories of two priests who gave witness to these ideals.

An unlikely and colorful pioneer priest was Fr. Demetrius Gallitzin. He was born as a prince in 1770. His father was a Russian prince, and his mother a Prussian countess. Fr. Gallitzin was raised an Orthodox Christian but became a Catholic after his mother's conversion to the Catholic Church. Upon completing his education, he emigrated to the United States.

In Baltimore, he met Bishop John Carroll, who interested him in missionary work. Fr. Gallitzin enrolled at Mount St. Mary's Seminary and was ordained a priest in 1795. He soon obtained permission to go to Captain Michael McGuire's settlement in western Pennsylvania. Once he arrived there, Fr. Gallitzin built a small church and celebrated the first Mass in it on Christmas Day, 1799.

He financed this and other projects from a subsidy he received from his mother. He encouraged migration by buying land and offering it to settlers at a low price. He declined several calls to become a bishop in order to stabilize his local community. In 1816, Fr. Gallitzin planned a town and laid out its two main streets. He changed the name of the area from "McGuire's settlement" to Loretto. He became vicar-general for western Pennsylvania. The strong Catholicism he established is reflected in the area's heavily Catholic population today. Called the "Apostle to the Alleghenies," Fr. Gallitzin planted a durable seed that became a great tree, a community of the baptized where the Eucharist nourished the faith.

Fr. James Fitton was born in Boston in 1805 to Abraham Fitton, an English wheelwright, and Sarah (Williams) Fitton of Wales. James Fitton attended public school in Boston, and Claremont Academy in New Hampshire. When he asked to become a priest, Bishop Benedict Joseph Fenwick of Boston oversaw his theological studies and ordained Fr. Fitton in 1827. He soon took up missionary assignments in Connecticut, Rhode Island, and central and western Massachusetts.

In 1831, Fr. Fitton was the only priest serving in what is today the Archdiocese of Hartford and the Dioceses of Bridgeport and Norwich in Connecticut and Springfield and Worcester in Massachusetts. He brought the Mass and the other Sacraments to two thousand Catholics scattered across that region. By contrast, today there are nearly two thousand priests serving about two million Catholics in that same territory.

Fr. Fitton was the typical circuit-riding priest of that early period. He was known to have celebrated the first Mass ever in many locations in what is now known as the Worcester diocese. A pioneer in Catholic education, he founded Mount St. James Seminary, Worcester, which became the College of the Holy Cross run by the Jesuits. Fr. Fitton was the first New England priest to celebrate his fiftieth anniversary as a priest. He died in 1881 and is called the "Apostle to New England."

These two men realized that observing the Day of the Lord meant providing the faithful the opportunity to attend Mass. They did it by establishing mission stations that eventually became chapels and then parish churches with resident pastors. Through God's providential care, devoted priests established stable communities where the Mass was offered, and equally devoted believers attended Mass.

❧ ⁓≈✦≋≋✦≈⁓ ❧

THE SABBATH DAY

The *Catechism* starts its reflection on the Third Commandment with the scriptural meaning of the Sabbath. Exodus 20:8-11 states that the Sabbath was the seventh day on which the Lord rested after the work of the previous six days. Deuteronomy 5:12 adds that the Sabbath is a day of our renewing the covenant with God. The Sabbath is connected to creation and covenant.

God's "rest" on the seventh day was his contemplative gaze enjoying the good of creation, especially its crown in man and woman. It was not a matter of divine inactivity, but rather the deeper "work" of contemplation and the restful act of loving us (cf. CCC, nos. 2184-2185). This is true also of ourselves. If we never stop working, when would we ever have time to contemplate and worship God and nourish a love relationship with him or with anyone else? Every human person, having been created by God, owes him worship and thanksgiving for what the Lord has done and continues to do.

The scriptural history of the Sabbath demonstrates that it was a day of worship of God and relaxation with one's family: "Then [on the Sabbath] you shall delight in the LORD / and I will make you ride on the heights of the earth" (Is 58:14). At their liturgies, the people of ancient Israel remembered the great works God performed on their behalf. They looked back on their history and family roots in the light of God's plans for them. They sang praises to God for his love and mercy. They recalled, "Everything belongs to God!" The Christian Sunday carries forward Sabbath themes of contemplative rest and worship.

THIS IS THE DAY THE LORD HAS MADE

*Jesus rose from the dead "on the first day of the week."
. . . For Christians it has become the first of all days, the
first of all feasts, the Lord's Day.*

—CCC, no. 2174

The Third Commandment calls us to keep holy the Sabbath day. For
Christians, the observance of the Sabbath is transferred to Sunday, the
day that Jesus rose from the dead. God, through the Church, obliges us
to make Sunday holy by participation in the Eucharist and by our being
prayerfully reflective as far as possible. Sunday observance fulfills the
interior law inscribed in the human heart to render to God visible and
public worship as a sign of radical dependence upon God and as gratitude for all the blessings we have received.

Every seven days, the Church celebrates the Easter mystery. This
tradition goes back to the time of the Apostles. It takes its origin from
the actual day of Christ's Resurrection. Sunday extends the celebration
of Easter throughout the year. It is meant to be illumined by the glory
of the Risen Christ. It makes present the new creation brought about
by Christ.

Sunday also recalls the creation of the world. The Genesis account
of creation, expressed in poetic style, is a hymn of awe and adoration of
God in the presence of the immensity of creation.

The Fathers of the Second Vatican Council explained how we should
celebrate the Eucharist on Sunday, or its vigil on Saturday evening:

> The Church, therefore, earnestly desires that Christ's faithful,
> when present at this mystery of faith, should not be there as
> strangers or silent spectators. On the contrary, through a good
> understanding of the rites and prayers they should take part in
> the sacred action, conscious of what they are doing, with devo-
> tion and full collaboration. They should be instructed by God's
> word and be nourished at the table of the Lord's Body. They
> should give thanks to God. Offering the immaculate victim, not
> only through the hands of the priest, but also together with

him, they should learn to offer themselves. Through Christ, the Mediator, they should be drawn day by day into ever more perfect union with God and with each other, so that finally God may be all in all. (SC, no. 48)

Our presence at Eucharist must be more than a passive experience of the work of the priest and the music from the choir. We should join actively in the worship, where everyone present pours out adoration of and love for God. The more we meditate upon what we are doing, the more we will worship in spirit and truth and benefit from the grace that flows from the Eucharist. We will grow in our love and worship of God as well as in respect and love for one another.

WHY GO TO CHURCH ON SUNDAY?

The intimate bond between Sunday and resurrection of the Lord is strongly emphasized by all the churches of East and West. In the tradition of the Eastern churches in particular, every Sunday is the anastaseos hemera, the day of resurrection, and this is why it stands at the heart of all worship.

—Pope John Paul II, *Day of the Lord*
(*Dies Domini*; DD), no. 19

While it is the first day of the week, Sunday is also called the "eighth day"—a day signifying eternity. Sunday fulfills and completes the Sabbath because it anticipates our eternal rest in God. The Sabbath remembered the first creation. Sunday recalls the new creation in Christ and the Spirit.

The heart of Sunday is the celebration of the Holy Eucharist. The practice of celebrating the Eucharist on Sunday dates from the earliest times. For example, St. Justin Martyr (AD 100-165) wrote as follows: "We all gather on the day of the sun, for it is the first day [after the Jewish sabbath, but also the first day] when God, separating matter from darkness, made the world; and on this same day Jesus Christ our Savior rose from the dead" (I *Apol.* 67: cf. PG 6, 429 and 432; cf. CCC,

FROM THE CATECHISM

1. What is our Sunday obligation?

Sunday "is to be observed as the foremost holy day of obligation in the universal Church. On Sundays and other holy days of obligation the faithful are bound to participate in the Mass." (CCC, no. 2192, citing CIC, cann. 1246 and 1247; see Glossary in this book for list of Holy Days of Obligation)

2. May we work on Sunday?

On Sundays and other holy days of obligation the faithful are bound . . . to abstain from those labors and business concerns which impede the worship to be rendered to God, the joy which is proper to the Lord's Day, or the proper relaxation of mind and body. (CCC, no. 2193)

3. What Sabbath principle governs rest and relaxation?

The Sabbath brings everyday work to a halt and provides a respite. It is a day of protest against the servitude of work and the worship of money. (CCC, no. 2172)

no. 2174). By their Sunday celebration of the Eucharist, the Catholic faithful fulfill both the Third Commandment to "keep holy the Lord's day" and the words of Jesus to his disciples at the Last Supper: "Do this in memory of me" (Lk 22:19).

The Third Commandment has been concretized for Catholics by one of the Precepts of the Church.

Because the faithful are obliged to attend Mass unless there is a grave impediment, pastors have the corresponding duty to offer everyone the real possibility of fulfilling the precept. . . . Yet more than a precept, the observance should be seen as a need rising from the depths of Christian life. It is crucially important that all the faithful should be convinced that they cannot live their faith or share fully in the life of the Christian community unless they take part regularly in the Sunday Eucharistic assembly. (DD, nos. 49, 81)

For a Catholic, the Sunday Eucharist must be the most important religious exercise of the week. In it, we offer our lives in sacrifice with Jesus to the Father, thereby participating directly in the great mysteries of our faith.

The Catholic parish, shepherded by the priest under the authority of the diocesan bishop, is the ordinary setting for Sunday worship and is central to the preparation for and celebration of all the Sacraments.

While Sunday is the time for worship, it is also an occasion for rest and relaxation. We should make time to be with one another in meals, conversation and activities that deepen family life. "Every Christian should avoid making unnecessary demands on others that would hinder them from observing the Lord's Day. Traditional activities (sports, restaurants, etc.), and social necessities (public services, etc.), require some people to work on Sundays, but everyone should still take care to set aside sufficient time for leisure" (CCC, no. 2187; cf. no. 2186). The Eucharistic celebration does not stop at the church door. Those who participate at Mass carry their joy, faith, and concern for others from the Mass into the rest of the day, and indeed into the week that follows.

RESTORE SUNDAY

After the Christian religion obtained its freedom under the Roman emperor Constantine in the fourth century, civil laws were passed to limit unnecessary work on Sunday. The greatest beneficiaries were the poor who otherwise worked long hours every day of the week. Centuries later, at the height of the Industrial Revolution, sweatshops were established in large cities where men, women, and children worked fifteen hours a day, often on Sundays.

Today in some places in our country, those seven-day sweatshops have returned. This is both an injustice to the poor and also an abuse of Sunday rest, and we need to find ways to correct this. "God's action is a model for human action. If God 'rested and was refreshed' on the seventh day, man too ought to 'rest' and should let others, especially the poor, 'be refreshed'" (CCC, no. 2172).

Millions of people in our culture deny themselves a day of rest. Incessant activity, so characteristic of a consumer society, means that Sunday is rarely a day of rest. Exceptions are made for those who must work for the public good, but this is not the problem. Too many people are just as busy and exhausted on Sundays as they are on weekdays. For many, Sunday is neither a day of rest nor a time for worship.

God built into human nature the rhythm between work and rest. We should treat this rest as sacred because it is our way of withdrawing from the demands of our work so that we have time to realize God's providential care of creation. Our remarkable progress in gaining control over the world can cause us to forget that God is the Creator upon whom everything depends. Science and technology are admirable gifts, but they must not be allowed to obscure the real author of all that is. Keeping the Lord's Day holy can also serve as a helpful corrective for a "consumer" society that tends to place value on people for their productivity and material possessions.

Sunday rest puts our whole life into perspective. It helps us stand back from material concerns and reflect on spiritual values. Taking a breather from the pressures of the workplace, we are freed to open our souls to matters that have eternal significance. Sunday rest allows us to look again at the wonders of nature and experience the harmony and peace placed there by God. It is a precious time for rediscovering the fundamental goodness of creation as it comes from God's providential hand.

Sunday also provides the opportunity for families to be together and to engage in common activities. Weekday schedules often require members of the family to spend much time away from each other. Participation in the Eucharist and other activities can renew the bonds of love and unity.

Athletic events for young people have sometimes interfered with the Sunday Mass observance of Catholic youth. Until recently, Sunday morning was a sacred time in most communities and neighborhoods, set aside for church attendance. Before this is abandoned on behalf of sports activities or other unexpected intrusions, it is hoped that Catholic pastors and other Christian religious leaders, with the support of their congregations, may prevail on sponsors of athletic events to adapt their programs to the religious needs of youth. We must preserve the opportunity to go to Mass on Sundays without competition from sporting events, work, or other temptations.

On Sunday, we can also seek out forms of culture and entertainment that enhance the message of the Gospel and foster spiritual growth. A proper observance of Sunday can thus be a prophetic stance in our culture, offering a witness that is both wholesome and healing for the great number of people who need to be less frantic and more willing to let go and settle down to what best corresponds to their spiritual nature and yearnings.

FOR DISCUSSION

1. What is your Sunday like? How can it become a balance of worship, restful reflection, and personal spiritual renewal? What pressures make this a challenge for you, and what can you do about them? How does Sunday Mass enrich your life, your relationships, and the rest of your week?
2. What can be done to free up poor people from unfair working practices that deprive them of the gift of the Christian Sunday? How can families reverse the trend sponsored by those who schedule athletic events for children and young people on Sunday morning?
3. How does consumerism eat away at the Christian ideals of Sunday? What are ways that family gatherings could again become a regular feature of Sunday life?

DOCTRINAL STATEMENTS

- "Take care to keep holy the sabbath day as the LORD, your God, commanded you. Six days you may labor and do all your work; but the seventh day is the sabbath of the LORD" (Dt 5:12-14).

- For Christians, the observance of the Sabbath has been transferred to Sunday, the day that Jesus rose from the dead. On Sundays and other holy days of obligation, the Catholic faithful are bound to participate in the Mass. A Catholic who deliberately fails to participate in Mass on Sundays and Holy Days of Obligation commits a serious sin.

- Sunday extends the celebration of Easter throughout the year. It is meant to be illumined by the glory of the Risen Christ. It makes present the new creation brought about by Christ.

- Sunday also recalls the first creation as well as the new creation. The Genesis account of creation, expressed in poetic style, is a hymn of awe and adoration of God in the presence of the immensity of creation. On Sunday, we remember the wonder of what the risen Son of God has done for us in his new creation.

- While Sunday is a time for worship, it is also an occasion for rest and relaxation. We should make time to be with one another in meals, conversation, cultural and social growth, and the deepening of family life.

MEDITATION

Church attendance and participation in worship has tended to decline in the modern industrial democracies, including the United States. However, there is still reason to have hope. There are more Catholics at Mass on a single weekend than all the fans that go to major league baseball games in an entire season. Maintaining and even increasing this level of attendance at Mass will be helped by a more fervent and active participation in the Eucharist.

Here are ways to help people prepare better for Sunday Mass:

- Go to Mass prepared to worship God.
- Approach the Mass with the intention of participating fully and actively in the celebration, singing the hymns and psalms and reciting the prayers with conviction and faith.
- Enter into the mystery of faith in the Mass. The sacrificial self-gift of Christ to the Father is made present through the Holy Spirit. If we

unite ourselves with him in his self-gift, we truly fulfill what is at the heart of being a priestly people.

• Read and pray over the Scripture texts for the Sunday liturgy in order to prepare for the Mass. Pray for light from God's Word on your needs.

• Spend time learning about the Mass: its structure, intentions, and the meanings within the prayers and its rituals.

• Come to Mass with a community-minded attitude. Keep in mind that liturgy is a communal act of worship in which faith is strengthened by contact with other believers in a context where the Holy Spirit is forming the worshipers into the unity of the Church, the Body of Christ.

• Always remember the sacrifice of the Mass is the Church's greatest prayer of praise and thanksgiving to God the Father in which the Lord Jesus is truly present as Savior of the world and is received in the Sacrament of the Eucharist as food for eternal life.

PRAYER

Come, let us sing joyfully to the LORD;
    cry out to the rock of our salvation.
Let us greet him with a song of praise,
    joyfully sing out our psalms.
For the LORD is the great God,
    the great king over all gods,
Whose hand holds the depths of the earth;
    who owns the tops of the mountains. . . .
Enter, let us bow down in worship;
    let us kneel before the LORD who made us.

—Ps 95:1-4, 6

Give to the LORD the glory due his name!
Bring gifts and enter his court.

—Ps 96: 8

28 THE FOURTH COMMANDMENT: STRENGTHEN YOUR FAMILY

HONOR YOUR FATHER AND YOUR MOTHER
—CCC, NOS. 2196-2257

THE MARRIED AMONG THE BLESSED

On October 21, 2001, Rome witnessed an unprecedented event when three siblings attended the beatification of their parents, the first husband and wife raised together to the rank of the Blessed.

Maria Corsini was born in Florence on June 24, 1884. Luigi Beltrame Quattrocchi was born in Catania on January 12, 1880. They met in Rome as teenagers and were married in the basilica of St. Mary Major on November 25, 1905.

Maria was the daughter of an army captain. A lover of music, she became a professor of education and wrote widely on the subject. A member of Women's Catholic Action, she spoke frequently to women's lay groups. She worked in relief efforts in Ethiopia during World War II.

Luigi was a talented lawyer whose career brought him into the Italian government as an assistant attorney general. He was close to many leaders of the government and worked with them in the reconstruction of Italy after the end of World War II.

Maria and Luigi had four children, two boys and two girls. The boys became priests. Filipo, now Fr. Tarcisio, is a diocesan priest in Rome. Cesare, now Fr. Paolino, is a Trappist. Enrichetta is a consecrated lay woman.

Stefania, who became Sr. Maria Cecilia, a cloistered Benedictine nun, died in 1963.

The Quattrocchis were a middle-class family whose home was a welcoming place and even became a shelter for refugees during World War II.

The couple went through a crisis in 1913 when Maria became pregnant. Doctors told her that she would not survive the pregnancy and that the child also would die. They said that an abortion could save her life. Maria and Luigi knew that if they followed the doctors' advice, they would be guilty of a grave sin. They simply put their trust in God's protection. Maria ultimately delivered Enrichetta safely. The whole experience brought the family to a new level of living their faith and trust in God.

In his homily at the beatification of this couple, Pope John Paul II cited this question of Jesus, "When the Son of Man comes, will he find faith on earth?" (Lk 18:8). The pope said that Luigi and Maria were an example of a positive reply to Christ's question. The husband and wife lived in the first half of the twentieth century, a time when faith was severely challenged. In this setting, they always said "yes" to Christ.

Throughout those difficult years, Luigi and Maria kept the lamp of faith burning and passed it on to their four children. Acknowledging the presence of three of them at the beatification, the pope quoted a line their mother had written about them: "We brought them up in the faith, so that they might know and love God."

The beatification was held on the twentieth anniversary of the publication of *On the Role of the Christian Family in the Modern World* (*Familiaris Consortio*; FC), a document from Pope John Paul II. *Familiaris Consortio* asks couples to follow the path of holiness by virtue of the sacramental grace "which is not exhausted in the actual celebration of the sacrament, but rather accompanies the married couple throughout their lives" (FC, no. 56).

Blessed Luigi and Blessed Maria walked that journey of holiness in the light of the Gospel and in a deeply human way. Their son Fr. Tarcisio remembered that "the aspect that characterized our family life was the atmosphere of normality that our parents created in the constant seeking of spiritual values."

No family is without its steady dose of disappointments and trials. Many are tempted to discouragement. There are those who face illness and those who endure the death of a child or a spouse. Luigi and Maria had their share of troubles and handled them with courage and faith.

Addressing the married couples at the beatification, the Holy Father asked them to learn from the example of Maria and Luigi, "as you face difficulties and trials in being faithful to your vocation, in cultivating conjugal and family harmony, in carrying out the mission of parents and participating in the life of society." Luigi died in 1951, Maria in 1965.

Luigi and Maria lived their ordinary life in an extraordinary way. They centered their life on the daily Eucharist. They also had a strong devotion to the Virgin Mary, to whom they prayed every evening. They met regularly with their spiritual director. Their fidelity to the Gospel and their heroic virtues were verified in their lives as spouses and parents. Their prayers and example can guide us in our reflection on the Fourth Commandment.

THE CHRISTIAN FAMILY

Marriage and family are ordered to the good of the spouses, to the procreation and education of children. . . . Children owe their parents respect, gratitude, just obedience, and assistance.

—CCC, nos. 2249, 2251

The first three Commandments help us to understand how to love God with our whole selves. The next seven Commandments teach us how to love each other as we love ourselves.

The Fourth Commandment deals with all aspects of family life— parental and filial duties and responsibilities, that is, those of love from child to parent. This includes the duties of children toward their parents, the duties of brothers and sisters toward each other, and the responsibilities of adult children toward their older parents. This Commandment also addresses the duties of government and the duties of citizens (cf. CCC, nos. 2234-2246), including the responsibility of the state and society to foster family values and to strengthen the family in every possible way.

THE DOMESTIC CHURCH—
THE CHURCH OF THE HOME

The Catholic family as a domestic church is the fundamental community or cell of the parish, the diocese, and the universal Church. Christ has called all family members to union with God through Baptism and the other Sacraments and to share in the mission of the whole Church. Family members carry out the Church's mission by fostering mutual love in the home and, through that love, by building up the community of the Church and society.

> The Christian home is the place where children receive the first proclamation of the faith. For this reason the family home is rightly called "the domestic church," a community of grace and prayer, a school of human virtues and of Christian charity. (CCC, no. 1666)

The Christian family forms an environment within which faith is professed and witnessed. When family members pray together, engage in lifelong learning, forgive one another, serve each other, welcome others, affirm and celebrate life, and bring justice and mercy to the community, they help each other live the faith and grow in faith. Some families may not understand themselves as a domestic church. Perhaps they consider their family too broken to be used for the Lord's purposes. They need to remember that a family is holy not because it is perfect, but because God's grace is at work in it.

What is a family? "A man and a woman united in marriage, together with their children, form a family" (CCC, no. 2202). A family as defined in the *Catechism* may be found in a considerable portion of the households in our nation. Other familial arrangements have developed, such as single-parent families, blended families, and families in which adult children care for their parents as well as their own children. All families are beset with many challenges. They deserve compassion and the hope that they can be faithful to Christ's way of love.

The Christian family is called to be a community of faith, hope, and love in an environment of prayer. Aided by a number of other virtues, such as prudence, justice, fortitude, and temperance, the family that practices them begins to actualize its spiritual calling as a domestic church. When a family becomes a school of virtue and a community of love, it is an image of the loving communion of the Father, Son, and Holy Spirit. It is then an icon of the Trinity.

CHILDREN'S LOVE FOR THEIR PARENTS

Respect for parents derives from a grateful heart toward those who gave us the gift of life and nourished, loved, and supported us throughout all our stages of growth. Filial love is shown by genuine obedience from children to their parents while living in their parents' home and by responsible concern of grown children toward their elderly parents.

> With your whole heart honor your father; / your mother's birth pangs forget not. / Remember, of these parents you were born; / what can you give them for all they gave you? (Sir 7:27-28)

God offers each member of the family the grace for creating family solidarity so that it may grow as a domestic church. Parents utilize the energies of their love, their education, and their experience for their children. In this way, they make a positive and essential contribution toward building a truly human and Christian family. Children respond in love and should work to reduce rivalries, angers, hurts, and hostilities among brothers and sisters.

Adult children of elderly parents are asked to care for them with a generous heart: "Listen to your father who begot you, / and despise not your mother when she is old" (Prv 23:22). The family remains a major source of support for the elderly. The elderly who have no adult children should be helped by the considerate care of others.

While adult children may sometimes experience a strain between raising their own children and caring for their parents, they must do what they can to help their parents. Still, not only do adult children help their parents, but many of the elderly parents also help their adult children by their continuing love, their example, and the benefit of their life-time experience. While it is right for society to help care for the elderly, the family remains the rightful source of support.

PARENTS' LOVE FOR THEIR CHILDREN

Parents exercise their love for their children by caring for their physical, spiritual, intellectual, emotional, and moral needs. Concern for these needs takes much time and commitment on the part of both mother and father. Giving proper example to children is the most powerful form of childrearing. Helping children to grow in virtue contributes to their character formation. Inspirational stories, good parental example, and repetition of acts of virtue are basic ways of forming the young.

Parents should teach their children to pray by praying with them from their earliest years. Parents, as the first and primary educators, must also ensure their children's Catholic religious education and regular participation in Mass and other aspects of parish life. Sharing with them the lives of the saints, bringing them to church, helping them to participate in the Mass, and encouraging them to go to Confession are necessary ways to help children grow in faith. Catholic schools and parish religious education programs can help parents fulfill their responsibility to educate their children in the Catholic faith. Parents are encouraged to use Catholic schools and parish programs whenever possible.

Parental example in all these areas is essential, for the young need to see a living faith in those they love. Emphasis on fundamental elements of the faith—such as fostering a relationship with Christ and devotion to Mary, the angels, and saints, along with love and concern for everyone they meet—gradually forms the religious life of the young in a productive and creative way.

When children become adults, they assume the responsibility of how they will live and work. Parents should not exert undue pressure on their children when the children are faced with these decisions (cf. CCC, no. 2230). However, since parents often know their children well, they can direct their children to make decisions in harmony with their gifts and education. Since the family is the domestic church, it is fitting that parents always encourage their children to make life decisions with serious consideration about the best ways to live out their faith. Parents, by their own faith and commitment to the Church, create an environment in their homes that is conducive to helping children begin to think about a religious vocation. They should not hesitate to invite a son or daughter to consider becoming a priest or a vowed religious. In particular, parents should always encourage and support a child who is discerning such a call.

THE FAMILY AND SOCIETY

Authority, stability, and a life of relationships within the family constitute the foundations for freedom, security, and fraternity within society. The family is the community in which, from childhood, one can learn moral values, begin to honor God, and make good use of freedom. Family life is an initiation into life in society.

—CCC, no. 2207

The family and society need to work together to defend the good of each human being. The state should encourage responsible initiatives for families and should provide them with all the economic, educational, political, and cultural assistance they need to exercise their responsibilities.

Civic authorities should defend and protect the family as created by God and based on the permanent and exclusive union of a man and woman in marriage. The first obligation of civil authorities is to establish laws that reflect and protect proper moral order. If the governing authority attempts to impose a law contrary to the moral order, then the citizens have a moral obligation to seek to try to change the law. If that fails, they should refuse to obey such a law.

The Church, too, has the mission and obligation to critique and challenge any civil laws, societal organizations, or political structures that infringe upon or deny the fundamental rights of human persons and

1. What is a family?
A man and a woman united in marriage, together with their children, form a family. This institution is prior to any recognition by public authority, which has an obligation to recognize it. It should be considered the normal reference point by which the different forms of family relationship are to be evaluated. (CCC, no. 2202)

2. What are the basic elements of filial love?
Children owe their parents respect, gratitude, just obedience, and assistance. Filial respect fosters harmony in all of family life. (CCC, no. 2251)

3. What is expected of parental love?
Parents have the first responsibility for the education of their children in the faith, prayer, and all the virtues. They have the duty to provide as far as possible for the physical and spiritual needs of their children. (CCC, no. 2252)

communities. Jesus spoke of the difference between serving God and the state when he said, "Then repay to Caesar what belongs to Caesar and to God what belongs to God" (Mt 22:21). Catholics have the duty to vote, to participate in the political arena, and to help shape society in light of Catholic teaching.

THE CHARTER OF FAMILY RIGHTS

In his apostolic exhortation *On the Role of the Christian Family in the Modern World* (*Familiaris Consortio*), Pope John Paul II cites a list of rights of the family. Among those rights, we note the following:

- the right to exist and progress as a family, that is to say, the right of every human being, even if he or she is poor, to found a family and to have adequate means to support it;
- the right to exercise its responsibility regarding the transmission of life and to educate children;
- the right to the intimacy of conjugal and family life;
- the right to the stability of the bond and institution of marriage;
- the right to believe in and profess one's faith and to propagate it;
- the right, especially of the poor and the sick, to obtain physical, social, political, and economic security;
- the right to housing suitable for living family life in a proper way;
- the right to form associations with other families and institutions, in order to fulfill the family's role suitably and expeditiously;
- the right to protect minors by adequate institutions and legislation from harmful drugs, pornography, alcoholism, etc;
- the right of the elderly to a worthy life and a worthy death;
- the right to emigrate as a family in search of a better life;
- the right to bring up children in accordance with the family's own traditions and religious and cultural values, with the necessary instruments, means and institutions. (FC, no. 46)

WITNESS FIDELITY IN MARRIAGE

God commands all couples to witness fidelity in their marriages. An enduring marriage is more than simply endurance. It is a process of growth into an intimate friendship and a deepening peace. Couples need to renew their commitment to each other regularly, to seek enrichment often, and to ask for pastoral and professional help when necessary. They need to welcome children lovingly from God, whether through birth or adoption.

There needs to be mutuality in the relationships, roles, and responsibilities of all members of the family. Each and every family member must work at giving love, respect, commitment, and support to and for each other.

Finally, family members need to take time to be with each other. Prayer and worship together is important, especially Sunday Mass and family prayers such as the Rosary. Shared meals should be a priority. A family can establish certain traditions and rituals that enrich and strengthen family life. They can also take part together in retreats or family education programs. They can watch television together and discuss the values being promoted.

Family members can also benefit from taking some time to be in solitude, to reflect on and to hear God's Word.

■ FOR DISCUSSION ■

1. Reflect on your family life. When have you felt God's presence in your midst? Why was this? What was happening?
2. What pressures have caused pain for your family? How did you deal with them? Did this bring you closer or drive you farther apart as a family?
3. What is it about your family that matters most to you? How well do your family members share themselves with each other? How are you balancing time and commitment to family, work, and community? What choices can be made to improve your family as a faith community?

■ DOCTRINAL STATEMENTS ■

- "A man and a woman united in marriage, together with their children, form a family. This institution is prior to any recognition by public authority, which has an obligation to recognize it. It should be considered the normal reference point by which the different forms of family relationships are to be evaluated" (CCC, no. 2202).

- "The Christian home is the place where children receive the first proclamation of the faith. For this reason the family home is rightly called "the domestic church," a community of grace and prayer, a school of human virtues and of Christian charity" (CCC, no. 1666).

- Children call forth the gifts of their parents who—through their love—use their education and experience to benefit their children. In this way, children make a positive and essential contribution toward building a truly human and Christian family.

- Adult children of elderly parents are asked to care for them with a generous heart. "Listen to your father who begot you, / and despise not your mother when she is old" (Prv 23:22).

- Parents exercise their love for their children by caring for their physical, spiritual, intellectual, emotional, and moral needs. Responding to these needs requires time and commitment by both mother and father. Parents have the first responsibility for the education of their children.

- The family is the basic unit of society. A healthy family is the prerequisite of a healthy society. The authority, stability, and loving relationships that are found in families are essential for a society that wants to sustain freedom, security, and community responsibility.

- Presidents, governors, legislators, judges, and other civil leaders are given their authority in order to serve people. Their decisions ought to reflect God's plan for humanity, the natural law, and the dignity of each person.

MEDITATION

Excerpt: Reflections at Nazareth by Pope Paul VI

Nazareth is the school in which we begin to understand the life of Jesus. It is the school of the Gospel. Here we learn to observe, to listen, to meditate, and to penetrate the profound and mysterious meaning of that simple, humble, and lovely manifestation of the Son of God. And perhaps we learn almost imperceptibly to imitate Him. Here we learn the method by which we can come to understand Christ. Here we discover the need to observe the milieu of His sojourn among us—places, period of time, customs, language, religious practices, all of which Jesus used to reveal Himself to the world. Here everything speaks to us; everything has meaning. Everything possesses twofold significance.

We cannot depart without recalling briefly and fleetingly some fragments of the lesson of Nazareth.

The lesson of silence: may there return to us an appreciation of this stupendous and indispensable spiritual condition, deafened as we are by so much tumult, so much noise, so many voices of our chaotic and frenzied modern life. O silence of Nazareth, teach us recollection, reflection, and eagerness to heed the good inspirations and words of true teachers; teach us the need and value of preparation, of study, of meditation, of interior life, of secret prayer seen by God alone.

The lesson of domestic life: may Nazareth teach us the meaning of family life, its harmony of love, its simplicity and austere beauty, its sacred and inviolable character; may it teach us how sweet and irreplaceable is its training, how fundamental and incomparable its role on the social plane.

The lesson of work: O Nazareth, home of "the carpenter's son." We want here to understand and to praise the austere and redeeming law of human labor, here to restore the consciousness of the dignity of labor, here to recall that work cannot be an end in itself, and that it is free and ennobling in proportion to the values—beyond the economic ones—which motivate it. We would like here to salute all the workers of the world, and to point out to them their great Model, their Divine Brother, the Champion of all their rights, Christ the Lord!

—Pope Paul VI, *The Pope Speaks* 9:3 (1964)

PRAYER

A Blessing by Parents for Their Children

Father,
inexhaustible source of life and author of all good,
We bless and we thank you
for brightening our communion of love by your gift
    of children.
Grant that our children will find in the life of this family
    such inspiration
that they will strive always for what is right and good
and one day, by your grace,
reach their home in heaven. . . . Amen.

—Book of Blessings, no. 190

[Jesus] went down with [Mary and Joseph] and came to Nazareth, and was obedient to them; and his mother kept all these things in her heart.

—Lk 2:51

29 THE FIFTH COMMANDMENT: PROMOTE THE CULTURE OF LIFE

YOU SHALL NOT KILL
—CCC, NOS. 2258-2330

THE DOROTHY DAY STORY

Dorothy Day was born on November 8, 1897, and died on November 29, 1980. Daughter of a journalist, she also chose journalism as a profession. As a young woman, Dorothy became involved in several love affairs, entered into a brief marriage, and also gave birth to a child out of wedlock. She also had an abortion for which she later deeply repented.

During World War I, she became a Socialist and was influenced by the Communist Party, believing this was the best way to help the poor. But after the birth of her daughter, Tamar, she became a Catholic and came under the influence of Peter Maurin, with whom she formed the Catholic Worker Movement. She embraced voluntary poverty, raised her daughter, devoted her life to the care of the poor, and struggled to remove both the causes and symptoms of poverty in society.

On November 9, 1997, Cardinal John O'Connor delivered a homily about sanctity and Dorothy Day on the occasion of the one-hundredth anniversary of her birth. We quote here some of the comments that he made:

> Dorothy Day died before I became archbishop of New York, or
> I would have called on her immediately upon my arrival. Few

people have had such an impact on my life, even though we never met.

A number of new books are appearing now, because of the centenary of her birth, but I still find her own book on St. Thérèse of Lisieux to reveal as much about Dorothy Day as anything else that I have read. Most particularly she seems clearly to recognize that Thérèse's "little way" was the way of suffering, and to understand with Thérèse that all suffering united with that of Christ on the Cross is of inestimable value for souls.

I wish every woman who has suffered an abortion . . . would come to know Dorothy Day. Her story was so typical. Made pregnant by a man who insisted she have an abortion, who then abandoned her anyway, she suffered terribly for what she had done, and later pleaded with others not to do the same. But later, too, after becoming a Catholic, she learned the love and mercy of the Lord, and knew she never had to worry about His forgiveness. This is why I have never condemned a woman who has had an abortion; I weep with her and ask her to remember Dorothy Day's sorrow but to know always God's loving mercy and forgiveness.

Not everyone who knew Dorothy at a distance is aware of her meetings with Mother Teresa of Calcutta, or of the esteem in which Mother Teresa held her. A new book by Jim Forest, *Love is the Measure*, includes a portion of a Mother Teresa letter written for Dorothy Day's seventy-fifth birthday: Mother Teresa wrote to her, "So much love—so much sacrifice—all for Him alone. You have been such a beautiful branch on the Vine, Jesus, and allowed His Father, the Vine dresser, to prune you so often and so much. You have accepted all with great love. . . ."

I wish I had known Dorothy Day personally. I feel that I know her because of her goodness. But surely, if any woman ever loved God and her neighbor, it was Dorothy Day! Pray that we do what we should do. (*Catholic New York* (November 13, 1997): 13-14)

The Vatican has begun proceedings that may lead to her canonization. She went down many blind alleys before she found the road that Christ was pointing out to her all the time.

As the archbishop of New York City, Cardinal John O'Connor pointed out in his endorsement of her cause for sainthood that she "anticipated the teachings of John Paul II" in her uncompromising devotion both to the Church and to the cause of social justice. The Cardinal said he considered her a model for everyone, "but especially for women who have had or are considering abortion."

Dorothy Day's life was dedicated to seeking holiness, defending life, and promoting social justice and peace. In valuing human life, she came to reject the violence of abortion and to abhor war and crushing poverty. Her story seems most suitable for our reflection on the Fifth Commandment.

RESPECT HUMAN LIFE

Human life is sacred because from its beginning it involves the creative action of God and it remains for ever in a special relationship with the Creator, who is its sole end. God alone is the Lord of life from its beginning until its end: no one can under any circumstance claim for himself the right directly to destroy an innocent human being.

—CCC, no. 2258; citing *The Gift of Life*
(*Donum Vitae*), no. 5

God's creative action is present to every human life and is thus the source of its sacred value. Each human life remains in a relationship with God, who is the final goal of every man and woman.

The Fifth Commandment calls us to foster the physical, spiritual, emotional, and social well-being of self and others. For that reason, it forbids murder, abortion, euthanasia, and any life-threatening acts. We are called to create the culture of life and work against the culture of death. This presents us with three challenges.

1. We need to counter the relativism that imperils human life, by recognizing that human freedom needs to be consistent with God's intentions and the laws that govern moral life.

2. We must witness God's providential presence to all creation and particularly to each human being. "Where God is denied, and people live as though he did not exist, or his commandments are not taken into account, the dignity of the human person and the inviolability of human life also end up being rejected or compromised" (Pope John Paul II, *The Gospel of Life* [*Evangelium Vitae*; EV], no. 96).

3. We need to confront the weakening of conscience in modern society. Too many people fail to distinguish between good and evil when dealing with the value of human life. Moral confusion leads many to support choices and policies that desecrate life. Choices that were once considered criminal and immoral have become socially acceptable. Many consciences that were once formed by the Ten Commandments, Christ's moral teachings, and the Holy Spirit's grace-filled guidance are now swayed by the moral confusion of the spirit of the times. We should deal with the weakening of conscience by helping people to understand the Church's teaching on conscience as the capacity to make judgments in agreement with God's law, to protect human dignity and reject anything that degrades it.

LIFE ISSUES THAT CONFRONT US

Murder

The deliberate murder of an innocent person is gravely contrary to the dignity of the human being, to the golden rule, and to the holiness of the Creator.

—CCC, no. 2261

God forbids murder. "The innocent and the just you shall not put to death" (Ex 23:7). The intentional murder of any person is strictly forbidden by this commandment (cf. CCC, nos. 2268-2269). Such actions are gravely sinful.

Self-defense against an unjust aggressor is morally permitted. There is also a moral duty for the defense of others by those who are responsible for their lives. Self-defense or the defense of others has the goal of protecting the person or persons threatened. Once the threat is eliminated, no further action is required. In such situations, the deliberate killing of the aggressor can be permitted only when no other solution is possible (cf. CCC, no. 2265). Any response to aggression must be proportionate to the nature of the threat or the act of aggression.

Abortion

Legalized abortion is having a destructive effect on our society; few other actions legalized by our public policy as profoundly undermine our values as a people or upset the moral compass by which we live. The Church has always condemned abortion. In the *Didache* (*The Teaching of the Apostles*), 2, 2, written toward the end of the first century and revered as an honored guide for Christian life, we read, "You shall not kill the embryo by abortion." This teaching has never changed and it will not change.

> From its conception, the child has the right to life. Direct abortion, that is, abortion willed as an end or as a means, is a "criminal" practice (GS, no. 27 §3), gravely contrary to the moral law. The Church imposes the canonical penalty of excommunication for this crime against human life. Because it should be treated as a person from conception, the embryo must be defended in its integrity, cared for, and healed like every other human being. (CCC, nos. 2322-2323)

Modern technology has enabled us to appreciate how quickly the growing child in the womb takes on human features. This has made many more people aware of the fact that human life begins at conception, the moment that the egg is fertilized. Many common forms of artificial birth control cause abortions by not allowing the newly conceived human child to implant in the mother's womb.

The pro-life commitment of the Church is reflected in her compassion for those who so often regret having had an abortion, her understanding for those who are facing difficult decisions, and her assistance for all who choose life. People who have been involved with an abortion are encouraged to get in touch with the Project Rachel ministry and other ministries that enable them to seek the mercy of God in the Sacrament of Penance and Reconciliation and to obtain the necessary counseling. Pro-life ministries work with expectant mothers who are considering abortion by encouraging them to choose life for their children. They also provide alternatives to abortion through prenatal care, assistance in raising children, and adoption placement services.

In Vitro Fertilization

While *in vitro* fertilization is more appropriately treated in relation to the integrity of the link between fertility and love, it deserves brief mention here. This is because very often in the process, eggs that have been fertilized and are beginning to grow as a human person are discarded or destroyed. This action is the taking of human life and is gravely sinful.

Stem-Cell Research and Cloning

Every human body contains stem cells, undifferentiated cells that have the potential to mature into a wide variety of body cells. They develop early in the human embryo after fertilization or conception. They are also found in the placenta, the umbilical cord, as well as in the adult brain, bone marrow, blood, skeletal muscle, and skin. Scientists theorize that these stem cells may be used for therapeutic purposes for curing diseases such as Parkinson's or Alzheimer's.

Some scientists, however, maintain that the best source for stem cells is the human embryo. The moral problem is that in order to retrieve the stem cells, the growing child must be killed. But every embryo from the moment of conception has the entire genetic makeup of a unique human life. The growing child must be recognized and treated as completely and fully human. He or she needs only time to grow and develop. To destroy an embryo is to take a human life, an act contrary to God's law and Church teaching.

Some argue that the good obtained by healing serious diseases justifies the destruction of some human embryos. But this reduces a human being to a mere object for use. It assumes there are no moral absolutes that must be held in all circumstances. It violates the moral principle that the end does not justify the means. Embryonic stem-cell research is an immoral means to a good end. It is morally unacceptable.

Similarly, cloning, whether for reproductive or therapeutic uses, is immoral on many levels, not the least of which is because it too involves the destruction of human embryos.

> No objective, even though noble in itself, such as a foreseeable advantage to science, to other human beings, or to society, can in any way justify experimentation on living human embryos or fetuses, whether viable or not, either inside or outside the mother's body. (Congregation for the Doctrine of the Faith, *Instruction on Respect for Human Life in its Origin and on the Dignity of Procreation* [Vatican City: Liberia Editrice Vaticana, 1987])

On the other hand, stem cells can be obtained from adults with their informed consent. The federal government has spent millions of dollars on this research. Stem cells from placenta, bone marrow, and the umbilical cord are being used to treat leukemia. This is a promising field of research and does not involve the moral implications of embryonic stem-cell research.

Euthanasia and Physician-Assisted Suicide

Intentional euthanasia, sometimes called mercy killing, is murder. Regardless of the motives or means, euthanasia consists of putting to death those who are sick, are disabled, or are dying. It is morally unacceptable. The emergence of physician-assisted suicide, popularized by the right-to-die movement, seeks to legalize what is an immoral act. Its advocates plan to achieve this on a state-by-state basis.

Suicide is gravely sinful whether committed alone or aided by a doctor. Serious psychological disturbances, anxiety, fear of suffering, or torture can diminish the responsibility of the one committing suicide. The question is often asked whether persons who have committed suicide receive eternal salvation. Although suicide is always objectively sinful, one "should not despair of the eternal salvation of persons who have taken their own lives. By ways known to him alone, God can provide the opportunity for salutary repentance. The Church prays for persons who have taken their own lives" (CCC, no. 2283). The pastoral care of family and friends of those who have taken their own lives is an important focus for the Church's healing and compassionate ministry.

Catholic moral tradition has always taught that we can discontinue medical procedures that are burdensome, extraordinary, and disproportionate to the outcome. However, respect for every human being demands the ordinary treatment of the dying by the provision of food, water, warmth, and hygiene. Ordinary treatment is always a moral requirement.

There is also extraordinary treatment. The Church recognizes that some medical treatment may not provide benefits commensurate with the risks of certain medical procedures. Extraordinary medical treatment may not be morally required and can even cease in certain cases, depending on the benefits to the sick person and the burdens it will or may impose. For example, in instances when a person has been declared brain-dead, the patient can be disconnected from mechanical devices that sustain breathing and the heart since there is little hope of the person's recovery.

The Death Penalty

Following the lead of Pope John Paul II's *The Gospel of Life*, the *Catechism* teaches that governmental authority has the right and duty to assure the safety of society, and to punish criminals by means of suitable penalties. This includes imposition of the death penalty if there is no other way to protect society (cf. CCC, no. 2267). But this principle has a very restrictive application:

> If, however, non-lethal means are sufficient to defend and protect people's safety from the aggressor, authority will limit itself to such means, as these are more in keeping with the concrete conditions of the common good and more in conformity with the dignity of the human person. Today, in fact, as a consequence of the possibilities which the state has for effectively preventing crime, by rendering one who has committed an offense incapable of doing harm—without definitively taking away from him the possibility of redeeming himself—the cases

in which the execution of the offender is an absolute necessity "are very rare, if not practically non-existent." (CCC, no. 2267, citing EV, no. 56)

When dwelling on legal and moral arguments concerning the death penalty, we should do so not with vengeance and anger in our hearts, but with the compassion and mercy of our Lord in mind. It is also important to remember that penalties imposed on criminals always need to allow for the possibility of the criminal to show regret for the evil committed and to change his or her life for the better.

The imposition of the death penalty does not always allow for one or both of the purposes of criminal punishment to be achieved. "Our nation's increasing reliance on the death penalty cannot be justified. We do not teach that killing is wrong by killing those who kill others. Pope John Paul II has said the penalty of death is 'both cruel and unnecessary' (Homily in St. Louis, January 27, 1999). The antidote to violence is not more violence" (USCCB, *Faithful Citizenship* [Washington, DC: USCCB, 2003], 19).

War

Blessed John XXIII wrote that peace is a gift from God:

> So magnificent is this aim [for peace] that human resources alone, even though inspired by the most praiseworthy good will, cannot hope to achieve it. God himself must come to man's aid with his heavenly assistance, if human society is to bear the closest possible resemblance to the Kingdom of God. (*Peace on Earth* [*Pacem in Terris*], no. 168)

The best way to avoid war is to safeguard peace by letting go of the anger and hatred that breed war and by eliminating the poverty, injustice, and deprivation of human rights that lead to war. Disarmament needs to be encouraged. "The arms race is one of the greatest curses on the human race and the harm it inflicts on the poor is more than can be endured" (CCC, no. 2329, citing GS, no. 81 §3).

While every possible means must be taken to avoid war, there are times when a use of force by competent authority may be justified to correct a manifest injustice, especially to defend against a threat to one's homeland. The tradition of the Church going back to St. Augustine (AD 354-430) has developed the conditions for war to be moral. These are known as the just-war conditions. They are listed as follows in the *Catechism*:

> The strict conditions for *legitimate defense by military force* require rigorous consideration. The gravity of such a decision makes it subject to rigorous standards of moral legitimacy. At one and the same time:
>
> —the damage inflicted by the aggressor on the nation or community of nations must be lasting, grave, and certain;
> —all other means of putting an end to it must have been shown to be impractical or ineffective;
> —there must be serious prospects of success;
> —the use of arms must not produce evils graver than the evil to be eliminated. The power of modern means of destruction weighs very heavily in evaluating this condition.
>
> These are the traditional elements enumerated in what is called the "just war" doctrine. The evaluation of these conditions for moral legitimacy belongs to the prudential judgment of those who have responsibility for the common good. (CCC, no. 2309)

War may never be undertaken from a spirit of vengeance, but rather from motives of self-defense and of establishing justice and right order. The government has the right and duty to enlist citizens in defense of the nation. Special provision should be made for those who refuse to bear arms for reasons of conscience. These men and women should serve their country in some other way.

The Church and human reason assert the permanent validity of the moral law during armed conflict. Civilians, wounded soldiers, and prisoners should be treated humanely. Exterminating people by ethnic cleansing is an intrinsic and grave moral evil.

In 1983, the bishops of the United States formally rejected nuclear war:

Under no circumstances may nuclear weapons or other instruments of mass slaughter be used for the purpose of destroying population centers or other predominantly civilian targets. . . . We do not perceive any situation in which the deliberate initiation of nuclear warfare, on however restricted a scale, can be morally justified. (United States Conference of Catholic Bishops, *The Challenge of Peace: God's Promise and Our Response*, nos. 147 and 150)

Terrorism

Terrorist attacks throughout the world have killed thousands of people. We are aware, along with all people of good will, of the unmitigated evil of such acts. These deeds have raised our awareness of similar acts of terror around the world.

There can be no religious or moral justification for such acts. Such claims by terrorists can be countered by the teachings of the world's religions and by the constructive actions of religious believers. At the same time, we are called to mitigate problems such as violations of human rights and poverty, which cause widespread frustration and anger. While never excusing acts of terrorism, we still need to address issues associated with poverty and injustice that are exploited by terrorists.

Scandal

In its focus on the preservation of life, the Fifth Commandment also is concerned with the care we show for each other's moral life. A person whose words or actions lead others to believe that evil or sinful behavior is acceptable and not morally wrong is guilty of the sin of scandal.

Scandal can also be caused by laws or institutions that legitimize sinful actions. An example from the history of the United States can be seen in laws that allowed slavery. A modern example is seen in those laws that allow abortion.

FROM THE CATECHISM

1. Why is suicide morally wrong?
Suicide contradicts the natural inclination of the human being to preserve and perpetuate his life. It is gravely contrary to the just love of self. It likewise offends the love of neighbor because it unjustly breaks the ties of solidarity with family, nation, and other human societies to which we continue to have obligations. Suicide is contrary to love for the living God. (CCC, no. 2281)

2. What are the roots of war?
Injustice, excessive economic or social inequalities, envy, distrust, and pride raging among men and nations constantly threaten peace and cause wars. . . . Insofar as men are sinners, the threat of war hangs over them and will so continue until Christ comes again; but insofar as they can vanquish sin by coming together in charity, violence itself will be vanquished. (CCC, no. 2317)

3. What are some reasons for punishing criminals?
Punishment, then, in addition to defending public order and protecting people's safety, has a medicinal purpose: as far as possible, it must contribute to the correction of the guilty party. (CCC, no. 2266)

The Right of the Dying to Live

There are cases where state and federal courts have ruled against the idea of a constitutional right to die. In doing so, they have been gradually assembling a defense against this so-called right-to-die movement. Following is a brief summary of some of these arguments:

- Many physicians take the Hippocratic Oath, by which they commit themselves to do no harm. The relationship between a physician and a patient should be marked by compassion. Physicians should not be the killers of their patients. It would perversely affect their self-understanding and would reduce their desire to look for cures for disease, if killing instead of curing were to become the option.

- We should not allow the elderly and infirm to be pressured to consent to their own deaths by assisted suicide or euthanasia.
- We should protect the poor and minorities from exploitation. Pain is a significant factor in the desire for physician-assisted suicide. The poor and the minorities often do not have the resources for the alleviation of pain.
- We should protect all people with disabilities from societal indifference, antipathy, and any bias against them.
- We should never present suicide as a socially acceptable solution to life's difficulties.

The Pontifical Academy for Life on March 8, 1999, issued a statement that included the following comments about euthanasia and the alleviation of the pain of the dying:

> With absolute conviction we vigorously reject any kind of euthanasia, understood as recourse to those actions or omissions which are intended to cause a person's death in order to prevent suffering and pain. At the same time, we want to express our human and Christian closeness to all the sick, especially to those who know they are approaching the end of their earthly life and are preparing to meet God, our beatitude. We ask that these brothers and sisters of ours be spared the "therapeutic neglect" which consists in denying them the treatment and care that alleviate suffering. Nor should this treatment and care be lacking for financial reasons.

Greater efforts are being made today to provide patients whose medical conditions cause great pain with medications or treatments that relieve their suffering. People are being encouraged to use advanced directives to make sure that medical treatment and end-of-life care is both humane and in conformity to the moral teachings of Christ and the Church. The personal presence, prayer, and love of relatives and friends, supporting their loved one through the final stages of life's journey, are also essential parts of the process of Christian dying. The Church, through her ministers, also accompanies the dying person through the Sacrament of the Anointing of the Sick, *Viaticum*, and Prayers for the Dying.

FOR DISCUSSION

1. How can individuals and families promote respect for life and the value of life in the world today?
2. How can Catholics promote peace and understanding in the face of terrorism and violence in the world today?
3. What are root causes of the culture of death? How can we promote the value of human life in all its stages in contrast to abortion, euthanasia, and capital punishment?

DOCTRINAL STATEMENTS

- God's creative action is present to every human life and is thus the source of its sacred value. Each human life remains in a relationship with God, who is the final goal of every man and woman. God alone is the Lord of human life from its beginning to its end.
- "The deliberate murder of an innocent person is gravely contrary to the dignity of the human being, to the golden rule, and to the holiness of the Creator" (CCC, no. 2261).
- "The prohibition of murder does not abrogate the right to render an unjust aggressor unable to inflict harm" (CCC, no. 2321).
- Direct abortion is the intended destruction of an unborn child and is an act gravely contrary to the moral law and the holiness of the Creator.
- Euthanasia consists in putting to death the sick, the disabled, or the dying. Regardless of the motives or means, it is never morally permissible.
- Physician-assisted suicide is suicide performed with the aid of a doctor. The emergence of physician-assisted suicide, popularized by the

right-to-die movement, seeks to legalize what is an immoral act. Suicide is wrong whether committed alone or aided by a doctor.

- The human embryo from the moment of conception has the entire genetic makeup of a unique human life. The growing child must be treated as completely and fully human. He or she needs only time to grow and develop. Killing the embryo is killing human life, an act contrary to God's law and Church teaching.

- "Today, in fact, as a consequence of the possibilities which the state has for effectively preventing crime by rendering the one who has committed the offense incapable of doing harm . . . the cases in which the execution of the offender is an absolute necessity 'are very rare, if not practically non-existent'" (CCC, no. 2267, citing EV, no. 56).

- While every possible means must be taken to avoid war, there are times when legitimate defense of one's homeland by military force may be taken under the strictest conditions.

- In addition to the respect for bodily life, there must also be reverence for the souls of others. One must always avoid scandal, which is a grave offense when, by deed or omission, one leads another to sin gravely (cf. CCC, nos. 2284-2287).

- The Fifth Commandment also forbids other sins: bigotry and hatred, physical or emotional abuse, violence of any kind against another person, inattention to one's health, or the abuse of alcohol or drugs (cf. CCC, nos. 2288-2291).

■ MEDITATION ■

Christ's blood reveals to man that his greatness, and therefore his vocation, consists in the sincere gift of self. Precisely because it is poured out as the gift of life, the blood of Christ is no longer a sign of death, of definitive separation from the brethren, but the instrument of a communion which is richness of life for all. Whoever in the Sacrament of the Eucharist drinks this blood and abides in Jesus (cf. Jn 6:56) is drawn into the dynamism of his love and gift of life, in order to bring to its fullness the original vocation to love which belongs to everyone (cf. Gn 1:27; 2:18-24).

It is from the blood of Christ that all draw the strength to commit themselves to promoting life. It is precisely this blood that is the most powerful source of hope, indeed it is the foundation of the absolute certitude that in God's plan life will be victorious. "And death shall be no more," exclaims the powerful voice which comes from the throne of God in the Heavenly Jerusalem (Rev 21:4). And Saint Paul assures us that the present victory over sin is a sign and anticipation of the definitive victory over death, when there "shall come to pass the saying that is written: 'Death is swallowed up in victory. O death, where is your victory? O death, where is your sting?'" (1 Cor 15:54-55).

—Pope John Paul II, *The Gospel of Life*
(*Evangelium Vitae*), no. 25

PRAYER

Lord, make me an instrument of your peace.
Where there is hatred, let me sow love; where there is
    injury, pardon;
where there is doubt, faith, where there is despair, hope;
where there is darkness, light; and where there is sadness, joy.
Grant that I may not so much seek to be consoled as
    to console,
to be understood as to understand, to be loved as to love;
for it is in giving that we receive, it is in pardoning that we
    are pardoned,
and it is in dying that we are born to eternal life.

—St. Francis of Assisi

I have set before you life and death. . . .
Choose life, then, that you and your descendants may live.

—Dt 30:19

30 THE SIXTH COMMANDMENT: MARITAL FIDELITY

YOU SHALL NOT COMMIT ADULTERY
—CCC, NOS. 2331-2400

POPE PAUL VI: A SHEPHERD FOR THE RENEWAL OF THE CHURCH

The Second Vatican Council was a major event in the life of the Catholic Church in the twentieth century. From 1962 until 1965, it brought together approximately 2,500 bishops from all over the world for four sessions in Rome—each session lasting about three months—to discuss and make decisions about the life of the Church in the modern world. Blessed John XXIII had convoked the Council and presided over its first session. When he died in June of 1963, the College of Cardinals elected as his successor Cardinal Giovanni Battista Montini, who took the name Paul VI. Pope Paul VI presided over the next three sessions of the Council and guided the Church through the time of change and renewal that followed the Council.

Giovanni Battista Montini was born in northern Italy in 1897. He was ordained a priest in 1920 and two years later began service in the Vatican's Secretariat of State. He worked very closely with Pope Pius XII until 1954, when he was named Archbishop of Milan. In 1958 Blessed John XXIII named him to the College of Cardinals.

His knowledge of the universal Church through his service in the Holy See, his intellectual abilities and wide reading in theology, and his pastoral experience in Milan all served him well when he was elected pope. His constant concern was to maintain the unity of the Catholic Church even in times of considerable controversy. He guided the Church through a series of reforms and the renewal of the liturgy. In 1970, he authorized the publication of a new *Roman Missal*. He fostered dialogue with other churches and ecclesial communities. He worked diligently for peace, even visiting the headquarters of the United Nations in New York in 1964 to deliver an urgent appeal against war.

Throughout his pontificate, Paul VI emphasized the importance of the family for the Church and society. In his apostolic exhortation *On Evangelization in the Modern World* (*Evangelii Nuntiandi*) of 1975, he wrote, "The family, just like the Church, must always be regarded as a center to which the Gospel must be brought and from which it must be proclaimed. Therefore in a family which is conscious of this role all the members of the family are evangelizers and are themselves evangelized" (no. 71).

Because of controversy in the Church surrounding the morality of artificial contraception, he issued his encyclical *On the Regulation of Birth* (*Humanae Vitae*; HV) in July of 1968. He reaffirmed the teaching of the Church that artificial contraception is gravely immoral because it contravenes God's will for the conjugal act, which unites the spouses in their love and must also be open to the creation of new life. He warned of the consequences for the moral tenor of society that would come from ignoring God's plan. He recognized the difficulties that married couples might have in following this teaching, but he encouraged them to have constant recourse to God's grace through the Sacrament of Penance and Reconciliation and the Sacrament of the Eucharist.

Pope Paul VI was a courageous shepherd for the renewal of the Church and the defense of her teaching. The cause for his beatification was initiated in 1993. Pope Paul VI's clear teaching on family, marriage, and moral issues such as artificial contraception shows him to be a most important figure in fostering the values and virtues embodied in the Sixth Commandment.

PRACTICE MARITAL FIDELITY

God created human beings as male and female. In so doing, he gave equal dignity to both man and woman. In his plan, men and women should respect and accept their sexual identity. God created both the body and sex as good. Hence, we do not approach sexuality with fear or with hostility to the flesh. It is a gift of God by which men and women participate in his saving plan and respond to his call to grow in holiness.

The *Catechism* states that sexuality involves the whole person. "*Sexuality* affects all aspects of the human person in the unity of his body and soul. It especially concerns affectivity, the capacity to love and to procreate, and in a more general way the aptitude for forming bonds of communion with others" (CCC, no. 2332).

The Sixth Commandment summons spouses to practice permanent and exclusive fidelity to one another. Emotional and sexual fidelity are essential to the commitment made in the marriage covenant. God established marriage as a reflection of his fidelity to us. The vows made by the spouses at their wedding to be faithful to one another forever should witness the very covenant God has made with us.

CHASTITY

All people—married, single, religious, and ordained—need to acquire the virtue of chastity. "Chastity means the successful integration of sexuality within the person and thus the inner unity of man in his bodily and spiritual being" (CCC, no. 2337). Chastity unites our sexuality with our entire human nature. It approaches sexuality as related to our spiritual natures so that sex is seen as more than a physical act. Sexuality affects the whole person because of the unity of body and soul. Jesus is the model of chastity. "Chastity includes an *apprenticeship in self-mastery* which is a training in human freedom" (CCC, no. 2339). The acquisition of chastity depends on self-discipline and leads to an internal freedom, which enables human beings to temper sexual desires according to God's plan for the appropriate expression of love in the marital relationship of a man and a woman.

The *Catechism* describes the acquisition of chastity in the following way:

> Self-mastery is a *long and exacting work*. One can never consider it acquired once and for all. It presupposes renewed effort at all stages of life. The effort required can be more intense in

certain periods, such as when the personality is being formed during childhood and adolescence. (CCC, no. 2342; cf. Ti 2:1-6)

Chastity has *laws of growth* which progress through stages marked by imperfection and too often by sin. (CCC, no. 2343)

Chastity presupposes respect for the rights of the person, in particular the right to receive information and an education that respect the moral and spiritual dimensions of human life. (CCC, no. 2344)

Chastity is a moral virtue. It is also a gift from God, a *grace*, a fruit of spiritual effort. The Holy Spirit enables one whom the water of Baptism has regenerated to imitate the purity of Christ. (CCC, no. 2345; cf. Gal 5:22, 1 Jn 3:3)

The virtue of chastity blossoms in friendship. . . . Chastity is expressed notably in *friendship with one's neighbor.* Whether it develops between persons of the same or opposite sex, friendship represents a great good for all. It leads to spiritual communion. (CCC, no. 2347)

There are a number of acts that are sins against chastity:

- *Lust* is a "disordered desire for or an inordinate enjoyment of sexual pleasure," especially when sought for itself (CCC, no. 2351).
- *Masturbation* is sinful because it misuses the gift of sexuality in an inherently selfish act, devoid of love. It is a problem for which a counselor, spiritual director, or a confessor can be of considerable help. A person often needs assistance to understand the causes of this behavior, which are often habitual or in response to emotional stress or unexamined underlying attitudes.
- *Fornication* (sexual intercourse between unmarried persons) is sinful because it violates the dignity of persons and the nuptial meaning and purpose of sexuality, which is ordered only to the unitive and procreative goals of married people.

- *Incest* (sexual relationships between close relatives) is always wrong, harming both the individuals involved as well as the family itself.
- *Sexual abuse* of any kind harms the victim on many more levels than only the physical. Forcing sexual intimacy of any type on a child or minor is an even graver evil (cf. CCC, no. 2356), which often scars the victim for life (cf. CCC, no. 2389).
- *Pornography* (sexually explicit material) has become even more available through the Internet. This presents real difficulties for both individuals and society, as viewing pornography is not only sinful in itself but can also become an addiction and lead to dangerous sexual behaviors. It has also led to a greater exploitation of children as sexual objects.
- *Prostitution* reduces the person "to an instrument of sexual pleasure," an object to be used. It increases the spread of sexually transmitted diseases. To protect innocent members of society, prostitution can legitimately be forbidden by civil authority. It is more prevalent where a culture exploits the physical and social vulnerability of women (CCC, no. 2355).
- *Rape* is an act of violence in which a person forces a sexual act on an unwilling partner. "Rape deeply wounds the respect, freedom, and physical and moral integrity to which every person has a right. . . . It is always an intrinsically evil act" (CCC, no. 2356).
- "*Homosexual acts* are intrinsically disordered" and immoral. "They are contrary to the natural law. They close the sexual act to the gift of life. They do not proceed from a genuine affective and sexual complementarity" (CCC, no. 2357). Having homosexual inclinations is not immoral. It is homosexual acts that are immoral.

    "The number of men and women who have deep-seated homosexual tendencies is not negligible. This inclination, which is objectively disordered, constitutes for most of them a trial. They must be accepted with respect, compassion, and sensitivity. Every sign of unjust discrimination in their regard should be avoided. These persons are called to fulfill God's will in their lives and, if they are Christians, to unite to the sacrifice of the Lord's Cross the difficulties they may encounter from their condition" (CCC, no. 2358).

THE LOVE OF HUSBAND AND WIFE

The spouses' union achieves the twofold end of marriage: the good of the spouses themselves and the transmission of life.

—CCC, no. 2363

The bond between husband and wife is both conjugal and procreative. Conjugal mutual love and fidelity is the *unitive* aspect of marriage. The *procreative* aspect of marriage concerns the conception, birth, and education of children. The bond between the unitive and procreative may not be broken.

Unitive Faithful Love

The unitive aspect of marriage involves the full personhood of the spouses, a love that encompasses the minds, hearts, emotions, bodies, souls, and aspirations of husband and wife. They are called to grow continually in unitive love and fidelity so that they are no longer two but one flesh. Their mutual self-giving is strengthened and blessed by Jesus Christ in the Sacrament of Matrimony. God seals the consent that the bride and groom give to each other in this Sacrament.

> The acts in marriage by which the intimate and chaste union of the spouses takes place are noble and honorable; the truly human performance of these acts fosters the self-giving they signify and enriches the spouses in joy and gratitude. (CCC, no. 2362, citing GS, no. 49)

Acceptance of a spouse's faults and failures as well as of one's own is a recognition that the call to holiness in marriage is a lifelong process of conversion and growth.

Procreative Love

God calls the married couple to be open to children, remembering always that having a child is not a right, but rather a gift from God (cf.

CCC, no. 2378). In this way, they share the creative power and fatherhood of God. In giving birth to children and educating and forming them, they cooperate with the love of God as Creator. Marital love by its nature is fruitful. The marriage act, while deepening spousal love, is meant to overflow into new life. Families are images of the ever-creative power and life of the Holy Trinity and the fruitfulness of the relationship between Christ and his Church.

Respecting the Link of Fertility and Love

"A child does not come from outside as something added on to the mutual love of the spouses, but springs from the very heart of that mutual giving, as its fruit and fulfillment. So the Church, which is 'on the side of life' teaches that 'it is necessary that each and every marriage act remain ordered *per se* to the procreation of human life'" (CCC, no. 2366, citing FC, no. 30, and HV, no. 11, respectively).

This passage underlines the Church's teaching that God established an inseparable bond between the unitive and procreative aspects of marriage. Each and every sexual act in a marriage needs to be open to the possibility of conceiving a child. Thus, artificial contraception is contrary to God's will for marriage because it separates the act of conception from sexual union. Efforts to achieve pregnancy outside of the act of sexual intercourse (e.g., *in vitro* fertilization) are morally wrong for the same reason—they separate conception from sexual intercourse.

Contemporary methods of natural family planning are making it possible for couples, in cases of legitimate need, to space the births of their children while remaining faithful to God's plan for marriage. These methods allow a couple to have a more precise knowledge of the time of ovulation to enable them to either avoid or achieve a pregnancy. "The regulation of births represents one of the aspects of responsible fatherhood and motherhood. Legitimate intentions on the part of the spouses do not justify recourse to morally unacceptable means (for example, direct sterilization or contraception)" (CCC, no. 2399).

In the course of their marriage, couples may, for serious reasons, decide to avoid a new birth for the time being or even for an indeterminate period, but they must not use immoral means to prevent conception. Couples should also be mindful of the fact that their love is expressed in more ways than just the conjugal act. Abstaining from intercourse at certain times can be an act of sacrifice which gives rise to a deeper relationship.

> In relation to physical, economic, psychological and social conditions, responsible parenthood is exercised either by the thoughtfully made and generous decision to raise a large family, or by the decision, made for grave motives and with respect for the moral law, to avoid a new birth for the time being or even for an indeterminate period. (HV, no. 10)

THREATS TO MARRIAGE

The *Catechism* lists the following behaviors as acts that undermine the purpose and dignity of marriage.

Adultery is gravely sinful because it violates God's call to a loving covenant of fidelity between a married man and woman. The act of adultery is an injustice to the wounded spouse. It weakens the institution of marriage and the stability of the family.

Divorce is contrary to the natural law for it breaks the promise "to which the spouses freely consented to live with each other till death" (CCC, no. 2384). Jesus clearly taught that God's original plan for marriage excluded divorce (cf. Mt 5:31-32, 9:3-9; Mk 10:9; Lk 16:18; 1 Cor 7:10-11). Marriage is an indissoluble union. Jesus removed the accommodations for divorce that had been tolerated under the Old Law.

The couple may be allowed a separation in certain cases, such as when adultery is occurring or some type of abuse is present. A separation can be, at times, a prudent action to take. "If civil divorce remains the only possible way of ensuring certain legal rights, the care of the children, or the protection of inheritance, it can be tolerated and does not constitute a moral offense" (CCC, no. 2383). In such cases, a Catholic can still receive the Sacraments.

Cohabitation (an unmarried couple living together) involves the serious sin of fornication. It does not conform to God's plan for marriage and is always wrong and objectively sinful. Cohabitation does not

FROM THE CATECHISM

1. What is the divine plan for marriage?
Each of the two sexes is an image of the power and tenderness of God, with equal dignity though in a different way. The *union of man and woman* in marriage is a way of imitating in the flesh the Creator's generosity and fecundity. (CCC, no. 2335)

2. What is the link between charity and chastity?
Charity is the *form* of all the virtues. Under its influence, chastity appears as a school of the gift of the person. Self-mastery is ordered to the gift of self. Chastity leads him who practices it to become a witness to his neighbor of God's fidelity and loving kindness. (CCC, no. 2346)

3. What is the marital covenant?
The covenant which spouses have freely entered into entails faithful love. It imposes on them the obligation to keep their marriage indissoluble. (CCC, no. 2397)

guarantee successful married life, as has been revealed in the painful experience of many, and is detrimental to future commitment.

Polygamy (having more than one spouse at a time) violates the understanding of the equal dignity that a man and woman bring to marriage and contradicts the unitive purpose of marriage.

Attempts to justify same-sex unions or relationships or to give them matrimonial status also contradict God's plan—as revealed from the beginning both in nature and in Revelation—for marriage to be a lifelong union of a man and a woman.

THE THEOLOGY OF THE BODY

The many ways in which one can depart from God's call to chastity and marital fidelity are more than evident in American culture. The exploitation of sexuality for commercial gain is manifested in countless ads and other means of engaging our attention through television and allied media. The cult of the body, not just for health reasons but for hedonistic attraction, is a prime example of the effect of an exaggerated focus on sex and sexuality.

What is needed is a healing vision of sexuality, the body, and the human person. Pope John Paul II offers us this perspective in his theology of the body. He begins with the idea that God willed each human being for his or her own sake. This means that none of us is merely a part of something else, or a means of gaining some result. God created us as free and unique human persons. We are not things to be used, but persons to be respected.

God created human beings to love one another. Since God is a communion of persons, it makes sense that we, being made in his image, would reach out to love others, forming our own communion of persons. Marital love witnesses the total self-giving of man and woman. The miracle is that in the act of self-giving, each spouse gains a greater sense of self while enriching the other spouse.

The Nuptial Meaning of the Body

We experience our selfhood through our bodies. We are embodied as man and woman. Genesis teaches that it is not good for man to be alone. We are rescued from our solitude by a complementary existence as man and woman. Pope John Paul II calls the capacity of the male body and the female body to serve mutual self-giving the nuptial meaning of the body.

Sin, particularly lust, obscures the nuptial meaning of the body and its capacity to witness the divine image. In this case, the woman's body ceases to reveal her as a person to be loved, but rather as an object to be used. Conversely, a man's body would not disclose him as a person to be loved, but rather as an instrument to be exploited. Sin erodes spousal love.

Shame may enter the relationship. Pope John Paul II notes there is an instinctive shame that can ward off utilitarian sex. Shame leads the woman to protect herself from the aggressive, lustful sexuality of the man. In the opposite case, shame causes the man to resist a sexual advance from the woman that is merely lustful. God calls for spousal love as the remedy for moving beyond the sex appeal of the body alone to its nuptial meaning, revealing the person as made in his image.

The Redemption of the Body

Pope John Paul II retrieves the nuptial meaning of the body by taking us back to life before the Fall, to a time of original innocence and original nakedness. The first man and woman did not experience any shame in their nakedness because the attraction of male and female served love alone. This was more than virtuous self-control. The man and woman dwelt so intimately in their bodies that each body expressed to the other the beauty of the human person and the image of God. Bodily sexuality was integrated into the energy of spousal love.

Original Sin caused a rupture in the unity of body and soul. The body now could *obscure* as well as reveal the person. Christ's saving act included the redemption of the body by which he restored the lost unity of soul and body. This is a *process of restoration*, partly completed here and fully restored in the next life. While there will not be marriage in the future life, masculinity and femininity will endure. Pope John Paul II relates this to consecrated celibacy and virginity in which the nuptial meaning of the body is not denied. The body's nuptial meaning serves love in ways other than marriage.

We seldom do justice to the ways in which our bodies share in and reveal our interior personal lives. We have drawn attention here to Pope John Paul II's meditation on the nuptial meaning of the body because we believe it is a vision of sex, marriage, and the person best suited to rebuilding a wholesome, faith-filled, and loving approach to these most precious gifts.[15]

---

15   See Pope John Paul II, *Love and Responsibility* (New York: Farrar, Straus, Giroux, 1981); and his *Original Unity of Man and Woman: Catechesis on the Book of Genesis* (Boston: St. Paul Editions, 1981).

▰▰▰▰ FOR DISCUSSION ▰▰▰▰

1. How can we best show respect for human sexuality in the light of a culture that demeans it? What are the ways of reversing the degradation of sexuality?
2. Why is marital fidelity so important for the stability of the family and society? What spiritual means does the Church offer to strengthen marriages or rebuild troubled marriages?
3. How does Pope John Paul II's theology of the body help you to appreciate the beauty of the gift of sexuality and its integration into your life?

▰▰▰▰ DOCTRINAL STATEMENTS ▰▰▰▰

- God is the author of marriage and the family. The Sacrament of Marriage, along with the Fourth, Sixth and Ninth Commandments, illustrate the principal ways in which God's plan for marriage and the family is to be lived.
- The Sixth Commandment summons the spouses to practice permanent and exclusive fidelity to one another. God established marriage as a reflection of his fidelity to us.
- The Sixth Commandment forbids adultery, which is sexual relations between a married person and someone other than one's spouse.
- Chastity integrates bodily sexuality within the broader human reality. It approaches sexuality as related to our spiritual natures so that sexuality is seen as more than a physical act. Sexuality affects the whole person because of the unity of body and soul. Jesus is the model of chastity. Every person is called to chastity according to one's state in life.
- "Among the sins gravely contrary to chastity are masturbation, fornication, pornography, and homosexual practices" (CCC, no. 2396).
- God calls married couples to grow continually in unitive love and fidelity so that they are no longer two but one flesh. Their mutual self-giving is strengthened and blessed by Jesus Christ in the Sacrament

of Matrimony. God seals the consent that the bride and groom give to each other in this Sacrament.

- "The acts in marriage by which the intimate and chaste union of the spouses takes place are noble and honorable; the truly human performance of these acts fosters the self-giving they signify and enriches the spouses in joy and gratitude" (CCC, no. 2362, citing GS, no. 49).

- God calls the married couple to be open to children. In this way, they share the creative power and fatherhood of God. In giving birth to children and educating and forming them, they cooperate with the love of God as Creator (cf. CCC, no. 2367).

- "In relation to physical, economic, psychological and social conditions, responsible parenthood is exercised either by the thoughtfully made and generous decision to raise a large family, or by the decision, made for grave motives and with respect for the moral law, to avoid a new birth for the time being or even for an indeterminate period" (HV, no. 10)

MEDITATION

At a time in history like the present, special attention must also be given to the *pastoral care of the family*, particularly when this fundamental institution is experiencing a radical and widespread crisis. In the Christian view of marriage, the relationship between a man and a woman—a mutual and total bond, unique and indissoluble—is part of God's original plan, obscured throughout history by our "hardness of heart," but which Christ came to restore to its pristine splendor, disclosing what had been God's will "from the beginning" (Mt 19:8). Raised to the dignity of a Sacrament, marriage expresses the "great mystery" of Christ's nuptial love for his Church (cf. Eph 5:32).

On this point the Church cannot yield to cultural pressures, no matter how widespread and even militant they may be. Instead, it is necessary to ensure that through an ever more complete Gospel formation Christian families show convincingly that it is possible to live marriage fully in keeping with God's plan and with the true good of the human person—of the spouses, and of the children who are more fragile. Families themselves must become increasingly conscious of the care due to children, and play an active role in the Church and in society in safeguarding their rights.

—NMI, no. 47

PRAYER

Father, to reveal the plan of your love, you made the union of
    husband and wife
an image of the covenant between you and your people.
In the fulfillment of this sacrament, the marriage of Christian
    man and woman
is a sign of the marriage between Christ and the Church.

—From the Nuptial Blessing

Set me as a seal on your heart, / as a seal on your arm.

—Sg 8:6

31 THE SEVENTH COMMANDMENT: DO NOT STEAL— ACT JUSTLY

YOU SHALL NOT STEAL
—CCC, NOS. 2401-2463

MOTHER JOSEPH: A FRONTIER NUN

Mother Joseph was born Esther Pariseau on April 16, 1823, in a farmhouse near the village of St. Elzear, Quebec. In her youth, she learned carpentry from her father, who was a carriage maker. When Esther was twenty, her father presented her to the newly formed Sisters of Providence in Montreal and told the mother superior, "Madam, I bring you my daughter Esther, who wishes to dedicate herself to religious life. She can read, write, figure accurately, sew, cook, spin and do all manner of housework. She can even do carpentry, handling a hammer and saw as well as her father. She can also plan for others and she succeeds in anything she undertakes. I assure you, Madam, she will make a good superior someday."

This was an accurate prophecy. In 1856, Mother Joseph, as she was now called, and a small band of four sisters set out from Montreal for Fort Vancouver, Washington—a trip of six thousand miles by land and water. It was not an easy journey. Once in Vancouver, the sisters inherited an old, abandoned Hudson's Bay company building and converted it into a convent. Mother Joseph built the chapel and the altar with her own hands.

The sisters began their works of mercy and evangelization. They visited the sick, cared for the Native Americans displaced by war, attended to orphans, and taught young people. Mother Joseph established Providence Academy, the first permanent school in the Northwest, and opened the four-bed St. Joseph Hospital, the Northwest's first permanent hospital.

Building hospitals and schools took money, and Mother Joseph proved to be an excellent fundraiser. She traveled for months through the mining camps begging for funds, often returning home with as much as five thousand dollars in cash. Fundraising was hard enough, but more so for Mother Joseph, who had to deal with harsh weather and fending off wolves and bandits.

When all of Mother Joseph's works are added up, they encompass the building of hospitals, orphanages, schools, homes for the aged, and shelters for the mentally ill in the states of Washington, Oregon, Idaho, and Montana.

The Seventh Commandment not only deals with matters of property and stealing, but also with issues of social justice and human dignity. The life of Mother Joseph illustrates this Commandment because it was one of dedication to the basic rights of individuals, economically and socially. She treated all people with dignity, justice, and mercy, opening all of her institutions to anyone who needed them. Mother Joseph died of cancer in 1902 in Vancouver, Washington.

In 1980, the United States Senate accepted a statue of her, a gift from the state of Washington, for inclusion in the national Statuary Hall Collection. The inscription on the statue reads: "She made monumental contributions to health care, education and social work throughout the Northwest." Today her legacy lives on in the mission of the Sisters of Providence, who are headquartered in Seattle, Washington.

Her dying words to the members of her religious community were, "Sisters, whatever concerns the poor is always our concern."[16] Her example helps us to understand better how to live out the Seventh Commandment.

---

16   Quoted in Eugene F. Hemrick, *One Nation Under God* (Huntington, IN: Our Sunday Visitor, 2001), 72-74.

RESPECT PEOPLE AND THEIR POSSESSIONS

The seventh Commandment forbids theft. Theft is the usurpation of another's goods against the reasonable will of the owner. . . . Every manner of taking and using another's property unjustly is contrary to the seventh commandment. The injustice committed requires reparation. Commutative justice requires the restitution of stolen goods.

—CCC, nos. 2453-2454

The Seventh Commandment forbids stealing or theft, which involves taking someone's money or property "against the reasonable will of the owner." Theft includes not only robbery but also actions such as embezzlement, computer theft, counterfeit money, fraud, identity theft, copyright violations (including pirating things such as music or computer software), and mail scams.

To keep this Commandment, we need to acquire the virtues of moderation in our possessions, justice in our treatment of others, respect for their human dignity, and solidarity with all peoples. Moderation curbs our attachment to worldly goods and restrains our appetite for consumerism. Justice helps us respect our neighbor's rights and be interested in their human well-being. Solidarity opens our hearts to identifying with the whole human family, reminding us of our common humanity.

We should not steal from each other, pay unfair salaries, cheat in business, or exploit people's weaknesses to make money. Promises should be kept and contracts honored to the extent that the issues are morally just (cf. CCC, no. 2410). We need to safeguard property rights, pay our debts, and fulfill obligations freely incurred. The government has the right and duty to safeguard legitimate ownership of money and property and to protect people from robbery and injury.

THE RIGHT TO RELIGIOUS FREEDOM

A basic duty every human person owes to God is regular worship. Because of this, and because of the basic longing each person has for God, a fundamental human right is the right to worship freely. No one should be prohibited from a free exercise of their faith, either in public or in private, and no one should ever be forced to worship in a manner that violates their beliefs and convictions. Because freedom of religion and worship is such an important and fundamental right, governments need to enact and enforce laws that respect and protect this right (cf. CCC, nos. 2105-2109).

PRACTICE THE CHURCH'S SOCIAL TEACHINGS

Man is himself the author, center, and goal of all economic and social life. The decisive point of the social question is that goods created by God for everyone should in fact reach everyone in accordance with justice and with the help of charity.

—CCC, no. 2459

For over a century, the Church, especially through the teaching of the popes, has given special attention to the development of her social doctrine. The Church's social doctrine is related to the understanding of what it means to be a human being, to the origin of human dignity, to the problem of the Fall, and to the promise of Redemption. We are seriously weakened by Original Sin and actual sin but are redeemed by Christ's saving death and Resurrection with its gift of divine life, a source of moral strength (cf. CCC, nos. 355-431).

The Church's social doctrine also relates to an understanding of participation in social life, the role of authority, the importance of the common good, natural law, social justice, and human solidarity (cf. CCC, nos. 1897-1948). Finally, there is the Seventh Commandment, which includes consideration of the relationship between the economy and social justice, the importance of solidarity among nations, and a preferential love for the poor (cf. CCC, nos. 2401-2463).

Catholic social teaching embraces both the Church's perennial concern for people's social needs since New Testament times as well as an explicit social doctrine.

> The Church makes a judgment about economic and social matters when the fundamental rights of the person or the salvation of souls requires it. She is concerned with the temporal common good of men because they are ordered to the sovereign Good, their ultimate end. (CCC, no. 2458)

The central focus of the Church's social teaching is justice for all, especially for the helpless and the poor. It involves the removal of the symptoms and causes of poverty and injustice.

The Church's social doctrine addresses a wide range of issues that include the dignity of work, the need of workers to receive a salary that will enable them to care for their families, a safe working environment, and the responsibility of the state for areas such as a stable currency, public services, and protecting personal freedom and private property. Church teaching also speaks to the need of business enterprises to consider the good of the employees, not just the profit motive. Wage earners should be able to represent their needs and grievances when necessary.

As can be seen in the summary that follows, the major themes of Catholic social doctrine build on each other and complement each other. All of the Church's social teaching is rooted in the fundamental principle of the sacredness of human life and the fundamental dignity of every single individual. Out of these truths flows the rest.

Reflections of the Catholic Bishops of the United States on the Church's Social Teaching: Major Themes

> The Church's social teaching is a rich treasure of wisdom about building a just society and living lives of holiness amidst the challenges of a modern society. Modern Catholic social teaching has been articulated through a tradition of papal, concil-

FROM THE CATECHISM

1. What should be the attitude of business toward the environment?

Those *responsible for business enterprises* are responsible to society for the economic and ecological effects of their operations. They have an obligation to consider the good of persons and not only the increase of *profits*. (CCC, no. 2432)

2. Who should have access to employment and professions?

Access to employment and to professions must be open to all without unjust discrimination: men and women, healthy and disabled, natives and immigrants. For its part society should, according to circumstances, help citizens find work and employment. (CCC, no. 2433)

3. When is a strike permissible?

Recourse to a *strike* is morally legitimate when it cannot be avoided, or at least when it is necessary to obtain a proportionate benefit. It becomes morally unacceptable when accompanied by violence, or when objectives are included that are not directly linked to working conditions or are contrary to the common good. (CCC, no. 2435)

iar, and episcopal documents. The depth and richness of this tradition can be understood best through a direct reading of these documents. In these brief reflections, we wish to highlight several of the key themes that are at the heart of our Catholic social tradition.

Life and Dignity of the Human Person

The Catholic Church proclaims that human life is sacred and that the dignity of the human person is the foundation of a moral vision for society. Our belief in the sanctity of human life and the inherent dignity of the human person is the foundation of all the principles of our social teaching. In our society, human life is under direct attack from abortion and assisted suicide. The value of human life is being threatened by increasing use of the death penalty. We believe that every person is precious, that people are more important than things, and that the measure of every institution is whether it threatens or enhances the life and dignity of the human person.

Call to Family, Community, and Participation

The person is not only sacred, but also social. How we organize our society—in economics and politics, in law and policy—directly affects human dignity and the capacity of individuals to grow in community. The family is the central social institution that must be supported and strengthened, not undermined. We believe people have a right and a duty to participate in society, seeking together the common good and well-being of all, especially the poor and vulnerable.

Rights and Responsibilities

The Catholic tradition teaches that human dignity can be protected and a healthy community can be achieved only if human rights are protected and responsibilities are met. Therefore, every person has a fundamental right to life and a right to those things required for human decency. Corresponding to these rights are duties and responsibilities—to one another, to our families, and to the larger society.

Option for the Poor and Vulnerable

A basic moral test is how our most vulnerable members are faring. In a society marred by deepening divisions between rich and poor, our tradition recalls the story of the Last Judgment (Mt 25:31-46) and instructs us to put the needs of the poor and vulnerable first.

The Dignity of Work and the Rights of Workers

The economy must serve people, not the other way around. Work is more than a way to make a living; it is a form of continuing participation in God's creation. If the dignity of work is to be protected, then the basic rights of workers must be respected—the right to productive work, to decent and fair wages, to organize and join unions, to private property, and to economic initiative.

Solidarity
We are our brothers' and sisters' keepers, wherever they live. We are one human family, whatever our national, racial, ethnic, economic, and ideological differences. Learning to practice the virtue of solidarity means learning that "loving our neighbor" has global dimensions in an interdependent world.

Care for the Environment
We show our respect for the Creator by our stewardship of creation. Care for the earth is a requirement of our faith. We are called to protect people and the planet, living our faith in relationship with all of God's creation. This environmental challenge has fundamental moral and ethical dimensions that cannot be ignored.

This summary should only be a starting point for those interested in Catholic social teaching. A full understanding can only be achieved by reading the papal, conciliar, and episcopal documents that make up this rich tradition. (USCCB, *Excerpts from Catholic Social Teaching* [card] [Washington, DC: USCCB, 1999])

THE POOR IN OUR MIDST

Our nation is one of the wealthiest on the earth, and yet we do not have to look beyond our borders to find the ravages of poverty. There are the homeless in the streets of our cities, destitute families in rural and urban areas, and neglected children. The causes of poverty are many, but they all call forth the compassion of the Church—through her members and through her various structures, such as Catholic Charities and the St. Vincent de Paul Society.

On his death bed, St. Vincent de Paul (1580–1660) was asked by a novice what was the best way to serve the poor. He responded by telling the novice that the most important thing is to love them because loving them makes it possible for the needy to forgive those who give food to them. St. John Chrysostom said this about ministry to the poor: "Not to enable the poor to share in our goods is to steal from them and deprive them of life. The goods we possess are theirs, not ours" (Homily on the Parable of Lazarus and the Rich Man).

Jesus teaches us, "Whoever has two cloaks should share with the person who has none. And whoever has food should do likewise" (Lk 3:11). St. James reinforces this truth. "If a brother or sister has nothing to wear and has no food for the day, and one of you says to them, 'Go in peace, keep warm, and eat well,' but you do not give them the necessities of the body, what good is it?" (Jas 2:15-16).

Acts of charity for the poor are a good way to start living the Church's social teaching. Personal contact with those who need our help fulfills Christ's command to love the poor most effectively. But we are called to heal not only the symptoms of poverty and injustice but also their causes. This requires participation in political and social processes to correct unjust laws and structures of injustice.

FOR DISCUSSION

1. How does the Seventh Commandment guide us to respect and care for property that is not our own, that belongs to others, or that is public property?

2. Why is it important to realize that you are more than an individual, that you are a social being meant to be in solidarity with others? What social justice issues have caught your attention recently? What did you do about them?

3. What insights have you gained from reflecting on the U.S. bishops' statement of themes related to Catholic social teaching? What are some stories you could share about people you admire who have helped you to acquire a social conscience?

DOCTRINAL STATEMENTS

- "The seventh Commandment forbids theft. Theft is the [taking] of another's goods against the reasonable will of the owner. Every manner of taking and using another's property unjustly is contrary to the seventh commandment. The injustice committed requires reparation. Commutative justice requires the restitution of stolen goods" (CCC, nos. 2453-2454).

- In creating the universe, God entrusted the resources of the earth to the stewardship of all people. The Church, applying this truth, upholds the principle that the universal destination of the goods of the earth is meant for the common good of all people. At the same time, the Church stands by the right of private property.

- The Church teaches that human dignity can be protected and a healthy community can be achieved only if human rights are protected and responsibilities are met. Therefore, every person has a fundamental right to life and a right to those things required for human decency. Corresponding to these rights are duties and responsibilities—to one another, to our families, and to the larger society.

- We show our respect for the Creator by our stewardship of creation. Care for the earth is a requirement of our faith. We are called to protect people and the planet, living our faith in relationship with all of God's creation. This environmental challenge has fundamental moral and ethical dimensions that cannot be ignored.

- The Church's social doctrine addresses a wide range of issues that include the ability to freely practice one's faith, the freedom to participate in cultural life, the dignity of work, the need of workers to receive a salary that will enable them to care for their families, the need for a safe working environment, and the responsibility of the state for areas such as a stable currency, public services, and the protection of personal freedom and private property.

- Church teaching also speaks to the need of business enterprises to consider the good of the employees, not just the profit motive. Wage earners should be able to represent their needs and grievances when necessary.

- It can never be stated often enough that love and care for the poor is a major priority for every Christian. "Giving alms to the poor is a witness to fraternal charity: it is also a work of justice pleasing to God" (CCC, no. 2462).
- The central interest of the Church's social teaching is justice for all, but especially for the helpless and the poor. It involves the removal of the symptoms and causes of poverty and injustice.
- "The moral law forbids acts which, for commercial or totalitarian purposes, lead to the enslavement of human beings, or to their being bought, sold or exchanged like merchandise" (CCC, no. 2455).
- True social and economic development is concerned with the whole person and with increasing each person's ability to respond to God's call.

MEDITATION

Certainly we need to remember that no one can be excluded from our love, since "through his Incarnation the Son of God has united himself in some fashion with every person."

Yet, as the unequivocal words of the Gospel remind us, there is a special presence of Christ in the poor, and this requires the Church to make a preferential option for them. This option is a testimony to the nature of God's love, to his providence and mercy; and in some way history is still filled with the seeds of the Kingdom of God which Jesus himself sowed during his earthly life whenever he responded to those who came to him with their spiritual and material needs.

In our own time, there are so many needs which demand a compassionate response from Christians. Our world is entering the new millennium burdened by the contradictions of an economic, cultural and technological progress which offers immense possibilities to a fortunate few, while leaving millions of others not only on the margins of progress but in living conditions far below the minimum demanded by human dignity. How can it be that even today there are still people dying of hunger? Condemned to illiteracy? Lacking the most basic medical care? Without a roof over their heads?

. . . We must therefore ensure that in every Christian community the poor feel at home. Would not this approach be the greatest and most effective presentation of the good news of the Kingdom? Without this form of evangelization through charity and without the witness of Christian poverty the proclamation of the Gospel, which is itself the prime form of charity, risks being misunderstood or submerged by the ocean of words which daily engulfs us in today's society of mass communications. The charity of works ensures an unmistakable efficacy to the charity of words.

—NMI, nos. 49-50

PRAYER

Father, we honor the heart of your Son, broken by our cruelty,
yet symbol of love's triumph, pledge of all that we are called
    to be.
Teach us to see Christ in the lives we touch and to offer him
    living worship
by love-filled service to our brothers and sisters.
We ask this through Christ, our Lord.

—Concluding Prayer, Consecration to the Sacred Heart of Jesus,
St. Margaret Mary Alacoque

Let justice surge like water,
    and goodness like an unfailing stream.

—Am 5:24

32 THE EIGHTH COMMANDMENT: TELL THE TRUTH

YOU SHALL NOT BEAR FALSE WITNESS
AGAINST YOUR NEIGHBOR
—CCC, NOS. 2464-2513

THE BISHOP TOLD AND DEFENDED THE TRUTH

The Catholic Church will always need a vehicle for telling the truth to the public and to her members about her positions on problems in society, her hopes for people's happiness, and her fresh insights into the eternal Gospel of Christ. This becomes acutely necessary when forces outside the Church distort her teachings, misrepresent her intentions for society, and attempt to diminish the Church's life and integrity. "In Jesus Christ, the whole of God's truth has been made manifest" (CCC, no. 2466).

One man who understood this need was Fr. John Francis Noll. Born in Fort Wayne, Indiana, in 1875, he knew early on he wanted to be a priest. After completing studies at St. Lawrence College, in Mount Calvary, Wisconsin, he attended Mount St. Mary's Seminary in Cincinnati, Ohio. Bishop Joseph Rademacher ordained him a priest for the Fort Wayne diocese in 1898.

Within two years, Fr. Noll became a pastor in the Fort Wayne area. A man of prodigious energies, he not only served his people with zeal, but he also found time to respond to the larger issues affecting the Church of his time. He discovered he had a special talent for journalism, a gift for writing that he put at the service of the apostolic needs of the Church.

In the beginning, his mind was focused on people outside the Church—those whom he wished to convert to Catholicism and those who specialized in anti-Catholic bigotry and propaganda. His first venture for converting non-Catholics was the booklet *Kind Words from Your Pastor*. He chose a welcoming title to disarm suspicious readers and offer them an inviting look at Catholic teaching.

In 1913, he wrote *Father Smith Instructs Jackson*, an imaginary dialogue between a priest and a potential convert. A bestseller for over sixty years, it was a huge publishing success as well as a remarkable evangelizing tool that brought countless numbers of people into the Church.

When it came to defending the Church against the various anti-Catholic attacks, Fr. Noll began to publish a four-page newspaper, *Our Sunday Visitor*. In the years that followed, this project became a general-interest Catholic newspaper with a national circulation that continues to serve the cause of Catholic truth to this day.

In 1925, Fr. Noll founded the magazine *Acolyte*, which in 1945 became *Priest*, a publication that continues to support and serve the needs of clergy. Eventually, these efforts were organized into Our Sunday Visitor Publishing Company, to which was added a full-scale book publishing section.

In 1925, Fr. Noll became the bishop of Fort Wayne. During his thirty-one–year tenure, he helped to make the Church's influence on society more visible. He was one of the original members of the bishops' committee that formed the Legion of Decency to combat immorality in the movies by evaluating films and rating their suitability or absence thereof for public viewing. Fr. Noll was the first chairman of the National Organization for Decent Literature. Ever the evangelizer, he served on the Board of Catholic Missions for twenty-five years. Pope Pius XII gave him the honorary title of "Personal Archbishop" in 1953. Bishop Noll died in 1956.

As priest and as bishop, John Francis Noll understood the implications of the Eighth Commandment. Not only should each person avoid lying and tell the truth, but individuals and the Church herself must publicly proclaim the truth and expose the deceit of those who willfully undermine the Church. He knew the value of presenting the truths of the Church in a clear manner and was unafraid to defend the Church against her detractors.

SPEAK THE TRUTH AND LIVE THE TRUTH

Truth or truthfulness is the virtue which consists in showing oneself true in deeds and truthful in words, and guarding against duplicity, dissimulation, and hypocrisy. . . . Respect for the reputation and honor of persons forbids all detraction and calumny in word or attitude.

—CCC, nos. 2505 and 2507

You shall not bear false witness against your neighbor.

—Ex 20:16

The Bible teaches that God is the source of truth. Jesus not only taught the truth; he also said, "I am the truth" (cf. Jn 14:6). The Hebrew word for truth, *emeth*, refers both to truth in words and truthfulness in deeds. Jesus both personalized truth and spoke nothing but the truth.

When Christ stood before Pilate, Pilate asked Jesus if he were a king. In his reply, Jesus declared that his Kingdom was not political but spiritual; he had come to bear witness to truth. A spiritual kingdom is based on truth. Pilate could not understand Christ's reply. Jesus reached out to him and offered him the possibility of change. Pilate could only say, "What is truth?" (Jn 18:38).

In our culture, relativism challenges our ability to tell the truth because it claims there is no objective truth. This attitude undermines the distinction between truth and lies; it leads to an environment of deceit. In such an atmosphere, even Christ's teachings, based on divine truth, fail to persuade those whose trust in the possibility of objective truth has disappeared. This is the climate in which the Church needs to call people back to the reality of objective truth and to the link between doctrinal truth and everyday life.

SINS AGAINST TRUTH

"Lying is the most direct offense against the truth. . . . By injuring man's relation to truth and to his neighbor, a lie offends against the funda-

INTEGRITY AND TRUTH

Pope John Paul II has named St. Thomas More the Patron Saint of Statesmen, Politicians, and Lawyers. This saint's willingness to die rather than compromise the truth serves as an example to all. Often, society tries to convince us that faith is personal and should not influence political or legal positions and decisions. St. Thomas More is someone who reminds us that this is a false understanding. His example reminds men and women who serve in public office or who practice law of the importance of personal integrity, which is, after all, a form of truth. Integrity requires that we allow our faith to shape every aspect of life, public as well as private.

mental relation of man and of his word to the Lord" (CCC, no. 2483). People sin against the truth when they are guilty of ruining the reputation of another by telling lies, when they practice rash judgment, or when they engage in detraction (the unjust telling of someone's faults), perjury (lying under oath), or calumny (telling lies about another).

Scripture is clear about the evil of lying. In the Sermon on the Mount, Jesus said, "Let your 'Yes' mean 'Yes' and your 'No' mean 'No.' Anything more is from the evil one" (Mt 5:37). This reminds us not only that we need to be truthful, but also that hypocrisy—saying one thing while doing the opposite—is a sin against truth.

In the Gospel of John, Jesus describes the devil as father of lies (cf. Jn 8:44). St. Paul discouraged lying: "Stop lying to one another" (Col 3:9); "Speak the truth, each one to his neighbor, for we are members one of another" (Eph 4:25).

Happily, history is filled with stories of people who valued the truth so highly that they were willing to die for it. St. John Fisher (1469-1535) and St. Thomas More (1478-1535) surrendered their lives rather than approve of the divorce of King Henry VIII or deny the truth that the pope is Christ's appointed head of the Church. During World War II,

FROM THE CATECHISM

1. **What principle guides us in revealing the truth to another?**
   The golden rule ["Do unto others as you would have them do unto you"] helps one discern, in concrete situations, whether or not it would be appropriate to reveal the truth to someone who asks for it. (CCC, no. 2510)

2. **What is the responsibility of the media regarding truth?**
   Society has a right to information based on truth, freedom, and justice. One should practice moderation and discipline in the use of the social communications media. (CCC, no. 2512)

3. **How do art and beauty help us with truth?**
   Arising from talent given by the Creator and from man's own effort, art is a form of practical wisdom, uniting knowledge and skill, to give form to the truth of reality in a language accessible to sight or hearing. To the extent that it is inspired by truth and love of beings, art bears a certain likeness to God's activity in what he has created. (CCC, no. 2501)

Franz Jagerstatter, an Austrian farmer, refused to accept the lies of the Nazis, and he was martyred for his commitment to Christ's truth. During the French Revolution, a convent of Carmelite nuns chose to ignore laws that disbanded their monastery and continued to live together as a community. They courageously went to the guillotine rather than abandon the truth for which their vows stood.

We can testify to the truths of our faith in our everyday living, especially when we come in contact with those who do not hold the fullness of faith taught by the Catholic Church. This is done by living out the responsibilities and implications of our faith, as well as by being prepared to dialogue with others on issues of doctrine and morality where differences occur. "Always be ready to give an explanation [of your faith] to anyone who asks you for a reason for your hope, but do it with gentleness and reverence" (1 Pt 3:15-16).

THE RIGHT TO KNOW THE TRUTH

"No one is bound to reveal the truth to someone who does not have the right to know it" (CCC, no. 2489). The security of others, their right to privacy, and a respect for the common good are reasons for keeping silent or being discreet in our language concerning matters that should not be disclosed. It is also for these reasons that gossiping is a sinful violation of the privacy of others.

Professionals such as politicians, doctors, lawyers, psychologists, and others in positions where confidences are entrusted should preserve confidentiality, unless there is a grave and proportionate reason for divulging the information. The same is true about ordinary personal relationships in which confidences are shared.

THE MEDIA

In our culture, the communications media hold an influential place in disseminating information, forming attitudes, and motivating behavior. Technological advances are increasing the role of the media and its capacity to shape public opinion. "The information provided by the media is at the service of the common good. Society has a right to information based on truth, freedom, justice, and solidarity" (CCC, no. 2494). In the assembling and publishing of news, the moral law and the lawful rights and human dignity of men and women should be followed.

The requirements of justice and charity must guide communications just as much as other public institutions. Those who undertake to form public opinion need to be governed by these principles. Human solidarity is one of the positive effects of media communications when a commitment to a right-minded policy is followed—one that supports a free circulation of ideas that advances knowledge and people's respect for each other. Mutually respectful dialogue also aids the quest for truth.

LIES HAVE DEVASTATING EFFECTS

Lying is linked to the tragedy of sin and its perverse consequences, which have had, and continue to have, devastating effects on the lives of individuals and nations. We need but think of the events of the past century, when aberrant ideological and political systems willfully twisted the truth and brought about the exploitation and murder of an appalling number of men and women, wiping out entire families and communities. After experiences like these, how can we fail to be seriously concerned about lies in our own time, lies which are the framework for menacing scenarios of death in many parts of the world. Any authentic search for peace must begin with the realization that the problem of truth and untruth is the concern of every man and woman; it is decisive for the peaceful future of our planet. (Benedict XVI, "Message for World Day of Peace," January 1, 2006)

TRUTH AND THE OP-ED PAGE

The more our culture has moved away from acceptance of objective truth, the more it has moved toward the culture of opinions. Each day, newspapers give us a diet of opinions on their op-ed page. Talk shows on television have turned the sharing of opinions into a national pastime. Editors and talk show hosts strive to give us a range of opinions that stretch from one end of the spectrum to another. At the high end of these presentations, experts and scholars are recruited to offer us their best current research. At another level, people are simply enlisted to share their thoughts and feelings publicly on any number of social, moral, and political matters. Sometimes debate degenerates into expressions of hatred.

Though the intuition remains that there is really such a thing as objective truth, it tends to be lost in a marathon of inconclusive discussions. As a result, some spend valuable time sharing only feelings or

uninformed opinions. Much of what passes for truth is the effort to justify individual behavior. In its unsettling form, this generates an attitude
of skepticism and even suspicion about any truth claims. Thus objective
truth is considered unattainable.

In this kind of cultural environment, how can we speak of the invitation of the Eighth Commandment to tell the truth and avoid lying?
Speaking the truth is the opposite of lying. The distinction between
lying and truth-telling presupposes that there is a truth that can be told.
Although a real problem is that some people lie, there is also the related
issue of skepticism about the possibility of knowing truth.

The best way to step outside the constriction of these biases is
through study, love, and practice grounded in faith. The Church never
ceases to urge, "Know the truth. Love the truth. Live the truth." And the
truth is Jesus Christ.

FOR DISCUSSION

1. Why do we believe what people say? What happens when we discover that someone has lied? What is the relationship between trust
   and truth?
2. When you encounter people who cause you to be skeptical about
   the truth of the Church's doctrinal and moral teachings, how should
   you react?
3. What steps can be taken to restore conviction about objective truth
   and concrete moral standards in our society? What are some inspiring stories about truth in word and deed that you can share?

DOCTRINAL STATEMENTS

- "You shall not bear false witness against your neighbor" (Ex 20:16).
  Scripture teaches that God is the source of truth. Jesus not only
  taught the truth; he also said, "I am the truth" (cf. Jn 14:16). At the
  Last Supper, Jesus identified himself with truth. Jesus both personalized truth and spoke nothing but the truth.

- The natural law requires all people to speak and live by the truth in words and deeds.
- "The golden rule ['Do unto others as you would have them do unto you'] helps one discern, in concrete situations, whether or not it would be appropriate to reveal the truth to someone who asks for it" (CCC, no. 2510).
- The right to know the truth is not absolute. Charity and justice govern what may be communicated. People's safety, respect for privacy, and the common good are reasons for being silent or using discreet language about what should not be known.
- "No one is bound to reveal the truth to someone who does not have the right to know it" (CCC, no. 2489).
- Members of the media have the responsibility to always be at the service of the common good.
- In the assembling and publishing of the news, the moral law and the lawful rights and human dignity of men and women should be upheld.
- "Arising from talent given by the Creator and from man's own effort, art is a form of practical wisdom, uniting knowledge and skill, to give form to the truth of reality in a language accessible to sight or hearing. To the extent that it is inspired by truth and love of beings, art bears a certain likeness to God's activity in what he has created" (CCC, no. 2501).
- "An offense committed against the truth requires reparation" (CCC, no. 2509).

MEDITATION

Truth is more than an idea. It reveals goodness and beauty. This is what moved Pope Paul VI to speak of the "inherent attractiveness of Gospel truth." Love beholds truth as a revelation of beauty. Once it is known and loved, truth is meant to be practiced. St. Ignatius offered this wise advice regarding the need to foster truth:

> Every good Christian ought to be more ready to give a favorable interpretation to another's statement than to condemn it. But if

he cannot do so, let him ask how the other understands it. And if the latter understands it badly, let the former correct him with love. If that does not suffice, let the Christian try all suitable ways to bring the other to a correct interpretation so that he may be saved. (St. Ignatius of Loyola, *Spiritual Exercises*, 22)

PRAYER

Blessing of Centers of Social Communication

Lord God Almighty,
We humbly praise you,
for you enlighten and inspire
those who by probing the powers implanted in creation
develop the work of your hands in wonderful ways.
Look with favor on your servants
who use the technology discovered by long research.
Enable them to communicate truth,
to foster love, to uphold justice and right,
and to provide enjoyment.
Let them promote and support
that peace between peoples
which Christ the Lord brought from heaven,
for he lives and reigns for ever and ever.
Amen.

—*Book of Blessings* (1990), no. 830

I do not sit with deceivers,
    nor with hypocrites do I mingle.

—Ps 26:4

33 THE NINTH COMMANDMENT: PRACTICE PURITY OF HEART

YOU SHALL NOT COVET YOUR NEIGHBOR'S WIFE
—CCC, NOS. 2514-2533

MARIA GORETTI: A MODEL OF PURITY

Maria Goretti was born in Corinaldo, Italy, on October 16, 1890. She was one of six children born to Luigi Goretti and Assunta Carlini. In 1896, the family moved to Ferriere di Conca, where the Gorettis became sharecroppers for Count Mazzolini. The Goretti family lived in an old cheese factory building on the estate, where Assunta worked hard to make a home for her family.

Due to the hard labor of draining the flooded estate, Luigi soon contracted malaria and was unable to adequately manage the land for which he was responsible. On account of this, Count Mazzolini sent Giovanni Serenelli and his son Alessandro to share half the work, half the profits, and half of the building which the Goretti family had made into a home.

The Goretti parents soon became aware that the Serenellis were not people of high moral character. As Luigi's malaria became more severe, Luigi and Assunta regretted their leaving Corinaldo.

The position of the Goretti family took a tragic turn upon Luigi's death in 1902. Since Assunta was now forced to work in the fields to provide for the family, she put Maria in charge of the duties at home. Maria had grown in virtue and grace throughout her childhood. She also had a great devotion to the Blessed Sacrament, which she received for the first time in May of that same year.

Alessandro began stalking Maria and making suggestive advances towards her, advances that she always unhesitatingly refused. Ultimately, her refusal sparked him to take matters into his own hands.

On July 5, 1902, Maria—who was not yet twelve years old—was peacefully stitching and caring for her little sister, Theresa. Alessandro, who was eighteen years old, grabbed Maria's arm, dragged her into the kitchen, and attempted to rape her. She fought him and pleaded with him to stop, exclaiming that what he was attempting was a sin forbidden by God. Her resistance infuriated Alessandro who, after failing to choke her into submission, stabbed her fourteen times.

Maria was taken to a hospital, where she suffered for an entire day. Upon gaining consciousness, she fixed her gaze on a statue of the Blessed Mother that was at the foot of her bed. Before receiving *Viaticum*, she forgave Alessandro for what he had done and expressed the desire that he might join her in heaven. She died of her wounds on July 6, 1902.

Alessandro Serenelli was soon apprehended, convicted, and sentenced to thirty years in prison for his crime. Eight years into his sentence, Maria appeared to him in a dream. In that dream, Maria gathered lilies, which she then handed to him. The lilies took on a radiance that assured him of her forgiveness. This vision led to a conversion, which brought him into reconciliation with God, the Church, and the Goretti family.

Pope Pius XII canonized Maria Goretti on June 24, 1950. Her mother Assunta and her murderer Alessandro Serenelli were both present. St. Maria Goretti has been named the Patroness of Modern Youth. Her love for her attacker—shown in her forgiveness of him—and her spiritual and physical purity of heart serve as a model for all Christians. Her purity exemplifies the Ninth Commandment.

THE MORALITY OF THE HEART

The heart is the seat of moral personality: "Out of the heart come evil thoughts, murder, adultery, fornication" (Mt 15:19). The struggle against carnal covetousness entails purifying the heart and practicing temperance.

—CCC, no. 2517

We experience tensions between spiritual and physical desires. This struggle belongs to the heritage of sin. This does not mean that we are to despise the body and emotions that, with the soul, constitute our nature. It does make us realize that we will face a daily spiritual struggle to acquire virtues that help us obey the saving action of the Holy Spirit and overcome vices that cause us to resist him.

The grace of Baptism purifies us from sins, but a certain tendency to sin remains. We must struggle against disordered desires by practicing purity of mind, heart, and body with daily vigilance. To do this, we need to examine our motives as well as our deeds, so that we always seek God's will. This will cause us to discipline our feelings and imagination. Finally, since purity is a gift of God, we need to pray for it, as St. Augustine did:

I thought that continence arose from one's own powers, which I did not recognize in myself. I was foolish enough not to know . . . that no one can be continent unless you grant it. For you surely would have granted it if my inner groaning had reached your ears and I with firm faith had cast my cares on you. (*The Confessions*, bk. 6, chap. 11, no. 20)

MODESTY

Modesty is a virtue necessary for purity. It flows out of the virtues of temperance, chastity, and self-control. A modest person dresses, speaks, and acts in a manner that supports and encourages purity and chastity, and not in as manner that would tempt or encourage sinful sexual behavior. Modesty protects the mystery of the person in order to avoid exploiting the other. This attitude instills in us the patience and reserve we need for avoiding unbecoming behavior. Modest relationships reflect the connection between the marital state and sexual behavior. Modest behavior respects the boundaries of intimacy that are imbedded in our natures by the natural law and the principles of sexual behavior laid out in Divine Revelation. Modesty ensures and supports purity of heart, a gift that enables us to see God's plan for personal relationships, sexuality, and marriage.

Recovering Modesty

Modesty protects the mystery of persons and their love. It encourages patience and moderation in loving relationships. . . . It inspires one's choice of clothing. It keeps silence or reserve where there is evident risk of unhealthy curiosity. It is discreet.

—CCC, no. 2522

We need to maintain the concern for chaste living prayerfully in our hearts. Faith is the proper foundation in the quest for a clean heart. Growth in modesty requires loving support from family and friends as well as wise counsel and the practice of virtues.

The attitude of modesty is difficult to maintain in a culture that prizes sexual permissiveness. Countless appeals for erotic satisfaction assail us daily from all the major forms of communication. This environment of indecency challenges all men and women of faith to choose and to witness to modesty as a way of life and as a method for healing a culture that has strayed from God's plan for sexuality and marriage.

Those who have accepted the approach of the permissive culture have been persuaded that freedom is the right to do what we want to do, not what we should do. At the beginning of Christianity, the Apostles preached and witnessed Christ's Gospel to the permissive cultures of Greece and Rome, a fact well-illustrated in St. Paul's Letters to the Corinthians. Difficult as it was, the first preachers prevailed over the allurements of the culture, won numerous converts, and encouraged the virtue of modesty.

FROM THE CATECHISM

1. What is the teaching of the Ninth Commandment?
"Everyone who looks at a woman lustfully has already committed adultery with her in his heart" (Mt 5:28). The ninth commandment warns against lust or carnal concupiscence. (CCC, nos. 2528-2529)

2. What is the antidote to lust?
The struggle against carnal lust involves purifying the heart and practicing temperance. Purity of heart will enable us to see God: it enables us even now to see things according to God. (CCC, nos. 2530-2531)

3. How do we purify our hearts?
Purification of the heart demands prayer, the practice of chastity, purity of intention and of vision. Purity of heart requires the modesty which is patience, decency, and discretion. Modesty protects the intimate center of the person. (CCC, nos. 2532-2533)

The Church calls us to be signs of contradiction in an overly eroticized society. All members of the Church should respond to the immodest aspects of society and culture with a deep and conscious spirituality. The Gospel can renew and purify what is decadent in our culture and gradually can displace the attraction of sin. We must assert Christ's Gospel by word and witness to transform the moral tone of our culture. This approach fosters virtue in the human heart and its development through the grace of the Holy Spirit.

As we have mentioned, in New Testament times, the Apostles encountered moral challenges every bit as awesome as ours. Faced with his own struggles, St. Paul appeared discouraged when he said, "Miserable one that I am! Who will deliver me from this mortal body?" In the same breath he praised God as he gave the answer: "Jesus Christ our Lord!"

(Rom 7:24, 25). The gifts of faith and grace enabled Paul to meet the demands of the Gospel of Jesus. They will do the same for us.

FOR DISCUSSION

1. What are modesty and purity of heart? What are ways you have found to help you acquire these virtues? Share stories of people you admire who witness to these values.
2. Why is it important to be as vigilant about our interior attitudes toward sexuality as we are about external acts? What are other examples you can cite about the link between inner attitudes and external behavior?
3. While it may seem daunting, what are strategies that could be adopted to turn back the cultural influences that undermine modesty and purity of heart? What will help you trust in the power of the Gospel of Jesus to bring this about?

DOCTRINAL STATEMENTS

- You shall not covet your neighbor's wife (Dt 5:21).
- "'Everyone who looks at a woman lustfully has already committed adultery with her in his heart' (Mt 5:28). The ninth commandment warns against lust or carnal concupiscence" (CCC, nos. 2528-2529).
- "Modesty protects the mystery of persons and their love. It encourages patience and moderation in loving relationships. . . . It inspires one's choice of clothing. It keeps silence or reserve where there is evident risk of unhealthy curiosity. It is discreet" (CCC, no. 2522).
- *Concupiscence* refers to our disordered desires and the inclination to sin that is a consequence of Original Sin. The term describes rebellion of our passions and desires against the dictates of right reason.
- "Purification of the heart demands prayer, the practice of chastity, purity of intention and of vision. Purity of heart requires the modesty which is patience, decency, and discretion. Modesty protects the intimate center of the person" (CCC, nos. 2532-2533).

- The Gospel can renew and purify what is decadent in our culture and gradually displace the attraction of sin. Asserting Christ's Gospel by word and witness helps to transform the moral tone of our culture. This approach fosters virtue in the human heart and its development through the grace of the Holy Spirit.

MEDITATION

At the conclusion of the Jubilee Year 2000, Pope John Paul II reflected on his meetings with young people throughout that year:

> And how could we fail to recall especially the joyful and inspiring gathering of young people? If there is an image of the Jubilee of the Year 2000 that more than any other will live on in memory, it is surely the streams of young people with whom I was able to engage in a sort of very special dialogue, filled with mutual affection and deep understanding. It was like this from the moment I welcomed them in the Square of Saint John Lateran and Saint Peter's Square. Then I saw them swarming through the city, happy as young people should be, but also thoughtful, eager to pray, seeking "meaning" and true friendship. Neither for them nor for those who saw them will it be easy to forget that week, during which Rome became "young with the young." . . .
>
> Yet again, the young have shown themselves to be for Rome and for the Church a special gift of the Spirit of God. Sometimes when we look at the young, with the problems and weaknesses that characterize them in contemporary society, we tend to be pessimistic. The Jubilee of Young People however changed that, telling us that young people, whatever their possible ambiguities, have a profound longing for those genuine values which find their fullness in Christ. Is not Christ the secret of true freedom and profound joy of heart? Is not Christ the supreme friend and the teacher of all genuine friendship? If Christ is presented to young people as he really is, they experience him as an answer that is convincing and they can accept his message, even when it is demanding and bears the mark of the Cross. For this reason, in response to their enthusiasm, I did not hesitate to ask them to

make a radical choice of faith and life and present them with a stupendous task: to become "morning watchmen" (cf. Is 21:11-12) at the dawn of the new millennium.

—NMI, no. 9

PRAYER

Prayer for Purity of Body and Mind
Lord, set aflame my heart and my entire being
with the fire of the Holy Spirit,
that I may serve you with a chaste body and pure mind.
Through Christ our Lord. Amen.

—*Daily Roman Missal*

Blessed are the clean of heart,
for they will see God.

—Mt 5:8

34 THE TENTH COMMANDMENT: EMBRACE POVERTY OF SPIRIT

YOU SHALL NOT COVET YOUR NEIGHBOR'S GOODS
—CCC, NOS. 2534-2557

I WANT TO LIVE AND DIE FOR GOD

Henriette Delille was born in 1813 in New Orleans. The daughter of a Catholic mother of African origin and a prosperous white father, she was a free, beautiful, and educated woman. She was raised a Catholic. As a child of mixed blood, she was known as a *quadroon*. White in appearance, she had the possibility of climbing the social ladder and of marrying a rich man. Quadroon balls were often held to facilitate such arrangements.

At age eleven, she met Sr. St. Martha Fontier, whose Christian faith and charitable devotion to African slave families greatly impressed her. Sr. St. Martha introduced her to the ideal of love as expressed in the vow of virginity.

By the time Henriette was fourteen, she was teaching religion to the slaves on the nearby plantations. She regularly visited and helped the sick and elderly among the freed blacks and slaves. Since it was against the law to educate slaves, such as teaching them to read, Henriette acted out stories from Scripture and Church history to teach them about salvation through Jesus Christ.

After her mother's death in 1836, Henriette sold all her property and began to fulfill her dream of founding a religious community. Eventually her dream came true. With the help of a priest friend, Fr. Etienne Rousselon, permission was received from the bishop to start a religious congregation of sisters for African American women. Devoted to poverty, chastity, obedience, and service to the poor and enslaved, they called themselves the Sisters of the Holy Family.

Henriette wrote at this time, "I believe in God. I hope in God. I love and I want to live and die for God." To gain financial support for her community, Henriette created the Association of the Holy Family with members from free families of African heritage. These associates benefited from the spiritual life and prayers of the sisters and in turn gave them moral support and financial assistance.

After a few years, Henriette opened a home for the elderly, the sick, and the poor. She purchased a house that would serve as a community center, where slaves and free blacks could come and socialize with each other as well as learn the teachings of the Church. In time she founded schools and orphanages for her people.

She found many ways to bring dignity to the life of black slaves. She taught them they were free in the eyes of God for they were created in his image. She devised ways to have the slaves enter into sacramental marriages—a practice considered illegal because under the law, slaves were not thought to be fully human, only property. Their marriages were not considered valid in civil law, but for the Church, they were valid in God's eyes.

Henriette Delille died on November 17, 1862. Her obituary stated, "The crowd gathered for her funeral testified by its sorrow how keenly felt was the loss of her who for the love of Christ had made herself the humble servant of slaves."

The bishops of the United States have voted unanimously to endorse the "the appropriateness and timeliness" of Mother Henriette's cause for sainthood. Today the Sisters of the Holy Family continue to operate in the United States and several South American countries.[17]

Mother Henriette Delille wanted nothing for herself and did not seek to acquire for herself the goods of this world. Her embrace of poverty freed her to seek the spiritual good of others.

---

17   Biography adapted from Ann Ball, *Modern Saints* (Rockford, IL: Tan Books, 1983).

WHERE YOUR TREASURE IS, THERE ALSO WILL YOUR HEART BE (MT 6:21)

The tenth commandment unfolds and completes the ninth, which is concerned with concupiscence of the flesh. It forbids coveting the goods of another, as the root of theft, robbery, and fraud, which the seventh commandment forbids. . . . The tenth commandment concerns the intentions of the heart.

—CCC, no. 2534

When Jesus began the Sermon on the Mount, he proclaimed the eight Beatitudes as the ways to authentic happiness. The first of these stated that poverty of spirit would enable us to inherit the Kingdom of God. In other words, the first step on the road to joy begins with a healthy detachment from material goods. Later on in the same sermon, Jesus taught that building up wealth for its own sake is foolishness. We should be more interested in spiritual riches.

> Do not store up for yourselves treasures on earth, where moth and decay destroy, and thieves break in and steal. But store up treasures in heaven, where neither moth nor decay destroys, nor thieves break in and steal. For where your treasure is, there also will your heart be. (Mt 6:19-21)

The financial scandals that periodically occur in our culture remind us that greed is a constant threat to moral behavior. It leads many to conclude that money is the root of all evils. But in fact, "the love of money is the root of all evils" (1 Tm 6:10). In the study of the Seventh Commandment, we dealt with the visible acts of stealing and injustice. The Tenth Commandment looks at the interior attitudes of greed and envy that lead us to steal and act unjustly.

On the positive side, the Tenth Commandment calls us to practice poverty of spirit and generosity of heart. These virtues liberate us from being slaves to money and possessions. They enable us to have a preferential love for the poor and to be witnesses of justice and peace in the world. They also enable us to adopt a simplicity of life that frees us from consumerism and helps us preserve God's creation.

Sinful inclinations move us to envy what others have and lead to an unrestrained drive to acquire all that we can. We do have a reasonable need to acquire the means needed to care for our families. Greed is the distortion of this desire. The greedy person will stop at nothing to get all the money and possessions possible.

We need to remember that envy is the companion of greed; it is an attitude that fills us with sadness at the sight of another's prosperity. Envious people can be consumed with so much desire for what others have that they will even commit crimes to get what they want.

Baptized people should counter envy with humility, thanksgiving to God for his gifts to oneself and to others, goodwill, and surrender to the providence of God (cf. CCC, no. 2554). "Christ's faithful 'have crucified the flesh with its passions and desires' (Gal 5:24); they are led by the Spirit and follow his desires" (CCC, no. 2555). Poverty of heart is a way to avoid greed and envy. "Abandonment to the providence of the Father in heaven frees us from anxiety about tomorrow. Trust in God is a preparation for the blessedness of the poor. They shall see God" (CCC, no. 2547, citing Mt 6:25-34).

TO BE A CHRISTIAN STEWARD: A SUMMARY OF THE U.S. BISHOPS' PASTORAL LETTER ON STEWARDSHIP

"As each one has received a gift, use it to serve one another as good stewards of God's varied grace" (1 Pt 4:10).

What identifies a steward? Safeguarding material and human resources and using them responsibly are one answer; so is generous giving of time, talent, and treasure. But being a Christian steward means more. As Christian stewards, we receive God's gifts gratefully, cultivate them responsibly, share them lovingly in justice with others, and return them with increase to the Lord.

Disciples as Stewards

Let us begin with being a disciple—a follower of our Lord Jesus Christ. As members of the Church, Jesus calls us to be disciples. This has astonishing implications:

- Mature disciples make a conscious decision to follow Jesus, no matter what the cost.
- Christian disciples experience conversion—life-shaping changes of mind and heart—and commit themselves to the Lord.
- Christian stewards respond in a particular way to the call to be a disciple. Stewardship has the power to shape and mold our understanding of our lives and the way in which we live. Jesus' disciples, as Christian stewards, recognize God as the origin of life, the giver of freedom, and the source of all things. We are grateful for the gifts we have received and are eager to use them to show our love for God and for one another. We look to the life and teaching of Jesus for guidance in living as Christian stewards.

Stewards of Creation

The Bible contains a profound message about the stewardship of material creation: God created the world, but entrusts it to human beings. Caring for and cultivating the world involves the following:

- Joyful appreciation for the God-given beauty and wonder of nature;
- Protection and preservation of the environment, which is the stewardship of ecological concern;
- Respect for human life—shielding life from threat and assault and doing everything that can be done to enhance this gift and make life flourish;
- Development of this world through noble human effort—physical labor, the trades and professions, the arts and sciences. We call such effort "work."

Work is a fulfilling human vocation. The Second Vatican Council points out that, through work, we build up not only our world but also the Kingdom of God, already present among us. Work is a partnership with God—our share in a divine human collaboration in creation. It occupies a central place in our lives as Christian stewards.

Stewards of Vocation

Jesus calls us as his disciples to a new way of life—the Christian way of life—of which stewardship is a part. But Jesus does not call us as nameless people in a faceless crowd. He calls individually, by name. Each one of us—clergy, religious, layperson, married, single, adult, child—has a personal vocation. God intends each one of us to play a unique role in carrying out the divine plan.

The challenge, then, is to understand our role—our vocation—and to respond generously to this call from God. Christian vocation entails the practice of stewardship. In addition, Christ calls each of us to be stewards of our personal vocations, which we receive from God.

Stewards of the Church

Stewards of God's gifts are not passive beneficiaries. We cooperate with God in our own redemption and in the redemption of others.

We are also obliged to be stewards of the Church, collaborators and cooperators in continuing the redemptive work of Jesus Christ, which is the Church's essential mission. This mission—proclaiming and teaching, serving and sanctifying—is our task. It is the personal responsibility of each one of us as stewards of the Church.

All members have their own roles to play in carrying out this mission.

- Parents who nurture their children in the light of faith
- Parishioners who work in concrete ways to make their parishes true communities of faith and vibrant sources of service to the larger community
- All Catholics, who give generous support—time, money, prayers, and personal service according to their circumstances—to parish and diocesan programs and to the universal Church

FROM THE CATECHISM

1. What two attitudes does the Tenth Commandment forbid?
The tenth commandment forbids *greed*. . . . It requires that envy be banished from the human heart. (CCC, nos. 2536 and 2538)

2. How can we acquire poverty of spirit?
Abandonment to the providence of the Father in heaven frees us from anxiety about tomorrow. Trust in God is a preparation for the blessedness of the poor. They shall see God. (CCC, no. 2547)

3. How can we be free of exaggerated dependence on material goods?
Desire for true happiness frees man from his immoderate attachment to the goods of this world so that he can find his fulfillment in the vision and beatitude of God. "The promise [of seeing God] surpasses all beatitude. . . . In Scripture, to see is to possess. . . . Whoever sees God has obtained all the goods of which he can conceive." (CCC, no. 2548, citing St. Gregory of Nyssa, *De Beatitudinibu*s 6: PG 44, 1265A)

Obstacles to Stewardship

People who want to live as Christian disciples and Christian stewards face serious obstacles. In the United States and other nations, a dominant secular culture often contradicts religious convictions about the meaning of life. This culture frequently encourages us to focus on ourselves and our pleasures. At times, we can find it far too easy to ignore spiritual realities and to deny religion a role in shaping human and social values.

As Catholics who have entered the mainstream of American society and experienced its advantages, many of us also have been adversely influenced by this secular culture. We know what it is to struggle against selfishness and greed, and we realize that it is harder for many today to accept the challenge of being a Christian steward.

It is essential, therefore, that we make a special effort to understand the true meaning of stewardship and live accordingly.

A Steward's Way
The life of a Christian steward models the life of Jesus. It is challenging and even difficult in many respects, yet intense joy comes to those who take the risk to live as Christian stewards. Women and men who seek to live as stewards learn that "all things work for good for those who love God" (Rom 8:28).

After Jesus, we look to Mary as the ideal steward. As the Mother of Christ, she lived her ministry in a spirit of fidelity and service; she responded generously to the call.

We must ask ourselves, do we wish to be disciples of Jesus Christ and Christian stewards of our world and our Church?

Central to our human and Christian vocations, as well as to the unique vocation each one of us receives from God, is that we be good stewards of the gifts we possess. God gives us this divine-human workshop, this world and Church of ours. The Spirit shows us the way. Stewardship is part of that journey. (USCCB, "To Be a Christian Steward," in *Stewardship: A Disciple's Response* [Washington, DC: USCCB, 2002], 45ff.)

BLESSED IS THE GENEROUS HEART

Some say that helping the poor involves only making sure that all their physical or material needs are addressed. But is this enough? Should we not also focus on helping people to develop to their utmost potential?

The first step in helping the disadvantaged is to acknowledge the sacred dignity and image of God found in each person. What is also required is a conscience formation from which flow the beliefs, attitudes, and actions that will help the poor. Having more is never enough. Being more is paramount.

Christian discipleship means, among other things, working to ensure that all people have access to what makes them fully human and fosters their human dignity: faith, education, health care, housing, employment, and leisure. Members of the Church are called to build up the resources of the Church herself and of civil society in making possible the sharing of God's blessings and social goods with others. This they do by their own generosity in the use of their time, talents, and treasures with others. Such generosity flows from hearts grateful to God for his generosity in creating and saving us.

FOR DISCUSSION

1. While it is necessary to acquire earthly goods for the care and well-being of our families, there are forces that motivate us to become overly attached to wealth. How does the media contribute to this? What role does envy play in this drive toward the love of money?
2. What habits have you developed to help you have a healthy detachment from worldly goods? How would generosity counter the tendency to be attached to material things?
3. What do you need to do as a Christian steward?

DOCTRINAL STATEMENTS

- "The tenth commandment unfolds and completes the ninth, which is concerned with concupiscence of the flesh. It forbids coveting the goods of another, as the root of theft, robbery, and fraud, which the seventh commandment forbids. . . . The tenth commandment concerns the intentions of the heart" (CCC, no. 2534).
- "For where your treasure is, there also will your heart be" (Mt 6:21).
- Envy is an attitude of sadness at the sight of another's prosperity. It can create a disordered desire to acquire such goods, even by unjust means. Envy tightens the heart and subdues love. For this reason, envy is considered a Capital Sin.
- "The baptized person combats envy through goodwill, humility, and abandonment to the providence of God. Christ's faithful 'have crucified the flesh with its passions and desires' (Gal 5:24); they are led by the Spirit and follow his desires" (CCC, no. 2555).

- "The tenth commandment forbids *greed* and . . . requires that *envy* be banished from the human heart" (CCC, nos. 2536 and 2538).
- The Christian practice of giving and sharing is a powerful alternative to greed and a positive contribution to a peaceful and just society.
- "Detachment from riches is necessary for entering the Kingdom of heaven. 'Blessed are the poor in spirit'" (CCC, no. 2556).
- "Envy often comes from pride; the baptized person should train himself to live in humility: 'Would you like to see God glorified by you? Then rejoice in your brother's progress and you will immediately give glory to God. Because his servant could conquer envy by rejoicing in the merits of others, God will be praised'" (CCC, no. 2540, citing St. John Chrysostom, *Homiliae in ad Romanos*, no. 71, 5).

MEDITATION

The Church witnesses the fact that human dignity cannot be destroyed, whatever the situation of poverty, scorn, rejection or powerlessness to which a human being has been reduced. [The Church] shows her solidarity with those who do not count in a society by which they are rejected spiritually and sometimes even physically. She is particularly drawn with maternal affection toward those children who, through human wickedness, will never be brought forth from the womb to the light of day, as also for the elderly, alone and abandoned. The special option for the poor . . . manifests the universality of the Church's being and mission.

—Congregation for the Doctrine of the Faith,
Instruction on Christian Freedom and Liberation (1986), no. 68

PRAYER

The Prayer of a Poor Man (The Canticle of the Sun)
Most high, all powerful, all good Lord!
All praise is yours, all glory, all honor, and all blessing.
To you, alone, Most High, do they belong.
No mortal lips are worthy to pronounce your name.

Be praised, my Lord, through all your creatures,
especially through my lord Brother Sun, who brings the day;
and you give light through him.
And he is beautiful and radiant in all his splendor!
Of you, Most High, he bears the likeness.
Be praised, my Lord, through Sister Moon and the stars;
in the heavens you have made them, precious and beautiful.
Be praised, my Lord, through Brothers Wind and Air,
and clouds and storms, and all the weather,
through which you give your creatures sustenance.
Be praised, My Lord, through Sister Water;
she is very useful, and humble, and precious, and pure.
Be praised, my Lord, through Brother Fire,
through whom you brighten the night.
He is beautiful and cheerful, and powerful and strong.
Be praised, my Lord, through our sister Mother Earth,
who feeds us and rules us, and produces various fruits with
    colored flowers and herbs.
Be praised, my Lord, through those who forgive
for love of you;
through those who endure sickness and trial.
Happy those who endure in peace, for by you, Most High, they
    will be crowned.
Be praised, my Lord, through our Sister Bodily Death,
from whose embrace no living person can escape.
Woe to those who die in mortal sin!
Happy those she finds doing your most holy will.
The second death can do no harm to them.
Praise and bless my Lord, and give thanks, and serve him with
    great humility.

—St. Francis of Assisi

He who is greedy of gain brings ruin on his own house.

—Prv 15:27

PART IV

PRAYER:
THE FAITH PRAYED

35 GOD CALLS US TO PRAY

THE FOUNDATIONS OF PRAYER
—CCC, NOS. 2558-2758

THE HOUR THAT MADE HIS DAY

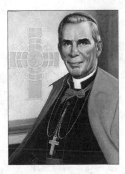

Archbishop Fulton J. Sheen believed that his daily hour of prayer before the Blessed Sacrament was essential for his ministry as a priest. For him it was like "an oxygen tank that revived the breath of the Holy Spirit." Sheen said the idea of having a daily hour of prayer came to him one evening in 1918 while he was a student at St. Paul Seminary in Minnesota. He began his Holy Hour observance the next day and maintained it for the rest of his life, usually early in the morning before Mass.

He was born in El Paso, Illinois, in 1895, to a hardware store owner and his wife. His parents first enrolled Fulton at St. Mary's grammar school in 1900. Later, he was educated at St. Viator's College in Bourbonnais, Illinois, and then at St. Paul's Seminary in Minnesota, before being ordained in 1919. Later, he pursued graduate studies in philosophy at the Catholic University of America and at Louvain University in Belgium.

His bishop brought him back to the Diocese of Peoria, where he served as a parish priest for a year. He was permitted to become a professor of philosophy at The Catholic University of America in Washington, D.C., where he taught for twenty-five years.

God had also given him the gift of preaching, a talent he used for the Church's work of evangelization, first on a radio program called the *Catholic Hour* for twenty-five years, and later on television's *Life Is Worth Living* series for five years. He is sometimes credited with inventing the medium of television evangelism.

Fr. Sheen was made head of the Propagation of the Faith in 1950 and was named a bishop the following year. In that role, he raised the consciousness of American Catholics to the material and spiritual needs of the Church's far-flung missions. He wrote a number of books, several of which focused on the Eucharist. In his pastoral work, he brought numerous converts into the Church and conducted countless retreats, especially for priests.

Archbishop Sheen constantly promoted meditative prayer before the Blessed Sacrament. "We become like that which we gaze upon. Looking into a sunset the face takes on a golden glow. Looking at the Eucharistic Lord for an hour transforms the heart in a mysterious way." In his autobiography, Archbishop Sheen wrote of "The Hour That Makes My Day":

> Neither theological knowledge nor social action alone is enough to keep us in love with Christ unless both are preceded by a personal encounter with him. I have found that it takes some time to catch fire in prayer. This has been one of the advantages of the Holy Hour. Sitting before the Presence is like a body exposing itself to the sun to absorb its rays. In those moments one does not so much pour out written prayers, but listening takes place. The Holy Hour became a teacher for me. Although before we love anyone we must have knowledge of that person, nevertheless, after we know, it is love that intensifies knowledge. (Archbishop Fulton J. Sheen, *Treasure in Clay* (San Francisco: Ignatius Press, 1993), 190-191)

In recent years, many parishes have introduced times set aside for adoration of the Blessed Sacrament. In addition, thousands of believers have discovered the spiritual benefits of meditative prayer and similar ways of prayer. The positive fruits of such deep prayer have been demonstrated in the personal lives of people committed to it, as well as in the spiritual vitality of parishes where this occurs. The Holy Spirit, teacher of prayer, is clearly present and active in these welcome developments in the prayer life of the Church.

Archbishop Sheen encouraged the practice of prayer before the Blessed Sacrament in his lifetime, and the heritage endures today. He died in 1979 and is buried in the crypt of St. Patrick's Cathedral in New York City.

GOD'S UNIVERSAL CALL TO PRAYER

"For me, prayer is a surge of the heart; it is a simple look turned toward heaven, it is a cry of recognition and of love, embracing both trial and joy."

—CCC, no. 2558, citing St. Thérèse of Lisieux, *Manuscrits Autobiographiques*, C 25r

Descriptions of prayer are abundant throughout Christian history. "True prayer," wrote St. Augustine, "is nothing but love." Prayer should arise from the heart. "Prayer," said St. John Vianney, "is the inner bath of love into which the soul plunges itself." "Everyone of us needs half an hour of prayer each day," remarked St. Francis de Sales, "except when we are busy—then we need an hour." Definitions of prayer are important, but insufficient. There is a huge difference between knowing about prayer and praying. On this issue, the Rule of St. Benedict is clear: "If a man wants to pray, let him go and pray."

St. John Damascene gave a classic definition of prayer: "Prayer is the raising of one's mind and heart to God or the requesting of good things from God" (CCC, no. 2559, citing St. John Damascene, *De Fide Orth.* 3, 24).

The *Catechism* clearly defines prayer as a "vital and personal relationship with the living and true God" (CCC, no. 2558). Prayer is Christian "insofar as it is communion with Christ" (CCC, no. 2565), and a "covenant relationship between God and man in Christ" (CCC, no. 2564).

It is important to remember that all of Part Two of the *Catechism* also deals with prayer as it is found in the celebration of the Sacraments and in the Liturgy of the Hours. Liturgical prayer, which is the action of the Church, joins us to Christ, interceding with the Father—in the Holy Spirit—on behalf of our salvation.

We should consider Part Four's reflection on the foundations of prayer and the meaning of the Our Father as essentially related to liturgical prayer and a basic complement to it. Because catechetical teaching may never be disconnected from prayer, which is the soul of truth, every chapter in this text includes a meditative section and a liturgical or scriptural prayer.

This chapter on prayer has four sections: Scripture, the sources and manner of praying, guides for prayer, and expressions of prayer.

SCRIPTURE

Scripture reveals the relationship between God and his people as a dialogue of prayer. He constantly searches for us. Our restless hearts seek him, though sin often masks and frustrates this desire. God always begins the process. The point where his call and our response intersect is prayer. The event is always grace-filled and a gift.

Old Testament People at Prayer

The Role of Faith in Prayer

Abraham, Isaac, and Jacob witnessed the role of faith in prayer. God's call came first. These patriarchs responded in faith, but not without a struggle. Essential to their prayer was trust in God's fidelity to his promises. Centuries later, God called Moses to be his instrument for the salvation of Israel from slavery. Moses dramatized the value of intercessory prayer as he vigorously begged God for mercy and guidance for the people making their journey to the Promised Land.

After the people had settled in the Promised Land, there were many powerful witnesses to the importance of faith in prayer. One example is the holy woman Hannah, who longed for a child. Year after year, she made a pilgrimage to the shrine at Shiloh, where she prayed to the Lord and made him a vow that if he would give her a child, she would dedicate the child to God. The Lord answered her prayer, and she conceived and bore a son, whom she called Samuel. He grew up to be a prophet and a judge, a religious leader of God's people. Her song of joy at the dedication of her son to God is a canticle of praise.

> My heart exults in the LORD, . . .
> The LORD makes poor and makes rich,
>   he humbles, he also exalts.

He raises the needy from the dust;
    from the ash heap he lifts up the poor, . . .
For the pillars of the earth are the LORD's. (1 Sm 2:1, 7-8)

Examples of Prayer

The People of God learned how to pray at the shrine of God's presence, before the Ark of the Covenant in the temple. God raised up priests, kings, and prophets to lead the people in prayer. The people assimilated the prayerful attitudes of awe, wonder, and adoration of God at the celebration of the various feasts and liturgies. The books of the Prophets in particular show them praising God in prayer, seeking his help, and crying out to him in times of opposition and persecution.

The Book of Esther is the story of a woman of faith who was an example for her people of the importance of relying on God in prayer. A prominent official in the Persian Empire conspired to destroy in a single day all the Jews in the empire. At the same time, a Jewish woman, Esther, was the queen. She sought the help of God, praying, "My LORD, our King, you alone are God. Help me, who am alone and have no help but you" (Est C:14).

With courage, she explained the plot to her husband the king: "I ask that my life be spared, and I beg that you spare the lives of my people" (Est 7:3). He heard her plea, canceled the massacre, and executed the official. The people praised God that their sorrow was turned into joy.

Esther's actions are remembered by the annual observance of the Feast of Purim. The feast celebrates God's providential care of his people in response to Queen Esther's prayers.

The Psalms: Prayers of the Assembly

Poets like King David and many other holy authors over a number of years composed the masterpiece of prayer known as the Psalms. These incomparable prayers nourished the people both personally and communally. They embraced every age of history, while being rooted in each moment of time. They were sung at the Temple, in local synagogues, in family settings, on pilgrimages, and in the solitude of personal prayer. They formed the basis of the prayer of Jesus and, as such, can be used to draw us into his prayer as well. The Psalms are part of every celebration of Mass. They also form the heart and soul of the Liturgy of the Hours, that public daily prayer of the Church which prolongs the Eucharistic celebration and gives praise to God.

The Canticle of Judith belongs to the genre of psalms and memorializes the vivid story of how God delivered his people through the leadership of the valiant woman Judith. The Book of Judith cites her example as a way to help God's people trust in the divine presence among them. Despite all the troubles the people of ancient Israel faced, they had trusted in him as the Lord of history.

This book describes how the Assyrian army besieged the Jewish people. Judith developed a successful plan to defeat the Assyrians. The emphasis in the narrative is on God's intervention to save his people. Judith led her people in a prayer of praise that has many features of the Psalms and was meant to be a prayer of the whole assembly:

> Strike up the instruments,
>> a song to my God. . . .
> A new hymn I will sing to my God.
>> O Lord, great are you and glorious,
>> wonderful in power and unsurpassable.
> Let your every creature serve you,
>> for you spoke, and they were made. (Jdt 16:1, 13-14)

Prayer in the New Testament

The Prayer of Jesus

As a child, Jesus first learned to pray from Mary and Joseph. As he grew in age, he also joined in prayer at the synagogue and at the Temple. But he also had his heavenly Father as the source of his prayer. It was a filial prayer he revealed when he was twelve: "I must be in my Father's house" (Lk 2:49). Jesus addressed his Father by the name "*Abba*," which in the language of his day was used by children to speak to their fathers.

The Gospels also describe the numerous times Jesus went away from the crowds and his disciples to pray by himself. In the Garden of Gethsemane, he prayed in agony to the Father knowing the Cross that awaited him, but also praying with acceptance of and obedience to the mission the Father had given him.

Jesus also taught his disciples to pray. In the Gospel of Matthew, for example, he instructed them to pray with simplicity of words and confidence in the Father (cf. Mt 6:5-15; 7:7-11).

Prayer in the New Testament Church

At Pentecost, after nine days of prayer in the Upper Room, the disciples experienced the gift of the Holy Spirit for the manifestation of the Church. The first community of believers in Jerusalem devoted themselves to the Apostles' teaching and fellowship, to the breaking of the bread, and to prayers (cf. Acts 2:42). The infant Church was born in prayer, lived in prayer, and thrived in prayer.

The Letters of St. Paul show him to be a man of intense prayer. Throughout his Letters, there are prayers of praise to God for blessings the Church and he himself have received. There are also prayers of intercession as he seeks God's grace for the communities he has evangelized. And he describes his own personal prayers to God, especially in times of difficulty.

The Holy Spirit taught the Church the life of prayer and led her to deeper insights into basic ways of praying: adoration, petition, intercession, thanksgiving, and praise.

Adoration

This form of prayer flows from an attitude that acknowledges we are creatures in the presence of our Creator. It is an act by which we glorify the God who made us. We adore God from whom all blessings flow.

Petition

This is a prayer that takes many forms: to ask, to implore, to plead, to cry out. In each case, it acknowledges how much we depend on God for our needs, including forgiveness and persistence in seeking him. We need to practice the prayer of petition, remembering Christ's call to ask in order to receive, to seek in order to find, and to knock in order that the door may be opened (cf. Mt 7:7).

The first movement of the prayer of petition is asking forgiveness of our sins as did the tax collector in the parable where he was compared to the Pharisee whose prayer lacked humility (cf. CCC, no. 2631). The tax collector begins his prayer with the words, "O God, be merciful to me a sinner" (Lk 18:13). Humility and repentance characterize a prayer that returns us to communion with Christ.

Intercession

This is the prayer that we make on behalf of the needs of others. Jesus Christ himself, our great High Priest, incessantly intercedes for us. God calls us also to intercede for each other and even for our enemies. Intercessions for others' needs are part of the Mass and the Liturgy of the Hours.

Thanksgiving

This form of prayer flows from the Church's greatest prayer, the celebration of the Eucharist. Every moment or event can become a thanksgiving offering. We are called to thank God for all the gifts we have received, including our joys and sorrows, all of which, through love, work towards our benefit.

Praise

"Praise is the form of prayer which recognizes most immediately that God is God. . . . It shares in the blessed happiness of the pure of heart who love God in faith before seeing him in glory" (CCC, no. 2639). Scripture is filled with outpourings of praise for God. When we exult in him with simplicity and an open heart, we obtain a glimpse of the joy of the angels and saints who glory in the ways of God.

THE SOURCES AND MANNER OF PRAYING

We must do more than rely on an impulse for our prayer life. St. Paul calls us to "pray without ceasing" (1 Thes 5:17). The will to pray in a daily, sustained, and structured manner is essential for becoming a prayerful person. The Holy Spirit guides the Church at prayer through her reading of Scripture, her celebration of the liturgy, and the practice of faith, hope, and love.

Daily familiarity with Scripture is a rich source of prayer. We need to do more than read or study Scripture; we should also converse with God, whose Spirit lies within the text and who draws us to appreciate "the supreme good of knowing Christ Jesus" (Phil 3:8).

By our active participation in the liturgy, the prayer of the Church, we encounter the Father, and the Son, and the Holy Spirit, who impart to us the gifts of salvation. Spiritual writers tell us our heart can be an altar of adoration and praise. Prayer internalizes the liturgy both during and after its celebration (cf. CCC, no. 2655).

Faith puts vitality in prayer because it brings us to a personal relationship with Christ. Hope carries our prayer to our final goal of permanent union with God. Love, poured into our heart by the Holy Spirit, is the source and destiny of prayer.

St. John Vianney (1786-1859) wrote: "My God, if my tongue cannot say in every moment that I love you, I want my heart to repeat it to you as often as I draw breath" (CCC, no. 2658, citing *Prayer*).

"Because God blesses the human heart, it can in return bless him who is the source of every blessing" (CCC, no. 2645).

Christian prayer is always Trinitarian. The sweep of our prayer should direct us toward the Father. But access to the Father is through Jesus Christ. Therefore, we also address our prayer to Christ and can do so using titles of Jesus found in the New Testament: Son of God, Word of God, Lamb of God, Son of the Virgin, Lord and Savior, etc. Christ is the door to God.

We must never tire of praying to Jesus. Yet it is the Holy Spirit who helps us to draw near to Jesus.

"No one can say 'Jesus is Lord,' except by the Holy Spirit" (1 Cor 12:3). The Church invites us to invoke the Holy Spirit as the interior Teacher of Christian prayer. (CCC, no. 2681)

Prayer in Communion with Mary

"Because of Mary's singular cooperation with the action of the Holy Spirit, the Church loves to pray in communion with the Virgin Mary, to magnify with her the great things the Lord has done for her, and to entrust supplications and praises to her" (CCC, no. 2682). This twofold movement of joining Mary in praising God for his gifts to her and seeking her intercession has found a privileged expression in the Hail Mary.

The Hail Mary

Along with the Lord's Prayer, the Hail Mary is one of the most widely used prayers in the Catholic Church. The first half of the Hail Mary comes from Luke's Gospel accounts of the Angel Gabriel's annunciation to Mary that she was called to be the Mother of God's Son (Lk 1:26-56). The second half is an intercessory prayer developed in the Church's tradition.

- "Hail Mary, full of grace." This is the greeting the Angel Gabriel spoke to Mary of Nazareth. Gabriel proclaims that Mary is full of grace, meaning that she is a sinless woman, blessed with a deep union with God, who had come to dwell in her.
- "The Lord is with thee." Mary has been chosen by God for this great privilege. He is with her, having already preserved her from sin and filled her with grace. This does not mean that Mary is deprived of her freedom. She lives in graced friendship with God and freely offers him her undivided heart.
- "Blessed art thou among women." This was the greeting given Mary by her cousin Elizabeth when Mary came to visit and help Elizabeth with the birth of her forthcoming child (Lk 1:42). As Scripture points out, Mary holds a singular place among all God's chosen ones in the history of salvation. Mary is the world's most honored woman.
- "Blessed is the fruit of thy womb, Jesus." This is another beatitude or blessing uttered by Elizabeth, who spoke these words after her child, John the Baptist, leaped in her womb at the moment she hears the greeting of Mary. Elizabeth is inspired by the Holy Spirit to bless Mary for believing the message of Gabriel. Elizabeth acknowledges

the presence of God in Mary's womb: "How does this happen to me, that the mother of my Lord should come to me?" (Lk 1:43). This is the first time in Scripture that Mary's faith is praised.

- "Holy Mary, Mother of God." Sometime in the Middle Ages, the second half of the Hail Mary, which begins by invoking her title of Mother of God, was composed. This title comes from the earliest days of Christian faith. Mary is the Mother of God, because she is the mother of Jesus who is true God and true man, as defined by the Council of Ephesus in AD 431. The Eastern Churches call Mary *Theotokos*, or "Birth-giver of God" (sometimes translated as "God-bearer"). Mary's response to God engages her in the plan of human salvation through motherhood of Jesus.

- "Pray for us sinners." We have noted that intercessory prayer concerns the needs and hopes of others. Jesus Christ, our High Priest, always intercedes for us before the Father, and he calls us to intercede for others as well. The saints and the Blessed Virgin Mary continue this prayer of intercession in heaven. As Mother of the Church, Mary continues to pray with a mother's care for the Body of her Son on earth. At Cana, Mary interceded with Jesus on behalf of the couple who had run out of wine. Jesus heard her prayer and turned water into wine. Mary's last words in Scripture are spoken to us: "Do whatever he [Jesus] tells you" (Jn 2:5). Our holy Mother always brings us to Jesus.

- "Now and at the hour of our death. Amen." In her life, Mary walked a pilgrimage of faith. Even with all the grace she received from God, she encountered the mysterious ways of God and profound suffering, especially at the death of her Son. She knows what a journey of faith entails, and she accompanies us with prayer as we make our journey to God throughout our lives and at death.

Other Prayers to the Blessed Virgin

In the Latin Church, the Rosary, a venerable and powerful form of prayer, developed out of popular piety. Praying the Rosary involves the recitation of vocal prayers, including the Our Father, the Hail Mary, and the Glory Be, while meditating on mysteries in the life of Jesus. In the

Eastern Churches, litanies and hymns to the Mother of God are more commonly prayed.

We do not pray to Mary in the same way we pray to God. In praying to Mary, we invoke her intercession on behalf of our needs, whereas when we pray to God we ask him directly for gifts and favors.

GUIDES FOR PRAYER

Throughout Church history, saints have left a heritage of prayer "by the example of their lives, the transmission of their writings," and their continued prayers in heaven on our behalf. Numerous schools of spirituality, such as Benedictine, Franciscan, or Ignatian, have come down to us as part of the heritage of the saints. This authentic diversity of spiritualities is united by the Holy Spirit within the living tradition of the Church (CCC, no. 2683).

Parents are the first teachers of prayer. Family prayer, practiced on a daily basis, in which the children witness the prayer of adults closest to them, is an excellent school of prayer. Priests and deacons have a public responsibility to lead people in prayer with genuine reverence. They should also teach people how to pray and encourage them by their example.

Men and women religious who embrace the consecrated life profess a commitment to prayer. Their example and willingness to dedicate themselves to Christ encourages us to pray with added fervor and dedication. Lay ministers have a unique opportunity to encourage and inspire the laity to incorporate prayer into their daily lives.

The lifelong religious education of Catholics at every level should always include training in how to pray as well as having time set aside for communal prayer. Prayer groups also have been admirable sources of the contemporary renewal of prayer. Places for prayer include the parish church, retreat centers, shrines, the home, and any situation in which people can achieve sufficient concentration of mind and heart.

EXPRESSIONS OF PRAYER

At Mass when the reading of the Gospel begins, we place the sign of the Cross on our foreheads, lips, and hearts and pray, "May the Lord be in our minds, on our lips, and in our hearts." Lips, minds, and hearts—these symbolize three kinds of prayer: vocal, meditative, and contemplative. These modes of prayer include formal and informal paths, personal and communal expressions, popular piety, and the liturgical prayer of the Church.

Vocal Prayer

The disciples were drawn to Jesus' own prayer. He taught them a vocal prayer, the Our Father. Jesus prayed aloud in the synagogues and the Temple and "raised his voice to express" personal prayers such as his surrender to the Father's will in Gethsemane. The seventeenth chapter of John's Gospel records a lengthy vocal prayer of Jesus, revealing the depth of his intimacy with his Father and his loving concern for his disciples (cf. CCC, no. 2701).

Since we are body as well as spirit, we need to express ourselves orally. Spoken and sung prayers arise from our souls; they can be complemented by bodily gestures such as the Sign of the Cross, genuflection, kneeling, and bowing. When we become inwardly aware of God, to whom we speak, our vocal prayer can become an initial step toward contemplative prayer.

Meditative Prayer

"Meditation is above all a quest. The mind seeks to understand the why and how of the Christian life, in order to adhere and respond to what the Lord is asking" (CCC, no. 2705). In meditative prayer, we use our minds to ponder the will of God in his plan for our lives. What does God ask of us? The Church provides many aids for meditation: "the Sacred Scriptures, particularly the Gospels, holy icons, liturgical texts of the day or season, writings of the spiritual fathers . . . the great book of creation, and that of history—the page on which the 'today' of God is written" (CCC, no. 2705). "Meditation engages thought, imagination, emotion,

LECTIO DIVINA

Lectio divina is a reflective reading of Scripture leading to meditation on specific passages. This is a centuries-old practice of prayer which relies on the guidance of the Holy Spirit within the heart as the person praying reads a Scripture passage and pauses to seek out the deeper meaning that God wants to convey through his Word.

"It is especially necessary that listening to the word of God should become a life-giving encounter in the ancient and ever valid tradition of *lectio divina*, which draws from the biblical text the living word, which questions, directs, and shapes our lives" (NMI, no. 39).

and desire" (CCC, no. 2708). It is meant to deepen our faith in Christ, to convert our hearts, and to strengthen us to do God's will.

"There are as many and varied methods of meditation as there are spiritual masters" (CCC, no. 2707). Most prominent among these are the *Lectio Divina* of St. Benedict, the radical simplicity of Franciscan spirituality, and the Spiritual Exercises of St. Ignatius. These spiritualities also include guidance for contemplation.

Contemplative Prayer

"Contemplative prayer . . . is a gaze of faith fixed on Jesus, an attentiveness to the Word of God, a silent love" (CCC, no. 2724). Like all prayer, this form requires a regular time each day. When one gives God time for prayer, he will give time for one's other responsibilities.

Contemplative prayer is a gift to which we dispose ourselves by resting attentively before Christ. It involves hearing and obeying God's Word. It is a time of silent listening and love.

FROM THE CATECHISM

1. What are some erroneous conceptions of prayer?

Some people view prayer as a simple psychological activity, others as an effort of concentration to reach a mental void. Still others reduce prayer to ritual words and postures. Many Christians unconsciously regard prayer as an occupation that is incompatible with all the other things they have to do. (CCC, no. 2726)

We must respond with humility, trust, and perseverance to these temptations that cast doubt on the usefulness or even the possibility of prayer. (CCC, no. 2753)

2. How is prayer connected to Christian life?

Prayer and *Christian life* are *inseparable*, for they concern the same love and the same renunciation, proceeding from love; the same filial and loving conformity with the Father's plan of love; the same transforming union in the Holy Spirit who conforms us more and more to Christ Jesus; the same love for all men, the love with which Jesus has loved us. (CCC, no. 2745)

3. What should we remember when our prayers seem unanswered?

Do not be troubled if you do not receive immediately from God what you ask him; for he desires to do something even greater for you, while you cling to him in prayer. (CCC, no. 2737, citing Evagrius Ponticus, *De Oratione*, 34: PG 79, 1173)

Filial trust is put to the test when we feel that our prayer is not always heard. The Gospel invites us to ask ourselves about the conformity of our prayer to the desire of the Spirit. (CCC, no. 2756)

THE WORK OF PRAYER

Prayer requires time, attention, and effort. We need to discipline ourselves for what spiritual writers call "spiritual combat." They cite problems such as *acedia* (a form of sloth or laziness) that arises from a lax ascetical behavior, a laxity that needs to be corrected. The Tempter will try to pull us away from prayer. Distraction and dryness will discourage us.

The remedy is faith, fidelity to times for prayer, constant conversion of heart, and watchfulness. The *Catechism*'s section "The Battle of Prayer" (CCC, nos. 2725-2745) answers many questions that beginners are likely to ask. Its advice is practical and experiential. For example, the section addresses the issue of distraction, a major obstacle for most beginners. Distractions interfere with all forms of prayer. The temptation to fight them entraps one; all that is needed is to turn back to the presence of the Lord in our hearts. A distraction reveals our attachments, but a humble awareness of this can move us to offer Christ our hearts for the needed purification.

PRAY ALWAYS (1 THES 5:17)

It is often said that we should pray as if everything depended on God and act as if everything depended on us. The "can-do" mindset of our culture inclines many believers to substitute self-reliance for prayer. People are not conscious of their need for God.

Despite the general cultural preference for an independent spirit that idealizes the achievements of the self in getting things done, studies about religion indicate a significant counter movement. Virtually all Americans claim they believe in God. A high number of people report they pray each day.

Within our Church, spirituality movements, including traditional schools of spirituality such as Benedictine, Carmelite, Franciscan, and Ignatian, stress the importance of liturgical and meditative prayer. In addition, new immigrants enrich the life of the Church through their traditions of popular piety. For example, devotion to Our Lady of Guadalupe, begun in Mexico, has spread to the point where her feast is now celebrated throughout the American continent.

Some people find spiritual strength in the Chaplet of Divine Mercy. There is a growing interest among many people from all walks of life in praying the Liturgy of the Hours. Parish missions, retreats, and spiritual movements such as Cursillo and Charismatic Renewal have helped many to begin the journey of prayer and have led people onward to meditation and contemplation. A significant number of people are attracted to the practice of *lectio divina* that weds scriptural reflection with elements of contemplation.

In our noisy and activist culture, prayer has brought Christ's peace and hope to many. Small faith communities, Scripture study groups, and charismatic groups make prayer a large component of their gatherings.

Another group of Americans is drawn to the rich prayer life of the Eastern Churches. Icon-inspired devotion, the Jesus prayer, and the mystical writings of the Greek Fathers have a transcendent appeal that is richly rewarding for these spiritual seekers.

Many parishes have instituted hours of adoration of the Blessed Sacrament, a form of prayer that is growing steadily. Popular piety attracts large numbers of the faithful, especially pilgrimages and devotions to Our Lady and the saints. Millions recite the Rosary regularly. A growing number of people are seeking spiritual direction. These are some highlights of the increasing turn to spirituality and prayer.

Bishops and pastors continue to emphasize the centrality of the liturgy in Catholic prayer life, while strongly supporting the wide-ranging aspects of personal prayer, piety, and meditation. They also provide constant reminders about the relationship between liturgy, other forms of prayer, and the call to witness Christ's Kingdom of love, justice, and mercy in our everyday lives. Prayer is the soul of discipleship and can strengthen us for a life of mission.

In the longstanding tradition of the Church, prayer is centered upon God. It is an emptying of oneself not for its own sake, but for the sake of being filled with God and entering into a deeper relationship with him. There are forms of spirituality in contemporary culture that focus more on one's own self and the achievement of a superficial tranquility. Genuine Christian prayer is attentive to the presence of God and seeks ways to be of greater service to God and others.

■■■■■ FOR DISCUSSION ■■■■■

1. Why do you pray? When do you pray? How do you pray?
2. If you practice some form of meditation regularly, how would you describe it? What means have you taken to persevere in meditation? How have you maintained a bond between prayer and an active Christian mission to others?
3. What are you doing to deepen your prayer life? What are you learning from spiritual reading to help you with your prayer? If you have a spiritual director, how has this been effective for your prayer?

■■■■■ DOCTRINAL STATEMENTS ■■■■■

- Prayer is the raising of one's mind and heart to God and the requesting of good things from him. It is an act by which one enters into awareness of a loving communion with God. "Prayer is the response of faith to the free promise of salvation and also a response of love to the thirst of the only Son of God" (CCC, no. 2561).

- Scripture reveals the relationship between God and people as a dialogue of prayer. God constantly searches for us. Our restless hearts seek him, though sin often masks and frustrates this desire. God always begins the process. The point where his call and our response intersect is prayer. The event is always a grace and a gift.

- Jesus taught his disciples "to pray with a purified heart, with lively and persevering faith, with filial boldness." He called them to vigilance and invited them "to present their petitions to God in his name" (CCC, no. 2621).

- The infant Church was born in prayer, lived in prayer, thrived in prayer. The Holy Spirit taught the community the life of prayer and led them to deeper insights into basic ways of praying: adoration, petition, repentance, intercession, thanksgiving, and praise.

- "The Word of God, the liturgy of the Church, and the virtues of faith, hope, and charity are the sources of prayer" (CCC, no. 2662).

- Christian prayer is always Trinitarian. The sweep of our prayer moves us toward the Father. But access to the Father is through Jesus Christ. Therefore we also address our prayer to Christ. Yet it is the

Holy Spirit who helps us to draw near to Jesus. The Church invites us to invoke the Holy Spirit as the interior teacher of Christian prayer.

- "Because of Mary's singular cooperation with the action of the Holy Spirit, the Church loves to pray in communion with the Virgin Mary, to magnify with her the great things the Lord has done for her, and to entrust supplications and praises to her" (CCC, no. 2682).

- The first teachers of prayer are parents or other members of the family, the domestic church.

- Our guides for prayer within the Church include ordained ministers, those in consecrated life, catechists, and spiritual directors.

- Places for prayer include the parish church, retreat centers and shrines, the home, and many other circumstances that afford the opportunity to pray.

- "The Church invites the faithful to regular prayer: daily prayers, the Liturgy of the Hours, Sunday Eucharist, the feasts of the liturgical year" (CCC, no. 2720).

- There are three kinds of prayer: vocal, meditative, and contemplative.

- Prayer requires humility, trust, and perseverance in order to battle temptations that cast doubt on the usefulness or even the possibility of prayer (see CCC, nos. 2726-2753).

- "Pray without ceasing" (1 Thes 5:17).

MEDITATION

"I Shall Keep the Silence of My Heart"

I don't think there is anyone who needs God's help and grace as much as I do. Sometimes I feel so helpless and so weak. I think this is why God uses me. Because I cannot depend on my own strength, I rely on him twenty-four hours a day. All of us must cling to God through prayer. My secret is simple: I pray. Through prayer I become one in love with Christ. I realize that praying to him is loving him.

We cannot find God in noise or agitation. Nature: trees, flowers and grass grow in silence. The stars, the moon, and the sun move in silence. What is essential is not what we say but what God tells others through us. In silence He listens to us;

in silence He speaks to our souls. In silence we are granted the privilege of listening to his voice.

Silence of our eyes.
Silence of our ears.
Silence of our minds.
. . . In the silence of the heart God will speak.

— Mother Teresa, cited in *The Power of Prayer*
(New York: MJF Books, 1998), 3, 7-8

PRAYER

I raise my eyes toward the mountains.
    From where will my help come?
My help comes from the LORD,
    the maker of heaven and earth.
God will not allow your foot to slip;
    your guardian does not sleep.
Truly, the guardian of Israel
    never slumbers nor sleeps.
The LORD is your guardian;
    the LORD is your shade
    at your right hand.
By day the sun cannot harm you,
    nor the moon by night.
The LORD will guard you from all evil,
    will always guard your life.
The LORD will guard your coming and going
    both now and forever.

—Ps 121

As the deer longs for streams of water,
    so my soul longs for you, O God.
My being thirsts for God, the living God.
    When can I go and see the face of God?

—Ps 42:2-3

36 JESUS TAUGHT US TO PRAY

THE LORD'S PRAYER: OUR FATHER
—CCC, NOS. 2759-2865

"THIS IS HOW YOU ARE TO PRAY" (MT 6:9)

Jesus prayed always. St. Luke, for example, tells us in his Gospel: "After . . . Jesus . . . had been baptized and was praying, heaven was opened" (Lk 3:21).

Jesus prayed before his choice of the Twelve Apostles and before he asked the Apostles who they thought he was. He prayed regularly in the synagogue and Temple. He prayed before the prediction of his Passion and during the Transfiguration. "While he was praying his face changed in appearance and his clothing became dazzling white" (Lk 9:29). Jesus prayed at the Last Supper, in Gethsemane, and on the Cross.

He prayed for long periods of time, sometimes for a whole night. "He went up on the mountain by himself to pray" (Mt 14:23). The Gospels rarely describe what his prayer was like, simply noting that he prayed often. One thing is clear, the Apostles were so moved by the constancy and depth of his prayer that they asked him to help them to pray: "Lord, teach us to pray" (Lk 11:1).

Jesus responded with what is now known as the Lord's Prayer. In St. Matthew's Gospel, he precedes his gift of this prayer with teachings about how *not* to pray. In St. Luke's Gospel, he adds advice about the need to pray with confidence that our prayer will be answered. The Gospel of Matthew introduces the Lord's Prayer with these words:

> When you pray, do not be like the hypocrites, who love to stand and pray in the synagogues and on street corners so that others might see them. Amen, I say to you, they have received their

reward. But when you pray, go to your inner room, close the door and pray to your Father in secret. And your Father who sees in secret will repay you. In praying, do not babble like the pagans, who think that they will be heard because of their many words. Do not be like them. Your Father knows what you need before you ask him.

This is how you are to pray:

Our Father in heaven, / hallowed be your name, / your kingdom come, / your will be done, / on earth as in heaven. / Give us today our daily bread; / and forgive us our debts, / as we forgive our debtors; / and do not subject us to the final test, / but deliver us from the evil one. (Mt 6:5-13)

The Gospel of Luke also offers counsel about prayer:

And I tell you, ask and you will receive; seek and you will find; knock and the door will be opened to you. For everyone who asks, receives; and the one who seeks, finds; and to the one who knocks, the door will be opened. What father among you would hand his son a snake when he asks for a fish? Or hand him a scorpion when he asks for an egg? If you then, who are wicked, know how to give good gifts to your children, how much more will the Father in heaven give the holy Spirit to those who ask him. (Lk 11:9-13)

It is clear, therefore, that Jesus framed his gift of the Lord's Prayer with guidance to help us pray more effectively.

St. Luke records another of Christ's instructions on prayer in the parable of the self-important Pharisee and a humble tax collector:

Two people went up to the temple area to pray; one was a Pharisee and the other was a tax collector. The Pharisee took up his position and spoke this prayer to himself, "O God, I thank you that I am not like the rest of humanity—greedy, dishonest, adulterous—or even like this tax collector. I fast twice a week, and I pay tithes on my whole income." But the tax collector stood off at a distance and would not even raise his eyes to heaven but beat his breast and prayed, "O God, be merciful to me a sinner." I tell you, the latter went home justified, not the former; for everyone who exalts himself will be humbled, and the one who humbles himself will be exalted. (Lk 18:10-14)

Jesus gave us not only the gift of the Lord's Prayer, but also the context in which it should be understood and prayed. With this in mind, we offer the following reflection on this, the greatest of prayers.

THE CENTRAL PRAYER OF SCRIPTURE

The Lord's Prayer is the most perfect of prayers. . . . In it we ask, not only for all the things we can rightly desire, but also in the sequence that they should be desired. This prayer not only teaches us to ask for things, but also in what order we should desire them.

—CCC, no. 2763, citing St. Thomas Aquinas, *Summa Theologiae*, II-II. 83, 9

The Our Father is called the "Lord's Prayer" because Jesus, our Lord and model of prayer, is its author. There are two versions of the Lord's Prayer in the Gospels. St. Luke's account of the event contains five petitions. St. Matthew's lists seven. The Church's liturgy follows Matthew's version.

St. Augustine wrote seven commentaries on the Our Father. So moved was he by its depth that he wrote, "Run through all the words of holy prayers [in Scripture], and I do not think you will find anything in them that is not contained in the Lord's Prayer" (*Letter*, 130, 12, 22). The Our Father is an integral part of sacramental liturgies (Baptism, Confirmation, and the Anointing of the Sick) and of the Eucharist itself. At Mass, it comes after the Eucharistic Prayer, summing up the intercessions of that prayer and preparing us for Holy Communion when we receive Jesus Christ, who is the Bread of Life. It is at the heart of every individual and communal prayer (cf. CCC, no. 2776).

We Address the Father

Before we make our own this first exclamation of the Lord's Prayer, we must humbly cleanse our hearts of certain false images drawn "from this world." Humility makes us recognize that "no one knows the Son except the Father, and no one knows the Father except the Son." . . . The purification of our hearts has to do with paternal or maternal images, stemming from our personal and cultural history, and influencing our relationship with God. God our Father transcends the categories of the created world. . . . To pray to the Father is to enter into his mystery as he is and as the Son has revealed him to us.

—CCC, no. 2779, citing Mt 11:27

Our Father

We call God "Father" only because Jesus, the Son of God made man, revealed him as such. Because of our union with Jesus through Baptism, we are given the grace of an adopted, filial relationship with the Father. This begets in us a new self-understanding due to this extraordinary intimacy with the Father and the Son. A term that our Lord uses for Father is "*Abba*!" This implies that Jesus is saying that a relationship with God should be like that of a child, very close, personal, and dependent.

While we recognize that there is no gender in God, we will be inclined to draw upon our experiences with our earthly fathers when thinking of this title for God. The image of a human father is generally a positive one, and this helps us to draw near to God as Father. Yet, sadly, there are cases of fathers who have fallen short of the responsibilities of fatherhood.

An understanding of God as Father is already evident in the Old Testament, where God describes himself as being in a special relationship of providential care for the people of Israel and in particular for their king. Jesus' revelation of God as his Father flows from a profound awareness not only of that same providential care but also of an indescribable intimacy (cf., e.g., Jn 14). "As proof that you are children, God sent the spirit of his Son into our hearts, crying out, 'Abba, Father!" (Gal 4:6).

When we say "Our," we recognize that we are a people bound together by the New Covenant that God has made with us through his Son in the Holy Spirit. While we are indeed individual persons, we are also persons in communion with each other because we have been baptized into communion with the Holy Trinity. The Our Father is a prayer of the Church, hence we pray with the Church when we recite these words, together calling God our Father.

Who Art in Heaven

"Who art in heaven" does not refer to a place but to God's majesty and his presence in the hearts of the just. Heaven, the Father's house, is the true homeland toward which we are heading and to which, already, we belong.

—CCC, no. 2802

Heaven is the culmination of our relationship with the Father, Son, and Holy Spirit begun in Baptism.

The Seven Petitions

In the Our Father, the object of the first three petitions is the glory of the Father: the sanctification of his name, the coming of the kingdom, and the fulfillment of his will. The four others present our wants to him: they ask that our lives be nourished, healed of sin, and made victorious in the struggle of good over evil.

—CCC, no. 2857

Hallowed Be Thy Name

Hallowed means "to be made holy." We do not make God's name holy; God is the source of his own holiness that is his perfection and glory.

But we give witness to his holiness by doing his will, being people of prayer, and establishing the earthly conditions by which his holiness is manifested.

God gradually revealed his name. First of all he revealed it to Moses, through whom he tells us that he is "I AM," a person who chooses to be close to us yet remains mysterious. As salvation history unfolded, the people of Israel developed other names they used to refer to God, such as Lord, Shepherd of Israel, and King.

But God's definitive revelation of who he is was through Jesus Christ, who taught us that God is his Father and he is the Son. Through Christ's salvation and the Sacrament of Baptism, we become adopted children of God by grace. Hence we can legitimately call God "Father."

Thy Kingdom Come

In this petition, we pray that the Kingdom promised us by God will come—the Kingdom already present in Christ's Passion, death, and Resurrection. In Matthew's Gospel, there is an extensive revelation of the many aspects of what Christ's Kingdom means in moral and spiritual terms as well as its relationship to the Church. It is a Kingdom of love, justice, and mercy, where sins are forgiven, the sick are made whole, enemies are reconciled, captives are freed, and the needs of the poor are met.

It is all these things and more, for ultimately the Kingdom is Jesus Christ and all he means for us. The Kingdom is already here because of the redemption of Jesus Christ. But in another sense, it is "not yet" here, since Christ's final transformation of individuals, society, and culture has yet to happen in its fullness. This is why we need to pray this petition every day and work for its coming.

Thy Will Be Done on Earth as It Is in Heaven

In the third petition, we ask our Father to unite our will to that of Jesus so as to fulfill the plan of salvation in the world. We need God's help and protection to make this possible (cf. CCC, no. 2860).

Jesus gave us an example of this when he was in Gethsemane on the eve of his Passion and death. He first asked that the cup of suffering might pass from him but also prayed, "Not my will but yours be done" (Lk 22:42).

What is God's will? In creating us, God established a plan for how to live in a fully human and spiritual manner. Jesus came to us to show us exactly what that means. The Lord Jesus asks us to be his disciples and shape our lives by faith. The Second Vatican Council reminds us that "the disciple is bound by a grave obligation toward Christ . . . to understand the truth received from him, faithfully to proclaim it and vigorously to defend it" (*Declaration on Religious Liberty* [*Dignitatis Humanae*], no. 14).

Give Us This Day Our Daily Bread

"'Our daily bread' refers to the earthly nourishment necessary to everyone for subsistence, and also to the Bread of Life: the Word of God and the Body of Christ" (CCC, no. 2861). We draw our life from the Eucharist each time we receive Holy Communion.

Just before he left this earth, the Lord Jesus promised to be with us every day. In a remarkable manner, Jesus is present to us in the Divine Sacrament, because he is himself the Bread of Life available to us. The Church's contemplation always centers itself on the Lord in this Sacrament, which contains the whole treasure of the Church, Jesus Christ.

At the same time, we ask for our material needs. While we seek what we need for our own maintenance and development, we must never forget the poor of the world, who so often lack daily bread. We are called to have solidarity with them and work for their physical and spiritual welfare. We pray for our "daily" bread, implying that we pray for what we need for today and will pray again each day for the needs of that day.

Forgive Us Our Trespasses as We Forgive Those Who Trespass Against Us

The fifth petition begs God's mercy for our offences, mercy which can penetrate our hearts only if we have learned to forgive our enemies, with the example and help of Christ.

—CCC, no. 2862

The best way to obtain mercy is to be merciful. As Jesus taught us, "Blessed are the merciful, for they will be shown mercy" (Mt 5:7). Failure to forgive others is a major human problem. Holding grudges is common. Failure to forgive routinely tears apart families, neighborhoods, and even nations. Jesus stressed mercy and forgiveness in numerous ways such as when he asked the Father to forgive those who crucified him (cf. Lk 23:34). We pray to God that we may be able to forgive as much as we are forgiven.

And Lead Us Not into Temptation

God wants to set us free from evil; he tempts no one (cf. CCC, no. 2846).

When we say "lead us not into temptation" we are asking God not to allow us to take the path that leads to sin. This petition implores the Spirit of discernment and strength; it requests the grace of vigilance and final perseverance. (CCC, no. 2863)

We know that preventive medicine is desirable so that curative medicine may not be needed. Preventing the possibility of sin is preferable to sinning with its negative impact on our lives. Traditionally we have been taught to avoid the occasions of sin, that is, persons or situations that may lead us to sin. Virtue grows stronger with its practice.

In this petition, we entrust ourselves to the Holy Spirit to keep us alert to the dangers of sin and give us the grace to resist temptation. A meditation on how Christ resisted temptation in the desert is a fruitful and inspiring example of how we should conduct ourselves in the face of temptation (cf. Mt 4:1-11; Lk 4: 1-12). "It is by his prayer that Jesus vanquishes the tempter, both at the outset of his public mission and in the ultimate struggle of his agony" (CCC, no. 2849).

But Deliver Us from Evil

> *In the last petition, "but deliver us from evil," Christians pray to God with the Church to show forth the victory, already won by Christ, over the "ruler of this world," Satan, the angel personally opposed to God and to his plan of salvation.*
>
> —CCC, no. 2864

As always throughout this prayer, we are reminded that we pray with the Church. We do not pray alone but in union with the community of believers around the world—all of us bound by our union with Jesus in the Spirit and with an adoptive filial relationship to the Father.

The *Catechism* emphasizes that we ask God to deliver us from the Evil One—Satan, the devil (cf. Jn 17:15). The evil we confront is not just an abstract idea, but an evil, fallen angel who wants to prevent our salvation. We entrust ourselves to God so that the devil may not lead us into sin.

"One who entrusts himself to God does not dread the devil. 'If God is for us, who is against us?'" (CCC, no. 2852, citing St. Ambrose, *On the Sacraments*, 5, 4, 30; cf. Rom 8:31). We ask God to deliver us from all evils—past, present, and future—of which Satan is the author or instigator.

Doxology

There is a final doxology which was added by the early Church: "For the kingdom, the power and the glory are yours, now and forever" (cf. *Teaching of the Twelve Apostles* [*Didache*] 8, 2; *Apostolic Constitutions*, 7, 24). It is recited by Latin Catholics after the prayer which follows the recitation of the Our Father during Mass. These words of praise echo the first three petitions, and we use them as words of adoration in union with the liturgy of heaven.

FROM THE CATECHISM

1. How is the Lord's Prayer related to the Gospel?
The Lord's Prayer is truly the summary of the whole Gospel. (CCC, no. 2774, citing Tertullian, *De Orat.* 1: PL 1, 1251-1255)

[It is] the quintessential prayer of the Church. (CCC, no. 2776)

2. What is contained in the first three petitions of the Our Father?
The first series of petitions carries us toward [God], for his own sake: *thy* name, *thy* kingdom, *thy* will! (CCC, no. 2804)

3. What is the focus of the last four petitions of the Our Father?
The four others present our wants to him: they ask that our lives be nourished, healed of sin, and made victorious in the struggle of good over evil. (CCC, no. 2857)

Amen

We conclude with the "Amen," which means, "So be it." We joyfully ratify the words that Jesus has taught us (cf. CCC, no. 2856).

PRAY IN ORDER TO BELIEVE, BELIEVE IN ORDER TO PRAY

A closer look at the *Catechism of the Catholic Church* will reveal its method of weaving prayer into presentations of doctrine. Though certain sections have been designated as dealing specifically with prayer, such as Part Two on the liturgy and this Part Four on prayer, there is a contemplative spirit to the whole presentation. Identifying certain parts with prayer does not imply some kind of false separation between doctrine and prayer.

The *Catechism* reminds us that the Lord Jesus asks us to believe in order to pray and to pray in order to believe. There is a complementarity in which knowing and loving God support each other. Belief in the Father, Son, and Spirit should be essentially and immediately connected to a prayerful and loving communion with the Trinity.

Belief in Catholic doctrine draws us to prayer and to a divine reassurance about the validity of these revealed truths of God to which we have responded in faith. We give ourselves to prayer to deepen our personal relationship with God in a loving communion. Experiencing God in prayer shows us the vitality of the truthfulness of doctrine and puts energy into our spiritual and moral witness.

Just as the understanding of doctrine requires study and effort, so also does the practice of prayer. "Prayer is both a gift of grace and a determined response on our part. It always presupposes effort" (CCC, no. 2725). Since prayer is a loving relationship with God, it places demands upon us. No love exists without sacrifice.

In our busy culture, time has become one of our most precious possessions. Of all the things we can give to the ones we love, among the best is our time. Often something else must be sacrificed to make this possible.

When it comes to prayer, we must choose regular times for prayer each day. We need to step aside from the rush of daily life and compose our souls before God, as Jesus did when he spent time with his Father.

How do we know when we really begin to pray? The different kinds of prayer have already been noted: liturgical and private; vocal, meditative, and contemplative prayer. Underneath all these forms should be our hearts actively opening to God.

> Where does prayer come from? . . . In naming the source of prayer, Scripture speaks sometimes of the soul or the spirit, but most often of the heart (more than a thousand times). According to Scripture, it is the *heart* that prays. If our heart is far from God, the words of prayer are in vain. (CCC, no. 2562)

In the biblical or Semitic mind, the heart is beyond the grasp of reason and deeper than our psychic drives. It is the very center of our selves, the mysterious place where we make our fundamental decisions. It is the ground of encounter with God. Unlike the busy-ness of mental life, the heart is a zone of silence.

The heart is the environment where our most serious dedication takes place. As the setting for meeting God, whether at liturgy or in meditation, the heart is the place for enjoying our covenant with him. It can be an awesome moment, as the author of the Book of Revelation tells us: "I fell down at his feet as one dead" (Rev 1:17).

Understanding the heart as the source of prayer should also help us realize how it affects our commitment to Christian teaching. If we treat doctrine simply as an academic study, we will have a tendency to miss its connection with our union with God. Jesus said, "I am the truth" (Jn 14:6). He also said, "Whoever loves me will keep my word" (Jn 14:23). Jesus never divorced his teaching from his person. The two went together.

Likewise, doctrine and prayer go together. The heart is the shrine of the Word and of Love. The heart links these gifts into one satisfying unity.

This focus on our efforts need not distract us from the humble realization that the prayer of the heart is prompted by the Holy Spirit. It is he who presides over our study of doctrine and our life of prayer. We will always find ourselves weaving between dependence on God and reliance on ourselves. But ultimately we will find ourselves echoing the saints who so often say, "All is grace."

FOR DISCUSSION

1. What is the link between belief and prayer? How do the teachings of Christ and his Church enrich our prayer?
2. How do we develop our dependence and reliance upon God in a world that promotes self-reliance?
3. What is the importance of the heart in prayer? How might one balance the intellectual and the intuitive approaches to God in prayer? How could you help others be open to the prayer of the heart?

■ DOCTRINAL STATEMENTS ■

- "The Lord's Prayer is the most perfect of prayers. . . . In it we ask, not only for all the things we can rightly desire, but also in the sequence that they should be desired. This prayer not only teaches us to ask for things, but also in what order we should desire them" (CCC, no. 2763, citing St. Thomas Aquinas, *Summa Theologiae*, II-II, 83, 9).

- The Church includes the Our Father in her liturgies. The communal praying of the Lord's Prayer at Mass gathers up the intercessions that accompany the consecration of the bread and wine into Christ's Body and Blood and prepares the worshipers for Holy Communion.

- The divine mystery is beyond our understanding and imagining. We call God "Father" only because Jesus, the Son of God made man, revealed him as such.

- Because of our union with Jesus through Baptism, we are given the grace of an adopted, filial relationship with the Father. This begets in us a new self-understanding based on this extraordinary intimacy with the Father and the Son.

- Prayer to the Father inclines us to be like him and to acquire a humble and trusting heart (cf. CCC, no. 2800).

- 'Who art in heaven' does not refer to a place but to God's majesty and his presence in the hearts of the just. Heaven, the Father's house, is the true homeland toward which we are heading and to which, already, we belong" (CCC, no. 2802).

- "In the Our Father, the object of the first three petitions is the glory of the Father: the sanctification of his name, the coming of the kingdom and the fulfillment of his will. The four others present our wants to him: they ask that our lives be nourished, healed of sin, and made victorious in the struggle of good over evil" (CCC, no. 2857).

- *Hallowed* means "to be made holy." We do not make God's name holy; God is the source of his own holiness that is his perfection and glory. We hallow God's name by showing honor, respect, and adoration to God (cf. CCC, no. 2807). We give witness to God's holiness by doing his will, being people of prayer, and establishing the earthly conditions by which God's holiness is manifested.

- "Thy kingdom come" turns our attention to the final coming of Jesus and the ultimate fulfillment of his Kingdom. This was the prayerful cry of the early Christians who had a vivid sense of Christ's final coming—Maranatha! "Come, Lord Jesus!" (Rev 22:20).
- "In the third petition, we ask our Father to unite our will to that of his Son, so as to fulfill his plan of salvation in the life of the world" (CCC, no. 2860).
- "'Our daily bread' refers to the earthly nourishment necessary to everyone for subsistence, and also to the Bread of Life: the Word of God and the Body of Christ" (CCC, no. 2861).
- "The fifth petition begs God's mercy for our offences, mercy which can penetrate our hearts only if we have learned to forgive our enemies, with the example and help of Christ" (CCC, no. 2862).
- "When we say 'lead us not into temptation,' we are asking God not to allow us to take the path that leads to sin. This petition implores the Spirit of discernment and strength; it requests the grace of vigilance and final perseverance" (CCC, no. 2863).
- "In the last petition, 'but deliver us from evil,' Christians pray to God with the Church to show forth the victory, already won by Christ, over the 'ruler of this world,' Satan, the angel personally opposed to God and to his plan of salvation" (CCC, no. 2864).
- We conclude with the "Amen," which means, "So be it." We joyfully ratify the words that Jesus has taught us (cf. CCC, no. 2856).

MEDITATION

The proper ordering of our external activities can only be achieved once we have re-established conscious contact with the center of all these activities and concerns. This center is the aim of our meditation. In St. Teresa's words, "God is the center of the soul." When our access to this center is opened up, the Kingdom of God is established in our hearts. That kingdom is nothing less than the present power and all-pervasive life of God Himself permeating all creation. In the words of John Cassian: "He who is the author of eternity would have men ask of him nothing that is uncertain, petty or temporal."

This is not because he does not want us to enjoy the good things of life, but because we can fully enjoy them only when we have received His gift of Himself who is goodness itself. The proof of his generosity is also what St. Paul calls "The ground of our hope." It is the love of God flooding our inmost hearts through the Holy Spirit he has given us (cf. Rom 5:5).

This is not an experience reserved for the selected few. It is a gift available to all men and women. To receive it we must return to the center of our being, where we find the infusion of God's love through the Spirit of Jesus.

— John Main, OSB, *Word into Silence*
(Mahwah, NJ: Paulist Press, 1981), 66-67

PRAYER

Our Father, who art in heaven,
hallowed be thy name.
Thy kingdom come.
Thy will be done on earth, as it is in heaven.
Give us this day our daily bread;
and forgive us our trespasses
as we forgive those who trespass against us,
and lead us not into temptation,
but deliver us from evil. Amen.

—cf. Mt 7:9-13

Worthy is the Lamb that was slain
    to receive power and riches, wisdom and strength
    honor and glory and blessing. . . .
To the one who sits on the throne and to the Lamb
    be blessing and honor, glory and might,
    forever and ever.

—Rev 5:12-13

CONCLUSION
AND
APPENDICES

CONCLUSION:
A SOURCE OF MEANING
AND HOPE

The Second Vatican Council declared that "the future of humanity is in the hands of those men who are capable of providing the generations to come with reasons for life and optimism" (GS, no. 31). No one can live without the hope that life has ultimate and lasting meaning beyond the concerns and struggles, the joys and satisfactions of each day. Catholics find that meaning and hope in Jesus Christ, whom God the Father has sent into the world for the salvation of all peoples.

But the world can be a disturbing place. There is war and anxiety because of terrorism. There is the fierceness of competition and the injustices that come from greed. There are continuous distractions that come from the media, the numerous hours given to television, radio, and Internet. There are the unrelenting demands of work and family life.

Yet in the midst of all this, people are generously loving within their families, with their friends, and for their communities. Nevertheless, a nagging question remains: Where is all this going? There is a persistent thirst for meaning and hope.

Many people find refuge in various types of spiritual activities and communities that promise serenity in a hectic world and refuge from its pressures. They look to meditation techniques and to well-publicized personalities for ways to find tranquility and some hope for themselves.

In the midst of such a culture, the Catholic Church offers a message that is not its own but comes from God's self-revelation in Jesus Christ two thousand years ago, yet is ever new and renewing as it is received, celebrated, lived, and contemplated today. The Church offers to all people the possibility of encountering the living God today and finding in him lasting meaning and hope.

God continues to be present in the Church as the Gospel of his Son, Jesus Christ, is proclaimed and received by her members through the life-giving power of the Holy Spirit. In the first part of this *United States Catholic Catechism for Adults*, we have studied the summary of faith in the Apostles' Creed and have learned how the Gospel of Jesus Christ is transmitted faithfully from generation to generation, continuing to be heard by countless believers in a way that leads them to an ever greater understanding of God's love and their destiny.

God continues to be present in his Church as her members are brought together by the Holy Spirit to celebrate the Seven Sacraments, most especially the Eucharist. In Part Two of this *Catechism*, we have learned how Jesus Christ continues to endow his people with his gifts of salvation. Through Baptism, he makes them children of the Father, his disciples, and members of the Church. Through Confirmation, he deepens within them the presence of the Holy Spirit. Through the sacrifice of the Eucharist, he nourishes them with his Body and Blood. Through Penance and Reconciliation, he brings them from sin to grace. Through the Anointing of the Sick, he helps them bear—and sometimes lifts from them—the burdens of serious illness. Through Marriage, he reveals the absoluteness of love and its life-giving creativity. Through Holy Orders, he establishes bishops, priests, and deacons to ensure his continuous shepherding of the Church.

God continues to be present in the Church as her members strive to live according to the example and teaching of Jesus Christ. In Part Three of this *Catechism*, we have learned how the Beatitudes and the Ten Commandments guide the consciences and lives of the members of the Church so that they make alive, in the midst of humanity, the power of God's love to transform society by the wisdom, compassion, justice, and fidelity that flow from God himself. The Holy Spirit is the dynamic presence of God, enabling the members of the Church to live a truly Christian life.

God continues to be present in the Church as her members contemplate the great things God has done through his Son by the power of the Holy Spirit for the salvation of all people. In Part Four of this *Catechism*, we have learned about the significance of prayer and popular piety as ways in which the members of the Church continue to encounter the living God within their own hearts and within their own communities.

The Church is a community of human beings who are still subject to sin, and so it is with humility that she offers herself as the meeting place with the living God. Her existence for two thousand years demonstrates the unceasing mercy and love of God in maintaining her in his grace as a faithful and repentant people. In a world of passing fads and transitory ambitions, she offers the substance of the wisdom of the Gospel and her growing understanding of it through two millennia. She offers the possibility of enriching the present moment with the gifts of a tradition rooted in God's self-revelation and with the hope and meaning for human life that come from God himself. In a world torn by war and injustice, she celebrates the death and Resurrection of Jesus Christ, the gift of himself made eternally present and effective, to make all peoples one with him as head of a reconciled and healed community. In a world of violence against human life, the Church mightily defends life by her works of justice and charity as well as by her advocacy for the protection of all human life.

Of her very nature, the Church is missionary. This means her members are called by God to bring the Gospel by word and deed to all peoples and to every situation of work, education, culture, and communal life in which human beings find themselves. The members of the Church seek to transform society not by power but by persuasion and by example. Through participation in political life—either as voters or as holders of public office—they work for increasing conformity of public policy to the law of God as known by human reason and Divine Revelation. This they do especially by showing the coherence of Catholic teaching with the fundamental yearnings and dignity of the human person.

From its foundation, the United States has maintained the freedom of its citizens to worship according to their consciences and has prohibited infringement upon religious freedom by the government. For some, this leads to the conclusion that religion is a purely private matter and should not exercise a public voice in debates about moral issues. That was not the intention of the founders of this nation. Catholics must participate in political life and bring to bear upon it—by their voice and their vote—what they have learned about human nature, human destiny, and God's will for human beings from his self-revelation. The Gospel of Jesus Christ is relevant for all times and all places.

This *Catechism* provides Catholics with a knowledge and understanding of the Gospel that enables them to give an account of their faith to all whom they meet with clarity and persuasiveness. They are more effectively enabled to proclaim what God has done for them through his Son in the Holy Spirit, and to explain the rich tradition of belief that is our heritage. This proclamation and catechesis are essential to the new evangelization to which the Church commits herself today: to bring the Gospel of salvation to those near and far.

APPENDIX A.
GLOSSARY

-A-

ABORTION: The intentional destruction of an unborn child; such an act is gravely contrary to the moral law and the will of the Creator.

ABSOLUTION: The act of the priest, using the power Christ entrusted to the Church, in the Sacrament of Penance by which he pardons sin(s) of the penitent.

ADVENT: A period of roughly four weeks prior to Christmas, during which the faithful prepare themselves spiritually for the celebration of the birth of Christ.

AGNOSTIC: One who claims to be unable to know whether or not God exists.

AMEN: A Hebrew word meaning "so be it" or "it is so"; its use serves as an affirmation of what was said previously; this term most often is used to conclude prayer.

ANAMNESIS (THE MEMORIAL): Prayer after the words of consecration at the Mass in which we recall the death and Resurrection of Christ and look forward to his glorious return.

ANGEL: A spiritual, personal, immortal creature with intelligence and free will, created by God to serve him unceasingly and to act as a messenger to carry out the plan of salvation.

ANGER: When considered as one of the Capital Sins, anger is that passion which leads one to either harm a person or want to harm a person because of a desire for vengeance.

ANNULMENT (DECLARATION OF NULLITY OF A MARRIAGE): The consent of the spouses entering into marriage must be a free act of the will, devoid of external or internal invalidating factors. If this freedom is absent, the marriage is invalid. For this reason, the Church, after an examination of the situation by a competent Church court, can declare the nullity of a marriage, i.e., that the sacramental marriage never existed. In this case, the contracting parties are free to marry, provided the natural obligations of the previous union are discharged (cf. CCC, 1628-1629; CIC, cann. 1095-1107; CCEO, cann. 1431-1449).

ANOINTING OF THE SICK, SACRAMENT OF: This Sacrament of healing is given to a person who is seriously ill or in danger of death due to sickness or old age. Elderly people may be anointed if they are in a weak condition though no dangerous illness is present.

APOSTASY: The term applied to a baptized person who has abandoned the Christian faith.

APOSTLE: The title traditionally given to those specially chosen by Jesus to preach the Gospel and to whom he entrusted responsibility for guiding the early Church. The names of the Twelve are Peter, Andrew, James, John, Thomas, James, Philip, Bartholomew (or Nathaniel), Matthew, Simon, Jude (or Thaddeus), and Matthias (who replaced Judas Iscariot after Judas betrayed Jesus and then took his own life). St. Paul, though not one of the Twelve, was also called later by the Lord to be an Apostle.

APOSTLES' CREED: A statement of the Christian faith, developed in the early centuries of the Church and used in the Sacrament of Baptism. It expresses the faith passed down to us from the Apostles.

APOSTOLIC SUCCESSION: The passing on of the office of bishop from the Apostles to bishops, and from them to other bishops down each generation, by means of ordination. This office includes the sanctifying, teaching, and governing roles within the Church.

APOSTOLIC TRADITION: Jesus entrusted his revelation and teachings to his Apostles. They passed it on by their preaching and witness. Along with others, they began writing the message down in what became the New Testament.

ARIANISM: The heresy in Church history that was widely spread by a man named Arius (AD 250-336), who argued that Jesus was not fully divine, but that God the Son was a kind of lesser God who became the man Jesus. His heresy was refuted by the Councils of Nicea (AD 325) and Chalcedon (AD 451).

ASCENSION: The entry of Jesus' humanity into divine glory to be at the right hand of the Father; traditionally, this occurred forty days after Jesus' Resurrection.

ASSUMPTION: The dogma that when the Blessed Virgin Mary's earthly life was finished, because she was sinless, she was kept from corruption and taken soul and body into heavenly glory.

ATHEIST: One who denies the existence of God.

ATONEMENT: By his suffering and death on the Cross, Jesus freed us from our sins and brought about our reconciliation with God the Father.

AVARICE: See "Greed."

-B-

BAPTISM: The first Sacrament of Initiation by which we are freed from all sin and are endowed with the gift of divine life, are made members of the Church, and are called to holiness and mission.

BEATIFICATION: The last step before being declared a saint. The main steps in the canonization process (determining eligibility for sainthood) are as follows: Servant of God (Venerable), Blessed, and Saint.

BEATITUDES: The eight Beatitudes form part of the teaching given by Jesus during the Sermon on the Mount, which set forth fundamental attitudes and virtues for living as a faithful disciple.

BIBLE: See "Sacred Scripture."

BISHOP: The highest of the three degrees of Holy Orders; a bishop is normally ordained to teach, to sanctify, and to govern a diocese or local church; a bishop is a successor of the Apostles.

BLASPHEMY: The use of the name of God, of the Virgin Mary, and of the saints in an offensive way.

BLESSINGS: Among the sacramentals, blessings hold a major place. There are blessings for persons, meals, objects, places, and ceremonial occasions such as graduations, testimonial honors, welcomes, and farewells. All blessings praise God for his gifts. Most blessings invoke the Holy Trinity along with the sign of the Cross, sometimes with the sprinkling of holy water.

BODY OF CHRIST: A name for the Holy Eucharist (see "Eucharist, Sacrament of"). It is also a title for the Church, with Christ as her head, sometimes referred to as the Mystical Body of Christ. The Holy Spirit provides the members with the gifts needed to live as Christ's Body.

-C-

CANONIZATION: The name for the solemn declaration by the pope that a deceased member of the faithful may be proposed as a model and intercessor to the Christian faithful and venerated as a saint, on the basis of the fact that the person lived a life of heroic virtue or remained faithful to God through martyrdom.

CAPITAL SINS: Those seven sins, sometimes called "deadly," that can lead us into more serious sin. The Capital Sins are lust, avarice (greed), envy, pride, sloth, gluttony, and anger.

CATECHESIS: The act of handing on the Word of God intended to inform the faith community and candidates for initiation into the Church about the teachings of Christ, transmitted by the Apostles to the Church. It also involves the lifelong effort of forming people into witnesses to Christ and opening their hearts to the spiritual transformation given by the Holy Spirit.

CATECHISM: The name given to a written work that contains a summary of all the beliefs of the faith and is used for catechetical instruction.

CATECHUMEN: An unbaptized candidate for the Sacraments of Initiation.

CATECHUMENATE: An extended period of preparation for the Sacraments of Initiation incorporating ritual, prayer, instruction, and spiritual and moral support by the parish community.

CHARITY (LOVE): The Theological Virtue by which we give love to God for his own sake and love to our neighbor on account of God.

CHASTITY: Connected to purity of heart, this is a virtue that moves us to love others with generous regards for them. It excludes lust and any wish to exploit them sexually. It helps us see and put into practice God's plan for the body, person, and sexuality. All people are called to pursue and live the virtue of chastity according to one's state in life.

CHRISM: Perfumed oil consecrated by a bishop at the annual Mass of the Chrism during Holy Week; it is used in those Sacraments which confer a permanent mark or character—Baptism, Confirmation, and Holy Orders.

CHRISMATION: The name for Confirmation in the Eastern Churches.

CHRIST: The title given to Jesus meaning "The Anointed One"; it comes from the Latin word *Christus*, which in its Greek root is the word for *Messiah*.

CHRISTMAS: The annual celebration of Jesus' Nativity or birth.

CHURCH: This term refers to the whole Catholic community of believers throughout the world. The term can also be used in the sense of a diocese or a particular parish.

CIVIC RESPONSIBILITY: Citizens should work with civil authority to build a society of truth, justice, solidarity, and freedom. In conscience, citizens may not obey civil laws that are contrary to the moral order.

COLLEGE OF BISHOPS (COLLEGIALITY): All bishops, with the Pope as their head, form a single college, which succeeds in every generation the college of the Twelve Apostles, with Peter at their head. Christ instituted this college as the foundation of the Church. The college of bishops, together with—but never without—the pope, has the supreme and full authority over the universal Church.

COMMON GOOD: By the "common good is to be understood, 'the sum total of social conditions which allow people, either as groups or as individuals, to reach their fulfillment more fully and more easily'" (CCC, no. 1906, citing GS, no. 26, §1).

COMMUNION, HOLY: See "Eucharist."

COMMUNION OF THE SAINTS: This refers to members of the Church through all time—those presently now in the Church and those members who have already gone before us and are either in Purgatory or heaven.

CONCUPISCENCE: The disorder in our human appetites and desires as the result of Original Sin. These effects remain even after Baptism and produce an inclination to sin.

CONFIRMATION, SACRAMENT OF: This is a Sacrament of Initiation in which the bishop or a delegated priest confers Confirmation through the anointing with chrism on the recipient's forehead, which is done by the laying on of the hand, while saying, "Be sealed with the gift of the Holy Spirit." Confirmation completes the grace of Baptism by a special outpouring of the gifts of the Holy

Spirit, which seals and confirms the baptized in union with Christ and calls them to greater participation in the worship and apostolic life of the Church.

CONSCIENCE: The practical judgment about the moral quality of particular humans acts as well as the inner ability to make such a judgment.

CONTEMPLATION: Wordless prayer in which a person focuses the whole person in loving adoration on God and his very presence.

CONTRITION: Sorrow for sin with a firm purpose of amendment, which is the intention to avoid sin in the future. Contrition is imperfect when a person is motivated by fear of punishment. Contrition is perfect when the motive is a response to God's love for us. Contrition on the part of the penitent, either imperfect or perfect, is a necessary part of the Sacrament of Penance and Reconciliation.

CORPORAL WORKS OF MERCY: These are charitable actions by which we help our neighbors in their bodily needs. The corporal (bodily) works of mercy are to feed the hungry, give drink to the thirsty, shelter the homeless, clothe the naked, visit the sick, visit the prisoners, bury the dead, and give alms to the poor.

COVENANT: A solemn agreement made between people or between God and a person or persons. In the Old Testament, God established covenants with Noah, Abraham, and Moses. The Prophets prepared people for the new and eternal covenant established by Jesus Christ. Marriage is a covenant of life and love.

CREATION: God—Father, Son, Holy Spirit—out of love for us made the world out of nothing, wanting to share divine life and love with us. The original creation became a new creation in Jesus Christ.

CREED: This term comes from the Latin word *credo*, meaning "I believe." It is used to refer to a statement of belief.

CREMATION: The Church permits cremation (the burning of a deceased human body into ashes), provided that it does not demonstrate a denial of faith in the resurrection of the body" (CCC, no. 2301). In cases where cremation is planned, the Church counsels that the body should be present for the funeral. On March 21, 1997, in response to a request from the

National Conference of Catholic Bishops (now the United States Conference of Catholic Bishops), the Vatican's Congregation for Divine Worship and the Discipline of the Sacraments published an indult (Prot. 1589/96/L) giving to each diocesan bishop in the United States of America the right to allow for the presence of the cremated remains of a body at the full course of Catholic funeral rites. Each diocesan bishop has the right whether or not to allow this practice.

-D-

DEACONS: Men ordained by the bishop to serve. They receive the Sacrament of Holy Orders but not the ministerial priesthood. Through ordination, the deacon is conformed to the Christ who said he came to serve, not to be served. Deacons in the Latin Church may baptize, read the Gospel, preach the homily, assist the bishop or priest in the celebration of the Eucharist, assist at and bless marriages, and preside at funerals. They dedicate themselves to charitable endeavors, which was their ministerial role in New Testament times.

DECALOGUE: Another name for the Ten Commandments.

DEISM: A worldview that admits that God created the world but denies that he has any further providential care or concern for it. (See also "Providence.")

DEPOSIT OF FAITH: The heritage of faith contained in Sacred Scripture and Tradition, handed on in the Church from the time of the Apostles, from which the Magisterium draws all that it proposes for belief as divinely revealed.

DEVILS: Angels who, in pride, turned away from God and have fallen from grace are named demons or devils, and they tempt human beings to sin.

DEVOTIONAL PRAYER: Devotional prayer refers to the numerous forms of personalized prayer that have grown up outside, but complementary to, the liturgical prayer of the Church. (See Chapter 22 on "Sacramentals and Popular Devotion.") These devotions include the rosary; the Stations of the Cross; pilgrimages to shrines in the Holy Land and Rome, Marian shrines, and those dedicated to saints; novenas; litanies; and similar expressions of faith.

DISCIPLE: Name given in the New Testament to all those men and women who followed Jesus and were taught by him while he was alive, and who, following Jesus' death, Resurrection, and Ascension, formed the Church with the Apostles and helped spread the Good News, or Gospel message. Contemporary members of the Church, as followers of Jesus, can also be referred to as disciples.

DIVINE FILIATION: An effect of Baptism and Confirmation: becoming adopted sons and daughters of God, participating in God's life and love.

DIVINE PERSON: The term used to describe the Father, Son, and Holy Spirit in their relation to and distinction from one another within the unity of the Trinity. Each of the three divine Persons is God in one divine nature.

DIVINE PROVIDENCE: God's loving care and concern for all he has made; he continues to watch over creation, sustaining its existence and presiding over its development and destiny.

DOCTOR OF THE CHURCH: A person from any era in Church history whose sanctity and writings have had a profound influence on theological and spiritual thought.

A person is declared a Doctor by the Pope.

DOCTRINE/DOGMA: The name given to divinely revealed truths proclaimed or taught by the Church's Magisterium; the faithful are obliged to believe these truths.

DOMESTIC CHURCH: "The Christian home is the place where children receive the first proclamation of the faith. For this reason the family is rightly called 'the domestic church,' a community of grace and prayer, a school of human virtues and of Christian charity" (CCC, no. 1666).

DOXOLOGY: The name given to a prayer of Trinitarian adoration in which the three Persons of the Trinity are invoked.

-E-

EASTER: The annual celebration of the Resurrection of Jesus.

EASTERN CHURCHES AND WESTERN CHURCHES: The Eastern Churches originated in that region of the world that was at one time part of the Eastern Roman Empire. These churches possess their own distinctive traditions that may be seen in their liturgy, theology, and law. The Western

Church, focused in Rome, is sometimes called the Latin Church. All individual churches, Eastern or Western, that are in communion with the Apostolic See (Rome) are part of the Catholic Church.

ECUMENICAL COUNCIL: This is a gathering of the world's bishops, exercising their collegial authority over the universal Church in union with the pope.

ECUMENISM: The efforts among all Christians to bring about the fulfillment of Christ's will for the unity of his followers.

ELECT: The name given to those who are already with the Lord Jesus in heaven. It also can refer to catechumens who are in the final stage of formation prior to entering the Church.

ENVY: One of the Capital Sins; it is the inordinate desire for the possessions of another, even to the point of wishing harm on the other or rejoicing in another's misfortunes.

EPICLESIS (INVOCATION): During the celebration of the Eucharist, the priest invokes the Father to send the Holy Spirit to come upon the gifts of bread and wine that they may be changed into Christ's Body and Blood. In

every Sacrament, the prayer asking for the sanctifying power of God's Holy Spirit is an *epiclesis*.

EPISCOPACY: The office of bishop.

EUCHARIST, SACRAMENT OF: During the celebration of the Mass, by the power of the Holy Spirit and the proclamation of Jesus' words by the priest, the bread and wine are changed into the Body and Blood of Christ, which is offered in an unbloody manner in sacrifice for us and in praise to the Father. The assembly actively participates by prayers, hymns, psalms, responses, and an inner self-offering along with Christ to the Father. All who are properly prepared can receive Holy Communion, by which Jesus gradually transforms the receivers into himself and which leads them to Gospel witness in the world.

EUTHANASIA: An action or an omission which purposely results in the death of sick, disabled, or dying persons. Regardless of the motives or means, it is always gravely wrong and morally unacceptable.

EVANGELICAL COUNSELS: Those vows taken by men or women who enter religious life; there are three vows: poverty, chastity, and obedience.

EVANGELIZATION: This is the ministry and mission of proclaiming and witnessing Christ and his Gospel with the intention of deepening the faith of believers and inviting others to be baptized and initiated into the Church.

EXCOMMUNICATION: A severe penalty imposed or declared by the Church upon a Catholic who has committed a grave crime or offense according to Church law; a person who is excommunicated is barred from celebrating or receiving the Sacraments. This penalty is imposed as a remedy for serious sin, not as a punishment. Remission of the penalty can be granted only by those authorized to do so by the Church.

EXEGESIS: The process used by Scripture scholars to determine the literal and spiritual meanings of the biblical text.

EXORCISM: "Exorcism is directed at the expulsion of demons or to the liberation from demonic possession through the spiritual authority which Jesus entrusted to his Church" (CCC, no. 1673, citing CIC, can. 1172). One needs to distinguish psychological illness from demonic possession. Illness is the domain of psychological and medical care, whereas the presence of the Evil One needs the attention of an exorcist. In the Rite of Baptism, there is also a Prayer of Exorcism prior to the anointing with the Oil of the Catechumens; in this prayer, the priest or deacon asks that the one about to be baptized be freed from Original Sin.

-F-

FAITH: This is both a gift of God and a human act by which the believer gives personal adherence to God (who invites his or her response) and freely assents to the whole truth that God has revealed.

FALL, (THE): A title for the event in which the first man and woman, traditionally called Adam and Eve, disobeyed God with the result that they lost their place in Paradise, passed Original Sin to all their descendants, and made Redemption necessary.

FAMILY: "A man and a woman, united in marriage, together with their children, form a family. This institution is prior to any recognition by public authority, which has an obligation to recognize it. It should be considered the normal reference point by which the different [authentic] forms of family relationships are to be [recognized]" (CCC, no. 2202).

FATHERS OF THE CHURCH:
Church teachers and writers of the early centuries whose teachings are a crucial witness to the Tradition of the Church.

FILIAL LOVE: The love that children owe their parents through respect, gratitude, just obedience, and assistance.

FORTITUDE: The Cardinal Virtue by which one courageously and firmly chooses the good despite difficulty and also perseveres in doing what is right despite temptation, fear, or persecution.

FRUITS OF THE HOLY SPIRIT:
The Tradition of the Church lists twelve fruits of the Holy Spirit: love, joy, peace, patience, kindness, goodness, generosity, gentleness, faithfulness, modesty, self-control, and chastity (cf. CCC, no. 1832).

FULL COMMUNION (RECEPTION INTO): This refers to the entrance of baptized Christians of other Christian ecclesial communions into full communion with the Catholic Church, through a profession of faith and the Sacraments of Confirmation and the Eucharist.

-G-

GIFTS OF THE HOLY SPIRIT:
These gifts are permanent dispositions that move us to respond to the guidance of the Spirit. The traditional list of these gifts is derived from Isaiah 11:1-3: wisdom, understanding, knowledge, counsel, fortitude, reverence (piety), and wonder and awe in God's presence (fear of the Lord).

GLUTTONY: The Capital Sin that describes actions of eating and drinking more than what is necessary.

GNOSTICISM: In the first Christian centuries, this blend of Christianity and paganism denied that Jesus was human and sought salvation through occult "wisdom." The earliest Church Fathers, especially St. Ignatius of Antioch, rejected the Gnostics and vigorously defended the humanity of Jesus Christ, conceived by the Holy Spirit in the womb of the Virgin Mary, who gave birth to Jesus.

GOD: The eternal unchanging being who created all that is and who continues to oversee and guide all things. Through the centuries, God has revealed himself to us as one being who is a Trinity of Persons—Father, Son, and Holy

Spirit. Traditionally, *God* has been used to refer to the Father, or the First Person of the Trinity, as well as to the whole Godhead.

GOSPEL: The proclamation of the entire message of faith revealed in and through Jesus Christ, the Son of God and the Second Person of the Trinity. The word *Gospel* also refers to one of the four books of the New Testament—Matthew, Mark, Luke, and John—that contain a record of the life, teaching, death, and Resurrection of Jesus.

GRACE: The help God gives us to respond to our vocation to become his adopted sons and daughters. The divine initiative of grace precedes, prepares, and elicits our free response in faith and commitment. Sanctifying grace is a habitual gift of God's own divine life, a stable and supernatural disposition that enables us to live with God and to act by his love. Actual graces refer to God's interventions in our lives, whether at the beginning of conversion or in the course of the work of sanctification.

GREED (AVARICE): An inordinate attachment to the goods of creation, frequently expressed in the pursuit of money or other symbols of wealth, which leads to sins of injustice and other evils.

-H-

HERESY: A religious teaching that denies or contradicts truths revealed by God.

HOLINESS: A state of goodness in which a person—with the help of God's grace, the action of the Holy Spirit, and a life of prayer—is freed from sin and evil. Such a person, when gifted with holiness, must still resist temptation, repent of sins that may be committed, and realize that remaining holy is a lifelong pilgrimage with many spiritual and moral challenges. The struggles evident in the lives of the saints are instructive when trying to explain and describe holiness.

HOLY DAYS OF OBLIGATION: In the United States, for Latin Catholics these days are: Mary, Mother of God (January 1); Ascension (forty days after Easter or the following Sunday); Assumption of Mary (August 15); All Saints Day (November 1); Immaculate Conception of Mary (December 8); Nativity of our Lord or Christmas (December 25). On these days, there is an obligation to attend Mass and to refrain from servile work as much as possible.

HOLY ORDERS, SACRAMENT OF: The Sacrament in which a

bishop ordains a man to be conformed to Jesus Christ by grace, to service and leadership in the Church. A man can be ordained a deacon, priest, or bishop. Through this Sacrament, the mission entrusted by Christ to his Apostles continues to be exercised in the Church. This Sacrament confers a permanent mark or character on the one who receives it.

HOLY SPIRIT: The Third Person of the Trinity who builds up, animates, and sanctifies the Church and her members.

HOPE: The Theological Virtue through which a person both desires and expects the fulfillment of God's promises of things to come.

-I-

ICONS: A form of sacred art developed in the Eastern Churches. The artists consider their calling a sacred vocation. Their works have a mystical impact meant to draw the one praying beyond the picture into the realm of the divine.

IMAGE OF GOD: God has made us in his image by giving us the capacity for intelligence, love, freedom, and conscience. By Baptism, our bodies are made temples of the Holy Spirit.

IMMACULATE CONCEPTION: A dogma of the Church that teaches that Mary was conceived without Original Sin due to the anticipated redemptive graces of her Son, Jesus.

IMMORTALITY: "The Church teaches that every spiritual soul is created immediately by God—it is not 'produced' by the parents—and also that it is immortal: it does not perish when it separates from the body at death and it will be united with the body at the final Resurrection" (CCC, no. 366).

INCARNATION: By the Incarnation, the Second Person of the Holy Trinity assumed our human nature, taking flesh in the womb of the Virgin Mary There is one Person in Jesus and that is the divine Person of the Son of God. Jesus has two natures, a human one and a divine one.

INDEFECTIBILITY: The Lord Jesus ensures that his Church will remain until the Kingdom is fully achieved. Indefectibility means that the Church does not and cannot depart from proclaiming the authentic Gospel without error in spite of the defects of her members.

INDISSOLUBILITY OF MARRIAGE: "What God has joined together, no human being must separate" (Mk 10:9). God's plan for marriage is a permanent covenant embraced by the spouses, hence the bond is indissoluble—not able to be dissolved (cf. CIC, can. 1055; CCEO, can. 776).

INDULGENCE: The remission of temporal punishment due to sin, granted to the faithful who recite specified prayers, visit a specified place of pilgrimage, or engage in a specified act of charity; punishment is remitted through the power of the Church and in the mutual exchange of spiritual goods, particularly the merits of Christ and the saints.

INERRANCY: Because the authors of Sacred Scripture were inspired by God, the saving meaning or truth found in the Scriptures cannot be wrong. (See also "Inspiration.")

INFALLIBILITY: This is the gift of the Holy Spirit to the Church whereby the pastors of the Church—the pope, and bishops in communion with him—can definitively proclaim a doctrine of faith and morals, which is divinely revealed for the belief of the faithful. This gift flows from the grace of the whole body of the faithful not to err in matters of faith and morals. The pope teaches infallibly when he declares that his teaching is *ex cathedra* (literally, "from the throne"); that is, he teaches as supreme pastor of the Church.

INSPIRATION: This is the divine assistance given to the human authors of the books of Sacred Scripture. Guided by the Holy Spirit, the human authors made full use of their talents and abilities while, at the same time, writing the truth that God intended.

-J-

JEALOUSY: An attitude related to envy as well as greed; a jealous person is possessive of what one has or thinks one should have, as well as resentful toward others for what they have.

JESUS: The name given to the Son of God, the Second Person of the Trinity. This name, which means "God Saves," was revealed to both the Blessed Virgin Mary and to St. Joseph (cf. Lk 1:31; Mt 1:21).

JUST WAR: *Just War* is the term used for the proper use of military force to defend against an unjust aggressor. The strict conditions for engaging in a just war are known as the Just War Conditions. These conditions require that at one and the same time:

- The damage inflicted by the aggressor on the nation or community of nations must be lasting, grave and certain;
- All other means of putting an end to it must have been shown to be impractical or ineffective;
- There must be serious prospects of success;
- The use of arms must not produce evils graver than the evil to be eliminated.
- The power of modern means of destruction weighs very heavily in evaluating this condition. These are the traditional elements in what is called the "just war" doctrine.
- The evaluation of these conditions for moral legitimacy belongs to the prudential judgment of those who have responsibility for the common good. (CCC, no. 2309)

JUSTICE: The Cardinal Virtue by which one is able to give God and neighbor what is due to them.

JUSTIFICATION: The term used to refer to the action of God by which we are freed from our sins and sanctified and renewed by the grace of God.

-K-

KINGDOM OF GOD: The actualization of God's will for human beings proclaimed by Jesus Christ as a community of justice, peace, mercy, and love, the seed of which is the Church on earth, and the fulfillment of which is in eternity.

-L-

LAITY: Members of the Church, distinguished from the clergy and those in consecrated life, who have been incorporated into the People of God through the Sacrament of Baptism.

LAST JUDGMENT: The moment at the end of time when everyone will appear before Christ and receive an eternal recompense in accord with their earthly life.

LAW: A code of conduct established by a competent authority. Moraland civil law should all be based on divine law, whether it is natural or has been revealed by God.

LECTIO DIVINA: A manner of praying with Scripture; the person praying either reflectively reads a passage from Scripture or listens attentively to its being read, and then meditates on words or phrases that resonate.

LECTIONARY: The official liturgical book of the Church containing Scripture passages for use in the Liturgy of the Word.

LENT: This is an annual period of forty days beginning on Ash Wednesday for Latin Catholics, which is set aside for penance, fasting, and almsgiving in preparation for the coming celebration of Easter. It is modeled in part on the forty days that Jesus spent in the desert prior to beginning his public ministry. The penance, fasting, and almsgiving are meant to help lead the believer to ongoing conversion and a deeper faith in the Lord who redeemed us.

LITANY: Literally a list, such as in the list, or litany, of saints. In such a prayer, the name of the saints is spoken or sung and the congregation responds with a repeated invocation, "Pray for us." For example, in the Litany of Loreto, the list of qualities of the Virgin Mary are recited or sung, again with the response, "Pray for us."

LITURGICAL YEAR: The calendar that guides the liturgies and prayers of the Church. It commences on the First Sunday of Advent and ends with the celebration of Christ the King. It includes Advent, the Christmas Season, Lent, the Easter Season, and Ordinary Time, as well as various Feasts of Mary, the Apostles, and many other saints.

LITURGY: From the Greek, meaning "public work." It refers especially to the public worship of the Church, including the Mass and the Liturgy of the Hours. By their Baptism, all God's people are called to offer a sacrifice of praise to God at liturgy. The ordained priest at liturgy acts in the person of Christ, the Head of the Church, to make Christ's saving grace present by the power of the Holy Spirit.

LITURGY OF THE HOURS: The public daily prayer of the Church which extends the praise given to God in the Eucharistic celebration.

LORD'S DAY, (THE): A name used synonymously for Sunday, the day of the Lord Jesus' Resurrection.

LORD'S PRAYER, (THE): Another name used for the prayer more commonly known as the Our Father. This prayer is sometimes called the Lord's Prayer because it is a prayer taught by Jesus to his Apostles and disciples.

LOVE: See "Charity."

LUST: One of the Capital Sins; it is an inordinate desire for earthly pleasures, particularly sexual pleasures.

-M-

MAGISTERIUM: The teaching office of the pope, and bishops in communion with him, guided by the Holy Spirit. The pope and bishops are the authoritative teachers in the Church.

MARKS OF THE CHURCH: The name given to four singular characteristics of the Church: the Church is one, holy, catholic, and apostolic.

MARRIAGE, SACRAMENT OF: "The matrimonial covenant by which a man and a woman establish between themselves a partnership of the whole of life, is by its nature ordered toward the good of the spouses and the procreation and education of offspring; this covenant between baptized persons has been raised by Christ the Lord to the dignity of a sacrament" (CCC, no. 1601, citing CIC, can. 1055 §1; cf. GS, no. 48 §1, CCEO, can. 776).

MARTYR: One who witnesses to Christ and the truth of the faith, even to the point of suffering.

MASS AS A SACRED MEAL: The Mass is a sacred banquet, like the Last Supper, in which bread and wine become Christ's Body and Blood, received in Holy Communion.

MASS AS A SACRIFICE: Through the ministry of the ordained priest, the Holy Spirit makes present at Mass Christ's Paschal mystery, his dying and rising in which Christ is offered to the Father to give him adoration and praise to save us from our sins and bring us divine life.

MATRIMONY: Another name for the Sacrament of Marriage.

MEDITATION: Prayer in which, in order to respond to the Lord, one tries to understand more fully or deeply God's Revelation of the truths of the faith.

MINISTERIAL PRIESTHOOD: This priesthood, received in the Sacrament of Holy Orders, differs in essence from the priesthood of the faithful. The ministerial priesthood serves the priesthood of the faithful by building up the Church in the name of Christ, who is head of the Body, by offering prayers and sacrifices to God on behalf of people. A priest is given the power to consecrate the Eucharist, forgive sins, and administer the other Sacraments, except Holy Orders.

MODESTY: A modest person dresses, speaks, and acts in a manner that supports and encourages purity and chastity and not in a manner that would tempt or encourage sinful sexual behavior.

MORALITY: In one sense, this is the goodness or evil of particular actions. For a Catholic, it also refers to the manner of life and action formed according to the teaching laid down by Christ Jesus and authoritatively interpreted by the Church.

MORTAL SIN: Mortal sin is when we consciously and freely choose to do something grave against the divine law and contrary to our final destiny. There are three conditions for a sin to be a mortal sin: grave matter, full knowledge, and deliberate consent (freedom). Mortal sin destroys the loving relationship with God that we need for eternal happiness. If not repented, it results in a loss of love and God's grace and merits eternal punishment in hell, that is, exclusion from the Kingdom of God and thus eternal death.

MOTHER OF THE CHURCH: "[Mary] is clearly the mother of the members of Christ . . . since she has by her charity joined in bringing about the birth of believers in the Church, who are members of its head" (LG, no. 53; CCC, no. 963).

MOTHER OF GOD: Mary is truly the Mother of God since she is the mother of the Son of God made man. In the Eastern Churches, Mary is honored as the *Theotokos*, or "Birth-giver of God" (sometimes translated as "God-bearer").

MYRON: The name given in the Eastern Churches to the Chrism used during the Sacrament of Confirmation, or *Chrismation*.

MYSTERY: The term has several complementary meanings. First, it reminds us that we can never exhaust God's divine and infinite meaning. Second, mystery tells us that God is "wholly other," (not us) and yet so near that in him we live and move and have our being. Third, the union of the divine and human in Christ is so unique that we revere it as holy mystery. Fourth, mystery also applies to the celebration of the Sacraments in which God, Father, Son, and Spirit, are present and active for our salvation.

-N-

NATURAL FAMILY PLANNING: A morally permissible system for the regulation of births, which employs the natural fertility patterns and can be used within certain conditions of marriage and family life. (See CCC, nos. 2366-2372.)

NATURAL LAW: The natural law is our rational apprehension of the created moral order, an ability we have due to our being made in God's image. It expresses the dignity of the human person and forms the basis of our fundamental rights.

NEOPHYTYE: This term designates an adult who has been newly received into the Catholic Church.

NESTORIANISM: A significant heresy affecting early Christianity, founded by Nestorius (who died around AD 451) who believed Mary gave birth to the human Jesus, to whom the Son of God was united in some way. Hence Mary would not be the Mother of God. The Council of Ephesus repudiated Nestorius and proclaimed Mary as *Theotokos*—Birth-giver of God (sometimes translated as "God-bearer").

NEW LAW: The title given to the manner of living and acting taught by Jesus. When we follow the New Law, we are maintaining our part of the covenant with God.

NEW TESTAMENT: The designation for the second part of the Bible; this part contains the four Gospels, the Acts of the Apostles, various Letters or Epistles, and the Book of Revelation.

NICENE CREED: This creed resulted from the deliberations of the bishops at the Councils of Nicea (AD 325) and First Constantinople (AD 381). These Councils clarified and defended the ancient teachings of the Church about the humanity and divinity of Christ and the divinity of the Holy Spirit.

NOVENA: Nine days of prayer, usually invoking the intercession of the Virgin Mary or a saint. The novena traces its development to the scriptural nine days of prayer by Mary, the Apostles, and disciples asking for the gift of the Holy Spirit after the Ascension of Jesus Christ into heaven.

-O-

OBEDIENCE OF FAITH: Faith is hearing the Word of God and resolving to obey what God is asking of us. Jesus said, "Blessed are those who hear the word of God and observe it" (Lk 11:28).

OIL OF THE CATECHUMENS: Oil blessed by the bishop during Holy Week to be used in preparing a candidate for the Sacrament of Baptism.

OIL OF THE SICK: Oil blessed by the bishop in Holy Week to be used for the Sacrament of Anointing of the Sick. In necessity, a priest may also bless this oil.

OLD LAW: The term refers to the Ten Commandments and the way a faithful Israelite was called to observe them; following this Law was the manner in which a believer held up their part of the old covenant with God.

OLD TESTAMENT: The first part of Sacred Scripture that contains the Pentateuch (the first five books), the Historical Books, Wisdom Literature and Prophetic books. These come to us from the people of Ancient Israel before the coming of Christ. The books of the Old Testament were inspired by God.

ORDINARY TIME: The designation for the period during the Church's Liturgical Year that falls outside the times of Advent, Christmas, Lent, and Easter.

ORIGINAL HOLINESS AND JUSTICE: The "grace of original holiness was to share in divine life" (CCC, no. 375). "The inner harmony of the human person, the harmony between man and woman, and finally the harmony between the first couple and all creation, comprised the state called 'original justice'" (CCC, no. 376).

ORIGINAL SIN: The personal sin of disobedience committed by the first human beings, resulting in the deprivation of original holiness and justice and the experience of suffering and death. It also describes the fallen state of all human beings, including the experience of concupiscence, ignorance of God, and suffering and death.

-P-

PARACLETE: A name, given to the Holy Spirit by Jesus, which means adviser or consoler.

PASCHAL MYSTERY: In the Sacraments Jesus Christ enacts his Paschal mystery. In speaking of the Paschal Mystery we present Christ's death and Resurrection as one, inseparable event. It is *paschal* because it is Christ's passing into death and passing over it into new life. It is a *mystery* because it is a visible sign of an invisible act of God.

PASSOVER: The name of the Jewish feast that celebrates the deliverance of Israel from Egypt and from the Angel of Death who passed over their doors marked by the blood of sacrificed lamb. Jesus Christ inaugurated the new Passover by delivering all people from death and sin through his own blood shed on the Cross. The celebration of the Eucharist is the Passover feast of the New Covenant.

PENANCE, SACRAMENT OF: Also called the Sacrament of Confession, Reconciliation, Conversion, and Forgiveness, this is the Sacrament in which sins committed after Baptism are forgiven. It results in reconciliation with God and the Church.

PENTECOST: Celebrated each year fifty days after Easter, Pentecost marks the day when the Holy Spirit came upon the Apostles and disciples. The first Pentecost is sometimes referred to as the birthday of the Church because it was on this day that the Apostles, inspired by the Holy Spirit, first publicly preached the Good News to others.

PEOPLE OF GOD: God calls the Church into existence as his people centered in Christ and sustained by the Holy Spirit. The visible structure of the People of God as the Church is the means intended by Christ to help guarantee the life of grace for the whole.

PERPETUAL VIRGINITY: Mary was a virgin in conceiving Jesus, in giving birth to him, and in remaining always a virgin ever after.

PHYSICIAN-ASSISTED SUICIDE: This is suicide performed with the aid of a doctor. The emergence of physician-assisted suicide, popularized by the right-to-die movement, seeks to legalize what is a gravely immoral act forbidden by God in the Fifth Commandment.

POPE: The successor to St. Peter who serves as the Bishop of Rome and as the visible and juridical head of the Catholic Church.

PRAGMATISM: A philosophy that asserts that acts have value only in terms of their usefulness and practicality.

PRAYER: The raising of one's mind and heart to God in thanksgiving and in praise of his glory. It can also include the requesting of good things from God. It is an act by which one enters into awareness of a loving communion with God. "Prayer is the response of faith to the free promise of salvation and also a response of love to the thirst of the only Son of God" (CCC, no. 2561).

PRECEPTS OF THE CHURCH: Laws made by the Church that indicate basic requirements for her members.

PREJUDICE: Negative preconceived judgment of another; irrational suspicion or hatred of another because the person belongs to a particular race, religion, or group.

PRESBYTER: A term referring to an ordained priest.

PRIDE: The Capital Sin that involves excessive self-esteem and a strong desire to be noticed and honored by others; excessive pride sets one in opposition to God.

PRIEST: A baptized man ordained through the Sacrament of Holy Orders. "Priests are united with the bishops in priestly dignity and at the same time depend on them in the exercise of their pastoral functions; they are called to be the bishops' prudent co-workers" (CCC, no. 1595). With the bishop, priests form a presbyteral (priestly) community and assume with him the pastoral mission for a particular parish. They serve God's People in the work of sanctification by their preaching, teaching, and offering the Sacraments, especially the Eucharist and the forgiving of sins.

PRIESTHOOD OF THE FAITHFUL: Christ gives the faithful a share in his priesthood through the Sacraments of Baptism and Confirmation. This means that all baptized and confirmed members of the Church share in offering prayer and sacrifice to God. The priesthood of the faithful differs in essence from the ministerial priesthood.

PRIVATE REVELATIONS: These are revelations made in the course of history that do not add to or form part of the Deposit of Faith, but rather may help people live their faith more fully.

PROCREATIVE PURPOSE OF MARRIAGE: The aspect of marriage that requires that a married couple be open to the children that God may send them and resolve to raise them as true followers of Jesus Christ. The unitive and procreative aspects of marriage form an unbreakable bond.

PROVIDENCE: See "Divine Providence."

PRUDENCE: The Cardinal Virtue by which one knows the true good in every circumstance and chooses the right means to reach that end.

-R-

RCIA: The Rite of Christian Initiation of Adults. This is the title of the process designed to prepare adults for entrance into the Catholic Church by the reception of the Sacraments of Initiation.

REAL PRESENCE: When the bread is consecrated, it is changed into Christ's Body. When the wine is consecrated, it is changed into Christ's Blood. Jesus Christ is substantially present in a way that is entirely unique. This happens through the power of the Holy Spirit and the ministry of the priest or bishop acting in the person of Christ during the Eucharistic prayer.

REDEMPTION: The salvation won for us by Jesus. By his Incarnation, ministry, death and Resurrection, Jesus has freed us from original and actual sin and won eternal life for us.

REINCARNATION: The false belief that a dead person's spirit returns to life in another body either of an animal or another person. This belief is not compatible with the Catholic faith, which teaches that every human person has only one body and one soul, and is unique and unrepeatable.

RELATIVISM: The position that there is no objective truth, only subjective opinions.

RELIGION, VIRTUE OF: The habit of adoring God, praying to him, offering him the worship that belongs to him, and fulfilling the promises and vows made to him are acts of the virtue of religion that fall under the obedience of the First Commandment.

RELIGIOUS OR CONSECRATED LIFE: A permanent state in life into which certain men or women freely commit themselves to a life of special service to Christ, marked by the profession of the evangelical counsels: poverty, chastity, and obedience.

RESURRECTION: This is the triumph of Jesus over death on the third day after his crucifixion. Christ's risen body is real, but glorified, not restrained by space or time.

REVEALED LAW: There is revealed law as seen in the Old Testament when God communicated to Moses the Ten Commandments. This law prepared the world for the Gospel. Jesus revealed the full meaning of Old Testament law.

REVELATION: God's communication of himself and his loving plan to save us. This is a gift of self-communication, which is realized by deeds and words over time and most fully by his sending us his own divine Son, Jesus Christ. Public Revelation, which must be believed, ended with the death of the last Apostle. There can still be private revelation, which is intended only for the good of the person who receives it and does not need to be believed by others.

-S-

SABBATH: In Scripture, the Sabbath was the seventh day of the week that the people of Ancient Israel were to keep holy by praising God for the creation and the covenant and by resting from their ordinary work. For Christians, the observance of the Sabbath has been transferred to Sunday, the day of the Lord's Resurrection. (See also "Sunday.")

SACRAMENT: An efficacious sign of grace, instituted by Christ and entrusted to the Church, by which divine life is dispensed to us by the work of the Holy Spirit (CCC, nos. 1131, 774).

SACRAMENT OF SALVATION: By God's gracious plan, the Church is a sacrament of salvation, that is, a visible community in and through which Jesus Christ offers salvation through the Seven Sacraments, the preaching of the word, and the spiritual and moral witness of the members.

SACRAMENTAL CHARACTER: An indelible spiritual mark that is the permanent effect of the Sacraments of Baptism, Confirmation, and Holy Orders. It brings a new conformity to Christ and a specific standing in the Church. The reception of these Sacraments is never repeated (cf. CCC, Glossary).

SACRAMENTALS: These are sacred signs instituted by the Church. These are sacred signs that bear a resemblance to the Sacraments. They signify effects, especially of a spiritual nature, that are obtained through the intercession of the Church (CCC, no. 1667).

SACRAMENTS OF HEALING:
Designation given to the Sacrament of Penance and Reconciliation and the Sacrament of the Anointing of the Sick.

SACRAMENTS OF INITIATION:
Designation given to those Sacraments that bring a person into membership in the Church—Baptism, Confirmation, and the Holy Eucharist.

SACRAMENTS AT THE SERVICE OF COMMUNION:
The term *communion* refers to the Community of the Church. Holy Orders and Matrimony are the Sacraments at the Service of Communion (the community of the Church). This means they are primarily directed toward the salvation of others. If they benefit the personal salvation of the ordained or married person, it is through service to others that this happens.

SACRIFICE: A ritual offering made to God by a priest on behalf of the people as a sign of adoration, gratitude, supplication, penance, and/or communion.

SAINT: A person who, after having lived a life of virtue, dies in the state of grace and has been granted the reward of eternal life by God. The saints enjoy the beatific vision and unceasingly intercede for those still in earthly life. They also serve as a model and inspiration to us. (See also "Canonization.")

SANCTIFYING GRACE: See "Grace."

SATISFACTION: An act by which a sinner makes amends for sin. The penance received from the priest in Confession is a form of satisfaction. All real satisfaction for sin needs to be a participation in the satisfaction for sin won for us by Christ.

SCRIPTURE (BIBLE): The books that contain the truth of God's revelation and that were composed by human authors, inspired by the Holy Spirit, and recognized by the Church.

SCRUTINIES: During three Sundays of Lent, those preparing for entrance into the Church are led through prayerful reflections designed to help them turn from sin and grow in holiness.

SENSES OF SCRIPTURE:
Tradition notes that there are two senses or aspects of Scripture—the literal and the spiritual. The literal meaning is that meaning conveyed by the words of Scripture and discovered by exegesis following rules of sound interpretation. The

spiritual meaning points to realities beyond the words themselves and is subdivided into three categories. These categories are:

- *Allegorical*—This recognizes the significance of the Scriptures in Christ, that is, the way in which images in Scripture serve as a type or foreshadowing of Christ and his actions.
- *Anagogical*—This views realities and events in Scripture in terms of their eternal significance.
- *Moral*—What is read in Scripture inspires or motivates one to live justly (cf. CCC, nos. 115-117).

SIN: Sin is an offense against God as well as against reason, truth, and right conscience; it is a failure in genuine love for God and neighbor caused by a perverse attachment to certain goods. It wounds the nature of man and injures human solidarity. It has been defined as "an utterance, a deed, or a desire contrary to the eternal law" (CCC, no. 1849).

SLOTH: One of the Capital Sins; it involves a lack of effort in meeting duties and responsibilities to God, to others, and to oneself.

SOCIAL JUSTICE: Society ensures social justice by providing the conditions that allow associations and individuals to obtain their due (CCC, no. 1943). Social justice deals with the essential needs of people if they are to live together in community with respect for each other's dignity. These needs include food, clothing, and shelter and an income that supports the family.

SOCIAL SIN: Sins that produce unjust social laws and oppressive institutions. They are social situations and institutions contrary to divine goodness. Sometimes called "structures of sin" they are the expression and effect of personal sins. They lead the victims to do evil. In a certain sense, they constitute a social sin (CCC, no. 1869).

SOCIAL TEACHINGS OF THE CHURCH: While the Church from New Testament times has always been concerned about the social needs of the orphan, widow, alien, and other helpless people, she began to develop an explicit social doctrine to respond to the social problems that have arisen because of the industrial and technological revolutions. These teachings are found in papal encyclicals beginning with Pope Leo XIII's 1891 encyclical *On Capital and Labor* (*Rerum Novarum*) to those of the present. They are also contained in conciliar and episcopal documents.

SOLIDARITY: "The principle of solidarity, also articulated in terms of 'friendship' or 'social charity,' is a direct demand of human and Christian brotherhood" (CCC, no. 1939). This involves a love for all peoples that transcends national, racial, ethnic, economic, and ideological differences. It respects the needs of others and the common good in an interdependent world.

SOUL: The immortal spiritual part of a person; the soul does not die with the body at death, and it is reunited with the body in the final resurrection.

SPIRITUAL WORKS OF MERCY: These are actions that help our neighbor in their spiritual needs. They include counseling the doubtful, instructing the ignorant, admonishing the sinner, comforting the sorrowful, forgiving injuries, bearing wrongs patently, and praying for the living and the dead.

STATE OF GRACE: A condition in which our sins have been forgiven and we are reconciled with God, though purification from sin's effects may still be needed. A person is first in a state of grace, sharing in God's life, following Baptism.

If a person falls out of that state, he or she can be subsequently reconciled to God, especially through the Sacrament of Penance.

SUBSIDIARITY: "A community of a higher order should not interfere in the internal life of a community of a lower order, depriving the latter of its functions, but rather should support it in case of need and help it to coordinate its activity with the activities of the rest of society, always with a view to the common good" (CCC, no. 1883).

SUNDAY: Christians celebrate the Sunday because it is the day of the Lord's Resurrection and the beginning of the new creation. Catholics are obliged to participate in the celebration of the Eucharist on Sundays and to devote the remainder of the day to rest, relaxation, spiritual reflection, and activities that are consonant with this.

-T-

TABERNACLE: A noble repository located in a prominent place in a Catholic church in which unconsumed hosts that have become the Body of Christ are reserved for later use as well as a focus for adoration and prayer.

TEMPERANCE: The Cardinal Virtue by which one moderates the desire for the attainment of and pleasure in earthly goods.

TEMPLE OF THE HOLY SPIRIT: The Holy Spirit dwells in the Church in each member, providing the gifts and fruits that make the Church's members holy.

TEN COMMANDMENTS: Laws guiding human actions given to Moses by God on Mount Sinai.

THEOLOGICAL VIRTUES: The Theological Virtues are faith, hope, and charity. They call us to believe in God, hope in him, and love him. The Theological Virtues relate directly to the living God.

THEOLOGY: Theology is the reflective study of Revelation as found in the Scripture, in Apostolic Tradition, and in Church teaching.

TRADITION: The living transmission of the message of the Gospel in the Church, flowing from the oral preaching of the Apostles and the written message of salvation under the inspiration of the Holy Spirit (Scripture). Tradition is preserved and handed on as the Deposit of Faith under the guidance of the bishops, successors to the Apostles.

TRANSUBSTANTIATION: A term used to describe the unique change of bread and wine into the Body and Blood of Christ. By the consecration, the substance of bread and wine is changed into the substance of Christ's Body and Blood.

TRIDUUM: In the Church's liturgical calendar, these are the three days that follow the conclusion of Lent. The Triduum begins with the Mass of the Lord's Supper on Holy Thursday and concludes with the celebration of Evening Prayer on Easter Sunday.

TRINITY: One God in three Persons—Father, Son, Holy Spirit.

TRUTH: Reality and authenticity according to God's design. Through God's revelation, truth is found in Apostolic Tradition, in Scripture, and in the Magisterium of the Church guided by the Holy Spirit. In the human order, truth is discovered by the light of reason and reinforced by love of truth and truthful behavior.

-U-

UNITIVE PURPOSE OF MARRIAGE: The aspect of marriage that requires that it be a lifelong union. God willed that husband and wife be united in a permanent communion of love. Their communion reflects and is strengthened by the Trinity's communion of love.

-V-

VENIAL SIN: A venial sin is an offense against God in a less serious matter. Though venial sin does not completely destroy the love we need for eternal happiness, it weakens that love and impedes our progress in the practice of virtue and the moral good. Over time, repeated venial sin can have serious consequences.

VIATICUM: The Holy Eucharist when received by a dying person as the spiritual food for one's passing from this world to the Father.

VICE: Vice is the habitual practice of repeated sin.

VIRTUE: "Virtue is a habitual and firm disposition to do good. . . . The human virtues are stable dispositions of the intellect and will that govern our acts, order our passions, and guide our conduct in accordance with reason and faith. They can be grouped around the four cardinal virtues: prudence, justice, fortitude, and temperance. . . . There are three theological virtues: faith, hope and charity. They inform all the moral virtues and give them life (CCC, nos. 1833, 1834, 1841).

VOCATION: The term given to the call to each person from God; everyone has been called to holiness and eternal life, especially in Baptism. Each person can also be called more specifically to the priesthood or to religious life, to married life, and to single life, as well as to a particular profession or service.

APPENDIX B.
TRADITIONAL
CATHOLIC PRAYERS

Sign of the Cross
In the name of the Father
and of the Son
and of the Holy Spirit. Amen.

Our Father
Our Father who art in heaven,
hallowed be thy name.
Thy kingdom come.
Thy will be done on earth, as it is
  in heaven.
Give us this day our daily bread,
and forgive us our trespasses,
as we forgive those who trespass
  against us,
and lead us not into temptation,
but deliver us from evil.

Hail Mary
Hail, Mary, full of grace,
the Lord is with thee.
Blessed art thou among women
and blessed is the fruit of thy
  womb, Jesus.
Holy Mary, Mother of God,
pray for us sinners,
now and at the hour of our death.
  Amen.

Glory Be (Doxology)
Glory be to the Father
and to the Son
and to the Holy Spirit,
as it was in the beginning
is now, and ever shall be
world without end. Amen.

—Traditional wording

Glory to the Father, and to the Son,
  and to the Holy Spirit.
As it was in the beginning, is now,
  and will be forever. Amen.

—wording as found in the
Liturgy of the Hours

The Apostles' Creed
I believe in God the Father
  almighty, Creator of heaven
  and earth.
And in Jesus Christ, His only Son,
  our Lord, Who was conceived by
  the Holy Spirit,
born of the Virgin Mary, suffered
  under Pontius Pilate,
was crucified, died, and
  was buried.
He descended into hell; the third
  day He rose again from the dead;

He ascended into heaven, and sits at the right hand of God the Father almighty, from thence He shall come to judge the living and the dead.

I believe in the Holy Spirit, the holy Catholic Church, the communion of saints, the forgiveness of sins, the resurrection of the body and life everlasting. Amen.

The Nicene Creed

I believe in one God, the Father, the Almighty, maker of heaven and earth, of all that is, seen and unseen.

I believe in one Lord, Jesus Christ, the only Son of God, eternally begotten of the Father, God from God, Light from Light, true God from true God, begotten, not made, one in Being with the Father. Through Him all things were made. For us men and for our salvation, He came down from heaven: by the power of the Holy Spirit He was born of the Virgin Mary, and became Man.

For our sake He was crucified under Pontius Pilate; He suffered, died, and was buried.

On the third day He rose again in fulfillment of the Scriptures; He ascended into heaven, and is seated at the right hand of the Father. He will come again in glory to judge the living and the dead, and His Kingdom will have no end.

I believe in the Holy Spirit, the Lord, the Giver of life, Who proceeds from the Father and the Son. With the Father and the Son He is worshiped and glorified. He has spoken through the prophets. I believe in one, holy, catholic, and apostolic Church. I acknowledge one Baptism for the forgiveness of sins. I look for the resurrection of the dead, and the life of the world to come. Amen.

Morning Offering

O Jesus, through the Immaculate Heart of Mary,

I offer you my prayers, works, joys and sufferings of this day

for all the intentions of your Sacred Heart,

in union with the Holy Sacrifice of the Mass throughout the world,

for the salvation of souls, the reparation for sins, the reunion of all Christians,

and in particular for the intentions of the Holy Father this month. Amen.

Act of Faith

O my God, I firmly believe that you are one God in three divine Persons, Father, Son, and Holy Spirit. I believe that your divine Son became man and died for our sins and that he will come to judge the living and the dead. I believe these and all the truths which the Holy Catholic Church teaches because you have revealed them who are eternal truth and wisdom, who can neither deceive nor be deceived. In this faith I intend to live and die. Amen.

Act of Hope

O Lord God, I hope by your grace for the pardon of all my sins and after life here to gain eternal happiness because you have promised it who are infinitely powerful, faithful, kind, and merciful. In this hope I intend to live and die. Amen.

Act of Love

O Lord God, I love you above all things and I love my neighbor for your sake because you are the highest, infinite and perfect good, worthy of all my love. In this love I intend to live and die. Amen.

An Act of Spiritual Communion

My Jesus, I believe that you
  are present in the Most
  Blessed Sacrament.
I love you above all things, and I
  desire to receive you into
  my soul.
Since I cannot at this moment
  receive you sacramentally,
  come at least spiritually into
  my heart.

I embrace you as if you were
  already there and unite myself
  wholly to you.
Never permit me to be separated
  from you. Amen.

Prayer to the Holy Spirit

V. Come, Holy Spirit, fill the hearts
  of your faithful.
R. And kindle in them the fire of
  your love.
V. Send forth your Spirit and they
  shall be created.
R. And you shall renew the face of
  the earth.

Let us pray:
O God, by the light of the Holy Spirit you have taught the hearts of your faithful. In the same Spirit, help us to know what is truly right and always to rejoice in your consolation. We ask this through Christ, Our Lord. Amen.

Prayer at Stations of the Cross

We adore you, O Christ, and we
  praise you,
because by your holy Cross you
  have redeemed the world.

Holy, Hail Queen

Hail, Holy Queen, Mother
  of Mercy,
our life, our sweetness and
  our hope.
To thee do we cry,
poor banished children of Eve.

To thee do we send up our sighs,
mourning and weeping in this
  valley of tears.
Turn then, most
  gracious advocate,
thine eyes of mercy toward us,
and after this exile
show unto us the blessed fruit of
  thy womb, Jesus.
O clement, O loving,
O sweet Virgin Mary.

Memorare

Remember, O most gracious Virgin
Mary, that never was it known that
anyone who fled to thy protection,
implored thy help, or sought thy
intercession, was left unaided.
Inspired by this confidence I fly
unto thee, O Virgin of virgins, my
Mother. To thee do I come, before
thee I stand, sinful and sorrowful.
O Mother of the Word Incarnate,
despise not my petitions, but in thy
mercy hear and answer me. Amen.

Angelus

V. The Angel of the Lord declared
  unto Mary.
R. And she conceived of the Holy
  Spirit.

Hail, Mary, full of grace,
the Lord is with thee.
Blessed art thou among women
and blessed is the fruit of thy
  womb, Jesus.

Holy Mary, Mother of God,
pray for us sinners,
now and at the hour of our death.
Amen.

V. Behold the handmaid of the
  Lord.
R. Be it done unto me according to
  thy word.
Hail Mary.

V. And the Word was made flesh.
R. And dwelt among us.
Hail Mary.

V. Pray for us, O holy Mother
  of God.
R. That we may be made worthy of
  the promises of Christ.

Let us pray:
Pour forth, we beseech thee, O
Lord, thy grace into our hearts; that
we, to whom the Incarnation of
Christ, thy Son, was made known
by the message of an angel, may by
his Passion and Cross be brought
to the glory of his Resurrection.
Through the same Christ, our Lord.
Amen.

Queen of Heaven
(Regina Caeli)

Queen of heaven, rejoice, alleluia.
The Son whom you merited to bear,
  alleluia,
has risen as he said, alleluia.
Pray for us to God, alleluia.

Rejoice and be glad, O Virgin
   Mary, alleluia!
For the Lord has truly risen,
   alleluia.
Let us pray:
O God, who through the
resurrection of your Son, our Lord
Jesus Christ, did vouchsafe to give
joy to the world; grant, we beseech
you, that through his Mother, the
Virgin Mary, we may obtain the
joys of everlasting life. Through the
same Christ our Lord. Amen.

Jesus Prayer

Lord Jesus Christ, Son of the
living God, have mercy on me,
a sinner.

Act of Contrition

O my God, I am heartily sorry
for having offended Thee, and I
detest all my sins because of thy
just punishments, but most of all
because they offend Thee, my God,
who art all good and deserving of
all my love. I firmly resolve with the
help of Thy grace to sin no more
and to avoid the near occasion of
sin. Amen.

—Traditional version

Act of Contrition (or Prayer of the Penitent)

My God,
I am sorry for my sins with all
   my heart.

In choosing to do wrong
and failing to do good,
I have sinned against you
whom I should love above
   all things.
I firmly intend, with your help,
to do penance,
to sin no more,
and to avoid whatever leads me
   to sin.
Our Savior Jesus Christ suffered
   and died for us.
In his name, my God, have mercy.

—Alternate version from the
Rite of Penance

Act of Contrition (or Prayer of the Penitent)

Lord Jesus, Son of God
have mercy on me, a sinner.

—Alternate version from the
Rite of Penance

Grace Before Meals

Bless us, O Lord, and these thy
gifts, which we are about to receive
from thy bounty, through Christ
our Lord. Amen.

Grace After Meals

We give thee thanks, for all thy
benefits, Almighty God, who live
and reign for ever.
[And may the souls of the faithful
departed, through the mercy of
God, rest in peace.] Amen.

The Divine Praises

Blessed be God.
Blessed be his holy Name.
Blessed be Jesus Christ, true God
and true Man.
Blessed be the name of Jesus.
Blessed be his most Sacred Heart.
Blessed be his most
Precious Blood.
Blessed be Jesus in the most holy
Sacrament of the altar.
Blessed be the Holy Spirit,
the Paraclete.
Blessed be the great Mother of God,
Mary most holy.
Blessed be her holy and Immaculate
Conception.
Blessed be her glorious Assumption.
Blessed be the name of Mary, Virgin
and Mother.
Blessed be Saint Joseph, her most
chaste spouse.
Blessed be God in his angels and in
his saints.

Anima Christi

Soul of Christ, be my sanctification.
Body of Christ, be my salvation.
Blood of Christ, fill all my veins.
Water of Christ's side, wash out
my stains.
Passion of Christ, my comfort be.
O good Jesu, listen to me.
In Thy wounds I fain would hide,
N'er to be parted from Thy side,
Guard me, should the foe
assail me.

Call me when my life shall
fail me.
Bid me come to Thee above,
With Thy saints to sing Thy love,
World without end. Amen.

Prayer for Peace

Lord, make me an instrument of
your peace.
Where there is hatred, let
me sow love; where there is
injury, pardon;
where there is doubt, faith; where
there is despair, hope;
where there is darkness, light; and
where there is sadness, joy.
Grant that I may not so much seek
to be consoled as
to console,
to be understood as to understand,
to be loved as
to love;
for it is in giving that we receive, it
is in pardoning that we
are pardoned,
And it is in dying that we are born
to eternal life.

—St. Francis of Assisi

Prayer for the Souls
in Purgatory

Eternal rest grant unto them, O
Lord, and let perpetual light shine
upon them.
May the souls of all the faithful
departed, through the mercy of
God, rest in peace. Amen.

Prayer to St. Michael the Archangel

St. Michael the Archangel, defend
us in battle,
be our protection against the
wickedness and snares of
the Devil.
May God rebuke him, we
humbly pray.
And do thou, O Prince of the
Heavenly Host, by the Power
of God,
thrust into hell Satan and all evil
spirits who wander the earth to
seeking the ruin of souls. Amen.

Prayer to One's Guardian Angel

Angel of God, my guardian dear,
to whom God's love commits
me here,
ever this day be at my side,
to light and guard, to rule and
guide. Amen.

How to Pray the Rosary

Make the Sign of the Cross.
Holding the Crucifix, say the
Apostles' Creed.

On the first bead, say an
Our Father.

Say three Hail Marys on each
of the next three beads. Say the
Glory Be.

Go to the main part of
the rosary. For each of the five
decades, announce the Mystery,
then say the Our Father. While
fingering each of the ten beads of
the decade, next say ten Hail Marys
while meditating on the Mystery.
Then say a Glory Be.

(After finishing each decade,
some say the following prayer
requested by the Blessed Virgin
Mary at Fatima: "O my Jesus,
forgive us our sins, save us from
the fires of hell, lead all souls to
Heaven, especially those who have
most need of your mercy.")

After saying the five decades,
say the Hail, Holy Queen, followed
by this dialogue and prayer:

V. Pray for us, O holy Mother of
God.
R. That we may be made worthy of
the promises of Christ.
Let us pray:
O God, whose only-begotten Son,
by his life, death and resurrection,
has purchased for us the rewards
of eternal life, grant, we beseech
thee, that meditating on these
mysteries of the most holy Rosary
of the Blessed Virgin Mary, we
may imitate what they contain and
obtain what they promise, through
the same Christ our Lord. Amen.

Mysteries of the Rosary

Joyful Mysteries
1. The Annunciation
2. The Visitation
3. The Nativity
4. The Presentation in the Temple
5. The Finding of the Child Jesus after Three Days in the Temple

Luminous Mysteries
1. The Baptism at the Jordan
2. The Miracle at Cana
3. The Proclamation of the Kingdom and the Call to Conversion
4. The Transfiguration
5. The Institution of the Eucharist

Sorrowful Mysteries
1. The Agony in the Garden
2. The Scourging at the Pillar
3. The Crowning with Thorns
4. The Carrying of the Cross
5. The Crucifixion and Death

Glorious Mysteries
1. The Resurrection
2. The Ascension
3. The Descent of the Holy Spirit at Pentecost
4. The Assumption of Mary
5. The Crowning of the Blessed Virgin as Queen of Heaven and Earth

APPENDIX C.
FOR FURTHER READING

The *United States Catholic Catechism for Adults*
draws from these resources.

Reference/Foundational Texts

Catechism of the Catholic Church. 2nd ed. Washington, DC:
Libreria Editrice Vaticana–United States Conference of Catholic
Bishops, 2000.

Code of Canon Law (Codex Iuris Canonici): New English Translation.
Washington, DC: Canon Law Society of America, 1998.

*Code of Canons of the Eastern Churches (Codex Canonum
Ecclesiarum Orientalium): New English Translation.* Washington,
DC: Canon Law Society of America, 2001.

Papal Documents

Unless otherwise noted, these and other papal documents may be found
on the website of the Vatican in multiple languages: *www.vatican.va.*

Pope John XXIII

Encyclical *Peace on Earth (Pacem in Terris).* April 11, 1963.

Pope Paul VI

Apostolic Exhortation *On Evangelization in the Modern World
(Evangelii Nuntiandi).* December 8, 1975.
Encyclical *On the Holy Eucharist (Mysterium Fidei).*
September 3, 1965.
Encyclical *On the Regulation of Birth (Humanae Vitae).* July 25, 1968.

Pope John Paul II

Apostolic Letter *At the Close of the Great Jubilee of the Year 2000
(Novo Millennio Ineunte).* January 6, 2001.

Apostolic Exhortation *The Church in America* (*Ecclesia in America*). January 22, 1999.

Encyclical *The Gospel of Life* (*Evangelium Vitae*). March 25, 1995.

Apostolic Exhortation *I Will Give You Shepherds* (*Pastores Dabo Vobis*). March 25, 1992.

Apostolic Letter *On the Coming of the Third Millennium* (*Tertio Millennio Adveniente*). November 10, 1994.

Encyclical *On Commitment to Ecumenism* (*Ut Unum Sint*). May 25, 1995.

Apostolic Letter *On the Dignity and Vocation of Women* (*Mulieris Dignitatem*). August 15, 1988.

Encyclical *On the Eucharist* (*Ecclesia de Eucharistia*). April 17, 2003.

Apostolic Letter *On Keeping the Lord's Day Holy* (*Dies Domini*). May 31, 1998.

Apostolic Letter *On the Most Holy Rosary* (*Rosarium Virginis Mariae*). October 16, 2002.

Apostolic Letter *On Reserving Priestly Ordination to Men Alone* (*Ordinatio Sacerdotalis*). May 22, 1994.

Apostolic Exhortation *On the Role of the Christian Family in the Modern World* (*Familiaris Consortio*). November 22, 1981.

Second Vatican Council Documents

A number of translations are available for documents from the Second Vatican Council. Unless otherwise noted, this book has consulted the translation of Austin Flannery, OP, *Vatican Council II: Volume 1: The Conciliar and Post Conciliar Documents*, new rev. ed. (Northport, NY: Costello Publishing, 1996).

Constitution on the Sacred Liturgy (*Sacrosanctum Concilium*). December 4, 1963.

Declaration on the Relation of the Church to Non-Christian Religions (*Nostra Aetate*). October 28, 1965.

Declaration on Religious Liberty (*Dignitatis Humanae*). December 7, 1965.

Decree on the Church's Missionary Activity (*Ad Gentes Divinitus*). December 7, 1965.

Decree on Ecumenism (*Unitatis Redintegratio*). November 21, 1964.

Decree on Priestly Life and Ministry (Presbyterorum Ordinis).
December 7, 1965.
Dogmatic Constitution on the Church (Lumen Gentium).
November 21, 1964.
Dogmatic Constitution on Divine Revelation (Dei Verbum).
November 18, 1965.
Pastoral Constitution on the Church in the Modern World (Gaudium et Spes). December 7, 1965.

Holy See Documents

Unless otherwise noted, these and other documents of the Holy See may be found on the website of the Vatican in multiple languages: *www.vatican.va*.

Declaration on the Admission of Women to the Ministerial Priesthood (Inter Insigniores). 1976. From the Sacred Congregation for the Doctrine of the Faith.
Instruction on Christian Freedom and Liberation. 1986. From the Congregation for the Doctrine of the Faith.
Instruction on Respect for Human Life in its Origin and on the Dignity of Procreation. 1987. From the Congregation for the Doctrine of the Faith.

USCCB Statements and Letters

Letters and statements of the Catholic bishops of the United States up through 1997 can be found in *Pastoral Letters of the United States Catholic Bishops*, 6 vols: 1792-1997 (Washington, DC: USCCB, 1984-1998). Many statements after 1997 can be found on the website of the United States Conference of Catholic Bishops: *www.usccb.org*.

ACKNOWLEDGMENTS

Images used with permission.

St. Elizabeth Seton, p. 1; St. Peter the Apostle, p. 111; St. Juan Diego, p. 141; St. Katharine Drexel, p. 151; St. Frances Cabrini, p. 201; St. John Neumann, p. 261; and St. Thomas More, p. 277: © Monastery Icons—www.monasteryicons.com

Moses, p. 11: Gustave Dore, Moses Coming Down from Mount Sinai, The Dore Bible Illustrations (New York, 1974), 40.

Pope John XXIII, p. 21, © 1986; Blessed Kateri Tekakwitha, p. 101, © 1986; and Blessed Junipero Serra, p. 125, © 1988: Brother Robert Lentz, courtesy of Trinity Stores, www.trinitystores.com, 800.699.4482.

Fr. Isaac Hecker, p. 35: Courtesy of the office of the Paulist History/Archives.

Orestes Brownson, p. 49: National Portrait Gallery, Smithsonian Institution/Art Resource, NY.

Rose Hawthorne Lathrop, p. 65: Courtesy of the Archives of the Dominican Sisters of Hawthorne.

Venerable Pierre Toussaint, p. 77: Courtesy of Christina Miller, iconfusion@earthlink.net.

Sr. Thea Bowman, p. 89: Artist: Tony Bryant; courtesy FSPA Thea Collection.

Msgr. Martin Hellriegel, p. 165: Courtesy of Notre Dame Archives.

John Boyle O'Reilly, p. 181: Thomas Larcom, photographer.

Blessed Carlos Manuel Rodriguez, p. 213: http://en.wikipedia.org/wiki/Carlos_Rodriguez.

St. Augustine (of The Confessions), p. 233: Scala/Art Resource.

Cardinal Joseph Bernardin, p. 249: The Archives of Chicago and Bachrat Portraits.

Fr. Patrick Peyton, p. 293: Courtesy of Holy Cross Family Ministries.

The Icon of Christ, p. 307: Theophanos of Crete (1546), Stavronikita Monastery, Mount Athos.

Cesar Chavez, p. 323: The Cesar Chavez Foundation and CNS.

Catherine de Hueck Doherty, p. 339: Madonna House Archives, Combermere ON Canada KOJ IL0, 613-756-1766, e-mail: archives@madonnahouse.org.

Job, p. 351: Scala/Art Resource, NY.

Fr. Demetrius Gallitzin, p. 361: http://en.wikipedia.org/wiki/Image:DAGallitzin.jpg.

Fr. James Fitton, p. 362: Courtesy of College of the Holy Cross Archives.

Blessed Luigi and Blessed Maria Quattrocchi, p. 373; Pope Paul VI, p. 403; Henriette Delille, p. 447: Courtesy of Catholic News Service.

Dorothy Day, p. 387: Courtesy of the Marquette University Archives.

Mother Joseph, p. 417: Courtesy of Providence Archives, Seattle, Washington.

Fr. John Francis Noll, p. 429: Courtesy of Our Sunday Visitor Archives.

St. Maria Goretti, p. 439: Fr. William Hart McNichols.

Archbishop Fulton J. Sheen, p. 461: W. F. Hardin, Peoria, Illinois.

Praying Hands, p. 481: Design Pics.

<hr/>

tion of the *Roman Missal* © 1973, ICEL; excerpts from the English translation of the *Liturgy of the Hours* © 1970, 1973, 1975, ICEL; excerpts from the English translation of the *Rite of Marriage* © 1969, ICEL. All rights reserved.

Biography of Henriette Delille adapted in part, with permission, from Ann Ball, *Modern Saints—Book One* (Rockford, IL: TAN, 1983).

Excerpt from Archbishop Fulton J. Sheen, *Treasure in Clay*, copyright © 1993 by Ignatius Press, San Francisco, CA. Reprinted with permission of Doubleday Books.

Excerpt from *The Gift of Peace* by Joseph Cardinal Bernardin (Loyola Press, 1997) reprinted with permission of Loyola Press. To order copies of this book, call 800-621-1008 or visit www.loyolabooks.org.

Excerpt from Boniface Hanley, OFM, *Ten Christians* (Notre Dame, IN: Ave Maria Press: 1979), used with permission of the author.

Excerpt from *Rose Hawthorne Lathrop: Selected Writings*, from Sources of American Spirituality, edited by Diana Culbertson, OP, copyright © 1993 by Diana Culbertson; excerpt from *Word into Silence*, copyright © 1981 by John Main, OSB; excerpt from *Love is the Measure*, copyright © 1986 by Jim Forest. Paulist Press, Inc., New York/Mahwah, NJ. Used with permission of Paulist Press: www.paulistpress.com.

Excerpt from *Catholic New York*, the newspaper of the Archdiocese of New York, used with permission.

Excerpt from the *Daily Roman Missal* used with permission from the publisher, Midwest Theological Forum.

Excerpts from the English translation of the *Code of Canon Law* used with permission of Canon Law Society of America, 108 N. Payne Street, Alexandria, VA 22314-2906.

Excerpts from speeches and articles by Sr. Thea Bowman, FSPA (1937-1990). Used with permission as indicated in the citations to Chapter 8.

Excerpts from Fr. Patrick Peyton taken from www.familyrosary.org used with permission of Holy Cross Family Ministries.

Excerpt from Ellen Tarry, *Saint Katharine Drexel*, copyright © 2000 by Pauline Books and Media, Boston, MA.

Excerpt from Mother Teresa, cited in *The Power of Prayer*, copyright © 1998 by MJF Books, New York.

SCRIPTURAL INDEX

The numbers following each citation refer to the text page numbers. An asterisk indicates that the citation has been paraphrased.

14:6	29*, 431*, 436*, 492*
14:23	492
15:12	87, 196
15:13	91
16	105*
16:12-15	210*
16:13	110
17:15	489*
17:21	21, 231
18:38	431
19:27	146*
20:1	178
20:8	94, 99
20:19-23	94*, 178*
20:21-23	236
20:22	101, 203
20:22-23	244
20:28	94
20:31	79
21:15-17	112*, 121*
21:15-19	236*

Acts of the Apostles

1:2	96
1:8	102, 108
1:9	96
1:11	97*
2	203*
2:1-4	103
2:1-14	210*
2:1-47	210*
2:17	203
2:36	109
2:42	467*
4:12	84, 85, 357
9:1-31	236*
9:3-6	94*

10:38	204
16:31	37
17:26	73
17:26-28	5*
17:28	53, 243

Romans

1:3-4	96
1:5	45*
1:19-20	54*
1:20	3
1:21-25	74*
5:5	103-104
5:12, 19, 20b	70
5:20	72, 74, 313
6:3-4	183
6:4	155*
6:22	338
7:15, 19	72
7:19	73
7:24	72
7:24, 25	443-444
8:11	155, 155*
8:19-23	157*
8:28	454
8:31	489
12:1	225
13:13-14	234
13:26	45
16:26	37

1 Corinthians

2:9	154
3:16-17	122*
7:10-11	280-281, 410*
10:11	28
11:17-34	225*
11:23-26	216*, 216-217
11:27	222

INDEX

Italicized numbers indicate location of definition in glossary.

Fertility and infertility, issues regarding:
392, 409-10
couples without children: 285
openness to fertility: 285-86, 290,
404, 408-9, 415
see also *specific topics,* e.g., Natural
family planning
Fertilization, *in vitro:* 392
Fidelity: see Faithfulness; Truth
Filial love: 375, 377, 380, *513*
Final Judgment: 156-58, 161, *517*
and call to conversion: 158
Fire: 457
eternal: 157 (see also Hell)
Holy Spirit, as symbol of: 107,
446, *535*
images of as portraying hell: 155
Pentecost, tongues of fire at:
103, 114
purifying: 154
First Vatican Council: see *specific topics,*
e.g., Papal infallibility
Fitton, Fr. James: 362
Flesh: see Body; *specific topics,* e.g.,
Marriage (two becoming
one flesh)
Flock
Church as: 114, 270
shepherds of: 258
Flood: 14
Following Christ: 91
in consecrated life: 135
Force: see Violence
Forgiveness of others
and compassion for others: 242
of enemies: 488, 494
in family: 376
given to whoever trespasses against
us: 129, 482, 488
"Go, first, be reconciled to your
brother": 239
holiness and: 196
in marriage: 285
number of times a person should
forgive: 243
Forgiveness of sin: 46, 234-35
of all sins, possibility of: 192,
196-97

and Anointing of the Sick (see
Anointing of the Sick)
asking for forgiveness in prayer:
129, 467-68, 482, 488, 494
Baptism and: 47, 192, 196-97, 235,
243, 245, *505*
bishops and priests as instruments
to forgive sins: 236, 240
Christ as meriting justification for
us: 328, 336
Christians as still needing: 129,
243, 245
and Christ's Kingdom: 486
Christ's mission of: 235-36
the Church's power to forgive
sins: 236
and compassion for others: 242
Eucharist and: 224, 226
forms of penance and ways
to obtain (see Penance and
Reconciliation)
God alone as able to forgive: 83,
236, 251
as a manifestation of Jesus as
Savior: 98
and mercy of God: 52, 235
offering of Christ to the Father for
our sins: 92, 96
power to forgive sins imparted to
the Apostles by the Risen Christ
on Easter: 236, 244-45
see also Penance
and Reconciliation
Formation
of catechumens: 186, 188
of conscience: 314-15, 319-20, 454
spiritual formation of children:
189, 378
Fornication: 406, 410-11, 414, 441
Fortitude: 317, *513*
as a Cardinal Virtue: 193
as a gift of the Holy Spirit: 108
Fortune-telling: 344
Four marks of the Church: see under
Church: four marks of the Church
Franciscan Order: xi, 89, 125-26, 136,
277, 472, 474

using discreet language to preserve
personal safety, respect for
privacy, and the common good:
434, 437
Last Judgment: see Final Judgment
Last Supper: 21, 52, 216-17, 436, 481
bread, wine, and: 219-20
"Do this in memory of me," as a
command to the Apostles and
their successors: 366
institution of the Eucharistic
Sacrifice: 215-17, 219-21, 228
Jesus' discourse at the: 80, 105,
217, 329
Jesus shown to be High Priest of
the New Covenant and perfect
sacrifice to the Father: 216
Jesus transformed the bread and
wine into his Body and Blood
(Mass as sacred meal): *519*
linked to Christ's sacrifice on the
Cross: 221
**Lathrop, Rose Hawthorne (Mother
Alphonsa):** 65-67, 278
Law: 332, *517*
Church law/canon law: *524* (see
also Precepts of the Church;
specific topics)
civil law: *517* (see also Political
authority)
the Church's mission and
obligation to critique and
challenge those that offend
against fundamental rights:
379-80
and civic responsibility: *507*
moral obligation to oppose laws
contrary to the moral order:
379-80
natural law should be reflected
in: 383
to promote social justice: 326
to reflect and protect proper
moral order: 379-80
divine wisdom as leading us to
various types of laws: 336
eternal law as wisdom ordering all
things rightly: 327

love as at the heart of all: 309
moral law: *517* (see also
specific topics)
in accord with reason and divine
law: 327
acts gravely contrary to: 391,
396-97, 400, 427
during armed conflict, validity
of: 396-97
assist us in determining good
from bad: 320
crimes against life and: 391, 396-
97, 400
following, divine assistance
with: 330
freedom and: 310-11
as given to us for our
happiness: 310
information and: 434, 437
love as the foundation for: 318
as not arbitrary: 310
reproduction and: 410, 415
salvation as leading us to: 330
and scientific research: 38, 58
sin as an act contrary to: 312
natural law: 327-28, 335, *521*
(see under *specific topics*,
e.g., Marriage)
acts contrary to: 280, 407, 410
as applying to all people at all
times: 327
in the Church's social
doctrine: 420
and civil law: 283
coming to know natural law
through human reason: 327
confirmed in Divine
Revelation: 327
consequence of being made in
the image of God: 327, 335
as at the core of what makes us
human: 327
definition: *521*
detectable because we are made
in the image of God: 335, 437
as expressing our human dignity:
327, 335

the Lord's death and Resurrection as the central event of: 221, 224

the means of salvation found in the Church: 128-29, 138

message of salvation preserved in the Deposit of Faith (see Deposit of Faith)

Messiah to bring: 18

mystery of: 188, 268

as necessary: 68

necessity of Jesus Christ for: 68

no salvation through anyone else: 84, 132, 357

Old Testament images pointed towards salvation by the Messiah: 18

out of Abraham's family: 13

"Outside the Church there is no salvation": 132

Sacred Scripture conserving without error the message of salvation: 27

suicides and possibility of: 393-94

those in purgatory assured of: 154, 161

Virgin Mary cooperated through free faith and obedience in human salvation: 145

Same-sex unions: 280, 286, 411

Sanctification: 338

acts of sanctification received in Baptism: 196

actual graces aiding us in the course of the work of: 329

all Three Persons of the Trinity working together in: 329

certain elements of sanctification outside the Catholic Church: 128

of God's name: 485, 493

justification and: 328, 336

Old Testament priest unable to provide definitive sanctification for the people: 264

our acceptance of the holiness of God: 328, 336

of the people and liturgy: 175

priests serving God's People in the work of: 264, *524*

thanksgiving for: 219

Sanctifying grace: see under Grace: sanctifying grace

Sanctus: 219

Satan: 55, 62, 157, 296, 489, 494

as the evil we confront: 489

as "father of lies": 432

as "prince of this world": 75

see also Demons; *specific topics,* e.g., Adam and Eve

Satanism: 344

Satisfaction: 92, 239-40, 245, *527*

Savior, Jesus as: 57, 68, 72, 84-85, 95, 98, 357, 371

see also Jesus Christ

Scandal: 397

caused by laws and institutions that legitimize sinful actions: 397

duty to avoid: 401

gravity of: 401

scandalous behavior of some believers driving some seekers of God away: 4-5

Schism: 342

see also Error

Schools: see Education

Schools of spirituality: see *specific Schools,* e.g., Benedictine; Franciscan; Ignatian

Science: 5

evolutionary theories: 58-61

faith and: 57-61

moral laws and: 58

and religion, no intrinsic conflict between: 58-59

see also Stem-cell research

Scripture, Sacred: 23, *527*

authors (human), role of: 26-27, 31-32 (see also Inerrancy; Inspiration)

Biblical literalism: 29-30

canon of: 24

Christ as fulfillment of: 47

Church, as source of constant nourishment and strength for: 29

Church as venerating: 24, 29, 32-33

as divinely inspired: 24, 32

beauty and: 433, 437

being truthful, admitting sin and:
312

being truthful, conscience and:
314-15

building a society of (see
Civic responsibility)

the Church and: 6-7, 42, 63, 129,
330, 337, 436

the Church's Magisterium in service
of: 25, 134, 330

confidentiality and: 434

the creed as a summary of the
principle truths of the faith: 309

ecumenism and: 128, 131

the Eighth Commandment: 429-38

eternal truths: 301

every human person as seeking: 4,
8, 16, 48, 67

existence of objective truth: 431, 435

faith and: 37-39, 44-45

God as: 7, 39, 61, 431, 436

of God, sharing in: 62

Gospel as source of: 23, 26

historical truth: 31

Holy Spirit and: 110, 185, 337

ignorance and: 70

inspired books of the Bible as
teaching: 27, 30, 32

Jesus Christ as: 16-17, 29, 43, 85,
87, 176, 270, 431, 436, 492

"Know the truth. Love the truth.
Live the truth": 436

mass media and: 433-37

of mystery of God: 51

natural law and: 327, 437

"No one is bound to reveal the
truth to someone who does not
have the right to know it":
434, 437

oath-taking (see Oaths)

offenses against truth: 432-34

of the Old Law, revelation of:
328, 336

openness to: 4, 8, 16, 48, 67, 192

and philosophy: 57-58

prayer as soul of: 463, 491

principles for revealing: 433-34, 437

and proofs for God's existence: 5

relativism: 431, 525

right to the communication of:
434, 437

science and: 57

skepticism: 436

truths of faith: 6-7, 17, 27, 491 (see
also *specific topics*)

understanding and handing on: 25

understanding, proclaiming, and
defending: 487

when it's inappropriate to reveal:
433-34, 437

worship in: 365

Twelve Apostles: see Apostles

Unbelievers: see Non-believers

Understanding
all the faithful as sharing in: 25
of the Apostles: 26
of created realities: 58
of doctrine: 22, 491
and faith: xvi, xxiv, 38, 58, 115, 500
as gift of the Holy Spirit: 45, 103,
108, 205, 207-9
religion as: 16
Revelation and: 14, 16, 38
of Scripture: xxiii, 28
see also Gifts of the Holy Spirit;
specific topics

Unemployment: see Work

Union, Church/Christian:
see Ecumenism

Unions (labor unions): 424

Unitarianism: 49

United States: ix-xii, 361, 397
September 11: 332-33
see also *specific topics,* e.g.,
September 11

Unity, Church/Christian: see Ecumenism

Universal destination of goods: 420, 426

Universe
seen as evidence of God's existence: 4
see also Creation; World

Unleavened bread: 229